History of Universities

VOLUME XXXVII/1-2

2024

History of Universities is published bi-annually

Editors:
Robin Darwall-Smith *(University and Jesus Colleges, Oxford)*
Mordechai Feingold *(California Institute of Technology)*

Editorial Board:
R. D. Anderson *(University of Edinburgh)*
Nigel Aston *(University of York)*
Judith Curthoys *(Christ Church, Oxford)*
L. J. Dorsman *(Utrecht University)*
Heather Ellis *(University of Sheffield)*
Thierry Kouamé *(Université Paris 1 Panthéon-Sorbonne)*
Mauro Moretti *(Università per Stranieri di Siena)*
S. Rothblatt *(University of California, Berkeley)*

A leaflet 'Notes to OUP Authors' is available on request from the editors.

To set up a standing order for History of Universities contact Standing Orders, Oxford University Press, North Kettering Business Park, Hipwell Road, Kettering, Northamptonshire, NN14 1UA
Email: StandingOrders.uk@oup.com
Tel: 01536 452640

History of Universities

VOLUME XXXVII/1–2
2024

EDITORS
ROBIN DARWALL-SMITH
AND
MORDECHAI FEINGOLD

OXFORD
UNIVERSITY PRESS

Great Clarendon Street, Oxford, OX2 6DP,
United Kingdom

Oxford University Press is a department of the University of Oxford.
It furthers the University's objective of excellence in research, scholarship,
and education by publishing worldwide. Oxford is a registered trade mark of
Oxford University Press in the UK and in certain other countries

© Oxford University Press 2025

The moral rights of the authors have been asserted

All rights reserved. No part of this publication may be reproduced, stored in a retrieval system, transmitted, used for text and data mining, or used for training artificial intelligence, in any form or by any means, without the prior permission in writing of Oxford University Press, or as expressly permitted by law, by licence or under terms agreed with the appropriate reprographics rights organization. Enquiries concerning reproduction outside the scope of the above should be sent to the Rights Department, Oxford University Press, at the address above.

You must not circulate this work in any other form
and you must impose this same condition on any acquirer

Published in the United States of America by Oxford University Press
198 Madison Avenue, New York, NY 10016, United States of America

British Library Cataloguing in Publication Data
Data available

Library of Congress Control Number: 2024946916

ISBN 9780198946519

DOI: 10.1093/oso/9780198946519.001.0001

Printed and bound by
CPI Group (UK) Ltd, Croydon, CR0 4YY

Links to third party websites are provided by Oxford in good faith and
for information only. Oxford disclaims any responsibility for the materials
contained in any third party website referenced in this work.

The manufacturer's authorised representative in the EU for product safety is
Oxford University Press España S.A. of el Parque Empresarial San Fernando de
Henares, Avenida de Castilla, 2 – 28830 Madrid (www.oup.es/en).

Contents

Articles

University *Rotuli* of Supplication before Submission to the Pope:
The University of Cambridge, 1371–1399, and the Picard Nation
at the University of Paris in 1414   1
William J. Courtenay

Memory and University Reform in the English Revolution   58
Alex Beeton

Revisioning John Sherman's *A Greek in the Temple:* Teaching
apologetic responses to pagan religion as confessionalised
polemic at Cambridge University, *c.*1627–1641   85
S. F. M. Head

Anthony Tuckney's Anti-Socinian Lecture on the Divinity of Christ   121
Sergiej Slavinski

Studies at Trinity College, Cambridge, *c.*1600–*c.*1750   173
Richard Serjeantson

George Costard (1710–1782) on the Book of Job: Orientalism
and Sacred History in Mid-Eighteenth-Century Oxford   238
Natasha Bailey

A History of the Concept of the University of Sussex:
From Balliol-by-the-Sea to Plate Glass University   257
David M. Berry

Reviews

Cornelia M. Rudderikhoff and Hilde de Ridder-Symoens (eds),
*Les registres-matricules de la nation germanique de l'ancienne
Université d'Orléans, 1602–1689. Avec un supplement 1721–1781*   287
Andrew Hegarty

Nigel Aston, *Enlightened Oxford: The University and the Cultural and Political Life of Eighteenth-Century Britain and Beyond* 292
Robin Darwall-Smith

William J. Ashworth, *The Trinity Circle: Anxiety, Intelligence, and Knowledge Creation in Nineteenth-Century England* 298
Sheldon Rothblatt

William C. Kirby, *Empires of Ideas: Creating the Modern University from Germany to America to China* 305
David Palfreyman

List of Illustrations

Fig. 1.1. Picard Rotulus of 1414.	14
Fig. 1.2. Rotulus of 1414 showing strips sewn to the margin.	14
Fig. 5.1. Representations of (left to right) the Faculties of Divinity, Law, Medicine, and Arts. Wren Library, Trinity College, Cambridge.	176
Fig. 5.2. Representation of the Faculty of Arts, Wren Library, Trinity College, Cambridge.	177
Fig. 5.3. Francis Cleyn, 'Dialectica' (1645).	179

University *Rotuli* of Supplication before Submission to the Pope

The University of Cambridge, 1371–1399, and the Picard Nation at the University of Paris in 1414

William J. Courtenay

It has long been assumed that supplication *rotuli*, that is, rolls containing petitions to the pope by masters at Paris and other universities asking for financial support in the form of a benefice, provide a copy of most if not all the supplications that were included in a *rotulus* that was submitted by a university. The rolls that are known are those that were recorded in the Registers of Supplication in the Vatican Archives.[1] And those from the University of Paris were edited in brief form by Heinrich Denifle and Emile Chatelain at the end of the nineteenth century, which until recently has been the principal source for our knowledge of such *rotuli*.[2] While not all successful supplication rolls were recorded in the volumes and quires of the Registers of Supplication that have survived, those that were are usually thought to reflect the order and content of the original roll sent to the pope. It was Donald Watt's conclusion that the papal curia viewed such *rotuli* as reflecting a pre-submission vetting process that did not require further scrutiny.[3] Consequently, popes accepted the judgment of the qualifications

---

[1] Vatican City, Archivum Apostolicum Vaticanum (formerly known as Archivum Segretum Vaticanum), Registra Supplicationes, cited subsequently as Reg. Suppl.
[2] *Chartularium Universitatis Parisiensis*, ed. H. Denifle and E. Chatelain, 4 vols. (Paris, 1889–97), subsequently cited as *CUP*. For masters in arts, the editors included only the supplicant's name and diocese in their edition, sometimes mentioning the position being sought.
[3] D. E. R. Watt, 'University Clerks and Rolls of Petition for Benefices', *Speculum*, 34 (1959), 213–29, at 213–14: 'The pressure of business of this kind [petitions for benefices] was such that the Popes came to find it convenient to signify assent to whole Rolls at a time

or worthiness of the supplicants and simply approved the list as submitted. This assumption, in turn, allowed historians to make statistical comparisons and conclusions based on those documents as to the number of regent masters in faculties and nations at the time of each *rotulus*, comparative regional or diocesan distribution among petitioners, and the catchment or regions from which particular universities recruited students.[4]

Approving all supplications as submitted, however, was not the case. In the late 1990s Charles Vuillez found a report of a meeting of the Picard nation in the faculty of arts in April 1335 after their *rotulus* was returned to Paris following 'approval' by Pope Benedict XII in February, at the beginning of his pontificate.[5] Of the sixty-four regent masters in the Picard nation who had paid to have their petition included in the *rotulus*, only eight masters had their supplication granted. Before submission, apparently knowing that the pope did not grant all requests in a *rotulus*, the masters had agreed among themselves that those masters who were successful would pay those who had received nothing the fee they had paid for the inclusion of their supplication. This constitutes a success rate of 14.3%. The fact that Picard masters made this agreement among themselves before their *rotulus* was submitted means that a small success rate was expected and had been the experience of Parisian masters during the pontificate of John XXII.[6]

without apparently concerning themselves much about the details of the petitions they contained. Of course, large numbers of individual petitions continued to be granted as well; but these Rolls of Petition were an administrative convenience, and the Popes may well have argued that, if suitable sponsors thought that the various clerks on their Rolls were worthy of papal help, then they should be ready to give their consent.'

[4] For one such example, see J. Verger, 'Le recrutement géographique des universités françaises au début du XVe siècle d'aprés les *suppliques* de 1403', *Mélanges d'archéologie et d'histoire, l'École française de Rome*, 82 (1970), 855–902, reprinted in Verger, *Les universités françaises au Moyen Âge* (Leiden: Brill, 1995), 122–73. Verger recognized, 128–136, that the approved supplications did not provide a complete picture of a university community during the Papal Schism because they did not include non-clerics, mendicants, those who adhered to the pope in Rome, and possibly others for personal reasons. But these non-reported cases occurred at the time of composition of a *rotulus*, not at the time of papal action. Before the twenty-first century, there was no particular reason to believe that the number of approved supplications did not correspond to the number of submitted supplications.

[5] C. Vuillez, 'Autour d'un *Rotulus* adressé par l'Université de Paris à Benoît XII (1335)', *Mélanges de l'École française de Rome. Moyen Âge*, 144 (2002/1), 359–369, which contains an edition of the document. The document is Paris, Archives nationales de France (subsequently cited as AnF), S 6201, #5. The editors of the *Chartularium Universitatis Parisiensis* did not consult AnF, S 6201 or S 6202, and were thus unaware of this document as well as the draft *rotulus* of 1414.

[6] In response to the first group of supplications submitted by the University of Paris in 1316, only three masters in the Picard nation received an expectation of a benefice. Nicholas de Ceccano was one of the three executors on those provisions, and his close family connection with members of the papal curia may mean that he played a role in their selection.

Because information on the number of supplications by university masters has been based on *rotuli* recorded in the papal Registers of Supplication, only in cases where we know both the number of pre-submission supplicants and the number of provisions granted can we know the rate of success. Vuillez's analysis of the results of the Picard *rotulus* in 1335 gives us a base line of 14.3% for the rate of success in the second quarter of the fourteenth century. Whether it was actually that low under John XXII, or whether Benedict XII was for whatever reason less generous, we have no way of knowing, but Picard masters assumed it would be low.

We have, however, similar evidence for the rate of success on a *rotulus* from the University of Cambridge in 1371, for which we have a pre-submission draft that includes the names and supplications of all those who petitioned.[7] Although we do not have a *rotulus* of approved supplications because the Registers of Supplication under Gregory XI are lost, we have results in the form of letters of provision recorded in the Registers of Common Letters.[8] The actual rate of success for the Cambridge *rotulus* is not as certain as for the Picard nation in 1335, since the draft of that *rotulus* was a work in progress, but as supplemented by evidence in the Vatican Archives it is close to its final form based on the results. Moreover, the name of one supplicant is lost because of damage to the document, so we do not know whether he received a provision or not. In any event, the approximate rate of successful supplications for the University of Cambridge in 1371 was 70%. In light of the increasing number of provisions for Parisian scholars from Clement VI in 1342 to Benedict XIII in 1403 as recorded in the Registers of Supplication as well as in the Registers of Common Letters, the rate of success increased substantially in the course of the fourteenth century, and, correspondingly, so does the reliability of statistical analysis based on that type of documentation.

If the original *rotuli* as submitted had survived, which were signed by the pope, who added 'let it be so' (*fiat*) or 'seek a benefice from a different collator' (*pete alibi*) to some entries while ignoring others, we would know the precise rate of success, as we do from the 1335 Picard document. Regrettably, those original documents, which were returned to the university,

---

From the *rotulus* of 1328 the Picard and Norman nations received nothing, and in the *rotulus* of 1329, none from the French or Norman nations received provisions, but two Picard masters did.

[7] The *rotulus* is edited in W. J. Courtenay, 'Supplications to the Pope from the University of Cambridge in the Fourteenth Century', *History of Universities*, 31/1 (2018), 1–40, at 26–38.

[8] Letters from Gregory's first year have been edited in *Grégoire XI (1370–1378), Lettres communes analysées d'après les registres dits d'Avignon et du Vatican*, Bibliothèque des Écoles françaises d'Athènes et de Rome, ed. A.-M. Hayez, J. Mathieu, and M.-F. Yvan, 3 vols. [year 1], (Rome, 1992–93), subsequently cited as *LC Grégoire XI*.

faculty or nation, have not survived, at least none has yet been discovered. Thus, the few pre-submission drafts of university *rotuli* that have survived are a particularly important, but unused source of information for the history of beneficial support for medieval university scholars. While the document of the meeting of the Picard nation in 1335 tells us the number of regent masters in that nation at that time, by itself it tells us nothing except the names of the fifty-six masters who were unsuccessful in receiving a papal expectation of a benefice. A pre-submission draft of a *rotulus*, however, just as in the case of lists of supplications in the Registers of Supplication, includes mention of the diocese from which the supplicant came, his faculty of study, his academic status and degrees, the institution or collator from whom he was requesting a benefice, and what benefices he already held, if any. Most importantly, it includes that information for those who supplicated but received nothing, which is information absent in the registered form of a *rotulus*.

A number of such pre-submission rolls have survived in the archives of the University of Cambridge, along with some preparatory lists. The earliest, named 'Vetustior' by a Cambridge archivist and often referred to by that name, is a draft of the *rotulus* sent to Pope Gregory XI in 1371 at the beginning of his pontificate, and has been edited in calendared form, as just mentioned. A second example is a draft of the *rotulus* sent to Boniface IX in 1390 at the beginning of his pontificate, and a third is a draft of a subsequent *rotulus* sent to Pope Boniface in 1399.[9] Dr. A. H. Lloyd and his daughter worked on the rolls and related documents in the 1930s and left summaries of their contents, which are preserved in the archives of the Cambridge University Library. One entry in the 1371 *rotulus* is damaged, and sections of the 1390 *rotuli* and much of the 1399 *rotulus* are severely damaged, with a consequent loss of names and other information. After their deaths, Dr. Lloyd's wife Jessie published biographical notices on the Cambridge scholars named in those documents.[10] A. B. Emden incorporated that information in his biographical register of Cambridge.[11]

---

[9] The rolls and related documents, formerly catalogued as Cambridge University Library, Add. MS 6759 and Add. MS 7207, are today catalogued under Luard 82**(1) ['Vetustior' *rotulus* of 1371]; Luard 82* and Luard 82**(2, a–g) [drafts of 'Coville' *rotulus* of 1390]; Luard 82**(3) [draft of 'Zouche' *rotulus* of 1399] in the University Archives in Cambridge University Library. The numbers are those assigned by H. R. Luard, *A Catalogue of the Manuscripts Preserved in the Library of the University of Cambridge* (Cambridge, 1856–67). For the fascinating history of these rolls from the Cambridge archives to private hands, and finally back to the Cambridge University Library, see Courtenay, 'Supplications', 27, note 120.

[10] J. Lloyd, 'Notes on Cambridge Clerks Petitioning for Benefices, 1370–1399', *Historical Research*, 20 (1944–1945), 75–96, 192–211.

[11] A. B. Emden, *A Biographical Register of the University of Cambridge to 1500* (Cambridge, 1963), subsequently cited as *BRUC*. The Lloyd notes were also used by E. F. Jacob, 'Petitions

While those works identified Cambridge scholars whose names might otherwise not be known, only the draft *rotuli* themselves tell us the order in which their supplications were placed in the *rotulus*. Moreover, each Cambridge draft *rotulus* is one roll from the university that included all faculties, beginning with masters in theology, doctors in canon law, civil law, medicine, and masters in arts, followed by licentiates and bachelors in the same order of faculties. This contrasts with Paris, which grouped together separate *rotuli* from each faculty and nation, again according to academic rank and seniority.

Recognizing that the percentage of masters who successfully supplicated in *rotuli* increased over the fourteenth century, especially during the Papal Schism when the claimants as pope were trying to retain and enlarge their support, *rotuli* in the period from 1379 to 1415 are a rich source of information on university masters. This is especially true for pre-submission drafts, which allow us to see a large number of supplications in a *rotulus* before papal action. The draft *rotulus* from the Picard nation in the faculty of arts at Paris in 1414 provides close to the total number of supplications before submission. Such documents are also our only source of information on petitioners who were not successful in obtaining a papal provision.

Before discussing the specific pre-submission drafts, the steps in the process of submitting a *rotulus* to the pope should be reviewed, using Paris as the example. By the mid-fourteenth century, the University of Paris submitted a *rotulus* of supplications every two or three years unless conditions did not appear favorable. The most successful *rotuli* were those submitted in the first year of a new pontificate. When news of the death of a pope reached Paris, preparations for a *rotulus* by each of the higher faculties and the four nations of the faculty of arts began immediately. The fear of being away from Paris in the event of the death of the pope led masters to seek an agreement from their fellow regent masters that their name and supplication would be included in any *rotulus*, whether they were in residence or not.[12]

The first step was the decision by the university to send a *rotulus* of supplications to the pope. Then, each higher faculty and each nation in the faculty of arts appointed one or more of their members to be *inrotulatores* to whom those wishing to be included gave their supplications and paid a

---

for Benefices from English Universities during the Great Schism', *Transactions of the Royal Historical Society*, 4th series, 27 (1945), 41–59, reprinted with some updating in Jacob, *Essays in the Conciliar Epoch*, 2rd ed. (Manchester, 1963), 223–39.

[12] Those absent were sometimes listed in a separate section, after regent and non-regent masters. This is the case in the *rotuli* submitted in 1403 by the faculty of medicine (*CUP* IV, 80), the Picard nation (*CUP* IV, 93–95), the Norman nation (*CUP* IV, 102–07), and the English-German nation (*CUP* IV, 109–10).

fee for inclusion, which ran around 10 to 12 *solidi*. Since the number alone of regent masters in a nation in the faculty of arts might number well over a hundred, collecting supplications usually took several weeks and occasionally more than a month. Speed at the time of a new papal election was important in order to be the first university *rotulus* or *rotuli* to reach the new pope, so collecting supplications for a *rotulus* began before the conclave of cardinals to elect a pope was held, and was submitted within weeks of his coronation.

Soon after the appointment of the *inrotulatores*, each faculty and nation would elect one or two *nuncii* to carry the *rotuli* to Avignon or Rome. This was a much sought-after appointment, since it gave those selected direct access to the pope to plead their own case or transact other business, as well as present the supplications of their fellow masters. Moreover, all expenses for the trip and their stay in Avignon were covered by the nation or faculty.

Depending on the degree of urgency felt, the *inrotulatores* eventually met with one or more university scribes to create a draft of the official *rotulus*. The lists by the *inrotulatores*, presumably with some negotiation, became the basis for a pre-submission draft for each faculty and each nation, from which the final submitted *rotuli* were prepared. The names and supplications would be written on sheets of parchment or paper, which were later sewn together in a specific order. That document reflected the agreed-upon order of supplicants, most of whom had the text of their supplication entered at that time, while for others, only their name and diocese was entered, with a space left for the text of the supplication to be entered when ready. Supplications that were not yet ready would be written on separate strips, or *schedulae*, and tied onto the *rotulus* at the place where their name had been entered. The sequence of entries was of significance to the masters, who perhaps assumed the pope might be more favorable to those higher in the list. The sequence of names in the early portion of the document was based on academic rank and seniority, but later entries could vary. Occasionally the process was held up by supplications being changed, or by disputes over one's position on the list, or when the submission coincided with a change of rector of the faculty of arts or proctors of a nation, which could lead to a dispute over which of the two should be listed first.

The submitted versions were responded to by the pope, who in his own hand wrote '*fiat*' or '*pete alibi*' in the margin of the entries he approved, or '*fiat*' the end of the *rotulus* if he approved all the supplications. The original submitted *rotulus* was sent back to the university with the *nuncii*. A 'reformed' *rotulus* was often prepared and submitted, which included the revised supplications of those told to seek something else, along with some scholars who failed to be included in the original *rotulus*. For various reasons, less than half of university *rotuli* were entered in the Registers of Supplication, but those that were retained the language and sequence of the entries in the original document but listed only those supplications to which the pope responded favorably. The papal '*fiat*' was included in the version of the *rotulus* copied into the register, while '*pete alibi*' is known only if mentioned by a petitioner in a 'reformed' *rotulus*.

THE *CAMBRIDGE* ROTULUS *OF 1371* REVISITED

The edition of the 1371 *rotulus*, published in 2018, was an edition of the manuscript roll, not an edition of what would have been in the final roll sent to the pope.[13] In the absence of registers of supplication for the pontificate of Gregory XI, the only information on supplications in the final draft comes from the Registers of Common Letters for his pontificate, and consequently only for those that were successful. A search through the common letters of Gregory XI adds 34 letters that were included in the final *rotulus*. Among those additional letters, in response to supplications that were approved, are letters of provision to the chancellor of the University of Cambridge in 1371, Johannes de Donewych, and two regent masters in theology, William Goreham and Adam de Lakinghith, all of whom would have been listed in the first part of the final draft. Similarly, among the letters dated 28 January is a letter of provision for the university bedel, William de Fishwych, whose supplication for a benefice would have been entered at the end of the *rotulus*. Finally, the manuscript roll begins with the petitions of three doctors in civil law, who would have been in the early part of the *rotulus*, but not before the chancellor or masters in theology. The manuscript roll also does not have a prologue addressed to the pope on behalf of the supplicating masters, an element found in the Cambridge *rotulus* of 1390, which excludes the

---

[13] Two corrections need to be made in the edition of the 1371 *rotulus*. In note 154, I adopted Emden's identification in *BRUC*, 54, of the Johannes Beneth in the Cambridge *rotulus* as being Johannes Benet alias Chestrie (*LC Grégoire XI*, n° 6986) as well as another Johannes Benet (*LC Grégoire XI*, n° 13777), both of whom received a letter of provision on 28 January 1371. The latter is the Cambridge scholar, who came from the Norwich diocese, was rector of a parish church in that diocese, and was a student in canon law. The former was an Oxford scholar who held no benefice, came from the Litchfield diocese, and was a student in civil law. The second correction is in note 163 and confuses two different Cambridge masters. Johannes Kynne (*LC Grégoire XI*, n° 6971; BRUC, 345) is the person in the manuscript draft of the *rotulus*. Johannes Lenne (*LC Grégoire XI*, n° 4415; BRUC, 363) was in the submitted copy of the *rotulus* and received a provision, but is not in the manuscript draft.

manuscript *rotulus* of 1371 from being a final draft.[14] The most complete Cambridge draft, namely the 1390 *rotulus*, although damaged, reflects the form of a final *rotulus*, beginning with an address to the pope on behalf of the university, the chancellor's supplication, followed by those of masters of theology, law, medicine, and arts, and those of lesser academic rank.

Those who supplicated in the surviving draft of the 1371 *rotulus* were almost all masters, licentiates, or bachelors in civil and canon law, with one master in medicine, three bachelors in theology, and two students in theology. The eighteen remaining were simply masters in arts. And because all the additional names of supplicants are taken from the Registers of Common Letters in the first year of Gregory XI's pontificate, which would of necessity be the same for the *rotuli* in 1390 and 1399, there would probably be others who petitioned, received nothing, and thus remain unknown.

The Lloyds were able through research in the Registra Avenionensia in the Vatican Archives to add names and information on supplicants in the submitted version of the 1371 *rotulus* that are not in the surviving draft. Further research allows the following names to be added, some of which are persons included by Emden in *BRUC*, without always mentioning that they petitioned in the 1371 *rotulus*.

Supplicants not in the draft copy of the 1371 rotulus:
28 Jan. 1371:

> Edmundo de Alderford, presb. Norwicen. dioc., bac. in art. [*LC Grégoire XI*, n° 7017; BRUC, 7, Corpus Christi College]
>
> Johanni de Antingham, Norwicen. dioc., bac. in artibus [*LC Grégoire XI*, n° 4518 (Anthoyngham); *BRUC*, 13 (Antyngham)]
>
> Waltero Assh, Norwicen. dioc., qui fere per sex annos in jure can. stud. [*LC Grégoire XI*, n° 8060. Not in *BRUC*]
>
> Johanni Attestret, mag. in art., stud. in jure can., by mandate to official at Ely [*LC Grégoire XI*, n° 8063. Not in *BRUC*]
>
> Roberto Aylesham, presb. Norwicen. dioc., mag. in art. et theol. scolari [*LC Grégoire XI*, n° 6895. Not in *BRUC*]
>
> Petro de Cestriton, Elien. dioc., bac. in art. [*LC Grégoire XI*, n° 8067. Not in *BRUC*]
>
> Johanni de Donewych, doc. decr., qui universitatis studii Cantebriggie cancellarius existit [*LC Grégoire XI*, n° 9225; *BRUC*, 191–92, Clare Hall]

---

[14] The draft *rotulus* of 1399 begins with the supplication of the chancellor, Eudo la Zouche, which is addressed to the pope, but there is not a prolog on behalf of the whole university.

Willelmo de Fishwyke, Eboricen. dioc., qui universitatis studii Cantabrigie, Elien. dioc., bedellus existit [*LC Grégoire XI*, n° 4427 (Ffyschwyko); *BRUC*, 231, mentions Fisshewicke as bedel by 1375, but not in 1371]

Petro Godari de Tyryngton, Norwicen. dioc., qui in art. bac. [*LC Grégoire XI*, n° 4442; *BRUC*, 260]

Willelmo de Goreham, presb.. mag. in theologia [*LC Grégoire XI*, n° 9221; *BRUC*, 266 (Gotham)]

Walter de Hilton, Lincolnien. dioc., bac. in legibus [*LC Grégoire XI*, n° 13737; *BRUC*, 305–6]

Willelmo de Irby, presb. Lincolnien. dioc., mag. in art. [*LC Grégoire XI*, n° 6923; *BRUC*, 327–8]

Johanni Lenne, presb. Norwicen. dioc., mag. in art. [*LC Grégoire XI*, n° 4415; *BRUC*, 363]

Ade de Lakynghith, presb., mag. in theol., qui in studio Cantebrigge in fac. theologie per quinque annos rexit [*LC Grégoire XI*, n° 9623; *BRUC*, 346]

Willermo de Okham, Lincolnien. dioc., bac. in art. [*LC Grégoire XI*, n° 4429; *BRUC*, 433]

Willermo de Preshale, mag. in art. [*LC Grégoire* XI, n° 13751; *BRUC*, 467 (Pyshale)]

Johanni de Rudby, Eboracen. dioc., bac. in leg. [*LC Grégoire XI*, n° 8074; *BRUC*, 494]

Willelmo de Sondsham, Norwicen. dioc., in art. bac. [*LC Grégoire XI*, n° 4438; *BRUC*, 542]

Johanni de Teveresham, Elien. dioc., licen. in art. [*LC Grégoire XI*, n° 7041 (Teneresham); *BRUC*, 579 (Teversham de Bodekesham)]

Roberto de Tunsted, Norwicen. dioc., bac. in art. [*LC Grégoire XI*, n° 13586 (Timsted); *BRUC*, 599]

Bartholomeo Tunstede, Norwicen. dioc., mag. in art., bac. in medicina [*LC Grégoire XI*, n° 7051 (Turistede); *BRUC*, 598]

29 Jan. 1371:

Edmundo de Baylham, Elien. dioc., bac. in legibus, [*LC Grégoire XI*, n° 4514; *BRUC*, 51 (Beilham), which cited information from Jessie Lloyd's biographical article, who claimed this to be an entry in a 1374 *rotulus*, but meant 1371, a mistake repeated by Emden]

Willelmo Bromi de Hingham, Norwicen. dioc., presb., bac. in decr., [*LC Grégoire XI*, n° 13809 (Hengham); *BRUC*, 99 (Browne de Hengham)]

Willelmo Colvile, Eboracen. dioc., licen. in art. [*LC Grégoire XI*, n° 4515; *BRUC*, 151]

Ricardo Moris, Londonien. dioc., bac. in art. [*LC Grégoire XI*, n° 4503; *BRUC*, 414 (Morys), which dates the *rotulus* as 23 Jan. 1371, a typographical error.]

> Rogerio de Pilliergh, presb. Norwicen. dioc., mag. in art., qui in studio Cantabrigie in eisdem regit, [*LC Grégoire XI*, n° 7092; *BRUC*, 466 (Pylleberw, *sic*)]
>
> Symoni Selle, Norwicen. dioc., bac. in leg. [*LC Grégoire XI*, n° 7097; *BRUC*, 503–4 (Salle)]
>
> Johanni Roberti de Uffordi comitis Suffolchie nato, presb., mag. in art., scol. in theol. [*LC Grégoire XI*, n° 8156; *BRUC*, 603]

30 Jan. 1371:

> Johanni de Redeham, presb. Norwicen. dioc., bac. in decr. [*LC Grégoire XI*, n° 8172; *BRUC*, 476]
>
> Roberto de Thurkywy, presb. Eboracen. dioc., lic. in art. [*LC Grégoire XI*, n° 4533; *BRUC*, 587 (Thurkylby)]
>
> Waltero de Tiryngton, Norwicen. dioc., bac. in art. [*LC Grégoire XI*, n° 7111; *BRUC*, 589]

31 Jan. 1371:

> Radulpho Stol, Eboracen., bac. in legibus, as mandate to prior of Barnwell, dioc. [*LC Grégoire XI*, n° 4546. Not in *BRUC*]
>
> Radulpho Cok, Lincolnien. dioc., bac. in leg., as mandate to official of Ely [*LC Grégoire XI*, n° 7111; *BRUC*, 147 (Coke)]

1 Feb. 1371:

> Willelmo Quye, Elien. dioc., bac. in art., [*LC Grégoire XI*, n° 7136; *BRUC*, 467–68]

By comparing those named in the manuscript draft with the additional supplicating masters, it is obvious that an initial sheet is missing in the draft *rotulus*, and a final sheet that would have listed the bachelors in arts is also missing. Moreover, in the draft roll those in civil law are listed before those in canon law, even as the traditional order of theology, law, medicine, and arts was maintained.

THE CAMBRIDGE ROTULI *OF 1390 AND 1399*

In addition to the pre-submission draft of the Cambridge *rotulus* in 1371, there are two more from Cambridge. One dates to 1390 during the first year of the pontificate of Boniface IX and the chancellorship of William Colville. It survives in two copies and some separate lists that may be lists prepared by *inrotulatores*, who collected supplications for inclusion in the *rotulus*. The other dates to 1399 during the chancellorship of Eudo la Zouche. Both *rotuli* were sent to Boniface IX in Rome, whom England recognized as the true pope, but whose chancery left no Registers of Supplications.[15] Boniface IX's chancery did, however, register letters, indults, and dispensations, which fill the first 118 volumes of the Registra Lateranensia and 9 volumes (312–320) of the Registra Vaticana. Despite the extent of those records, no letters of provision resulting from the *rotuli* of 1390 and 1399 appear in those registers. Individual petitioners, however, did receive dispensations from Pope Boniface to farm one or more benefices while studying at a university, for holding incompatible benefices, for the right to hold a mass at a portable altar, or appointment as an apostolic notary. Without a registered copy of a *rotulus* or of letters resulting from one that provide information on successful supplications, we are left with only the names and wishes of Cambridge masters, along with information on any parish rectorships or canonical prebends they held as of those dates. That is crucial biographical information, and for individuals who petitioned in both *rotuli* it can reveal what benefices they obtained during that decade. It cannot, however, tell us anything about the response of the pope.

The 'Coville' *rotulus* of 1390 is close to the text that would have been sent to Rome. It contains the prefatory address to the pope, the supplication of the chancellor, followed by those of masters of theology, doctors of canon law, doctors of civil law, doctors of medicine, licentiates in theology, bachelors in theology, regent masters in arts, beginning with the current and previous rectors of the university, then bachelors in the law faculties, and finally bachelors in arts. Although the longer copies are written in a formal hand, they have marginal notes for insertion of supplications not yet entered and thus are not the final drafts from which the submission copy would have been prepared, unless accompanied by *schedulae* with the missing supplications.[16]

We do know that some, perhaps most of the supplications in the 1390 *rotulus* were approved. Thomas Eskeved, one of the petitioners in the *rotulus*, received a dispensation in Nov. 1390, months after papal action on the *rotulus*, in which the pope mentions his having recently granted him a provision.[17] The fact that some petitioners in 1399 who also petitioned in 1390 have parish churches or benefices that they did not have in 1390 may

---

[15] Throughout the Papal Schism, the papal archives and much of the bureaucracy remained at Avignon, pending a resolution of the crisis. Thus the archival record of the Avignon line of popes is more extensive than the Roman or Pisan lines. No registers of supplications and very few registers of common letters survive from the pontificate of Urban VI (Reg. Vat. 310–312).

[16] The more complete draft is on separate parchment sheets, while the other copy is composed of six parchment sheets sewn together but lacking the last group of supplications.

[17] *Calendar of Entries in the Papal Registers relating to Great Britain and Ireland. Papal Letters*, ed. W. H. Bliss and C. Johnson, vols. 1–3 (London, 1893–97), IV, 377.

have been a result of supplications that were successful, although there were other means of acquiring benefices apart from papal provision.

The 1399 draft *rotulus* was similarly structured to that of 1390. It also begins with masters in theology, a doctor in decrees and one in civil law, followed by licentiates in theology, decrees, formed bachelors in theology, bachelors in theology, licentiates in civil and canon law, masters in arts beginning with the current and previous rectors, bachelors in both laws, in decrees, and in civil law.

The 1399 *rotulus* and the most complete copy of the 1390 *rotulus* are close to final drafts from which the submission copy of the *rotulus* would have been transcribed. As mentioned, one of the 1390 *rotuli* has a marginal note marking the spot where two supplications should be entered, supplications that are found in the other copy, which was therefore copied later. In the latter as well as the 1399 draft, there are no blank spaces awaiting a supplication not yet entered, and in order to avoid any misunderstanding, a blank portion of a line in the 'Zouche' *rotulus*, has a line drawn through it, connecting the text. Despite the damaged portions, these pre-submission *rotuli* deserve editing, especially the 'Covill' *rotulus*, which contains 264 supplications.

THE ROTULUS *OF THE PICARD NATION IN 1414*

Turning next to Paris, the university continued to send *rotuli* to the pope in Avignon, except when the king of France withdrew obedience. While no mention of submitting a *rotulus* of supplications to Clement VII's successor, Benedict XIII, in 1394 shows up in the proctors' register for the English-German nation at Paris (surprising, since the university as well as many groups within the university submitted one),[18] that register does mention the preparation and submission of a *rotulus* in 1403.[19]

---

[18] For the results, see *Rotuli Parisienses. Supplications to the Pope from the University of Paris*, vol. 3: *1378–1394*, ed. W. J. Courtenay and E. D. Goddard (Leiden/Boston: Brill, 2013), part 1, subsequently cited as *Rot. Par.* III.

[19] For a time, Charles VI (1380–1422) acknowledged the pope in Rome, Boniface IX (1389–1404), and the University of Paris in July and August 1403 prepared a *rotulus* to be sent to him, of which nothing remains (*Auctarium Chartularii Universitatis Parisiensis*, vol. I: *Liber procuratorum nationis Anglicanae (Alemanniae) in Universitate Parisiensi*, ed. H. Denifle and E. Chatelain (Paris, 1894), 863–64, subsequently cited as *AUP* I). After further deliberations in early August, that nation prepared a *rotulus* to be sent to Benedict XIII in Avignon (*AUP* I, 864), and the signed *rotulus* was brought back to Paris at the beginning of October (*AUP* I, 870). The supplications of those who received a provision were recorded in the papal Registers of Supplication and their names are listed in *CUP* IV, 61–125, n° 1786–1799; see also Verger, 'Le recrutement géographique des universités françaises', cited above in note 4.

It also mentions the composition of a *rotulus* in 1409–10, the first and last year of Alexander V's pontificate, which was not acted on because of the death of Alexander.[20] A revised version of the latter was undertaken in 1410, and sent to Alexander's successor, John XXIII.[21] The entry for Frominus le Hure in the 1414 draft *rotulus* indicates that bachelors in the faculty of arts sent a separate *rotulus* to John XXIII in 1410, just as they had done in 1403.[22] The university organized a second group of *rotuli* to be sent to the same pope in 1414.[23]

For the last of these, a pre-submission draft of the *rotulus* for the Picard nation has survived, drafted between June and October, 1414, and discovered by Vuillez in the same box of documents in which he found the 1335 document.[24] Unlike the April 1335 document, which provides the names of all regent masters, including the majority who received nothing, pre-submission drafts additionally inform us of the diocese from which the master came, his academic discipline and rank, the position or positions he was seeking, and the specific benefices or positions he currently held.

The beginning of the scroll has been eaten away and begins in the middle of a supplication. The right margin throughout the scroll is also damaged. The roll has many *schedulae* or strips containing a supplication sewn onto the left margin of the *rotulus* where the individual's name and diocese is written, and space was left for the entry. There are also seventeen separate *schedulae* kept with the *rotulus*, which had once been attached to the *rotulus*,

---

[20] A *rotulus* was planned in July and August 1409, but not sent to Pope Alexander until January 1410; *AUP* II (Paris, 1897), 57–58, 66. It was never signed (*AUP* II, 77n: 'rotulus Universitatis in curia Romana propter mortem papae non expeditus est'). The university followed the policy of King Charles VI, who supported Alexander V, the pope declared at the council of Pisa in 1409, as well as his successor, John XXIII.

[21] *AUP* II, 80–81, 85–87.   [22] *CUP* IV, 116–125, n° 1799.

[23] Planning for the *rotulus* was begun in September 1413, but not sent until late 1414 or early 1415 (*AUP* II, 158–59, 162, 180, 182). In the face of the proposal that the current three popes resign, John XXIII fled the Council of Constance in March 1415, was subsequently deposed by the Council, and imprisoned while still in German territory. If the *rotuli* of the faculties and nations at Paris reached him, he was occupied with more immediate concerns. If any *rotuli* were signed, which is doubtful, the papal chancery, which had remained in Avignon, may have been uncertain about the confection of letters under these circumstances.

[24] C. Vuillez, 'Un *rotulus* original de la nation Picarde de l'Université de Paris au temps du Pape Jean XXIII', in *Suppliques et Requêtes*, ed. H. Millet (Rome: EFR, 2003), 165–173. The document is found in Paris, AnF, carton S 6201. Vuillez began his essay with the remark that the Picard nation 'fait un peu figure de parente pauvre parmi les autres nations du studium parisien.' On the contrary, it was usually second only to the French nation in the number of masters, and was placed second among the nations in a university *rotulus*. Vuillez dated the *rotulus* draft between January 1414 and the spring of 1415 based on the academic rank acknowledged by several masters studying in medicine and law. A closer look at that type of information permits the dating to be narrowed. The entry for Peter Brachii identifies him as licensed in medicine, which happened in March 1414 (*CUP* IV, 287, n° 2020). Since he was regent master in medicine in November 1414 (*CUP* IV, 294, n° 2030), the *rotulus* was drafted between those dates, most likely between June and October 1414.

14   *History of Universities*

Fig. 1.1. Picard Rotulus of 1414.

Fig. 1.2. Rotulus of 1414 showing strips sewn to the margin.

as the holes in the left margin of the *schedulae* as well as the *rotulus* reveal.[25] In addition, notes were occasionally written in the margin to indicate the place for a separate supplication strip to be attached, or to bring the order of entries in line with the list of supplications prepared by an *inrotulator*, who had collected them and prepared them for inclusion.[26] The draft was therefore written after the sequence of names had been initially determined, but before all the supplications were ready for inclusion. These elements suggest that this roll is probably the penultimate draft of the *rotulus* of the Picard nation from which, when complete, the final roll to be submitted would be prepared and sent to the pope along with those of the other nations and faculties. There are also three short lists of supplications found in Paris, AnF, S 6201 and 6202, which correspond to sections of the pre-submission *rotulus* and are almost certainly the work of *inrotulatores*, three of the few known examples of that stage in the process.[27]

The work of *inrotulatores* as well as of the scribe entering the information in a pre-submission draft were not without error. Johannes Cardonis complained that his supplication in 1410, recorded by an *inrotulator*, failed to be entered in the final draft of the *rotulus*. The entry for Johannes Fare in the present *rotulus* shows that the entry in the pre-submission draft was incomplete because the scribe skipped from one 'non obst.' to the next. The same scribe failed to transfer, or chose not to transfer, three entries from the third *inrotulator*'s list.

---

[25] Four supplication strips whose location in the *rotulus* could not be determined have been placed at the end of the edition.
[26] See, for example, remarks opposite entries for Johannes de Monte, Cosimo Nukaert, Johannes de Atrio, Johannes Cornepin, Nicolaus de Mota, and Arnuldus de Uden.
[27] The first of these *inrotulator* lists in the order in which they are found in the pre-submission *rotulus*, begins with Balduinus Andree and ends with Johannes de Novavilla alias Ployardi (AnF, S 6201, #10). The second list begins with Johannes Sandrini and ends with the entry of Petrus Gorguechon, with some changes in the order of entry (AnF, S 6201, #9). A third list begins with Wilhelmus Steenwinkel and ends with Johannes Gossumy (AnF, S 6202, unnumbered). The wording of the supplications in the lists of *inrotulatores* was sometimes standardized, and the sequence of entries was occasionally altered when entered into the *rotulus* itself. For example, in the first list (AnF, S 6201, #10), Martinus Questel, fifth in sequence in the i*nrotulator*'s list, was moved down two places in *rotulus*, and Cosimo Nukart, seventh in the initial list, was moved up in the *rotulus*, with Johannes Merrerii's supplication added. In the second *inrotulator*'s list (AnF S 6201, #9), the position of Johannes Fare and Adam Bourgin were changed, and the supplication of one master, Guillelmus Lupi, was substituted in place of Martinus de Varsenare. For whatever reason, several petitioners, such as Michael Malicorne, Jacobus de Belloramo, and Egidius de Woestina, had their supplication on a strip attached to the margin of the *rotulus* where an earlier version of their supplication had already been entered. The *inrotulator*'s list had authority, and both the insertion of a new entry into that sequence in the penultimate draft and marginal notes in the latter regarding placement of entries reflect a struggle between the *inrotulator* and his 'constituents' on the one side, and the power or influence of an individual master on the other.

The current draft is composed of sheets of paper on which the supplications were written, and then sewn together to form a roll. The sequence of entries, along with the incomplete entries, the marginal comments, and the three lists from inrotulators give us a rare glimpse of the process of preparation. This draft was written after the *rotulus* scribe had received lists of supplications from the inrotulators, but before all supplications were in his possession. He knew and entered the name and diocese of many of those who had not yet completed their supplication, and left space for the supplication to be entered later. In almost every case, the supplication, when received, was simply tied into the left margin of the *rotulus* at the designated place. Because of the size of these supplication strips, they covered other supplications, but the scribe or scribes responsible for the final submission copy could easily hold up the attached supplication in order to copy the supplications already in the draft copy. Further adjustments were made by marginal comments informing the final scribe of the agreed upon sequence of supplicants.

Well back into the fourteenth century Parisian masters sought permission from their colleagues to be included in a *rotulus* if one was prepared and submitted when they happened to be away from Paris. The proctors' registers for the English-German nation contain numerous examples of this practice. The question of where to place the supplications of absent masters, however, posed a problem, since those preparing the *rotulus* were actively teaching, while those who were absent might not be engaged in matters that served the interests of the nation or university. In 1403 separate *rotuli* with the supplications of absent masters were submitted by the faculties and the nations in the faculty of arts.[28] The draft of the 1414 *rotulus* occasionally notes in the margin when a master was absent, and some of the individual supplication strips are marked at the top with 'presens' or 'absens'. Whether this was to result in two different *rotuli*, or a difference in the placement of supplications in one *rotulus* is not evident.

The number of Picard masters was sizable, composed of regent and non-regent masters in arts. In 1335 the number of supplicating regent masters in the Picard nation was 64. In their *rotulus* in 1379, at the beginning of Clement VII pontificate, the number was 116, most of whom were regent masters. In the 1403 *rotulus* for the Picard nation, the number had grown to 126 masters in residence in Paris, again most of them regent, and 58 masters listed as being absent, for a total of 184. The draft *rotulus* of 1414 contains the names, most with supplications, of 214 or 215 Picard masters, depending on whether Johannes Tegularii and Johannes Tegularii

---

[28] See *CUP* IV, 80, n° 1795 (faculty of medicine); 93–95, n° 1796 (Picard nation); 102–07, n° 1796 (Norman nation); 109–10, n° 1796 (English–German nation).

alias Caboti are one and the same person, and whether the latter and Johannes Cabot are the same or different persons. An additional three names that are struck through and not included elsewhere were also Picard masters and may or may not have been included in a final *rotulus*. However, the total number of masters was certainly larger than 214/215 (or 219/220, if the struck-through names and those mentioned in a marginal note are counted), since we are missing a section at the beginning.

Since all masters were in the same faculty and nation, there does not seem to have been a fixed rule in terms of priority, but regency and seniority appear to have been important. At the point at which the roll in its present state begins, all supplicating masters affirm that they are regent masters, actively teaching, the last of whom claimed to have been a regent master for forty years. After that, a prioritized order breaks down, with students, bachelors, and licentiates in the higher faculties entered randomly. Those listed in the last third of the roll were masters of arts, most of whom were studying in one of the three higher faculties, with a few holding the degrees of bachelors or licentiates in those faculties. All supplicants were masters in arts, and the fifty-eight who are listed only as masters in arts appear in the last quarter of the document. No bachelors in arts are listed, and they would presumably have been placed in a separate *rotulus*, as was done in 1403.

Sixty-four masters were studying in the faculty of theology, twenty of whom were bachelors in theology and two, licentiates. Sixty-four were studying in the faculty of decrees, i.e. canon law, twenty-four of whom were bachelors in decrees, and eight of whom, licentiates. Five of them also held a degree in civil law, one as a bachelor and four as licentiates. Those degrees would have been earned elsewhere, most likely at Orléans, since civil law was not offered at Paris. Three held predoctorate degrees in both civil and canon law. Two held degrees in different faculties, one a bachelor of theology and canon law, and one a bachelor of theology and licentiate in canon law. Finally, twelve masters were studying medicine, five of whom held the degree of bachelor and one was a licentiate in medicine.

One of the most remarkable features of the 1414 *rotulus* of the Picard nation is that the supplicants asked for provision from many different collators in many different dioceses in northern France. Throughout most of the fourteenth century, it was expected that a supplicant would seek a benefice or canonical prebend in the gift of one collator, never more. Moreover, supplicants usually asked for either a benefice (parish church, chaplaincy, custody) or a canonical prebend in a cathedral chapter or a collegiate church, but almost never a benefice and canonical prebend in the same supplication. If a benefice was sought, the type was usually left open, e.g. with or without cure of souls (*cum cura vel sine cura*), a cathedral position (*si cathedralis dignitatus, personatus, archipresbyteratus*, etc.), as well as the actual collator, e.g. bishop, dean, individual canons together or separately (*episcopi, decani, canonici, communiter vel divisim*). By 1379 one encounters an example of someone asking for a provision from persons in two different institutions and dioceses, e.g. Johannes Filliastri, priest in the Chartres diocese, who asked for a canonical prebend at Chartres, or a benefice in the gift of the bishop, dean or chapter at Paris.[29] Asking for provision from multiple collators at different ecclesiastical institutions (bishops in different dioceses, abbots of different monasteries) is the predominant pattern in the *rotuli* of 1403, which were registered and therefore granted by Pope Benedict XIII. Presumably this practice was continued in the *rotuli* of 1410. It is the pattern for all supplicants in the Picard *rotulus* in 1414. The number of collators requested ranged from two or three up to eight or more, and included dioceses in the provinces of Rouen and Sens as well as those in Picardy in the province of Reims.

One example of asking for a provision from multiple collators is the supplication of Martin Questel from the diocese of Beauvais. He supplicated for one or more benefices, canonical prebends, or a position as rural dean or archpriest, or something in a hospital, house of lepers, or school, from any male or female collator, secular or in religious orders, in any city or diocese in the provinces of Reims, Rouen, Bourges, or Sens. He might as well have said 'give me anything from anyone anywhere in the northern half of France.'

THE DRAFT ROTULUS OF 1414: EDITORIAL PRINCIPLES

The length of the supplications in the edition has been reduced by omitting much of the formulaic language, abbreviating the rest, and excluding, with a few exceptions, positions being sought, because the supplicants asked for an unrealistic number of different types of benefices in the gift of many different collators in many different institutions and dioceses. While most Picard masters asked for positions in Picardy and adjacent areas in northern France in the ecclesiastical province of Reims,[30] several of them asked for a provision in the diocese of Le Mans in the province of Tours,

---

[29] *Rot. Par.* III, 39.
[30] In addition to dioceses in the province of Reims: Amiens (Ambianensis), Arras (Atrebatensis), Beauvais (Belvacensis), Cambrai (Cameracensis), Noyon (Noviomensis), Senlis (Silvanectensis), Soissoins (Suessionensis), Thérouanne (Morinensis), Tournai (Tornacensis), many Picard masters came from the diocese of Liège (Leodiensis) in the ecclesiastical province of Cologne.

and some held benefices at or in the diocese of Coutances on the edge of Brittany in the province of Rouen. The positions sought in multiple dioceses and provinces of northern France are too numerous to be a guide to what the individual most wanted, or thought might be possible to gain from a papal grace. Moreover, since the *rotulus* was never acted on and may not even have been submitted, there is no way to connect the requests with what the pope might have been willing to grant. The information on the petitioner, however, as well as any benefices or positions he already held and their non-resident value-limit (*in portatis*, or *in absentia*), have been included. The length of entries for those who have yet to receive a benefice are therefore short, even though in the manuscript they are often quite long because of the large number of potential collators requested. The modern name for places that might not be familiar has been included in backets.

Some of the entries on attached strips have retained the opening language of the petitioner, beginning with the '*Supplicat*' and his name in the nominative, while others have already been changed into the language of *rotulus* entries, beginning with 'Item' and his name in the dative. Some spelling variants used throughout the *rotulus*, such as *nundum* for *nondum*, *Attrebaten.* for *Atrebaten.* and *cappellania*, have been retained. As often occurs with drafts, some entries or parts of an entry have been struck through. These passages have been retained in that form, especially since they reproduce the character of the document, and in some cases contain the names of Picard masters who otherwise would not be recorded. When addressing the pope, *Sanctitas Vestra* and its other forms are often abbreviated as *S. V.* in the document and have been standardized that way in the edition.

Because of the minim problem (a sequence of vertical strokes that makes it difficult to distinguish 'n' from 'u' or 'v' and 'in' from 'ni' or 'm') and because 'c' and 't' often appear identical, alternative spellings of names have been separated with a '/'.

The abbreviations used in the calendared form in the following entries are, for the most part, those adopted by the editors of papal letters for the École Française de Rome, the Analecta Vaticano-Belgica, and as modified in the edited supplications from the University of Paris in the fourteenth century.[31] The elements are: name; diocese of origin; academic degree and current studies; and the requests for a benefice or a canonical prebend in

---

[31] For example, *Urban V (1362–1370), Lettres communes analysées d'après les registres dits d'Avignon et du Vatican*, Bibliothèque des Écoles françaises d'Athènes et de Rome, M.-H. Laurant, M. and A.-M. Hayez, et al. (eds), Rome, 1954–1089; Analecta Vaticano-Belgica, vol. VII: *Suppliques d'Urbain V (1362–1370)*, ed. A. Fierens, Rome, 1924; and *Rot. Par.* (see above, note 18).

the gift (*ad collat.* clause) of a bishop, cathedral dignitary, abbot, or other patron, concluding in the expanded version with the plea to the pope to provide what was asked (*dignemini misericorditer providere*). This section, with the large number of collation requests, has not been included for the reasons stated. This is followed by listing any benefice presently held (*non obst.* clause), along with its value or income in Roman numerals, although Arabic is used in the edition. This section also includes requests that current benefices be allowed to be retained in addition to ones newly granted, and dispensations that multiple incompatible benefices, e.g. two or more churches with care of souls, be permitted. Finally, the standard request that the letter of provision include all the normal chancery language and protections (the *non obstantibus clausulis opportunis, ut in forma* clause at the end) has been omitted because it is present in all supplications. The first two complete entries in the edition, however, are not abbreviated to illustrate the expanded form.

The Picard *Rotulus* of 1414

[Item Johanni]...theologia studenti dign[emini]...cuiusque existat... communiter vel divisim ad collationem, provisionem, presentationem... episcopi, capituli singulorumque canonicorum et personarum eccl. Belvacen., vel de consimili gratia ad collat.... eccl. Ambianen., vel de consimili gratia ad collat.... eccl. Noviomen., vel de consimili gratia ad collat..... [Non] obst. parroschiali (*sic*) ecclesia de Angicuria [Angicourt, Oise] in diocesi Belvacen., quam predictus Johannes obtinet, cuius valor annuum.... Cum non obst.....

Item Johanni de Novavilla, clerico Ambianensis diocesis, magistro in artibus, actu regenti in eadem facultate, gratiam specialem sibi facientes de beneficio ecclesiastico cum cura vel sine cura, etiam si canonicatus et prebenda, dignitas, personatus, administratio, vel curatus et electus, etc. fuerit, spectan. communiter vel divisim, etc. ad collationem, presentationem, provisionem, etc. episcopi, decani, et ca[pituli singulorumque] canonicorum ecclesie Ambianensis, aut ad collationem, etc. episcopi, decani, etc. ecclesie Noviomensis, aut ecclesie Belvacensis. Non obstantibus cappellania in parroschiali ecclesia de Guisencourt [Guizancourt, Somme], ~~cuius fructus xl f. non excedunt~~, et prebenda [in ecclesia] sancti Nicholai in claustro [Amiens], Ambianen. dioc., quam ~~gratia~~ vigore g[ratie] per V[estram] S[anctitatem] sibi facte in primo rotulo universitatis Parisiensis acceptavit in qua pretendit hinc ius, licet nundum pacifice assecutus...[*margin*: et parrochiali ecclesia de Chaudon [Chaudon, Eure-et-Loir], diocesis Carnotensis], cuius fructus annuus in portatis valorem lxv librarum parisien. non excedunt. Intuitu pietatis dignemini eidem misericorditer providere, cum ceteris non obstantibus clausulis opportunis, ut in forma.[32]

Item Nicolao Amici, subdiacono Ambianen. diocesis, magistro in artibus, actu regenti in dicta facultate, studenti in facultate theologie, gratiam specialem de beneficio ecclesiastico cum cura vel sine cura, vacante vel vacaturi, spectan. communiter vel divisim, ad collationem, provisionem, presentationem, seu quamvis aliam dispositionem episcopi, decani, capituli singulorumque canonicorum ecclesie Belvacen., etiam si canonicatus et prebenda cathedralis ecclesie vel collegiate, administratio, personatus seu officium extiterit, vel ad collationem episcopi etc. ecclesie Ambianen. vel ecclesie Parisien., vel ecclesie Silvanecten., vel decani et capituli Sancti Germani Autissiodoren., Parisien. dioc., dignemini misericorditer providere. Non obstante parrochiali ecclesia de Buneriis [Bonnières, Oise], Belvacen. dioc., cuius valor in portatis xxx lib. annuatim non excedit. Cum clausulis opportunis, ut in forma.[33]

Item Simon Baute/Bante, cler. Attrebaten. dioc., mag. in artibus actu regenti ac bac. in theologia, gratiam de benef..... Non obst. quadam cappellan. in eccl. colleg. s. Petri de Duaco [Douai, Nord], que deserviri consuevit in falla dicte ville Duacen., [*inserted at end*: quam assecutus est vigore gratie per E. S. V. sibi facte in alio rotulo universitatis V. S.,], (20 lib. parisien.).

Item Johanni Pergamenarii, cler. Laudunen. dioc., mag. in artibus actu regenti Parisius, de benef. ecclesiast. ad collat. episc., etc. eccl. Laudunen., Suessionen., Noviomen., Cenomanen., Carnoten., aut decani et capit. eccl. s. Marcelli prope Parisius, vel abb. et conv. s. Germani de Pratis prope Parisius, O.S.B., dignem. providere, aut gratiam eidem factam in rotulo univ. studii Parisien. ad predict. benef. c.c. vel s.c., etiam si canon., etiam sit tum quod canon. et preb. etc. uno duntaxat benef. computentur extendentes de eodem dignem. providere.[34]

~~Item Jodoco de Liza~~[35]

---

[32] He was licensed in canon law in 1416 (*CUP* IV, 314, n° 2063).

[33] He held a burse in the Collège des Chollets before 1419 and was cursor in theology in 1423. He read the *Sentences* in 1423–24 and was licensed in 1428. See T. Sullivan, *Parisian Licentiates in Theology, A.D. 1373–1500. A Biographical Register*, vol. II: *The Secular Clergy* (Leiden and Boston, 2011), 57–58.

[34] In 1403 he was a student in arts at Paris and held a burse in the Collège de Laon (*CUP* IV, 289n). He served as a procurator for the University of Paris in 1412 (*CUP* IV, 250, n° 1964), and at some point after 1414 studied at Angers and was licensed in civil law when he carried letters from Angers to the University of Paris (*CUP* IV, 289, n° 2026).

[35] Followed by a blank space for his supplication, which is among the loose strips and is inserted here, at the place where it was once attached.

Item Judoco de Liza, cler. Tornacen. dioc., mag. in artibus, gratiam de benef..... Non obst. cappellan. de Dedelem,[36] Tornacen. dioc., (20 lib. turon.).[37]

Item Johanni de Monte, mag. in artibus actu regenti Parisius in eadem facultate, cler. Leodien. dioc., providere dignemini de benef..... Non obst. canon. b. Marie Hoyen. [Huy, Liège, Belgium] in quo prefatus pretendit habere ius, licet nundum plene assecutus sit (10 march. argent.).[38]

Item Johanni Balduini, presb. dioc. Belvacen., mag. in artibus actuque regenti in eisdem, gratiam de benef..... Non obst. cura de Rullyaco [Rully, Oise] et Chamechiaco [Chamicy, Oise] unitis, dioc. Silvanecten., quam obtinet (24 lib. parisien.), etiam cum dispensatione duorum aliorum ad tenendum due beneficia iure inparabiliam.[39]

Item Balduino Andree, cler. Cameracen. dioc., mag. in artibus actu regenti Parisius studentique in facultate theologie, nullum benef. obtinet.[40]

Item Johanni Cantoris, Tornacen. dioc., mag. in artibus. actu regenti Parisius, gratiam de benef. vel officio....

Item Cosimo Nukaert, Cameracen. dioc., mag. in art., de benef..... Non obst. quadam cappellan. in eccl. s. Georgii [*in Cambrai*?], Cameracen. dioc. (15 lib. turon.). Non obst. quod sit de illegitimo matrimonio procreatus.[41]

Item Olivero Longi, cler. Tornacen. dioc., mag. in art., regenti in predicte facultate, de benef..... Non obst. quod ipse vestre creationis idem Oliverus in decimo octavo sue etatis anno existit, super quo dignemini secum misericorditer dispensare.

---

[36] The name is clear, but nothing resembling it appears in the Pouillés for the Reims province.

[37] He gave his second lectures as cursor in theology in 1422, read the *Sentences* in 1423–24, was licensed in theology in January 1428, and incepted as regent master in 1428 (*CUP* IV, 419, n° 2217 and 2218 [Lisa]; 470, n° 2301; 478, n° 2315; 486, n° 2331; 500, n° 2351; Sullivan, *Parisian Licentiates* II, 328–29).

[38] Marginal note in *rotulus* on left at end of Johannes de Monte entry: 'Nota quod Johannes Merrerii sequitur immediate Johannes de Monte.' He may be the Johannes de Monte, bachelor in canon law in 1416, mentioned in M. Fournier, *La Faculté de Décret de l'Université de Paris au XVe siècle*, vol. I (Paris, 1895), 152, subsequently cited as Fournier, *FDecr.*

[39] He is to be distinguished from two other Johannes Balduini, one from the diocese of Bayeux and one from the diocese of Amiens, both of whom were also students in the faculty of theology and petitioned in the *rotulus* of 1403 (*CUP* IV, 91 & 98, n° 1796). Rully and Chamicy are neighboring villages northeast of Senlis.

[40] The entries from Balduinus Andree through that of Johannes de Novavilla alias Ployardi are also in a list of one of the *inrotulatores* (AnF, S 6201, #10), from which it was copied into the *rotulus*, with some changes in placement.

[41] In the list of the *inrotulator* his entry followed that of Martinus Questel but was entered earlier in the draft *rotulus*. A marginal note in the *rotulus* opposite Nukaert's entry states: 'Nota quod ille debet poni immediate post Martinum Questel.'

Item Petro Gondemant, acolito Laudunen. dioc., mag. in artibus actu regenti Parisius, gratiam de benef..... Non obst., eccl. parroch. de Fontanis [Fontaine, Aisne], Laudunen. dioc. (30 lib. parisien.).[42]

Item Johanni Merrerii, mag. in artibus actu regenti, subdiac. Leodien. dioc., de benef..... Non obst. parroch. eccl. de Bayves [Baives, Nord], Cameracen. dioc. (15 lib. turon. parv.).[43]

Item Martino Questel, Belvacen. dioc., mag. in artibus actu regen. Parisius, de uno aut pluribus beneficio seu beneficiis.... Non obst. quadam gratia eidem per S. V. facta in cancellaria declaranda dispensus eo de quatuor annis super etate si opus fuerit.[44]

Item Ade Baudry, cler. Ambianen. dioc., mag. in artibus actu regenti, stud. in facultate theologie sibi providere de benef..... Non obst. parroch. eccl. de Senentes [Senantes, Oise], Belvacen. dioc., de qua sibi provisum est virtute gratie apost. sibi facte et de qua tanquam litigiosa competitorem habet (40 lib. parisien.).

Item, Johanni Haneron, cler. Noviomen. dioc., mag. in artibus actu regenti, gratiam de canon. sub expect. preb.....[45]

Item, Simoni Baillon, cler. Ambianen. dioc., mag. in artibus actu regenti Parisius, nullum beneficium obtinen., gratiam de benef.....

Item, Alexandro de Montibus, cler. Noviomen. dioc., mag. in artibus actu regent, de benef...., secum dispens. super deffectum annorum, quem patitur in xxii° anno sue etatis mundum ponitus.

Item, Johanni Cardonis de Craonna, Laudunen. dioc., presb., mag. in artibus sunt xl anni elapsi vel circiter, sibi gratiam de benef.,.... Necnon de simili beneficio ad collat. etc. abbatis et conventus monast. s. Vincentii extra muros Laudunen., O.S.B., communiter vel divisim, pertinen. de et super data v kal. Junii anni V. S. creationis. Cum per deffectum vel negligentiam inrotulatorum rotuli universitatis Parisien. filie humilis S. V., descriptus fuit seu ponitus, non fuerit in eodem rotulo mandare providere.

---

[42] He went on to study theology and began his second *cursus* on a book in the Bible in July 1433 (*CUP* IV, 554, n° 2434 [Godement]), read the *Sentences* 1433–34 (*CUP* IV, 554, n° 2435), was licensed in second place in December 1437 (*CUP* IV, 602, n° 2517), incepted as master in March 1438 (*CUP* IV, 602, n° 2517, n. 2), and began lectures as regent in theology in September 1438 (*CUP* IV, 607, n° 2526); Sullivan, *Parisian Licentiates* II, 260 [Godeme]).

[43] Merrerii entry occurs here in *rotulus*. The scribe who wrote the marginal note at the end of the entry for Johannes de Monte (see above) thought that it should be placed earlier, after de Monte. Merrerii's supplication was not included in the *inrotulator*'s list, as were the others in this section.

[44] He studied theology and became dean of the cathedral chapter at Beauvais by 1446 (*CUP* IV, 671, n° 2610).

[45] Presumably identical with Johannes Hanneron, who served three times as rector of the university before being licensed and incepting as master in theology in 1446 (*CUP* IV, 665, n° 2605; Sullivan, *Parisian Licentiates* II, 271–72).

Non obst. cappellan. perpetua s. Blasii de Ponteavaro [Pontavert, Aisne] predicti dioc. quam obtinet (40 lib. parisien.).[46]

Item, Johanni Vavassoris, presb., Ambianen. dioc., mag. in artibus, de benef..... Non obst. eccl. parroch. s. Luciani prope Sanctum Dionysium, Parisien. dioc., (30 lib. parisien.), et quadam gratia expectativa per S.V. facta in primo rotulo universitatis, de qua gratia nundum sibi provisum pacifice.[47]

Item, Philippo Ogierii, presb. Noviomen. dioc., in theologia et iure canonico bac. ac in artibus venerabilisque collegii scolarium de Dainvilla Parisius fundati mag. in decretis, stud. et alias rectore alme universitatis studii Parisius, de beneficio..., et quod dignitas sive personatus aut officium in eadem eccl. cum prebenda ipsius pro uno beneficio computentur,... ad collat., presentationem, etiam cuiuscumque seu quorumcumque collatorum et collatarum seu habentium conferre vel presentare, etc., in civitatibus et provinciis Remen. vel Rothomagen. aut Senonen., vel in civitate et dioc. Cenomanen.,.... Non obst. quod ipse Philippus canon. et preb. eccl. Attrebaten., et cappellan. s. c. de Plesseyo Godini [Plessis-Godin, Aisne], et duas cappellan. etiam s. c., unam videlicet in eccl. parroch. b. Martini de Calniaco supra Ysaram [Chauny-sur-Oise, Aisne] et aliam in cappella leprosarie de Fromitare Belyardi [?Firmitas Bliardy = La Ferté-sur-Péron, Aisne], Noviomen. et Laudunen. dioc., (30 lib. parisien.), ac canon. et preb. eccl. Noviomen. assecutus fuerit vigore gratie per E.S.V. sibi de canon. sub expect. preb., ac officii etc. eiusdem eccl. Noviomen. in alio rotulo dicte universitatis V.S. presentato factus, super

---

[46] He therefore incepted as a master in arts in 1374. He petitioned in the *rotulus* of 1379/80 as a master of arts in his third year as a student in canon law (*CUP* III, 261; *Rot. Par.* III, 201–02). He also petitioned in the second *rotulus* of 1382. In the *rotulus* of 1387 he still described himself as master in arts and a student in decrees, by then holding a portion of an altar in the church at Mons-en-Laonnois (*CUP* III, 455; *Rot. Par.* III, 649). From 1389 to 1393 he served as an apostolic notary (*CUP* II, 480, n° 1549; 521, n° 1574; 525, n° 1576; 528, n° 1577; 530, n° 1578; 551, n° 1603). In the *rotulus* of 1403 he described himself as master of arts and a student in theology, by then holding a chaplaincy at Pontavert in the diocese of Laon, near the village of Craonne (Archivio Vaticana, Reg. Suppl. 98, fol. 201r; CUP IV, 91, n° 1796).

[47] In 1380 he petitioned in a special *rotulus* of Parisian masters, at which time he identified himself as a student in theology and sought provision from the dean and chapter at Amiens as well as from the abbot of Saint-Wulfranni in Abbatisvilla (*CUP* III, 272; *Rot. Par.* III, 435). In 1387 he petitioned in the third *rotulus* of the University of Paris during the pontificate of Clement VII, in which he stated he had been a student in theology for seven years, i.e. since 1380, by which time he had obtained the parish church of Saint-Lucien [La Courneuve, near Saint-Denis] (*CUP* III, 455; *Rot. Par.* III, 649–50). In the same year he also petitioned as a fellow of the Collège des Chollets (*Rot. Par.* III, 727). His studies must have been interrupted, since in a *rotulus* in 1394 he stated he had studied theology for eight years (Reg. Suppl. 88, fol. 187r). His name does not appear among Picard masters in the *rotulus* of 1403. In this supplication, he was still rector of Saint-Lucien, but does not identify himself as a student in either theology or decrees.

quibus de presente litigat et timet evincere, nam a possessione sua licet de facto spoliatus est, quorum canon. et preb. Noviomen. abscen. deductis omnibus xxx lib. parisien. est valorem annuum non excedunt. Et in casu evictionis dicti Philippi ab eadem preb. vel aliis prebende acceptis virtute dicte gratie si sibi de iure non debeantur, eidem Philippo intuitu pietatis concedere dignemini quod ambabus gratiis huiusmodi sub datis et prerogativis earum saltim quo ad beneficia invices compatibiliam ut possit et gaudere, et ea simul assequi et retinere.[48]

Item, Nicolao du Sautoir, Ambianen. dioc., mag. in artibus, bac. in theologia, stud. in eadem, gratia de benef..... Non obst. quod parroch. eccl. de Blaquevilla [Blaqueville, Seine-Maritime], Rothomagen. dioc., et cappellan. ad altare b. Thome martyris in ecclesia b. Marie in castro de Gamachiis [Gamaches, Somme] fundatis, Ambianen. dioc., necnon et canon. et preb. eccl. Silvanecten. obtineat (90 lib. turon.).[49]

Item, Nicolao Robaut, diacono Attrebaten. dioc., mag. in artibus, in iure canonico licen., ac bac. in theologia Parisius continuari in eadem facultatem, de benef..... Non obst. quatuor cappellan. in Attrebaten. et Lensen. ecclesiis, ac in parroch. eccl. de Ghelesi [?Gœulzin, Nord] Ostrevano archidiac., Attrebaten., et in leprosaria Montis Sancti Desiderii [Montdidier, Somme], Ambianen. dioc., perpetuo fundatis, quos de presenti obtinuit (40 lib. parisien.). Non obst. expect. per S.V. nuper in rotulo devote filie vestre univ. Parisien. ultimo de data v° kal. Junii anno primo creationis S.V. eidem supplicanti facta, cum aliis et concessa, virtute cuius gratie adhuc sibi non est provisum ullatenus qua quidem prima [gratia] in vigore suo integra permanente cum hac secunda gratia vestra concedenda valeat eadem uti commode et gaudere.[50]

---

[48] He petitioned in two *rotuli* at the beginning of Clement VII's pontificate, and again in the second *rotulus* in 1382, was mentioned in the context of the proceedings against Chancellor Blanchard in 1385, and petitioned in the *rotulus* of 1387 (*Rot. Par.* III, 190–91, 468, 540, 643–44; *CUP* IV, 398). He also petitioned in the *rotulus* of 1403, by which time he had been a regent in arts for 26 years, was receptor for the Picard nation, and was on the verge of becoming a bachelor in theology and in canon law (Reg. Suppl. 98, fols. 199r–199v; *CUP* IV, 90, n° 1796). He petitioned in one or more *rotuli* at the beginning of John XXIII's pontificate (*CUP* IV, 196, n° 1908). In 1403 he held the parish church of La Couture in the diocese of Arras, canonical prebends in the collegiate church of Noyelles-sur-Mer, Amiens dioc., and a half prebend in St. Omer in Lillers, Thérouanne dioc., and a chaplaincy in the cathedral at Arras, valued at 54 lib. parisen., and three other chaplaincies of little value (*parvi valorum*), which he was willing to give up in return for something better.

[49] He was already master in arts when he petitioned in the first university *rotulus* sent to Clement VII in 1380 (*Par. Rot.* III, 214–15). He also supplicated in the *rotulus* of 1403, at which point he was a priest, regent master in arts, and bachelor in theology, who held a parish church in the diocese of Rouen and two chaplaincies, one at Gamaches and the other in the diocese of Laon (Reg. Suppl. 98, fols. 201v–202r; *CUP* IV, 91, n° 1796 [Santon]).

[50] Like Sautoir, Robaut was at Paris in the 1380s and petitioned in a separate *rotulus* of licentiates, bachelors, and students at the beginning of Clement VII's pontificate (*Rot. Par.*

Item, Johanni de Novavilla alias Ployardi, subdiac. Laudunen. dioc., mag. in artibus Parisius, stud. in facultate decretalium, gratiam de benef..... Non obst. quod parroch. eccl. de Bussiaco s. Martini [Bussy-Saint-Martin, Seine-et-Marne], Parisien. dioc., cum quadam cappellan. b. Gervasii de Guisya [Guise, Aisne], Laudunen. dioc., noscatur obtinuit, et quod in altera cappellan. ad altare s. Pauli in eccl. Laudunen. ius hinc pretendat (80 lib. parisien.). Necnon de benef. ad collat. episcopi, etc. eccl. Parisien. eadem S. eidem mandaverit provideri.[51]

Item, Egidio de Sancto Quintino, mag. in artibus, subdiac. Attrebaten. dioc., scholari actu Parisius in facultate decretorum, de benef..... Non obst. eccl. parroch. de Vitriaco [Vitry-en-Artois, Pas-de-Calais], cappellanis perpetuis de Warandino [Warendin, Nord] et de Huluch [Hulluch, Pas-de-Calais], una cappellan. habuit distributiones in eccl. s. Petri in Duaco, quod deservitur in magno altari cappelle b. Marie Magdalene situate prope eccl. s. Petri, et alia cappellan. ad collat. prepositi, decani, et capituli s. Petri non habente distributiones in eadem eccl., cum deservitur in altare s. Johannis Baptiste prope fontes eccl. s. Petri, Attrebaten. dioc. (60 lib. parisien.).[52]

Item, Michaeli de Rivo similem gratiam facientes devoto oratori vestro Hugoni Vavassoris, Morinen. dioc., mag. in artibus, stud. Parisius in facultate theologie, de benef..... Non obst. parroch. eccl. de Apibus?, Morinen. dioc., et canon. et preb. Attrebaten. litigiosi, quos vigore gratie per eandem S. V. eidem in rotulo univ. facte sub data v° kal. Junii pontificatus S. V. anno primo nundum pacifice possidet (30 lib. parsien.).[53]

Item, Petro Juppin, presb. Laudunen. dioc., mag. in artibus, de benef..... Non obst. quod canon. et preb. eccl. Cenomanen. noscatur obtinere (50 lib. parisien.).

Item, Jacobo de Flandria, presb. Cameracen. dioc., mag. in artibus et bac. formato in theologia, cum quo alias auctoritate ordinaria ut non obst.

III, 359). He testified in the proceedings against Chancellor Blanchard in 1385 (*CUP* III, 361). He petitioned in the *rotulus* of 1403, at which point he was licentiate in canon law and had studied in the faculty of theology for four years (Reg. Suppl. 98, fol. 202r; *CUP* IV, 91, n° 1796 [Robaudi]). He already held the chaplaincies in Arras, Lens, and in the parish church of Goeulzin [*ms*: Gueulesin] in 1403.

[51] His entry is on a strip, tied to the left margin. He petitioned in the *rotulus* of 1403, at which time he held only the chaplaincy in the collegiate church at Guise (Reg. Suppl. 98, fols. 202r–202v; *CUP* IV, 91, n° 1796).

[52] In the *rotulus* of 1403 he was master in arts and had been a student in theology for seven years without having obtained a benefice (Reg,. Suppl. 98, 203r; *CUP* IV, 91, n° 1796). At that time, he held a chaplaincy in the church of Warendin near Douai, and between 1403 and 1414 he had acquired the parish church at Vitry-en-Artois, a chaplaincy at Hulluch near Lens, and the other chaplaincies.

[53] He was principal of the College of Becoud at Paris and canon at Arras by 1413 (*CUP* IV, 268, n° 1997).

deffectu natalium quem patiebatur de milite soluto genitis et solute ad omnes ordines minores promoveri..... Non obst. gratia exspectativa dicto ~~magistro~~ Jacobo facta in ultimo rotulo univ. de qua nundum est sibi provisum, qui Jacobus prefatus presens est in prefato studio ut asserit, non obst. defectum huius natalium et non obst. beneficiis suis superius declaratis (100 coronarum auri).[54]

Item, ~~Dionysio Feullart~~[55] Michaeli de Rivo[56]

Item Michaeli de Rivo, cler. Cameracen. dioc., licen. in iure civili et bac. in iure canonico, ac mag. in artibus, in decretis nunc stud., de benef..... Non obst. cura seu admin. leprosarie b. Michaelis prope civitatem Constantien. [Coutances, Manche] et eiusdem diocesis ac provincie Rothomagen., ac canon. et preb. eccl. colleg. s. Gaugerici Cameracen., super qua timet sibi litem mov. (70 lib. turon.), secum misericorditer dispensari ut parroch. eccl. et admin., cum alia cura seu quocumque alio benef. incompatibili valeat retinere ipsique cum alio seu aliis simili vel dissimili permutare.[57]

Item, Petro de Hangardo, Ambianen. dioc. presb., mag. in artibus et bac. in theologia, gratiam de benef..... Non obst. canon. et preb. eccl. Silvanecten., necnon cura parroch. de [eccl.] Montatere [Montataire, Oise], Belvacen. dioc. (30 lib. parisien.). Et quod super incompatibilitate beneficii vel beneficiorum quid vel que virtute presentis gratie ipse obtinebit, ita quod ipsa simul tenere et possidere valeat.[58]

Item Thome de Atrio, presb. Morinen. dioc., mag. in artibus et licen. in decretis, curato eccl. parroch. de s. Clemente [Saint-Clément, Aisne], Laudunen. dioc., gratiam de benef..... [Non obst.] prefata parroch. eccl. de s. Clemente, canon. et preb. s. Gervasii de Guisia, Laudunen. dioc., cappellan. s. Vincentii in ecclesia Laudunen., quos obtinet (28 lib. turon.),

---

[54] He is mentioned in a document as mag. Jacobus de Flandria, dated April 1405 (*CUP* IV, 134, n° 1816).

[55] In his petition in the *rotulus* of 1403 he described himself as priest from the diocese of Beauvais, master in arts and bachelor in theology, at which time he held a portion of the parish church at Briteuil-sur-Noye (Reg. Suppl. 98, fol. 204r; *CUP* IV, 91, n° 1796 [Feuillart]). He petitioned John XXIII in a separate *rotulus* of masters of arts in 1410 (*CUP* IV, 196, n° 1908).

[56] De Rivo's supplication is among the loose supplication strips and is entered here, as was intended.

[57] He is mentioned in documents in 1408 and 1412 (*CUP* IV, 154, n° 1852; 232, n° 1943; 233, n° 1944). He was one of the four principal *librarii* of the university by 1418 and died in the capacity in or by 1426 (*Auctarium Chartularii Universitatis Parisiensis*, ed. H. Denifle and E. Chatelain, vol. 2 (Paris, 1897), 344–45).

[58] He petitioned in the *rotulus* of 1403 as master of arts and a student in theology, by which time he held the parish church at Montataire and an expectation of benefice from Saint-Martin-des-Champs (Reg. Suppl. 98, fol. 204r; *CUP* IV, 91, n° 1796).

et gratia expectativa dudum sibi in primo rotulo univ. Parisien. per S. V. facta, nundum sortita est suum effectum.[59]

Item Johanni de ~~Choques~~ Cloques, Tornacen. dioc. presb., mag. in artibus, bac. in iure canonico, de benef..... Non obst. eccl. parroch. de Rumiegne [?Rumegies, Nord], Tornacen. dioc., ac cappellan. altaris secundi in dicta eccl. Tornacen., quarum fructus....[60]

Item, Johanni Yonis, Leodien. dioc.

Item Johanni Yonis, presb. Leodien. dioc., mag. in artibus et bac. formato in theologia, stud. Parisius in facultate theologie, de canon. Leodien. sub expect. preb..... Non obst. decan., canon. et preb. b. Marie Tolnensis [Tholen, Zeeland, Netherlands] Leodien. dioc., et parroch. eccl. de Vlake [Vlake, Zeeland, Netherlands] partium Zuntbevelandie [Zuid Beveland], Traiecten. dioc. quam ex speciali gratia et dispen. per S. V. usque ad quinquennium una cum dicto decanatu facta optinet (14 march. argent.); non obst. etiam quadam gratia per eandem S. sibi concessa in rotulo Parisien. ad collat. prepositi, decani, etc. b. Marie Traiecten., de qua nundum sibi extitit provisum in cancellaria S. V., si opus fuerit latius declaranda, misericorditer dignemini providere.[61]

Item Anselmo Carelarii, subdiac. Tornacen. dioc., mag. in artibus et bac. in decretis, actuque stud. Parisius in facultate decretorum, de benef..... Non obst. quod canon. et preb. eccl. colleg. s. Piati Siclinien., quamdam cappellan. ad altare b. Marie in eccl. parroch. de Avelin [Avelin, Nord], Tornacen. dioc., et aliam cappellan. ad altare b. Quintini in eccl. parroch. de b. Quintini Tornacen., necnon aliam cappellan. in leprosaria de Hamo in Viromandia [Ham, Somme], Noviomen. dioc. (70 lib. parisien.).[62]

Item Eustacio de Manillo, Ambianen. dioc.

---

[59] He petitioned in the *rotulus* of 1410 (*CUP* IV, 196, n° 1908).

[60] He petitioned in the *rotulus* of 1403, at which time he was bachelor in decrees in his fourth year and rector of a parish church 'de Runa' and a chaplaincy in the church of St-Amé at Douai (Reg. Suppl. 98, fols. 204r–204v; *CUP* IV, 91, n° 1796 [Choques]). He is mentioned in a note in *CUP* IV, 180, n° 1883.

[61] The text is from the loose supplication that was once attached at this place. He was bachelor in theology in 1412 and regent master by 1425 (*CUP* IV, 232, n° 1943; 445, n° 2258). Because the editors of *CUP* thought Yonis was the same person as Johannes Dominici, a.k.a. Privis, a Norman master, Yonis is erroneously said to have been licensed in 1413 (*CUP* IV, 268, n° 1998). On Privis, see Sullivan, *Parisian Licentiates* II, 444–45.

[62] He petitioned in the *rotulus* of 1403 as an acolyte, master of arts and a bachelor in canon law in his third year of lectures, at which time he held the canonical prebend in the collegiate church of St. Piat [*ms*: S. Petri] at Seclin and two chaplaincies (Reg. Suppl. 98, fol. 204v; *CUP* IV, 92, n° 1796 [Carlerii]). He was licensed in 1419 (*CUP* IV, 95, n. 12).

Item pro Eustacio de Mannillo, presb. Ambianen. dioc., mag. in artibus et in facultate theologia licen., can. Suessionen., de benef..... Non obst. canon. et preb. Suessionen. et cappellan. Novi Cenobii Insulen., Tornacen. dioc.[63]

Item Bertrando de Mota, Laudunen. dioc.[64]

Item, Roberto de Chiny alias de Visello, Laudunen. dioc., mag. in artibus et bac. in utriusque iure, de benef..... Non obst. parroch. eccl. b. Germani de Drenceyo [Drancy, Seine-Saint-Denis], Parisien. dioc. (15 lib. parisien.).

Item, Petro Bernite/Bervite, cler., mag. in artibus, Laudunen. dioc., gratiam de benef..... Non obstan. cappellan. subscriptis, videlicet cappellan. b. Marie Magdalene in eccl. parroch. de Briengnia [Brienne-sur-Aisne, Ardennes],[65] Laudunen. dioc. (100 sol. parisien.). Item cappellan. b. Ludovici de Radnello[66] (40 sol. parisien.). Item cappellan. b. Anthonii fundata in domo dei de Brana [Braine, Aisne], Suessionen. dioc. (15 lib. parisien.). Item, non obst. predicta domus dei de Brana, Suessionen. dioc., cum domus datur per patronum laycum (24 lib. parisien.), et non obstan. quadam gratia predicto concessa de rotulo universitatis.

Item, Johanni Rousselli, cler. Belvacen. dioc., mag. in artibus, stud. Parisius in facultate decretorum, gratiam de benef..... Non obst. quod quandam cappellan. ad altare b. Nicolai in eccl. Ambianen. (12 lib.) obtineat, et quod vigore cuiusdam gratie expectative per E. S. V. dudum sibi factum in rotulo univ. Parisien. ad collat. abb. et conv. monast. b. Marie de Beccho Heluini, O. S. B., Rothomagen. dioc., adeptus fuerit possessionem parroch. eccl. de Plesseio Mahielli [Le Plessis-Mahiet, Eure], Ebroicen. dioc. (40 lib. parisien.), super quaquid parroch. eccl. lis seu controversia verisimili moveri speratur, de quaquid gratia ista simul aut successive possit et valeat uti et gaudere, etiam quo ad duo benef. curata eo causa quo dicta parroch. eccl. Plesseio Mahielli ab eo emerentur quod

---

[63] This supplication is among the separate supplication strips and was once attached at this place. He petitioned in the *rotulus* of 1403 as master in arts and a student in theology (Reg. Suppl. 98, fol. 205r; *CUP* IV, 92, n° 1796 [Mesnilio]). His petition consists solely of a list of four collators from whom he sought provision. He had read the *Sentences*, was *baccalarius formatus* by the fall of 1411 (*CUP* IV, 231, n° 1943), and was licensed in December 1413 (*CUP* IV, 268, n° 1998). He was regent master in theology at Paris by 1416 (*CUP* IV, 321, n° 2072), dean of the faculty in 1437 and again dean in 1445 (*CUP* IV, 334. n° 2092; 403, n° 2192; 406, n° 2195 [Extacio de Mesnillo]; 420, n° 2219; 445, n° 2258; 457, n° 2281; 478, n° 2315; 479 n° 2318; 600, n° 2510; 636, n° 2580; 656, n° 2595). He held canonical prebends at Soissons and Laon. Sullivan, *Parisian Licentiates*, II, 366–67 [Mesnillo].

[64] The strip with the supplication is not among those in S 6201. He petitioned in the *rotulus* of 1403 as master in arts and bachelor in decrees, at which time he held the parish church of Montigny-en-Arrouaise, northeast of Saint-Quentin (Reg. Suppl. 98, fols. 205r–205v; *CUP* IV, 92, n° 1796).

[65] *Recueil des Historiens de la France. Pouillés*, vol. 6: *Pouillés de la Province de Reims*, ed. A. Longnon, part 2 (Paris, 1897), 687: 'Capellania Beate Marie Magdalenes de Briaignie.'

[66] A village in the archdeaconate of Neufchâtel, unidentified in *Pouillés de la Province de Reims*, 687: 'capellania Sancti Ludovici de Radone.'

vigore gratie facte ad aliud benef. curatum seu non curatum liberum habeat et regressum, proviso quod unum ipsorum beneficiorum curatorum, si forte vigore huiusmodi gratiarum duo fuerit assecutus cum alio benef. compatibili non curato infra biennium teneatur permutare.[67]

Item, Roberto Lostelier.

Item, Roberto Lostelier, presb. Belvacen. dioc., mag. in artibus et bac. formato in theologia, de canon. sub expect. preb., dignitatis, ... Non obst. eccl. parroch. b. Marie de Moreto [Moret-sur-Loing, Seine-et-Marne] in Vastino [Gâtinais], Senonen. dioc., ac cappellan. b. Ludovici sita in villa de Canectecourt, Belvacen. dioc., ac canon. et preb. eccl. Suessionen. (100 lib. turon.), ac etiam quadam gratia expectativa eidem per S. V. sibi facta in rotulo univ. Parisien. virtute cuius gratie adhuc sibi non est provisum ullatenus qua quidem prima [gratia] in vigore suo integra permanente cum hac secunda gratia vestra concedenda valeat eadem uti commode et gaudere cum aliis, secum dispensantes quod simul tenere possit beneficia incompatibilia, etiam curate usque ad septennium.[68]

Item, Johanni Cordigeri, cler. Cameracen. dioc., mag. in artibus, licen. in iure canonico, benef..... Non obst. gratia apost. sibi facta in ultimo rotulo univ. de qua nundum provisus est.[69]

Item, Johanni de Bony, presb. Ambianen. dioc., mag. in artibus et bac. in theologia, actu legenti Sententias, gratiam de benef..... Non obst. cura Dathechy, Suessionen. dioc., et cappellan. in castelleto (60 lib. parisien.).[70]

Item Nicolao de Bihais, presb. [Atrebaten.], mag. in artibus, bac. in decretis, actu stud. Parisius in facultate decretorum, gratiam de benef..... Non obst. eccl. parroch. de Vry [?Ury, Seine-et-Marne],

[67] He petitioned in the *rotulus* of 1403, at which time he held a chaplaincy in the cathedral of Amiens and sought a benefice from collators in the dioceses of Evreux and Lisieux (Reg. Suppl. 98, fol. 205v; *CUP* IV, 92, n° 1796). Possibly identical with Johannes de Rosello (Fournier, *FDecr*. I, 180). See biographical sketch in T. Kouamé, *Le collège de Dormans-Beauvais à la fin du Moyen Âge* (Leiden/Boston, 2005), 589–90 [Roussel, Jean II]
[68] The text of his supplication is on a strip tied to the left margin of the *rotulus*. In his supplication he requested many different types of benefices or canonical prebends, from every type of collator, 'in eccl. Belvacen., Cameracen., Ambianen., Tornacen., Laudunen., Noviomen., Baiocen., Morinen., Silvanecten., Senonen., Melden., Andegaven.' He petitioned as master in arts and a student in theology in the *rotulus* of 1403, immediately after Johannes Rousselli, at which time he held the parish church of Rouvroy-en-Santerre, Somme (Reg. Suppl. 98, fols. 205v–206r; *CUP* IV, 92, n° 1796).
[69] His petition in the *rotulus* of 1403, five places after L'Ostelier, was entered twice. The first entry was struck through, with the marginal note: 'Cancellatus quia superflua.' At that time, he was a bachelor in canon law. In the first entry he claimed to be the rector of the parish church of Saint-Aubin in the diocese of Arras. In the second entry he claimed to be the rector of St. Quentin de Clariaco in the diocese of Cambrai (Reg. Suppl. 98, fol. 206v; *CUP* IV, 92, n° 1796).
[70] The full text of his supplication suggests that he held several chaplaincies, all unnamed. He may be identical with the Johannes de Bony, junior, who petitioned in the *rotulus* of 1403 (Reg. Suppl. 98, fol. 211r; *CUP* IV, 93, n° 1796).

Parisien. dioc., cappellaniis, una in Parisien. et alia Laurentii de Bellomonte [Beaumont-sur-Oise, Val-d'Oise], Belvacen. dioc., ecclesiis fundatis (70 lib. turon. parv.).[71]
Item Johanni Cabot. *Incomplete supplication strip sewn in left margin, beginning with*: ad collat. abbatis et conventus s. Audoeni, Rothomagen. dioc., O. S. B., vel ad collat. abbatis et conv. s. Wandrigisilli, Rothomagen. dioc..... Non obst. cura de Bovin Provin [Bauvin-Provin, Nord], Tornacen. dioc. (24 lib. parisien.), et non obst. gratia sibi facta per dominum nostrum papam in ultimo rotulo univ. ad collat. abbatis et conv. s. Martini Tornacensis, Tornacen. dioc. *In the lower right margin of schedula*: Item Johanni Tegularii alias Caboti, presb. Cameracen. dioc., mag. in artibus et bac. in theologia.
Item Jacobo Cati, subdiac. Noviomen. dioc., mag. in artibus et licen. in iure canonico Parisius, stud. in facultate decretorum, gratiam de benef...., secum dispen. ut parroch. eccl. de Bigoria [Bigottière, Mayenne], Cenomanen. dioc., quam obtinet.... Non obst. quod dictam parroch. eccl. ac canon. et preb. in eccl. colleg. s. Quintini de s. Quintino in Viromandia, Noviomen. dioc., obtinuit dignoscatur (120 [c xx] lib. turon. parv.).[72]
Item Johanni Figuli, presb. Cameracen. dioc., mag. in artibus et bac. in iure canonico, gratiam de benef. canon. sub exp. preb..... Non obst. canon. et preb. s. Quintini, Melbodien. [Maubeuge, Nord], cappellan. b. Marie de Terwiningue in parroch. eccl. de Stornaco, et cappellan. b. Marie de Fegnies [Feignies, Nord], Cameracen. dioc., et cappellan. s. Jacobi in eccl. s. Christi [Saint-Sauveur at Ghent], s. Christine in ecclesia sancti Johannis, Ganden., et subdiac. de Heyne, Tornacen. dioc., et gratia sibi facta per E. S. V. in rotulo univ. Parisien. sub data de v° kal. anno primo ad collat. episc., prepositi, decani, tresaurarii et capituli eccl. Cameracen., de qua nundum sibi extitit provisi (40 scutorum, residendo in loco privilegiato).[73]
Item Thome Fresne alias de Peneuche, diac. Cameracen. dioc., mag. in artibus, licen. in utroque iure cum rigore examinis, gratiam de canon..... Non obst. canon. et preb. eccl. Cameracen., quos dictus supplicans obtinuit virtute gratie apost. per S. V. eidem in rotulo univ. studii Parisien.

---

[71] He petitioned in the *rotulus* of 1403, at which time he was subdeacon and rector of the parish church of Lardiaco in the Paris diocese (Reg. Suppl. 98, fol. 207r; *CUP* IV, 92, n° 1796 [Bihars]). He was licensed in canon law by 1420 (*CUP* IV, 95, n.16).

[72] He petitioned in the *rotulus* of 1403, two entries after Tegularii alias Caboti, at which time he was a bachelor in canon law and held a canonical prebend in the collegiate church at Nesle in the diocese of Noyon (Reg. Suppl. 98, fol. 207r; *CUP* IV, 92, n° 1796). He described himself similarly in his supplication in 1419 (*CUP* IV, 95, n. 18).

[73] He was licensed in canon law in 1416 (*CUP* IV, 314, n° 2063; Fournier, *FDecr.* I, 149, 153).

nuper et iure facto concesse, ac parroch. eccl. b. Nicolai in Valenciennen., Cameracen. dioc., quo dictus supplicans obtinet (120 lib. parv. turon.), cum eodem ut unam dignit. cum dicta parroch. eccl. aut alio incompatibili, quamvis vixerit recipere et retinere valeat easdemque consimilibus aut dissimilibus beneficiis permutare dispensare.[74] Item ~~Guillelmo Wichgen, Leodien. dioc.~~[75] Reginaldo de Lequieze, presb. Belvacen. dioc., mag. in artibus, licen. in decretis in rigore examinis, bac. in legibus, gratiam de benef..... Non obst. canon. et preb. eccl. colleg. s. Amati de Duaco, parroch. eccl. de Jaux [Jauz, Oise], Belvacen dioc., et cappellan. nostre domine in eccl. s. Petri de Duaco (50 lib. parisien.).[76]

Item Egidio de le Glisuelle [la Glisuelle, Nord], nobili viro, subdiac. Cameracen. dioc., mag. in artibus, actu Parisius stud. in facultate decretorum, gratiam de beneficio.... Non obst. canon. et preb. b. Marie Hoyen, Leodien. dioc., canon. et preb. s. Hursmary Lobien. [Saint Wulmer, Lobbes, Belgium], et thesauraria b. Marie de Anthonio [Antoing, Hainaut, Belgium], Cameracen. dioc. (13 march. argen.).

Item Johanni Tegularii *and blank space for entry.*[77]

Item Johanni de Galeyda, subdiac. Tornacen. dioc., mag. in artibus, bac. in legibus et licen. in iure canonico, gratiam de benef..... Non obst. deffectum natalium, quem patitur de presb. et soluta super qua sede apost. benef. unum benigne dispen. obtinuit.... Necnon benef. curato s. Johannis in Scluza [L'Écluse/Sluys, Holland, *or* L'Écluse, Nord] ac cappellan. perpetua in eccl. s. Pharahildis, Gauden., sepe dicte Tornacen. (120 franc.).[78]

Item Michaeli Malicorne, mag. in artibus, licen. in legibus et bac. in decretis, Ambianen. dioc. subdiac., gratiam de benef..... Non obst. quod habeat curam de Aussouvilla [Auzouville, Seine-Maritime, *of which there are several*], Rothomagen. dioc. (70 franc.), et cappellan. de Alneto leprosarie

---

[74] He petitioned in 1403 in a *rotulus* for bachelors and licentiates in canon law (*CUP* IV, 69, n° 1790 [Frene]). He became a doctor in canon law in 1426 and participated in the trial of Joan of Arc (*CUP* IV, 451, n° 2269 [Fievé]; 465, 475, 492, 493, 500, 520, 523, 744).

[75] He petitioned in the rotulus of 1403, eighth in order after the proctor of the nation (*CUP* IV, 91, n° 1796 [Withgen de Gravia]), which suggests seniority.

[76] In his petition in the *rotulus* of 1403 he described himself as a bachelor in civil law in his fourth year of study in canon law, at which time he held a canonical prebend in the collegiate church of St. Vedast in Beauvais, and an expectation received from Benedict XIII in response to the *rotulus* of 1394 (Reg. Suppl. 98, fol. 207v; *CUP* IV, 92, n° 1796 [Leqmeze], but in 1414 *rotulus* the 'm' is clearly 'ui').

[77] He petitioned in the *rotulus* of 1403 in tenth place (Reg. Suppl. 98, fol. 200r; *CUP* IV, 91, n° 1796), at which time he was regent master in arts, a student in theology, and held the parish church of S. Audomari de Bisseghen [Bissegem, Kortrijk, Belgium], Tornacen. dioc.

[78] He is marked absent in the margin. He petitioned in the *rotulus* of 1403 among those declared absent from Paris, at which time he held a chaplaincy in the collegiate church of Ste. Pharailde in Ghent (Reg. Suppl. 98, fol. 216v; *CUP* IV, 95, n° 1796).

de Roya [Roye, Somme], Ambianen. dioc. (4 franc.), cum canon. et preb. eccl. Ambianen. (40 franc.).[79]
Item Johanni Buridani, Cameracen. dioc.[80]
Item, Ludovico de Billemont, Cameracen. dioc.[81]
Item Anthonio Chastenici/Chasteniti, cler. Belvacen. dioc., mag. in artibus, stud. Parisius in facultate theologie et domini nostri Regis notario et secretario, gratiam de benef..... Non obst. canon. et preb. s. Leodegarii de Peronna, Noviomen. dioc. (16 lib.), et cappellan. s. Blasii sita in castro Carcassone (16 lib.), cappellan. s. Jacobi sita in eccl. s. Benedicti Parisien. (6 lib.), cappellan. s. Johannis Baptiste in villa s. Clodoaldi [Saint-Cloud, Hauts-de-Seine], Parisien. dioc. (6 lib.). Necnon quadam gratia speciali expectativa per E. S. V. dudum sibi facta in rotulo univ. Parisius ad collat. episcopi, etc. Parisien., de quo nullatenus est sibi provisum, de qua gratia unacum ista simul aut successive possit, et valeat uti et gaudere.[82]
Item Michaeli Fabri, mag. in artibus, Ambianen. dioc., Parisius stud. in facultate decretorum, sibi gratiam de benef..... Et velitis ex habundante

---

[79] He received the canonical prebend at Amiens earlier in 1414 (*Fasti Ecclesiae Gallicanae, 1200–1500*, vol. I: *Diocèse d'Amiens* (Turnhout: Brepols, 1996), 171), subsequently cited as FEG. In addition to his supplication written in the *rotulus*, there is a supplication strip tied in the margin with an expanded petition that does not mention currently held positions: 'Supplicat S. V. devotus orator vester Michaeli Malicorne, subdiac. Ambianen. dioc., mag. in artibus, licen. in legibus, et in decretis bac., quatenus sibi gratiam facientes de canon. sub expect., unius preb. ac dignit., person., vel officii curatis et electis semel vel successive, vacan. vel vacat., omni et singularum metropolitanarum cathedralium et collegiatarum ecclesiarum Rothomagen. et Senonen. provinciarum; vel de benef., c. c. vel s. c., etiam si canon. et preb. ac person. vel office. in metropolitan. vel cathedrali eccl. fuerit, ad collat. etiam omni et singulorum collatorum et collatarum secularium et regularium provinciorum et dioc. predictarum. Cum omnibus et singulis non obst. in confectione litterarum declarandis, quas prosufficiter expressis hic habere dignemini, et clausulis in portunis et cum dispensatione duorum aut trium incompatibilium, etiam si due dignitates in ecclesiis cathedral. post pontificales principales et in collegiatis principales, aut due parroch. eccl. fuerint per ipsum perpetuo obtinendum, et unam vel ambas totiens quotiens voluerit, cum alio nec alius beneficio seu beneficiis compatibili seu compatibilibus permutare et permutata retinere, iure constitutionibus apostolicis contrarie et glossis et aliis in contrarium editis non obst. quibuscumque.'
[80] This is obviously not the famous Jean Buridan, who was from the Bayeux area in Normandy and lived more than a half-century earlier.
[81] He was of noble parentage, regent master in arts, and a student in canon law when he petitioned in the *rotulus* of 1403, at which time he held two chaplaincies in the diocese of Cambrai (Reg. Suppl. 98, fol. 208r; *CUP* IV, 92, n° 1796 [Buillemont]).
[82] He petitioned in the *rotulus* of 1403 immediately after Billemont, at which time he had studied in the faculty of theology for five years, held a chaplaincy in the castle at Carcasonne and an expectation of benefice in the gift of the bishop and chapter at Paris, granted earlier by Pope Benedict, but in which he had little hope (Reg. Suppl. 98, fol. 208r; *CUP* IV, 92, n° 1796 [Chastemer])

S. V. eundem obtinere duo benef. incompatibilia pacifice pro biannum, et alterum permutare in aliud benef. compatibile.[83]

Item Egidio de Prisces, Cameracen. dioc. presb., mag. in artibus et bac. in theologia, gratiam de canon. sub exp. preb..... Non obst. eccl. parroch. de Namaing [Namaing, Nord], Tornacen. dioc., necnon preb. eccl. b. Gaugerici, Cameracen. (50 lib. turon. parv.).[84]

Item, Johanni Sandrini, presb. Laudunen. oriundus, mag. in artibus et bac. in decretis, gratiam de benef..... Non obst. quadam gratia eidem Johanni facta ad collat. decani, capituli s. Laurentii de Roseto in Thierasta [Rozoy-sur-Serre, Aisne], Laudunen. dioc., de rotulo univ. de qua nundum sibi est provisum quia absens. Et etiam canon. et preb. eccl. colleg. s. Petri in Foro, Laudunen. (16 lib. parisien,); necnon eccl. parroch. de Apya [Eppes, Aisne], quam dictus Johannes possit permutare infra septem annos a tempore date predicti rotuli, et cappellan. b. Marie situate in eccl. parroch. de Guissya, Laudunen. dioc. (18 lib. parisien.).[85]

Item, Ade Bourgin, cler. Ambianen. dioc., mag in artibus et bac. formato in theologia, de canon. sub expect. preb..... Non obst. canon. et preb. s. Amati in Duaco, quadam cappellan. b. Marie de Lenso [Lens, Pas-de-Calais], Atrebaten. dioc., fundata ad altare b. Marie in aurora, et cappella seu cappellan. de Chassins supra maternam [Chassins-sur-Marne, Aisne], Suessionen. dioc. (60 lib. turon.).[86]

Supplicat S. V. ... Johannes Fare, presb. Ambianen. dioc., et mag. in artibus, stud. Parisius in facultate theologie, quatenus sibi gratiam de benef..... Non obst. cura de Cappyaco [Cappy, Somme], Ambianen.

[83] He petitioned in the *rotulus* of 1403, at which time he held a chaplaincy in the collegiate church in Fouilloy in the diocese of Amiens, and an expectation from Benedict XIII (Reg. Suppl. 98, fol. 208v; *CUP* IV, 92, n° 1796).

[84] He was in his fourth year of theological study when he petitioned in the university *rotulus* in 1403, by which time he already held the parish church of Moregem, spelled Mauring in the register entry in 1403 (Reg. Suppl. 98, fol. 208v; *CUP* IV, 92, n° 1796 [Priches]). He was still bachelor of theology in 1416 (*CUP* IV, 322, n° 2072) and was not licensed in theology until March 1424 and incepted as regent master in October 1424 (*CUP* IV, 428, n° 2234). See also Sullivan, *Parisian Licentiates* II, 443–44)

[85] He petitioned in the *rotulus* of 1403 among those declared absent from Paris (Reg. Suppl. 98, fol. 215v; *CUP* IV, 94, n° 1796). As bachelor in canon law, he began lecturing on the Decretals in 1415–16 (Fournier, *FDecr*. I, 158, 175). He was licensed in canon law in January 1418 (*CUP* IV, 335, n° 2094; Fournier, *FDecr*. I, 187). The supplications from here through Petrus Gorguechon correspond to the document of the *inrotulator* in AnF, S 6201, #9.

[86] This entry was left blank after Bourgin's name and diocese, and the text included here is from the *inrotulator*'s list. Bourgin petitioned in the *rotulus* of 1403 in tenth place (Reg, Suppl. 98, 200r; *CUP* IV, 91, n° 1796), at which point he had studied in the faculty of theology for four years and was still without a benefice. He petitioned in the first *rotulus* sent to John XXIII (*CUP* IV, 196, n° 1908 [Burgin]). As formed bachelor in theology he was a delegate at the Council of Constance in 1417–1418, and was licensed in theology between 1418 and 1422 (*CUP* IV, 91, n.4).

[*ms*: Noviomen.] dioc., quam obtinet (20 lib. turon.). Non obst. etiam quod gratia expectativa per S. V. nuper in rotulo devote filie vestre univ. Parisien. de data v° kal. Junii anno primo creationis S. V. eidem supplicanti facta cum aliis et concessa, virtute cuius gratie adhuc sibi non est pacifice provisum, quamvis tamen virtute ipsius vero acceptaverit duo beneficia cum protestatibus requisitis ac de ipsis sibi provisum extiterit, scilicet quandam cappellan. ad altare s. Anne in eccl. parroch. s. Jacobi de Carnificio [Saint-Jacques de la Boucherie] Parisius (25 lib. turon.), et curam s. Laurentii prope Parisius, Parisien. dioc. (100 lib. turon.), de quibus duobus beneficiis credit ipse supplicans infallibiliter evince, in quo casu eidem supplicanti intuitu pietatis concedere dignemini quod ipsa prima gratia in suo vigore remanen. cum hac secunda gratia vestra sibi concedenda valeat uti commode et gaudere....[87]

Item devoto vestro Odoni de Fouilliaco [Fouilloy, Somme], cler. Ambianen. dioc., mag. in artibus, bac. in decretis, de canon. sub exp. preb. cinq aut plurium Aurelianen., Turonen., Noviomen., Suessionen., Carnoten..... Non obst. cura Danquetonville [Anctoville-sur-Boscq, Manche], Constantien. dioc., [et] preb. eccl. colleg. s. Salvatoris Blesis [Blois], Carnoten. dioc., [et] cappella s. Guillelmi in eccl. Suessionen., et prebenda b. Marie in Vineis, Suessionen. (100 lib. parisien.).[88]

Item Guillelmo Lupi, mag. in artibus, bac. in decretis ac vestrarum apostolicarum abbreviatori, de canon. sub expect. preb. ac dignit., personat..... Non obst. canon. et preb. Rothomagen. et Belvacen. (140 lib. parisien.), et gratia expectativa in cancellaria declaranda, dispensan. cum eo ut duas dignitates aut personatus vel duo alia beneficia incompatibilia, si sibi vigore gratie haberi conferantur, recipere et retinere valeat quod adiunxerit vel dignetur E. S. gratiam eidem Guillelmo factam sub eadem data extendere ad canon. et preb. et dignit. unius aut plurium eccl. provinciarum predictarum.[89]

Item quatenus Martino de Varsenare, Tornacen. dioc., de legitimo matrimonio procreato, licen. in legibus de rigore examinatis, mag. in artibus et bac. in decretis, stud. Parisius in facultate theologie, gratiam de

---

[87] This supplication is attached in the left margin of the *rotulus*. In the *introtulator*'s list, Fare's supplication preceded that of Bourgin. He petitioned in the *rotulus* of 1403, at which time he was rector of parish church of Cappy, near Bray-sur-Somme (Reg. Suppl. 98, fol. 205r; *CUP* IV, 92, n° 1796).

[88] This supplication is also on a strip tied on the left margin of the *rotulus*. He petitioned in the *rotulus* of 1403 (Reg. Suppl. He began his lectures as bachelor in canon law at Paris in 1415 (Fournier, *FDecr*. I, 160, 173 [Fouilliaco]).

[89] He petitioned in the *rotulus* of 1403, at which point he was studying in the faculty of theology and only held a chaplaincy (Reg. Suppl. 98, fol. 208v; *CUP* IV, 92, n° 1796). His name does not appear among holders of prebends in *FEG* II: *Diocèse de Rouen* (Turnhout, 1998).

benef..... providere. Cum eodem supplicante misericorditer et de speciali gratia dispen. ut octo beneficia ecclesiastica quorum tamen fructus pro tempore obtinenti et apud eos non residenti ultra tricentas libras turon. parv. non valeant annuatim obtinere et simul quoad iuxerit retinere libere et licite valeat, generalis concilii et quibuscumque aliis constitutionibus apostolicis... nequaquem obstantibus. Non obst. quod obtinet parrochialem ecclesiam de Heurne [Heurne, East Flanders, Belgium], quam dictus supplicans obtinuit virtute gratia apostolice per eandem S. V. in rotulo universitatis studii Parisien. nuperrime sibi concesse, et personatum de Houthelm sancta Crucis [Kruishoutem, East Flanders, Belgium], et quamdam in parrochiali sancti Salvatoris et aliam in parrochiali sancti Jacobi ecclesiis, et cappelan. sancti Amandi per se fundatam opidi Brugen., dicte Tornacen. dioc., perpetuas cappellanias, et super quadam alia perpetua cappellan. in parroch. eccl. sancti Wawingis, dicti opidi Brugen. fundata, Parisius noscitur litigare, qui quidam personatus et cappellanie sine cura sunt (98 lib. turon. parv.). Et non obst. etiam quod habet dispensationem in qua sit mentio de omnibus predictis beneficiis, et eorum valore ad tenendum in simul quoad iuxerit duo beneficia ecclesiastice curata seu alias incompatibilia, etiam si parrochiales ecclesie, dignitates, personatus perpetue administrationes vel officia in metropolitan. vel cathedralibus aut collegiatis ecclesiis et dignitates ipsa in metropolitan. vel cathedralibus maiores post pontificales, aut in collegiatis ecclesiis huiusmodi principalis fuerint et ad eas consueverint, qui per electionem assume si sibi alias canonice conferantur vel assumatur ad illa et ad dimittendum illa, simul vel successive, simpliciter vel ex causa permutandis et loco dimissi vel dimissorum aliud vel alia, simile vel dissimile, aut simulia vel dissimilia, duo dum taxat invicem incompatibilia beneficium seu beneficia ecclesiasticum seu ecclesiastica recipiendum, et etiam quoad iuxerit insimul libere et licite retinendum, generalis concilii et quibuscumque aliis constitutionibus apostolicis, etc. contrariis nequaque obstantibus.[90]

Item Matheo Lourmier, presb. Laudunen. dioc., mag. in artibus, gratiam de benef..... Non obst. cura parroch. eccl. de Congrastro, custodia clericali in ecclesia Laudunen., ac cappellan. s. Martini in eccl. parroch. s. Boeciani de Petriponte [Pierrepont, Aisne], de Laudunen. dioc., quas idem Matheus noscitur obtinere (24 lib.).

Item Jacobo de Belloramo, subdiac. Ambianen. dioc., mag. in artibus, licen. in legibus et bac. in decretis, actu stud. Parisius in eadem facultate

---

[90] Varsenare's supplication was included in the list of the *inrotulator* at this place in sequence but is absent in the *rotulus*. Lupi's supplication is in the *rotulus*, but not in the *inrotulator*'s list. Whether this was an intentional switch, or an accidental omission cannot be determined. Varsenare petitioned in the *rotulus* of 1403 as master in arts and a student in canon law (Reg. Suppl. 98, fol. 210v; *CUP* IV, 93, n° 1796 [Varsevare]). He presumably came from the village of Varsenare, on the southwest edge of Bruges.

decretorum, gratiam de benef..... Non obst. canon. et preb. Ambianen., et canon. et preb. s. Vulfranni in Abbatisvilla, eiusdem dioc. (60 lib.).[91]

Item Balduino Galle, cler. Morinen. dioc., de legittimo matrimonio procreatis, mag. in artibus et in utroque iure licen., Parisius stud. in facultate theologie, gratiam de benef..... Non obst. altera portione parroch. eccl. s. Petri Bergen. [Bergues, Nord], quadam cappellan. in eccl. colleg. s. Audomari [Saint-Omer, Pas-de-Calais] ad altare s. Thome martiris, et quadam alia cappellan. in eccl. parroch. s. Martini Bergen., communiter et vulgariter nuncupata 'quinta cappellan.' (40 lib. parv. turon.).[92]

Item Johanni Darques, presb. Ambianen. dioc., mag. in artibus et bac. in theologia, gratiam de canon. sub. expect..... Non obst. parroch. eccl. s. Vedasti [Saint-Vaast] prope Monsterolum supra mare [Montreuil-sur-Mer, Pas-de-Calais], Ambianen. dioc., et personatu de Drovino [Drouvin, Pas-de-Calais], Attrebaten. dioc., quem adeptus est virtute gratie eidem per S. V. facte in primo rotulo univ. (50 lib. parisien.).[93]

Item Petro Gorguechon, presb. Ambianen. dioc., mag. in artibus, actu stud. Parisius in facultate theologie, gratiam de benef..... Non obst. cura s. Johannis Evangeliste fundata Parisius in collegio Cardinalis Monaci (15 franc.), et duabus cappellan., scilicet una in eccl. colleg. s. Vulfranni in Abbatisvilla, Ambianen. dioc., et altera in eccl. nostre domine de Dymontecourt, extra muros Abbatisvilla, (16 franc.).[94]

Item Johanni Bertandi, cler. Ambianen. dioc., mag. in artibus et bac. in iure canonico, actu stud. Parisius in predicta facultate, gratiam de canon. sub expect. preb.....[95]

---

[91] The text of his supplication in the *inrotulator*'s list asked for a canonry with expectation of prebend rather than a benefice, and makes no mention of his canonical prebends at Amiens and Abbeville. The text of that supplication is repeated in a strip attached to the left margin, covering the supplications of Lourmier and Belloramo. Only the version in the *rotulus* itself includes the required list of ecclesiastical positions currently held. He petitioned in the *rotulus* of 1403 among those declared absent from Paris, at which time he was studying civil law at Orléans and held a chaplaincy in the diocese of Amiens (Reg. Suppl. 98, fol. 215v; *CUP* IV, 94, n° 1796) and in the *rotulus* of 1410 (*CUP* IV, 196, n° 1908). He was licensed in both laws in 1421 (*CUP* IV, 94n). *FEG* I, 133 [Beaurains].

[92] He petitioned in the *rotulus* of 1403 (Reg. Suppl. 98, fol. 209v; *CUP* IV, 93, n° 1796)

[93] He petitioned in the *rotulus* of 1403, immediately before Galle (Reg. Suppl. 98, fol. 209v; *CUP* IV, 93. n°1796). He was a regent master in theology by 1422 (*CUP* IV, 406. n° 2195) and was still teaching in the faculty of thelogy at Paris in 1429 (*CUP* IV, 420, n° 2219; 445, n° 2258; 457, n° 2281; 467, n° 2296; 483, n° 2323); Sullivan, *Parisian Licentiates in Theology*, II, 190–91.

[94] He petitioned in the *rotulus* of 1403, at which time he was in litigation over an expectation granted by Benedict XIII in the gift of the dean of Saint-Vulfrani in Abbeville (Reg. Suppl. 98, fol. 209v; *CUP* IV, 93, n° 1796).

[95] He listed no benefices held. He should probably be distinguished from Johannes Bertandi, corrected to Bertrandi, a student in theology, who petitioned in the *rotulus* of 1403 and held two chaplaincies at that time (Reg. Suppl. 98, fols. 209v–210r; *CUP* IV, 93, n° 1796).

Item Gerardo Hemmere, subdiac. Cameracen. dioc., mag. in artibus et bac. in decretis, gratiam de benef..... Non obst. prebende s. Petri Insulen. [Lille, Nord], Tornacen. dioc., s. Quintini in Sancto Quintino, ac cappellan. b. Nicolai sita in eccl. parroch. s. Quintini et cappella in Peronna, Noviomen. dioc., necnon preb. sanctorum Gervasii et Prothasii de Guisi [Guise, Aisne], Laudunen. dioc., (60 lib. parisien.).

Item Egidio de Quorrouble [Quarouble, Nord], Cameracen. dioc. subdiac., mag. in artibus et bac. in decretis Parisius, gratiam de canon. sub expect. preb..... Non obst. parroch. eccl. de Oysiaco [Oysi, Pas-de-Calais], preb. b. Marie Condaten. [Condé-sur-l'Escaut, Nord], et b. Marie ad aulam in Valen[ciennen.], necnon cappellan. b. Marie site in eccl. b. Marie Maioris omni sanctorum in eccl. s. Johannis Valenchienn., Cameracen. dioc., et cappellan. situate ad maius altare in eccl. b. Jacobi eiusdem ville Valen[ciennen.], Cameracen. [*ms.* Attrebaten.] dioc., (70 lib. parisien.).

Item Johanni de Malafiducia, mag. in artibus et bac. in decretis, cler. Morinen. dioc., gratiam de benef..... Non obst. quadam gratia expectativa per S. V. sibi concessa in alio rotulo univ. Parisien. vigore cuius acceptavit et possidi canon. et preb. eccl. s. Petri Arien. [Aire, Pas-de-Calais], Morinen. dioc., canon. et preb. s. Petri de Lutosa [Leuze, Hainaut, Belgium], Cameracen. dioc., ac tribus cappellaniis, una in castro de Lucheu [in deanery of Saint-Pol-sur-Ternoise, Pas-de-Calais], et alia in castro de Frevench [Frévent, Pas-de-Calais], et alia latius in confect. litterarum declarandum (20 lib. parv. turon.).[96]

Marginal note at end of Malafiducia entry: Hic ponatur Gobertus Lanchart, Noviomen. dioc.[97]

Item Johanni de Atrio alias Clerici, cler. Cameracen. dioc., mag. in artibus, bac. in theologia studentique Parisius in predicta facultate theologie a decem annis circa, quatinus sibi gratiam de benef..... Non obst. quadam gratia expectativa ad predictam collationem Cameracen. in alio rotuli univ. Parisien. per S. V. sibi facta virtute cuius gratie acceptationem, provisionem et possessionem cappelle episcopalis palacii Cameracen., de qua litem patitur adeptus est (40 lib. parv. turon.), etiam cappellan. ad altare nostre domine in eccl. parroch. de Liis [Lys-lez-Lannoy, Nord], Tornacen. dioc. (30 lib. turon.), capellan. ad altare b. Andree in eccl. colleg. s. Petri de Luthosa (10 lib. turon.), et cappella nostre domine de Reulay/Renlay

---

[96] He petitioned in the *rotulus* of 1403, by which time he held a chaplaincy in the church of Notre-Dame in Thérouanne (Reg. Suppl. 98, fol. 211r; *CUP* IV, 93. n°1796 [Malfience]).

[97] His supplication, once attached here, is not among the separate supplication strips. Gobertus petitioned in the *rotulus* for bachelors in arts in 1403 (Reg. Suppl. 100, fol. 109r; *CUP* IV, 120, n° 1799).

sita infra metas parrochie de Sommaing [Sommaing, Nord], Cameracen. [*ms*: Attrebaten.] dioc., (6 lib. turon.).[98]
Item Jacobo de Mota, subdiac. Cameracen. dioc., mag. in artibus et licen. in decretis Parisius, gratiam de canon. sub expect. preb.....Non obst. eccl. parroch. de Hermis [Hermies, Pas-de-Calais] super qua litigat, necnon cappellan. s. Nicolai in eccl. parroch. de Villari domini Polii [Villers-Pol, Nord], et cappellan. s. Georgii in eccl. parroch. de Binchio [Binche, Hainaut, Belgium], Cameracen. dioc. (16 lib. turon.).[99]
Item Henrico de Barcheron, mag. in artibus, necnon in iure canonico bac., actu stud. Parisius in facultate decretorum, Cameracen. dioc., gratiam de benef.....necnon obst. cappellan. situate in eccl. s. Amati de Duaco, Attrebaten. dioc., que est consecrata altare b. Marie retro magnum altare illius eccl. s. Amati, quequid cappellania vulgariter nuncupata 'Gallem du Four', super qua presens Henrico pretendit ius hinc virtute sue nominatoris sibi concesse per S. P. (20 coronarum).
Supplicat...Johannes de Monstreleto [Monstrelet, Somme], presb. Ambianen. dioc., mag. in artibus ac bac. in theologia, actu studens Parisius in eadem facultate, quatinus sibi gratiam de benef.....Non obst. cura s. Johannis de Soyseyo iuxta Caprosiam [Chevreuse, Yvelines], Parisien. dioc., et cappellan. in cappella pauperum clericorum in suburbiis Ambianen., necnon cappellan. seu commenda in cappella Choletorum Parisius [collège Cholet] fundata (40 lib. parisien.).[100]
Item Johanni Andree, cler. Cameracen. dioc., mag. in artibus, bac. in decretis Parisius actu stud. in facultate decretorum, gratiam de benef..... Non obst. parroch. eccl. sancti Amandi de Helderghem [Heldergem, East Flanders, Belgium], dicte Cameracen. dioc., quam obtinet (27 lib. parisien.).[101]
Item Johanni de Gondainvillier, cler. Ambianen. dioc., mag. in artibus et bac. formato in theologia, presenti et continuo scolari Parisius in eadem facultate, ut asserit nullum benef. sibi provideri, de benef.....Non obst. gratia apost. in rotulo univ. Parisien. per S. V. sibi concessa de data v[to] kal. Junii anno primo, de qua nundum sibi pacifice provisum est. Non obst. etiam quadam cappellan. pro nunc litigiosa per dominum cardinalem

---

[98] The text of this entry is from his separate supplication strip, whose marginal note places it here. He petitioned in the 1403 *rotulus* for bachelors in arts, at which time he held two chaplaincies (Reg. Suppl. 100, fol.109v; *CUP* IV, 120, n° 1799).
[99] The text of this supplication follows that of Johannes de Atrio on the same separate strip.
[100] This separate supplication is marked at top as 'Presens', and in the upper left-hand margin: 'sequitur immediate post Henricum de Barcheron'.
[101] He petitioned in the *rotulus* for bachelors in arts in 1403 (Reg. Suppl. 100, fols. 110v–111r; *CUP* IV, 121, n° 1799). As a bachelor in canon law he lectured in the Decretals in 1415–16 (Fournier, *FDecr.* I, 157).

Pisan.,[102] legatum vestrum a latere, etiam sibi concessa fundata in eccl. sanctorum Innocentium Parisius ad altare b. Marie (20 lib. parisien.).[103]

Item Olivero Caminii, cler. Ambianen. dioc., mag. in artibus, actu stud. Parisius in iure canonico, gratiam de benef...., ita quod dignitas cum preb., sive simul sive successive, pro uno benef. sibi conputentur valeat, que post acceptationem preb. virtute gratie sue dignitatem acceptare vel viceversa, preb. s. Petri Namurcen., Leodien. dioc., et preb. nostre domine Laudunen., et s. Petri Arien., Morinen. dioc., in quibus ius licet pretendit (61 lib. turon. parv.).

Marginal comment at beginning of next entry: 'Renerus Scat, Leodien. dioc. inscribatur immediate ante Simonem de Morilio, et supplicatio eius inveniet inter absentes.' *This probably relates to an attached supplication for a 'Renerus', since there is a tie for an attached supplication in the margin, but no such supplication is among the separate supplications.*

Item Simoni de Morolio, cler. Ambianen. oriundi, mag. in artibus et licen. in iure canonico, gratiam de benef.... ad collat. episc., decani, etc. Ambianen., Parisien., Noviomen., Rothomagen..... Non obst. personatu de Campaignes Morinen. [Campagne-lés-Boulonnais or Campagne-lès-Guines, Pas-de-Calais], et canon. et preb. s. Mathei Foilliacen. [Fouilloy, Somme], Ambianen. dioc., quas idem Simoni assecutus est vigore gratie expectative per S. V. sibi factis in rotulo magistrorum univ. Parisien., necnon quedam cappellan. ad altare b. Michaelis in parroch. eccl. Rieu [Rieux, Oise], Belvacen. dioc., et quod alia in eccl. colleg. b. Marie de Nigella [Nesle, Somme] ad altare s. Johannis, Noviomen. dioc., (60 lib. turon. parv.).

Item Petro Brachii, cler. Laudunen. dioc., mag. in artibus et licen. in medicina, de canon. sub expect. preb..... Non obst. quod a S. V. gratiam expectativam in rotulo univ. et studii Parisien. obtinuerit eiusque vigore acceptaverit canon. et preb. (20 lib. parisien.).[104]

---

[102] Alamannus Adimarius, former bishop of Pisa, cardinal priest s. Eusebii from June 1411 until his death in Sept. 1422.

[103] He was still a formed bachelor in 1416, when he petitioned in a *rotulus* of the faculty of theology (*CUP* IV, 322, n° 2072). He was licensed between 1416 and 1420, probably in 1419 or 1420 (see Sullivan, *Parisian Licentiates* II, 261–62 [Gondevillier]). He was regent master in theology at Paris by 1426 and still active in 1438 (*CUP* IV, 457, n° 2281; 467, n° 2296; 486, n° 2331; 530, n° 2395; 563, n° 2453; 600, n° 2510; 607, n° 2526). His place of origin is presumably Godenvillers, Oise, south of Montdidier.

[104] This supplication, once attached here, is among the separate supplication strips. Petrus Brachii's name occurs in the margin of the *rotulus* at this point. A note in the margin of the supplication strip reads: 'ponatur in principali rotulo immediate post Simonem de Morolio.' 'Principali rotulo' refers to the university *rotulus*, which would include the *rotulus* of the Picard nation, as distinct from those from colleges or specific groups, such as bachelors of theology. Brachii was licensed in medicine in March 1414 and was regent master in November (*CUP* IV, 287, n° 2020; 294, n° 2030). He was still active in that faculty in 1423

Item Eligio Mainebode, presb. Morinen. dioc., mag. in artibus, actu present. stud. in facultate decretorum, gratiam de benef..... Non obst. parroch. eccl. b. Marie de Popinghes [Poperinghes, West Flanders, Belgium], dicte dioc., quam vigore cuiusdam gratie per E. S. V. eidem Eligio sub data v° kal. Junii pontificis E. S. V. anno primo facta obtinet, etiam non obst. quadam cappellan. b. Laurentii in eccl. s. Johannis in s. Audomaro (54 lib. parv. turon.).[105]

Item Reginaldo Remy, preb. Belvacen. dioc., mag. in artibus et bac. in theologia, dignemini providere canon. sub expect. preb. ac dignitas, etc. in eccl. Belvacen., Rothomagen., Melden., Silvanecten., Suessionen., Ambianen., Morinen. aut Noviomen., aut abbatis et conv. monast. s. Dionysii in Francia, O. S. B., Parisien. dioc., aut prioris s. Eligii Parisien. eiusdem ordinis..... Non obst. quod eccl. parroch. de Liencourt [Liancourt, Oise] et cappellan. monast. b. Marie de s. Paulo prope Belvacum, ac etiam domum dei cappellan. dicti domus dei s. Genovefe, Belvacen. dioc., dictus supplicans noscatur obtinere (80 lib. parisien.).[106]

The following entry is on a strip sewn onto the left margin of the rotulus, *with a marginal note at beginning of Cornepin entry*: 'ponitur hic supplicatio Victoris de Baenst.'

Item Victori de Baenst, cler. Tornacen. dioc., mag. in artibus, bac. in theologia, gratiam de benef..... Non obst. quadam cappellan. sita in eccl. parroch. de Lissvoeghe [Lisseweghe, West Flanders, Belgium], et quadam custodia in eadem eccl., Tornacen. dioc., ad quam nondum haberi ius vigore collationis facte per ordinarium, et non obst. gratiam per S. V. ... ad collat. etc. abbatis s. Bertini in s. Audomaro, Morinen. dioc., vigore cuius acceptavit, et si fecit provideri de altera portione parroch. eccl. s. Margarete in s. Audemaro, dicte Morinen. dioc., (80 lib. parisien.).

Item Johanni Cornepin, presb. Ambianen. dioc., mag. in artibus et bac. in theologia, de canon. sub expect. preb.... eccl. Parisien., Ambianen., Belvacen., Suessionen, Tornacen., Silvanecten., Rothomagen., Melden..... Non obst. canon. et preb. b. Marie de Nigella, Noviomen. dioc., (20 lib. turon.), non obst. etiam gratia expectativa de data v° kal. Junii anno primo per S. V. eidem supplicanti facta, virtute cuius gratie non sibi adhuc provisum, qua quidem gratia in vigore suo integra permanente cum hac gratia vestra concedenda valeat uti et gaudere.

(*CUP* IV, 308, n° 2050; 325, n° 2094; 355, n° 2119; 374, n° 2147; 400, n° 2184; 407, n° 2197; 424, n° 2228); E. Wickersheimer, *Dictionnaire biographique des médecins en France au Moyen Age* (Paris, 1936; repr. 1979), 644 [Lebras].

[105] He petitioned in the *rotulus* for bachelors in arts in 1403 (*CUP* IV, 120, n° 1799).

[106] He was the *temptator* for licentiates in the Picard nation in 1418 (*CUP* IV, 472, n° 2304).

42   *History of Universities*

~~Item Arnoldo de Gibbeque, presb., mag. in artibus, stud. Parisius in facultate decretorum, gratiam de benef...... Non obst. cappella nostre domine de Henim situata in eccl. parroch. de Boussuto, Cameracen. dioc., cuius fructus non excedunt in portatis annuatim 3 franc., vel ad collat. episc. etc. eccl. Parisien.~~

Supplicat...Arnoldus de Gibeque, presb. Cameracen. dioc., mag. in artibus, presens et inscriptus in rotulo univ. et studens in facultate decretorum, gratiam de benef..... Non obst. cappella nostre domine de Hemerip(?) situata in eccl. parroch. de Boussuto [Boussoit, Hainaut, Belgium], diocesis Cameracen. (6 franc.), et non obst. gratia expectativa ad collat. etc, decani et capituli nostre domine Anthonien., dioc. Cameracen., sub data quinto kalendas etiam in rotulo Parisien. univ. eidem Arnoldo facta per S. V. virtute cuius acceptavit et fecit sibi provideri de canon. et preb. Anthonien. super quibus litigium patitur (40 lib. parv. [turon.].[107]

Item Johanni de Fonte, presb. dioc. Attrebaten., mag. in artibus, stud. Parisius in facultate decretorum, gratiam de benef..... Non obst. cappellan. Du Bies, dicte Attrebaten. dioc., quam obtinet (30 lib. parv. turon.).[108]

Item Leonio de Baest, presb., mag. in artibus actu stud. in facultate theologie, rectori seu investiti parroch. eccl. de Vechel [Veghel, North Brabant, Netherlands], Leodien. dioc., gratiam de benef..... Non obst. dicta parroch. eccl. quam obtinet (20 march. agent.), ac gratia expectativa in cancellaria E. S. V. exprimenda.

~~Item Johanni(?) de Fonte, Attrebaten. dioc.~~

In margin at beginning of next entry: inscribatur supplicatio Georgii Cantoris[109] immediate post supplicationem Leonii de Baest.

Item Nicolao de Mota, Morinen. dioc. cler., mag. in artibus ac bac. in decretis, gratiam de benef..... Non obst. canon. et preb. b. Marie Casleten., Morinen. dioc., quos assecutus est virtute gratie apost. sibi per S. V. facte sub data v° kal. anno primo rotulo univ., et cappellan. b. Marie de Novo Opere in eccl. Cathalaunen., (27 lib. parisien.), secum dispen. quod duo incompatibilia benef. possit tenere coadiuxerit.[110]

Item Johanni Avantaige, Morinen. dioc., mag. in artibus et bac. in medicina, actu stud. Parisius in facultate medicine, gratiam de

---

[107] This version of his supplication is among the separate supplication strips, and entered here. He petitioned in the 1403 *rotulus* for bachelors in arts (Reg. Suppl. 100, fol. 110v; *CUP* IV, 120, n° 1799).

[108] He became a bachelor in canon law in December 1417 (Fournier, *FDecr.* I, 188, 190, 212, 220, 222, 229) and licensed in 1424 (Fournier, *FDecr.* 244).

[109] A supplication for Georgius Cantoris, a master in arts and bachelor in medicine, was supposed to be placed here, but it occurs later, after that of Johannes Juvenis.

[110] He was licensed in canon law in 1415 (*CUP* IV, 306, n° 2048); aee also Fournier, *FDecr.* I, 134, 141).

benef..... Non obst. parroch. eccl. de Merquenes [Merck-Saint-Liévin, Pas-de-Calais], Morinen. dioc., (50 lib. parv. turon.).[111]
Item Alberico de Sabbit, mag. in artibus, necnon in iure canonico bac., actu stud. Parisius in facultate decretorum, Cameracen. dioc., nullum benef. obtinen., gratiam de benef.....
Item Johanni Galet, Ambianen. dioc., mag. in artibus, actu stud. Parisius in facultate theologie, nullum obtinet benef., gratiam de benef..... Non obst. quadam gratia eidem per S. V. facta in rotulo Parisien. univ., de qua non est provisus.[112]
Item Johanni Hubry, subdiac. Laudunen. dioc., mag. in artibus, de benef..... Non obst. quod canon. et preb. eccl. colleg. s. Quintini de Sancto Quintino in Viromandia, Noviomen. dioc. noscatur obtinere (16 lib. parisien.), et quod per alias litteras vestras eidem de benef. ut mandatum extitit provideri, quod que earum vigore in altera cappellanarum ad altare s. Pauli in ecclesia Laudunen. (24 lib. parisien.), ius habere pretendat, licet ipsius possessionem pacifica nundum fuerit assecutus.[113]
Item Johanni Chuffart, Tornacen. dioc.[114]
Supplicat S. V. devotus orator vester Johannes Chuffart de Tornaco, mag. in artibus et bac. in decretis actu legens Parisius in dicta facultate decretorum, quatinus sibi gratiam de benef..... Non obst. quod optineat cappellanias, unam in eccl. colleg. b. Marie de Brugis, Tornacen. dioc., aliam in eccl. colleg. s. Gaugerici de Valencenis, aliam in eccl. parroch. de Havesies [Havinnes, Hainaut, Belgium], Cameracen. dioc., aliam in eccl. monialium b. Marie de Barra [la Barre, near Château-Thierry, Aisne], Suessionen. dioc., et non obst. cappellan. in loco infirmarie in monasterio s. Dionysii in Francia, Parisien. dioc., licet pacifice non possideat, et quod etiam de canon. et preb. eccl. colleg. s. Gaugerici Cameracen. per S. V. sibi mandatum extitit provideri (80 parv. turon.).

[111] Johannes de Avantage, or l'Avangage, was licensed in medicine in 1418 (*CUP* IV, 344, n° 2105n) and remained active in the faculty of medicine until at least 1425 (*CUP* IV, 384, n° 2164; 390, n° 2169; 400, n° 2184; 407, n° 2197; 437, n° 2246; 446, n° 2261); Wickersheimer, *Dictionnaire*, 355–56, who, not knowing this document, dated his baccalaureate in medicine to 1416. He was physician to Philip, Duke of Burgundy by 1420 and was bishop of Amiens from 1437 until his death in 1456 (*FEG* I, 77–79).
[112] Possibly identical with the Johannes Galet from the diocese of Amiens who, as a student in canon law, petitioned in a special *rotulus* of students at Paris in 1403 (*CUP* IV, 112, n° 1797).
[113] This supplication is among the separate supplication strips, and entered here because the note in the margin of the strip states: 'presens; ipse precedit Chuffart.'
[114] His supplication is among the separate strips and is placed here, where threads in the margin of the *rotulus* and corresponding holes in the margin of the supplication show it was once attached. He was bachelor in canon law in 1415 and licensed in 1416 (*CUP* IV, 307–08, n° 2050; 314, n° 2063; Fournier, *FDecr*. I, 149, 157). He had a distinguished career as regent master and later served as *nuncius* for the University of Paris at the papal court in Rome; see numerous entries in *CUP* IV and Fournier, *FDecr*. I.

Item Jacobo Canis, subdiac. Cameracen. dioc., mag. in artibus et bac. in decretis Parisius, gratiam de canon. sub expect. preb.....Non obst. parroch. eccl. de Felines [Flines-lés-Raches, Nord], Attrebaten. dioc. (36 lib. turon.).
Item Petro Rouselli, cler. Belvacen. dioc., mag. in artibus, actu stud. Parisius in facultate decretorum, gratiam de duobus beneficiis....Non obst. quadam gratia expectativa ad collat. etc. episc., decani...eccl. Ambianen. per E. S. V. sibi in primo et principali rotulo alme matris nostre univ. Parisien. sub data v kal. Juniii pontificatus E.S.V. anno primo concessa, super qua litteras apost. et processus inde ferat nundum expediri facere voluit.
Item Arnuldo de Uden [Uden, North Brabant, Netherlands], cler. Leodien. dioc., mag. in artibus et bac. in medicina, actu legenti in dicta facultate, rectori altaris s. Johannis Evangeliste in eccl. parroch. de Beke [Beek en Donk], prope Aerle [Aarle-Rixtel, North Brabant, Netherlands], et sancta crucis in eccl. parroch. de Alken [Alken, Limbourg, Belgium] sitorum dicte Leodien. dioc., de gratiam de benef.....Non obst. dicte altaris [cappellan.], que noscitur obtinere.[115]
Item Jacobo Jovin/Jonin, Cameracen. dioc. subdiac., mag. in artibus, de benef.....Non obst. preb. b. Marie ad aulam in Valen[cienn.], Cameracen. dioc., necnon cappellan. situate ad magnum altare in eccl. b. Jacobi eiusdem ville, Attrebaten. dioc., (30 lib. parv. turon.)..., necnon quadam gratia expectativa a domino nostro ultimate in rotulo Parisien. sibi concessa, de qua nundum est provisus.[116]
Item Guillelmo Blumel, subdiac. Noviomen. dioc., mag. in artibus Parisius, stud. in facultate decretorum, gratiam de benef...., secum dispen. ut parroch. eccl. de Villaribus in Boscagio [Villers-Bocage, Somme], Ambianen. dioc., quam obtinet simul cum dignitate, etc. seu curato benef. huiusmodi aut quemcumque alia duo incompatibiliam...simul recipere ac retinere possit. Non obst. eadem eccl. parroch. de Villaribus in Boscagio (15 lib. parisien.).[117]
Item Hugoni Maupin, cler. Ambianen. dioc, mag. in artibus, actu stud. Parisius in facultate theologie, gratiam de benef.....Non obst. quadam

---

[115] He was licensed in medicine in 1416 (*CUP* IV, 311, n° 2059); Wickersheimer, *Dictionnaire*, 44–45. The editors of the *Chartularium* placed him in the English-German nation, but without providing any source (*CUP* IV, 311, n. 2).
[116] This supplication is on a strip sewn into the left margin, with a marginal note: post immediate Arnuldum Uden.
[117] He became a bachelor in canon law in 1416 (Fournier, *FDecr*. I, 150, 161, 178, 197, 213) and was licensed in canon law in April 1426 (*CUP* IV, 450, n° 2267; Fournier, *FDecr*. I, 276).

gratia expectativa per S. V. sibi facta de rotulo univ. de qua sibi nundum provisum est.

Item Johanni de Fonte alias Borreman, presb. Cameracen. dioc., mag. in artibus, stud. actu Parisius in facultate decretorum a tribus annis citra, gratiam de benef..... Non obst. quod parroch. eccl. de Materna [Maeter, East Flanders, Belgium], predicte dioc. (16 coron. francie), noscitur obtinere, et non obst. gratia alia sibi facta in rotulo alme univ. Parisien. de qua nondum sibi provisum est.[118]

Item Petro Wisonis, Traiecten. dioc. cler., mag. in artibus et bac. in medicina, nullum beneficium obtenenti, gratiam de benef..... Non obst. gratia facta per rotulum univ. Parisien., super qua nundum bullas levavit.[119]

Item Andree Vavassoris, cler. Ambianen. dioc., mag. in artibus et in decretis bac., gratiam de benef..... Non obst. gratia eidem rotulo univ. Parisien. per S. V. facta, virtute cuius nullum benef. est assecutus.[120]

Item Johanni Franchi hominis, cler. Ambianen., mag. in artibus, actu stud. Parisius in facultate theologie, gratiam de benef..... Non obst. duabus cappellaniis quas obtinet, una videlicet fundata ad altare s. Petri in eccl. colleg. s. Furcei in Peronna, et alia in parroch. eccl. s. Johannis Evangeliste fundata ad altare s. Firmini, Noviomen. et Parisien. dioc., (16 lib. parisien.), necnon canon. et preb. in ecclesia s. Firmini confessoris in Ambianen., quorum canon. et preb. litem patitur (50 lib. parisien.).[121]

Item Balduino Lathomi, cler. Attrebaten. dioc., mag. in artibus, stud. in facultate decretorum, gratiam de benef..... Non obst. quadam gratia per eandem S. V. eidem Balduino facta de benef. eccl., c.c. vel s. c., etiam si prebenda etc., ad collat. prepositi, decani, et capituli s. Amati de Duaco, prefate dioc. Attrebaten., prout latius in litteris apost. inde confectis apparet, de qua numme sibi constat esse provisum.

Item Guillelmo Mets, presb. Cameracen. dioc., mag. in artibus et scolari Parisius, actu stud. in facultate decretorum, gratiam de benef..... Non obst. cura parroch. de Camphin [Camphin-en-Pevele, Nord, or Champhin-en-Carembault, Nord], Tornacen. dioc., qua dictus supplicans noscitur obtinere (26 lib. parv. turon.).[122]

Item Dominico Plaghe, cler. Morinen. dioc., mag. in artibus, actu stud. Parisius in facultate decretorum, gratiam de benef..... Non obst. quadam

---

[118] Possibly identical with the Johannes de Fonte, Cameracen. dioc., who was bachelor in canon law in 1420 (Fournier, *FDecr.* I, 211).

[119] Wickersheimer, *Dictionnaire*, 667.

[120] He was among a large group of scholars licensed in canon law in 1416 (*CUP* IV, 314, n° 2063; Fournier, *FDecr.* I, 149, 157).

[121] He was in his first year as cursor in theology in March 1423 (*CUP* IV, 419, n° 2217 [Francihominis]).

[122] He was bachelor in canon law in 1421 (Fournier, *FDecr.* I, 219 [Mets], 222, 228) and licensed in 1424 (*CUP* IV, 435 [Mers]; Fournier, *FDecr.* I, 244).

gratia speciali de v° kal. anno primo pontificatus S. V., qua extitit improvisus.

Item Simoni de Sancto Vedasto, cler. Ambianen. dioc., mag. in artibus ac bac. in iure canonico, gratiam de benef..... Non obst. quod personatus de Herentals [Herenthals, Antwerp, Belgium], Cameracen. dioc., obtineat in ecclesia Standei(?) (60 lib. parisien.). Non obst. quadam gratia etiam sibi facta in rotulo univ. Parisien., de qua nundum provisus est.[123]

Item Johanni Baudri, subdiac. Ambianen. dioc., mag. in artibus, actu stud. in facultate theologie, gratiam de benef..... Non obst. parroch. eccl. de Saicuto(?), Ambianen. dioc., (40 lib. parisien.).

Item Nicolao de Castris, mag. in artibus, Cameracen. dioc., actu stud. in facultate theologie, gratiam de canon. sub expect. preb..... Non obst. quod cappellan. de Sepmeries [Sepmeries, Nord] obtineat (10 coron. francie), et cappellan. s. Quintini in eccl. b. Aldegundis Melbodien. (10 d.).

Item Johanni Juvenis, Laudunen. dioc. cler., mag. in artibus et bac. in medicina, gratiam de benef..... Non obst. canon. et preb. ac thesauraria eccl. colleg. s. Petri in Foro, Laudunen., in quibus pretendit habere ius [*marginal insertion*: quamvis non fuerit possessionem pacificam assecutus] (40 lib. parisien.).[124]

Item Georgio Cantoris [*ms*: Cantre], cler. Tornacen. dioc., mag. in artibus et bac. in medicina, actu legenti in dicta facultate medicine, gratiam de benef..... Non obst. quadam martiraria in eccl. parroch. b. Marie de Dam [Damme, West Flanders, Belgium], (12 lib. parisien.), non obst. defectum natalium, quorum patitur ex soluto et soluta.[125]

Item Johanni de Garmeguy/Garmegny, mag. in artibus, preb. Belvacen. dioc., gratiam de benef..... Non obst. canon. et preb. eccl. colleg. s. Bartholomei in civitate Belvacen., et cappellan. s. Nicolai in eccl. nostre domine de Monciaco castro [Mouchy-le-Châtel, Oise] (22 lib.), et etiam eccl. de Tricot [Tricot, Oise], de qua nundum possessionem pacificam habet (20 lib.).

Item Simoni Maule/Manle, cler. Noviomen. dioc., mag. in artibus, gratiam de benef..... Non obst. gratia sibi facta sub data v° kal. [Junii] in rotulo univ. Parisien. ad collat. episcopi Noviomen., de qua nundum sibi

---

[123] As bachelor in canon law, he began his lectures in 1415–16 (Fournier, *FDecr.* I, 158, 173).

[124] He petitioned in the 1403 *rotulus* for bachelors in arts (Reg. Suppl. 100, fol. 110v; *CUP* IV, 120, n° 1799) and may have received a burse in the Collège de Laon in 1408 (*CUP* IV, 311n). He was licensed in medicine in 1416 (*CUP* IV, 311, n° 2059), after which he was regent master in medicine (*CUP* IV, 325, n° 2074; 333, n° 2090; 355, n° 2119; 374, n° 2147); Wickersheimer, *Dictionnaire*, 427.

[125] He was licensed in medicine in 1416 (*CUP* IV, 311, n° 2059; Wickersheimer, *Dictionnaire*, 181).

pacifice provisum est, et aliis non obst. in cancellaria declaranda, vel ad collat. etc. archiepiscopi Senonen.

Item Petro Soullardi, cler. Ambianen. dioc., mag. in artibus, actu stud. in facultate theologie, gratiam de benef..... Non obst. cappellan. s. Nicolai fundata in castro de Houssoy [la Houssoye, Somme], Ambianen. dioc., (8 lib. parisien.), et parroch. eccl. de Fontanis iuxta Vrervin [Fontaine-lès-Vervin, Aisne], Laudunen. dioc., de quarum provisum est virtute gratie apost. in ultimo rotulo univ. Parisien. per S. V. sibi facta, et de qua tanquam litigiosa competitiorem habet (30 lib. parisien.).

Item Guillelmus Brevis, mag. in artibus, cler. Tornacen. dioc., actu stud. in facultate decretorum, de benef..... Non obst. quadam cappellan. quam obtinet in eccl. b. Marie ad maius altare Curtracen. [Courtrai, Belgium] (6 lib. turon.).

Item Eustrando de Vallibus, cler. Attrebaten. dioc., mag. in artibus, actu stud. in facultate decretorum, gratiam de benef..... Non obst. canon. et preb. eccl. Attrebaten., de qua litem patitur ac cappellan.

Item Johanni de Venissia, cler. Noviomen. dioc., mag. in artibus, stud. Parisius in facultate decretorum, gratiam de benef..... Non obst. quadam gratia speciali pro eandem sibi S. V. facta de data v° kal. [Junii] anno primo, de qua sibi nundum provisum extitit.[126]

Item Ade de Doigny. Laudunen. dioc.

Item Johanni Angny, Laudunen. dioc.

Item Engelberto alias dicto Liemanno Nycolai, cler. Leodien. dioc., mag. in artibus actuque stud. Parisius in facultate medicine, gratiam....[127]

Item Michaeli de Merula, Tornacen. dioc., mag. in artibus, gratiam de benef..... Non obst. gratia expectativa de data vi° kal.[128] ad collat. Seclinien. eccl., et b. Marie Singen. [Synghem, East Flanders, Belgium], Tornacen. dioc., [et] non obst. cappellan. s. Jacobi quam obtinet in eccl. parroch. s. Amandi [Saint-Amand-les-Eaux, Nord], Tornacen. dioc., (10 lib. turon.).

Item Simoni Patoul, cler. Morinen. dioc., mag. in artibus actu stud. Parisius in facultate decretorum, gratiam de benef..... Non obst. personatu de Villariviridi, Ambianen. dioc., (23 lib. parisien.), ac quadam gratia expectativa eidem per S. V. sub data vestre coronationis ad collat. [episc., etc.] Melden. et Silvanecten., de qua sibi nundum est provisum facta.

---

[126] He was bachelor in canon law in 1415 (*CUP* IV, 306, n° 2048; Fournier, *FDecr.* I, 141).

[127] This supplication was on a separate strip attached here by paperclip, but nothing in the text or margin of the *rotulus* confirms this location. He was BMed in 1416 and licensed in 1418 (Wickersheimer, *Dictionnaire*, 129 [Engelbert Nicholai]).

[128] Probably refers to the *rotulus* of 1410, which was v kal.

Item Johanni Bertrandi de Ponte, cler. Leodien. dioc., mag. in artibus, Parisius stud. in facultate theologie, gratiam de canon. sub expect. preb..... Non obst. canon. et preb. eccl. Aquen. in provincia Provincie (30 lib. parisien.).

Item Fronimo le Hure, cler. Ambianen. dioc., mag. in artibus, stud. in theologia, nullum beneficium obtinen., gratiam de benef..... Non obst. quadam gratia de rotulo univ. baccalariorum sibi facta expectativa ad collat. decani et capituli etc. b. V[u]lfranni in Abbatisvilla, de qua nundum sibi provisum est.

Item Johanni Caron, cler. Ambianen. dioc., mag. in artibus, actu stud. in facultate theologie, nullum beneficium, gratiam de benef.....

Item Gerardo de Hoya, cler. Cameracen. dioc., mag. in artibus, actu stud. Parisius in facultate decretorum, ex nobili gener. procreato, gratiam de benef..... Non obst. tribus cappellaniis, quarum uno in parroschia de Esche [Essche-Saint-Liévin], Cameracen. dioc., sita est, alia in parroschia de Artevelde [?Achterveld, Utrecht, Netherlands], Traiecten. dioc., alia in parroschia de Pallis [le Pallet, Loire-Atlantique], Nanneten. dioc., (34 scutorum sive coronorum francie)..., [et] non obst. etiam gratia sibi alias in rotulo ducis Britannie facta, de qua nundum sibi extitit provisum.[129]

Item Petro de Aleurs, cler. Ambianen. dioc., mag. in artibus, actu stud. Parisius in facultate theologie, gratiam de benef..... Non obst. quadam cappellan. fundata ad altare s. Eligii in villa de Maucourt [Maucourt, Somme], Ambianen. dioc., (4 lib. parisien.).

Item Johanni de Morbeka, cler. Morinen. dioc., mag. in artibus, actu stud. Parisius in facultate medicine, nullum beneficium obtinen., gratiam de benef.....[130]

Item Henrico Tsermertens, mag. in artibus, stud. in facultate theologie, Cameracen. dioc., nullum beneficium obtinen., gratiam de benef..... Non obst. quod sit minor annus ob obtinendum benef. cum cura.

Item Bernardo Nivard, mag. in artibus, stud. in facultate medicine, Ambianen. dioc., gratiam de benef.[131]

---

[129] He began his lectures as a bachelor in canon law in 1416 (Fournier, *FDecr.* I, 161 [Haya], 180 [Hoya], 194 [Haya], 214 [Haya], 220 [Heya], 222 [Hoya], 228). He petitioned in the second *rotulus* sent to Martin V in 1424 and is mentioned in a letter of Eugenius IV in 1432 (*CUP* IV, 369, n° 2409).

[130] He was BMed in 1416 (Wickersheimer, *Dictionnaire*, 456 [Noerbeka]; D. Jacquart, *Supplément au 'Dictionnaire biographique des médecins' d'Ernst Wickersheimer* (Geneva, 1979), 188–89).

[131] He was licensed in medicine under unusual circumstances in June 1418 (*CUP* IV, 344, n° 2105 [Nivardi]). He continued as regent master in medicine and served once as dean until 1436 (*CUP* IV, 407, n° 2197; 424, n° 2228; 437, n° 2246; 461, n° 2285; 468, n° 2298; 500, n° 2352; 593, n° 2493); Wickersheimer, *Dictionnaire*, 77.

Item Johanni Potaige, cler. Ambianen. dioc., mag. in artibus, actu stud. Parisius in facultate theologie, gratiam de benef..... cum dispen. duorum annorum, si opus fuerit.[132]

Item ~~Jacobo Henicat, Laudunen. dioc.~~[133] Wilhelmo Steenwinkel, mag. in artibus, stud. Parisius in facultate decretorum, cler. Cameracen. dioc., nullum benef. obtinen., gratiam de benef.... aut canon.....[134]

Item Johanni de Ponte, Cameracen. dioc. cler., mag. in artibus, stud. Parisius in facultate theologie, gratiam de canon. sub expect. preb..... Non obst. cappellan. Animarum in eccl. b. Marie, Antwerpien., Cameracen. dioc., et cappellan. s. Johannis in Gratulo monte extra muros Geldonien. [Jodoigne, Brabant, Belgium], Leodien. dioc., (40 lib. parisien.).[135]

Item Johanni de Malda de Tornaco, mag. in artibus, stud. Parisius in facultate decretorum, nullum benef. obtinen., gratiam de benef.....[136]

Item Thome Barbery, presb., mag. in artibus, Ambianen. dioc., actu stud. in facultate theologie, gratiam de benef..... Non obst. cura de Fluiaco [Fluy, Somme], Ambianen. dioc., (20 lib.), et cappellan. quam habet in eccl. b. Martini de Pinconio [Picquigny, Somme] (8 lib.).

Item Johanni Sterkerade, cler. Cameracen. dioc., mag. in artibus, bac. in decretis Parisius, stud. in facultate decretorum, gratiam de uno vel duobus benef.....

Item Karolo de Pevenchi [Punchy, Somme], cler. Noviomen. dioc., mag. in artibus, Parisius actu stud. in facultate decretorum, gratiam de benef..... Non obst. quadam gratia sibi per S. V. facta ad duas collatores et duo benef. virtute cuius una pro sortita est effectum, videlicet de preb. eccl. b. Marie de Nigella, Noviomen. dioc., (12 lib. turon.), ac secum de

---

[132] He gave his first biblical lectures as cursor in theology in 1421, and his second lectures as cursor in 1424 (*CUP* IV, 399, n° 2182 [Potage]; 436, n° 2244; 465, n° 2292). He is to be distinguished from Johannes Potaige, who belonged to the Norman nation (*CUP* IV, 98, n° 1796).

[133] Perhaps a mistake for Johannes Helicant, a Picard master who was licensed in medicine in 1420 (*CUP* IV, 377, n° 2154).

[134] The supplications from here through Johannes Gossumy correspond to the list of the *inrotulator* found in S 6202.

[135] There were two Johannes de Ponte in theology in this period. One began his bachelor lectures on the Bible in January 1426 (*CUP* IV, 456, n° 2279) and the other in 1428 (*CUP* IV, 497, n° 2313). On the latter, see Sullivan, *Parisian Licentiates* II, 439–440. There was also a Johannes de Ponte who belonged to the French nation and petitioned in the 1403 *rotulus* of bachelors in arts (CUP IV, 314, n° 1799), whom Denifle incorrectly assumed was the younger of the two theologians (*CUP* IV, 551, n° 2429); see Z. Kaluza, 'Les débuts d'Albertisme tardif', in *Albertus Magnus und der Albertismus. Deutsche philosophische Kultur des Mittelalters* (Leiden, 1995), 207–302, at 265; idem, 'Les cours communs sur l'Éthique à Nicomaque à l'Université de Paris', in *Ad Ingenii Acuitionem.' Studies in Honour of Alfonso Maierù*, Stefano Caroti et al., eds. (Louvain-la-Neuve, 2006), 147–81, at 173.

[136] In the margin of this entry: 'ista supplicatio debet sequi immediate Karolum de Pevenchy', as is the case in the *inrotulator*'s list.

super deffectum etatis, quem patitur cum in xxiii° sue etatis anno constitutus extitit.

Item Johanni de Haemstede de nobili prosapia procreato, cler. Traiecten. dioc., mag. in artibus, nullum benef. obtinen., gratiam de benef.....

Item Franchisco de Casleto [Cassel, Nord], cler. Morinen. dioc., mag. in artibus, stud. Parisius in facultate theologie, nullum benef. obtinen., gratiam de benef.....

Supplicat...Jacobus Vrediel, mag. in artibus, in facultate medicine Parisius studens, cler. Cameracen. dioc., quatenus sibi specialem gratiam de benef. c.c. vel s.c.....[Non obst.] quadam gratia expectativa sub data quinto kal. Junii pontificatus vestri anno primo generose concessa, non obst. in cancellaria E. V. S. exprimenda.[137]

Item Johanni Albi, cler. Tornacen. dioc., mag. in artibus, stud. Parisius in facultate decretorum, nullum benef. obtinen., gratiam de benef.....

Item Michaeli Burgundi, cler. Laudunen. dioc., mag. in artibus, gratiam de benef.....Non obst. quod quandam gratiam de data v° kal. Junii anno primo a V. S. obtineat, de qua sibi nundum provisum extitit.[138]

Item Johanni Ponion, cler. Cameracen. dioc., mag. in artibus, de benef.....[139]

Item Nicholao de Baest, cler., rectori altaris b. Marie in castro de Gansoeyen. [Gansoijen, North Brabant, Netherlands], Leodien. dioc., mag. in artibus actuque stud. in facultate decretorum, de benef.....Non obst. dicto altare quid obtinet (2 march. argenti)....[140]

Item Johanni Dabbere, cler. Tornacen. dioc., mag. in artibus, actu stud. Parisius in facultate decretorum, gratiam de benef.....Cum dispensatum quatuor annos, si indigeat.[141]

Item Egidio de Woestina, cler. Tornacen. dioc., mag. in artibus scolarique Parisius in facultate theologie, gratiam de benef.....Necnon super

---

[137] This entry is missing in the *rotulus* but appears at this place in the *inrotulator*'s list and is among the separate supplication strips. Holes in the left margin of the *rotulus* between Haemstede and Casleto and on the supplication strip show that it was once attached. He is not mentioned by Wirkersheimer or Jacquart.

[138] In the *inrotulator*'s list, the date of the papal grace is given as iv kal. Junii, which is incorrect. He was a bachelor in canon law in 1418 (Fournier, *FDecr.* I, 200).

[139] His supplication appears at this place in the list of the *inrotulator* but is missing in the *rotulus*.

[140] He was a bachelor in canon law in 1418 (Fournier, *FDecr.* I, 197 [Vaest], 222, 228, 249, 262) and was licensed in April 1426 (*CUP* IV, 450, n° 2267; Fournier, *FDecr.* I, 276 [Vaest]).

[141] The last phrase on a dispensation for age is missing in the list of the *inrotulator*. He became a bachelor in canon law in 1416 and still lectured as a bachelor in 1425 (Fournier, *FDecr.* I, 151, 152, 163, 266). He served as procurator for the University of Paris at the Roman *curia* in 1426 (*CUP* IV, 464, n° 2290).

deffectibus natalium quos patitur de soluto et soluta genitus, et quia minor annus est, secum misericorditer dispensare.

On a separate strip, attached on the left margin that covers the last entry: Item devote oratori vestro Egidio de Woestina, cler. Tornacen. dioc., mag. in artibus et scolari Parisius, actu stud. in facultate decretorum, de benef..... Non obst. quod idem Egidius de legitimo non est matrimonio, sed soluta et soluto procreatus. Et quod tempore vestre coronationis in decimo octavo sue etatis anno extitit, super quibus dignemini secum dispensare.[142]

Item Alexandro Barbitonsoris, cler. Morinen. dioc., mag. in artibus actuque stud. Parisius in facultate decretorum, de benef..... providere, secum dispen. super deffectum etatis duorum annorum, quod possit benef. curatum obtinere.

Item Nicolao Callvaert, cler. Traiecten. dioc., mag. in artibus, nullum benef. obtinen., gratiam de benef.....

Item Johanni Simonis, Leodien. dioc. *In margin*: absens est.[143]

Supplicat S. V. humilis orator vester Philippus de Prenmont, cler. Noviomen. dioc., mag. in artibus, Parisius stud. in facultate theologie, cappellan. in eccl. b. Marie, Noviomen. (12 lib. parisien.), de benef.....[144]

Item Franco Rappe, cler. Tornacen. dioc., mag. in artibus, stud. Parisius in facultate decretorum, gratiam de benef..... Non obst. cappellan. fundata in eccl. s. Donatiani de Brugis ad altare b. Johannis Evangeliste, dicte dioc., (10 lib. parv. turon.).

Item Guillermo Coquillan, mag. in artibus, Morinen. dioc., stud. in facultate medicine, gratiam de benef.....[145]

Item Johanni de Marcha, alias Machuque/Mathuque, presb. Cameracen. dioc., mag. in artibus, de benef..... Non obst. parroch. eccl. de

---

[142] The text in the list of the *inrotulator* parallels that of the supplication strip attached here, not the initial entry in the *rotulus*. He began his lectures in canon law at Paris in 1415 (*CUP* IV, 305, n° 2048 [Westina]). See also Fournier, *FDecr*. I, 132 [Westina], 140, 159, 174, 249, 262.

[143] The parchment tie on the left margin indicates that a supplication was once attached. A supplication for Johannes Simonis was not included in the *inrotulator*'s list for this section, but one for Philippus de Premont was, which has been included here.

[144] The text given here is from a loose supplication marked at the top as 'presens', in contrast to the Simonis entry, which was marked 'absens est.' The text of Prenmont's supplication was included at this place in the *inrotulator*'s list and is identical with the text in the supplication strip, with the exception that it begins 'Item Philippo de Prenmont.' He sought a provision from seventeen different bishops, cathedral chapters, and monasteries. The holes in the margin of the *rotulus* and on the supplication strip indicate that it was once attached.

[145] Wickersheimer, *Dictionnaire*, 238.

Mainsencouture [Metz-en-Couture, Pas-de-Calais], Cameracen. dioc., (24 lib. turon.).[146]
Item Johanni Huberti, Cameracen. dioc. acolito, mag. in artibus, stud. Parisius in facultate decretorum, gratiam de benef..... Non obst. cappellan. ad altare b. Elizabeth in eccl. Cameracen., et cappellan. ad altare b. Marie in eccl. parroch. de Stamburg [Stambruges, Hainaut, Belgium], dicte Cameracen. dioc., (15 lib. parisien.). Cum eadem dispen. ut parroch. eccl. dum vacare contingerit obtinere et habere valeat. Non obst. quod solum sit in xxii° etatis sue anno constitutus.[147]
Item Mathie de Foetin, cler. Tornacen. dioc., mag. in artibus, gratiam de benef..... Non obst. cappellan. s. Stephani in eccl. s. Furcei de Perona, Noviomen. dioc., et cappellan. s. Andree sitis in eccl. b. Marie Magdalene, quas dignoscitur obtinet (24 lib. turon. parv.).[148]
Item Johanni Gossumy, diac., mag. in artibus, Ambianen. dioc., gratiam de benef..... Non obst. gratia sibi in nominationibus magis dignemini misericorditer providere.[149]
Supplicat S. V. devotus vester Egidius Caniveti, cler. Laudunen. dioc., mag. in artibus studens Parisius in facultate medicine, quatenus sibi providere dignemini de benef.....[150]
Item, Johanni Cinsinot, cler. Laudunen. dioc., mag. in artibus, actu stud. Parisius in facultate theologie, nullum benef. obtinen., gratiam de benef..... Non obst. gratia speciali per S. V. sibi facta de 4° kal. [*no month or year mentioned*], de qua nundum provisus est.[151]
Item Nicolao Beguemere, subdiac., mag in artibus et bac. in decretis, curato parroch. eccl. de Pisis [Poix, Ardenne], Remen. dioc., gratiam de benef..... Non obst. quadam gratia expectativa in cancellaria declaranda,

[146] This supplication is absent in the *rotulus*, but is in the list of the *inrotulator* at this place.
[147] He began lectures in his second year as a bachelor in canon law at Paris in 1416 (Fournier, *FDecr.* I, 178, 197, 206, 222, 228).
[148] The Foetin entry was left blank in the *rotulus*, but his supplication is in the *inrotulator*'s list and included here.
[149] This entry for Gossumy is absent in the *rotulus*. The text has been entered from the *inrotulator*'s list.
[150] The text of Caniveti's supplication is not in the *rotulus*, but is among the separate supplication strips. It is placed here because of the marginal note in the *rotulus*: 'ponatur Egidius Caniveti et immediate Johannes Cinsinot, Laudunen.' He sought a provision from many different collators, but mentioned no current benefice. He was licensed in medicine in March 1422 (*CUP* IV, 403, n° 2189). He continued as regent master in medicine from 1423 to at least 1435 (*CUP* IV, 437, n° 2246; 446, n° 2261n; 447, n° 2263; 461, n° 2285; 471, n° 2303; 500, n° 2352; 574, n° 2471); Wickersheimer, *Dictionnaire*, 196.
[151] This supplication is on a strip sewn on the left margin at this place.

ac dicta parroch. eccl., cuius fructus in portatis in eadem cancellaria declarabuntur.[152]

Item Henrico de Nedoncel [Nedonchel, Pas-de-Calais], cler. Morinen. dioc., mag. in artibus, actu stud. in iure canonico, gratiam de benef.....

Item Johanni de Vertaing [Vertaing, Nord], cler. Cameracen. dioc., mag. in artibus Parisius, gratiam de benef..... Non obst. preb. Leodien., necnon preb. s. Vincentii, Senogien. [Soignies, Hainaut, Belgium], Cameracen. dioc.

Item Theobaldo de Puteo, cler. Ambianen. dioc., mag. in artibus ac stud. Parisius in theologia, gratiam de benef. ....

Item Waltero Godefridi, cler. Cameracen. dioc., mag. in artibus, actu stud. Parisius in facultate theologie, gratiam de benef..... Non obst altare valore unius march. argenti in portatis in eadem dioc. Attrebaten.

Item Johanni Hircy/Hirty, cler. Leodien. dioc., mag. in artibus, stud. Parisius in facultate theologie, gratiam de benef..... secum de etate aliisque misericorditer dispensan. Non obst. quadam cappellan. in eccl. Cymacen. [Chimay, Hainaut, Belgium], Leodien. dioc., (1 march. argenti).

Item Marco Knedere, cler. Tornacen. dioc., mag. in artibus, gratiam de benef..... Non obst. cappellan. quadam obtinet in eccl. parroch. s. Michaelis, Ganden. (10 lib. turon.), non gaudivit.

Item Johanni Morelli dicto de Riria, cler. Ambianen. dioc., mag. in artibus, nullum benef. obtinen., gratiam de benef.....

Item Judoco Panden/Pauden, cler. Morinen. dioc., mag. in artibus, nullum benef. obtinen., gratiam de benef.....

Item Henrico Lips, cler. Tornacen. dioc., mag. in artibus, gratiam de benef.....

Item Johanni de Haenere, alias dicto de Asca [Assche-lés-Bruxelles, Belgium], cler. Cameracen. dioc., mag. in artibus, actu stud. in facultate theologie, gratiam dignemini providere de benef.....

Item Johanni de Ponte, acolito Belvacen. dioc., mag. in artibus, presenti in studio Parisien., gratiam de benef.....

Item Johanni de Salicibus, cler. Noviomen. dioc., mag in artibus, stud. in facultate decretorum, gratiam de benef.....[153]

Item Johanni de Grintre, cler. Tornacen. dioc., mag. in artibus, presens in studio Parisien., gratiam de benef..... Canon. et preb. b. Marie Curtracen., Tornacen. dioc., non obstante (100 lib. parisien.)

---

[152] As bachelor in canon law, he began his second year of lectures on the Decretals in September 1415 (Fournier, *FDecr.* I, 163 [Begue Mere, alias Grandis], 177, 195).

[153] He became a bachelor in canon law in February 1418 (Fournier, *FDecr.* I, 189, 191, 205). Not to be confused with the Johannes de Salicibus, who held a burse in the Collège de Navarre; see N. Gorochov, *Le collège de Navarre de sa foundation (1305) au début du XVe siècle (1418)* (Paris, 1997), 719.

Item Ludovico Kerbeghe, mag. in artibus, Tornacen. dioc., nullum benef. obtinen., gratiam de benef..... Non obst. quod sit minor annus ad obtinendum benef. cum cura.

Item Matheo de Poulanville [Poulainville, Somme], cler. Ambianen. dioc., mag. in artibus, presen. in studio [Parisien.], gratiam de benef.....

Item Johanni Routier, cler. Ambianen. dioc., mag. in artibus, actu stud. in facultate theologie, gratiam de benef.....

Item Johanni Fabri, cler. Belvacen. dioc., mag. in artibus, stud. in theologia, gratiam de benef...., cum dispensatione quinque annorum super etate.[154]

Item Johanni Gonye, dioc. Belvacen., mag. in artibus, nullum benef. obtinen., gratiam de uno aut pluribus benef..... Non obst. quadam gratia per S. V. facta in cancellaria declaranda dispen. cum eo de quinque annis super etate.

Item Petro Aubert, cler. Belvacen. dioc., mag. in artibus, actu stud. in facultate theologie, nullum benef. obtinen., gratiam de benef.....

Item Judoco de Binckem, cler. Leodien. dioc., mag. in artibus, stud. in facultate theologie, gratiam de benef..... Non obst. canon. et preb. Fossen [Fosse, Liège, Belgium] ac [cappellan. ad] altare b. Nicolai in castro de Clermont [Clermont, Liège, Belgium], Leodien. dioc. noscitur obtinere.

Item Johanni Avisse, cler. Ambianen. dioc., mag. in artibus, actu stud. Parisius in facultate theologie, nullum benef. obtinen., gratiam de benef.....

Item Johanni de Sanctis, cler. Ambianen. dioc., mag. in artibus, actu stud. Parisius in facultate theologie, nullum benef. obtinen., gratiam de benef..... Non obst. gratia de octavo kalendas [*no month or year mentioned*] per S. V. sibi facta, de qua nundum provisus est.[155]

Item Jacobo Damman, cler. Morinen. dioc., mag. in artibus, stud. Parisius in facultate theologie, nullum benef. obtinen., gratiam de benef..... et secum dispensare [*presumably for age, but no reason mentioned*].

Item Henrico Willems/Willenis, cler., mag. in artibus, Leodien. dioc., stud. in theologia, nullum benef. obtinen., gratiam de benef.....

Item Nicolao Stanke, cler. Morinen. dioc., mag. in artibus, actu stud. Parisius in facultate theologie, gratiam de benef.....

---

[154] He should be distinguished from the Johannes Fabri from the diocese of Amiens, who petitioned in the *rotulus* of 1403 as master of arts and a student in the faculty of theology (Reg. Suppl. 98, fol. 211r; *CUP* IV, 93, n° 1796). He may, however, be identical with the Johannes Fabri who was a biblical cursor in theology in 1433 (*CUP* IV, 562, n° 2451).

[155] He asked for collation from bishops and deans in six different dioceses and from priors and deans in eight different collegiate churches.

Item Egidio Commere/Commeve, mag. in artibus, gratiam de benef.....[156]

Item Arnulpho Carpentarii, cler. Belvacen., mag. in artibus, nullum benef. obtinen., actu stud. Parisius in facultate theologie, gratiam de benef.....

Item Johanni de Trengue/Trengne, cler., mag. in artibus, Leodien. dioc., gratiam de benef..... Non obst. eccl. parroch. b. Martini de Senzelle [?Sonzeel = Terheijden, North Brabant, Netherlands], Leodien. dioc., (7 march. Argenti).

Item Balduino Dalennes, subdiac. Attrebaten. dioc., mag. in artibus, gratiam de benef...., dispen. cum ipso ut duo beneficia incompatibiliam etc. si due parroch. eccl. fuerunt usque ad tenendum retinere et infra illud tempus unum illorum incompatibilium cum altero compatibili, simili vel dissimili, permutare licite et libere possit et valeat, etiam si vigore gratie expectative vel alias quovismodo iuste illa assecutus fuerit. Non obst. parroch. eccl. de Hersinio [Hersin-Coupigny, Pas-de-Calais], Attrebaten. dioc., et quadam cappellan. leprosarie de Albigniaco sita iuxta Albigniacum [Aubigny-en-Artois, Pas-de-Calais], Attrebaten. dioc., (40 lib. parisien.).

Item Jacobo Dippre, cler. Ambianen. dioc., mag. in artibus, gratiam de benef...., secum dispen. de tribus annis super etate si opus fuerit.

Item Petro Rogrant, cler. Attrebaten. dioc., stud. Parisius in facultate decretorum, gratiam de benef...., secum dispen. ut parroch. eccl. de Huluch [Hulluch, Pas-de-Calais], Attrebaten. dioc. qua obtinet simul cum dignitate seu curato benef. huiusmodi aut quecumque alia duo incompatibiliam coadiuxerit simul retinere possit. Non obst. eadem parroch. eccl. de Huluch (50 parv. turon.).

Item Petro Buteux, cler. Ambianen. dioc., mag. in artibus, stud. in facultate theologie, nullum benef. obtinen., gratiam de benef.....

Item Johanni Hellicam, cler. Laudunen. dioc., mag. in artibus, gratiam de benef...., ac cum eo qui xx^{mum} etatis sue annum non transcendit dispensare quod huiusmodi etatis deffectum, non obst., benef. cum cura valeat optuerit.[157]

Item Nicolao de Garmegny [Gierbigny, Somme], cler. Belvacen. dioc., mag. in artibus, gratiam de benef...., cum dispen. duorum annorum.

Item Nicolao Musy/Musery, cler. Cameracen. dioc., mag. in artibus, actu stud. Parisius in facultate theologie, litigan. pro cura b. Marie de castello in Cameracen. (30 lib. parv. turon.), gratiam de benef.....

---

[156] He asked for benefices in the diocese of Tournai.
[157] Possibly identical with Johannes Hellicant, who was licensed in medicine in 1420 (*CUP* IV, 377, n° 2154; 384, n° 2164; 390, n°; 407, n° 2197; 421, n° 2222); Wickersheimer, *Dictionnaire*, 418.

Item Johanni Prepositi, presb., mag. in artibus, Ambianen. dioc., gratiam de benef..... Non obst. parroch. eccl. de ~~Viller~~ Onviller [Onvillers, Somme], Ambianen. dioc., (10 lib. turon.). Non obst. etiam quadam gratia apost. de data v⁰ kal. vel vi⁰ sibi per S. V. concessa, de qua nundum est sibi pacifice provisi.

Item Roberto de Molendino, mag. in artibus, Tornacen. dioc., actu stud. Parisius in facultate decretorum, gratiam de benef..... Non obst. cappellan. situata infra limites parroschie de Berichghem [Berghem, *of which there are four in Belgium*], Cameracen. dioc., (20 lib. parisien.).

Item Johanni de Massemine [Massemen, East Flanders, Belgium], cler. Cameracen. dioc., mag. in artibus.

Item Cunno Andree, mag. in artibus, Cameracen. dioc., gratiam de benef.....

Item Johanni Tameson, cler. Leodien. dioc., mag. in artibus, gratiam de benef.....

Item Guillermo de Meclinia, Cameracen. dioc., mag. in artibus.

Supplicat V. S. vester devotus Johannes Steenbren, mag. in artibus, actu studens in facultate decretorum, cler. Cameracen. dioc., quatenus sibi gratiam de benef..... Non obst. cappellaniis nostre domine in eccl. de Mollem [Molhem, Brabant, Belgium], et cappellan. s. Nicolay et s. Mergarete in eccl. s. Gauderici [Cameracen.], et cappellan. s. Mathei in eccl. s. Gudele, Bruccellen. [Bruxellen.] (30 lib. parisien.).[158]

Item Johanni Saunin, cler. Attrebaten. dioc., mag. in artibus, gratiam de benef.....

Item Gaufrido de Brantint/Brautuit, cler. Belvacen. dioc., mag. in artibus, gratiam de benef...., cum dispen. quatuor annorum super etate dignemini providere.

Item Gerardo Canneti, cler. Laudunen. dioc., mag in artibus, gratiam de benef..... Non obst. quod cappellan. perpetuam ad altare b. Johannis Baptiste in eccl. parroch. b. Marie de Marla [Marle, Aisne], Laudunen. dioc., (10 lib. parisien.) noscatur obtinere.

Item Petro Rapondi, Tornacen. dioc., mag. in artibus, stud. in facultate decretorum, gratiam de benef..... Non obst. quod fuerit de soluto et solita procreatus, et quod cum eodem per sedem apost. alias fuit dispen. ut, non obst. deffectum natalium quem patiebatur, valeat obtinere duo benef., etiam si curam animarum alterum ipsorum haberet, et illa alius ex causa permutationis vel alterus, simul vel successive semel dimittere, vel alia duo benef. similia vel dissimilia libere recipere et retinere possit.

Item Guillelmo Bolkin, cler. Morinen. dioc., mag. in artibus, nullum benef. haben., gratiam de benef.....

---

[158] This supplication is on a strip attached to the *rotulus* at this place.

Item Dide(?) Porti, clerico Morinen. dioc., mag. in artibus, gratiam de benef.....

Separate supplication strips, whose location in the rotulus is uncertain:
Item Gerardo de Perfontibus, Cameracen. dioc. presb., mag. in artibus, et ab octo annus circa stud. in theologia facultate, de canon. sub expect. preb..... Non obst. parroch. eccl. de Thulin [Thulin, Hainaut, Belgium] pacifica, et preb. litigiosa b. Marie, Anthonien. (50 lib. parisien. absenti).

S[upplicat] devote vestre Jacobus Galet, cler. Laudunen. dioc., mag. in artibus, de benef..... Non obst. quod canon. et preb. eccl. colleg. b. Marie Bethmontis, Belvacen. dioc., et cappellan. ad altare s. Johannis Baptiste in castro Darciansart(?), Laudunen. dioc., noscatur obtinere (8 lib. parisien.), et quod eidem de benef. per alias litteras mandatum extitit eidem provideri.[159]

Item Johanni Duberriau, cler. Laudunen. dioc., mag. in artibus, de benef.....

Supplicat... Robertus Denis, presb. Ambianen. dioc., mag. in artibus, actu studens in facultate theologie, gratiam de benef..... Non obst. cura de Cumons, Ambianen. dioc., de qua sibi provisum virtute gratie expectative in rotulo univ. per S. V. sibi facte, necnon cappella perpetua fundata in parroch. eccl. b. Johannis Evangeliste Parisien. ad altare s. Firmini (24 lib. parisien.).[160]

---

[159] He was licensed in canon law in 1428 (*CUP* IV, 474, n° 2308; see also 408, n° 2198; 422, n° 2224, n. 1; 455, n° 2275, n.; 480, n° 2320; 551, n° 2429; 557, n° 2440; 576, n° 2473).

[160] He was a biblical cursor in 1427–28, was licensed in 1436, and regent master in theology in 1436 (*CUP* IV, 477, n° 2313; 574, n° 2469; 576, n° 2474; 593, n° 2492; 600, n° 2510).

Memory and University Reform in the English Revolution

Alex Beeton*

In recent years, scholarship of the relationship between memory and the English Revolution has grown exponentially. Valuable studies by Imogen Peck, Edward Legon, Matthew Neufield, and others have revealed the ways in which the 'remembering' of the Civil Wars became contested almost immediately after it occurred.[1] Rival authorities attempted to create official memories of what the three nations had endured, intending these to retrospectively explain the turmoil of the revolutionary decades. These attempts to create new orthodoxies often had to battle the memories created by private individuals as well as efforts by later generations to reinterpret the past to suit the needs of the present. The remembrance of times past in the English Revolution also shaped the discourse of later historians of the revolutionary decades, as Blair Worden's seminal study of

---

* I am very grateful to Waseem Ahmed, Emily Kent, Ellen Paterson, and William White for all reading various drafts of this piece and providing valuable feedback. Any mistakes are my own.

[1] Lloyd Bowen and Mark Stoyle (eds), *Remembering the English Civil Wars 1646–1700* (London, 2021); Andrew Hopper, 'The Farnley Wood Plot and the Memory of the Civil Wars in Yorkshire', *HJ*, 45:2 (2002), 281–303; Edward Legon, *Revolution Remembered: Seditious Memories After the British Civil Wars* (Manchester, 2019); Matthew Neufeld, *The Civil Wars After 1660: Public Remembering in Late Stuart England* (Woodbridge, 2013); Imogen Peck, *Recollection in the Republics: Memories of the British Civil Wars in England, 1649–1659* (Oxford, 2021); Erin Peters, *Commemoration and Oblivion in Royalist Print Culture, 1658–1667* (Cham, 2017); William White, 'Remembering Episcopalian Conformity in Restoration England', *EHR* (forthcoming). I am grateful to Dr White for allowing me to read this important article prior to publication; Blair Worden, *Roundhead Reputations: The English Civil Wars and the Passions of Posterity* (London, 2001). See also, Sarah Betts, 'Roundhead Reputations Twenty Years On: Cultural Memory Studies and the English Civil Wars', *EHR* (early access, 2024). Roundhead Reputations Twenty Years On: Cultural Memory Studies and the English Civil Wars | The English Historical Review | Oxford Academic (oup.com) (accessed 7/1/2024).

Civil War historiography has shown.[2] The message of his work, and that of similar studies, is clear: the memories of the mid-century conflicts are as dangerous to historians in their potential to mislead as they are important.

Can the lessons of Worden and others be turned to the topic of university reform during the English Revolution? As is well-known to historians of the subject, a major source for life inside Interregnum Oxford and Cambridge are the biographies and autobiographies of scholars. The texts, part of the seventeenth-century boom in biographical writings, were written in the decades following the Restoration of the Stuart monarchy in 1660 as the generation who had lived through English Revolution began to die.[3] The lives of significant figures ejected from their university positions by Parliament—and of those who either retained their places or entered the universities under the Interregnum regimes—form a well-used body of evidence which offers important information on an underdocumented issue. Since so much evidence about life inside the two universities during the period has been lost, either because of the haphazard record-keeping practices of college authorities as a result of the political turmoil of the 1640s, the natural loss of materials, or deliberate destruction, research on this particular era has been especially difficult. Consequently, texts which purport to give us an insight into collegiate life during such a mysterious period are tantalising.

As this piece argues, the genre of Restoration biographies is one which must be treated with caution because they have had a profoundly misleading effect on the historiography of university reform during the English Revolution, albeit often indirectly and in ways not intended by their authors. The writers of these biographical texts set out to justify the conduct of individuals who had lived through the Interregnum. In the process, and as is to be expected, they frequently presented Parliament in a negative light. However, their depiction of the 1640s and 1650s has influenced perceptions of university reform in more subtle ways, leading historians to marginalise the role of the parliamentary state in university reform, to ignore its aims, to overlook how parliamentary structures shaped reform, and to see the Interregnum universities as fiercely divided along 1640s political lines. Work by Charles Webster amongst others has presented a largely pessimistic interpretation of parliamentary educational reform, depicting it as narrowly political and lacklustre compared to the grand plans for pedagogical innovation suggested by those associated with

---

[2] Worden, *Roundhead Reputations*.
[3] Allan Pritchard, *English Biography in the Seventeenth Century: A Critical Survey* (Toronto, 2005), 9–29.

the Hartlib Circle.[4] This piece argues that parts of this negative characterisations are due to the biographical texts analysed in this piece. They may therefore be challenged. Additionally, a more positive view of Interregnum university reform may be presented. The following article also makes a contribution to the genre of English Civil War memory studies. Although recent works have shown the deliberate ways in which authorities and communities shaped memory, a key theme of this piece is the accidental consequences the texts analysed below had for later understandings of the period.

This article will begin by arguing that the royalist literature of the 1640s influenced the Restoration biographies by establishing certain tropes about parliamentarian attitudes to Oxford and Cambridge. These texts have diverted historians from considering the motivations behind parliamentary university reform. Next, this piece considers how the biographies obscure the importance of parliamentary structures in shaping reform. Finally, it will examine allegedly divisive consequences on life inside the universities as described in the biographies. The result of such an overview of the Restoration biographies is both pessimistic and optimistic: although this piece highlights many of the dangers inherent within this body of literature, it also argues that an appreciation of such shortcomings opens a door to further studies of university reform during the revolutionary period and gives a clearer insight into the often-overlooked role of the parliamentary state in the fate of Oxford and Cambridge.

I

The ideas and motifs employed by Restoration authors when discussing the recent past of the universities were not new. Much of the rhetoric in the post-1660s literature on the topic was formed during the 1640s and then later reused having perhaps survived in royalist circles during the 1650s. Therefore, although the writings of the Restoration era reflected their own contextual pressures, it is still important to begin in the 1640s when examining memories of the Civil Wars university reform. As first Cambridge and later Oxford fell to parliamentarian forces and purges of royalist personnel took place, pamphlets were produced denigrating Parliament's ability to rule over places of learning.[5] Several common tropes

[4] Alex Beeton, "'Not Infected with the Venime of the Times': The Rump Parliament and Places of Learning, 1649–53', Ph.D. thesis (Oxford, 2023), 10–21.
[5] [John Allibond,] *Rustica Academiae Oxoniensis nuper reformatae...* (London, 1648); [Thomas Barlow,] *Pegasus or the Flying Horse from Oxford...* (Mongomery [i.e. Oxford], 1648); [John Barwick et al.,] *Querela Cantabrigiensis...* (1647); [John Birkenhead,] *News*

emerged in these works. Accusations of stupidity, even of madness, were common as Parliament was accused of making 'Eloquence dumbe, Phylosophie sottish, [of having] widdowed the Arts, and [of driving] the Muses from their ancient habitation'.[6] As Lloyd Bowen has noted, madness was a motif of libellous literature stretching back to Reformation-era England and was frequently used in the 1640s.[7] As parliamentarian officials went about the business of purging the universities, they became easy targets for accusations of irrational violence or insanity, especially when contrasted against the supposedly cool rationality of royalist scholars. Francis Cheynell, a presbyterian minister and leading figure in the Oxford visitation with a fiery temper, was roundly mocked as '*Bedlam* seven stories high' while figures like Richard Bailey, master of St John's, or Gilbert Sheldon, warden of All Souls, were depicted as meeting their ejections with patience and reason.[8]

Such attacks not only mocked parliamentary aspirations to govern learning but sought to delegitimise the right of Parliament to conduct university reform. This was a contextually important issue as the Parliament had made the reformation of the universities under their aegis a recurrent demand of their peace proposals to the king during the 1640s, stating their intention to 'reform and purge the fountains of learning, the two Universities'.[9] Royalist attacks via pamphlets undermined this claim and made clear their opinion that, as well as being incompetent, parliamentarians would be dangerous to the universities. One typical remark was to give parliamentarians the role of the '*Goths* and *Vandalls*, or even the Turks' who were ranged against the 'poore Christians' of the universities and who could be expected to destroy both scholars and education. As the ejections of the universities took place, the death of learning in England was

---

from Pembroke and Mongomery... (Mongomery [i.e. Oxford], 1648); [Richard Braithwaite,] *A Letter from a Scholar in Oxford, to his Friend in the Countrey*... (1647); [John Cleveland,] *Midsummer-Moone, or Lunacy Rampant*... (1648); *Halifax Law Translated to Oxon*... (1648); [Adam Littleton,] T*ragi-Comoedia Oxoniensis* (1648); *Lord Have Mercy Upon Us*... (Pembrook and Mongomery [i.e. Oxford], 1648); *Mercurius Bellicus*, 14 (25 April– 2 May 1648); *Oxonii Lachrymae*... (London, 1649); [Thomas Pierce,] *A Third and Fourth Part of Pegasus*... (1648); [Thomas Swadlin] *Mercurius Academicus*... (London, 1648); [Thomas Winyard,] *An Owle at Athens*... (1648).

[6] [Barwick et al,.] *Querela Cantabrigiensis*, 26.
[7] Lloyd Bowen, 'The Bedlam Academy: Royalist Oxford in Civil War News Culture', *Media History*, 23:2 (2017), 199–217, 206.
[8] [Barlow,] *Pegasus or the Flying Horse*, 4; [Cleveland,] *Midsummer-Moone*, 1; [Swadlin,] *Mercurius Academicus*, 6.
[9] *The Constitutional Documents of the Puritan Revolution, 1625–1660*, ed. Samuel R. Gardiner, (3rd edn Oxford, 1906), 277, 293; *LJ*, x, 526. The quote is in *Constitutional Documents*, 230.

forecast.[10] *Querela Cantabrigiensis*, produced by several scholars at Cambridge in 1647, lamented that 'through our sides such a fatall stroke is given to one of the most famous Universities of Christendome'.[11]

There is some evidence that these royalist tropes continued to be used through the 1650s. As the work of John Twigg and Thomas Reinhart has shown, the purges of royalist scholars in the universities were not as wide-ranging or impossible to avoid as was previously thought.[12] Those royalists remaining in place seem to have acted as conduits for earlier Civil War terminology, their use of such terms supporting Peck's findings and a recent comment by Lloyd Bowen and Mark Stoyle that '[c]ivil war memory... was not something which emerged only after decades of reflection but was also an integral feature of the 1640s and 1650s'.[13] The correspondence of George Stradling, later dean of Chichester Cathedral, endorses this argument. Stradling was a fellow of All Souls whose ejection had been ordered in 1648 but never implemented thanks to the influence of parliamentarian family members.[14] Some of Stradling's letters from after 1649 have survived in his commonplace book and show that royalist perceptions of the parliamentarians as unlearned and dangerous to learning remained current after the visitations. In early 1650, Stradling lamented how the rules of Priscian, the sixth-century Latin grammarian, were broken regularly within the newly reformed university and he mocked the inability of Joshua Sprigg, a former chaplain and apologist for the New Model Army recently installed as a fellow at All Souls, to 'understand any language beyond his native one'.[15] Cambridge scholars the same year wrote to one another that they would write 'in Latin, but that I think the times neither deserve it nor understand it.'[16] Although the sparsity of information about royalist scholars during the Interregnum prevents conclusions being drawn about how typical such anti-parliamentarian rhetoric was, the comments of someone like Stradling do provide a possible indication of how the tropes used in the 1640s survived in royalist circles through the 1650s.

---

[10] [Barlow,] *Pegasus or the Flying Horse*, unnumbered page; [Barwick et al.,] *Querela Cantabrigiensis*, 2.

[11] [Barwick et al.,] *Querela Cantabrigiensis*, advertisement to the reader.

[12] Thomas E. Reinhart, 'The Parliamentary Visitation of Oxford University, 1646–1652', Ph.D. thesis (Brown University, 1984), 391; John D. Twigg, 'The Parliamentary Visitation of the University of Cambridge, 1644–1645, *EHR*, 98 (1983), 521–2.

[13] Bowen and Stoyle, 'Introduction: Remembering the English Civil Wars', in their *Remembering the English Civil Wars*, 1–22, 10.

[14] *Sermons and Discourses upon Several Occasions by G. Stradling... with an Account of the Author*, ed. James Harrington (London, 1692), preface.

[15] Bodl., MS Add. B 109, fols. 135v–136/150v–151 (this document has two foliations).

[16] *Memorials of the Great Civil War in England from 1646–1652*, ed. Henry Cary (2 vols, London, 1842), ii, 226.

Whether or not they were kept alive or simply were rediscovered, motifs lampooning Parliament and its ability to govern Oxford and Cambridge resurfaced after 1660. The biographies and memoirs of those who had lived through the Interregnum in places of learning often made use of such rhetoric, agreeing with the earl of Clarendon's famous remark that the Interregnum rule of the universities was one of 'stupidity and negligence'.[17] A life of Henry Hammond, the Oxford theologian and canon of Christ Church College ejected in 1648, written by John Fell, referred to the 'hunters' stomachs' of the parliamentary visitors who came to 'devour the prey' supported by their 'janizaries [i.e. the soldiers]', while another biography by Fell, this time of Richard Allestree, characterised the intruded fellows at Oxford as an 'illiterate rabble'.[18] Peter Barwick, brother of the royalist scholar and agent John, attacked the 'Barbarities' committed against Cambridge colleges by Oliver Cromwell, 'attended with a Company of hair-brain'd mad Fellows' with 'Blockheads...and senseless Scoundrels' put into the places of 'considerable and learned Men'.[19] The biographer of Stradling described the visitation of Oxford as a time when the 'Fury of the Conquerors was turn'd into deliberate Revenge' with the parliamentarians not having 'forgot their hatred' for the royalists.[20] Even the specific accusation that Francis Cheynell was 'not only mad, but also furious', returned in Restoration literature.[21] As such texts indicated, the language used in the circles of royalist scholars in the 1640s to discuss parliamentarians had not been forgotten during the Interregnum.

Although post-Restoration biographies may have owed much to the Civil War years, the reasons for utilising them differed. Whereas in the 1640s royalist pamphlets had been concerned with the present and the future, to a great degree those texts produced after 1660 were backward-looking and concerned with justifying the conduct of their protagonist during the Interregnum. This desire to excuse was often prompted after the return of the monarchy by the criticism received by those who had remained in their institutional places during the Interregnum. Ralph Bathurst,

---

[17] Edward Hyde, *The History of the Rebellion and Civil Wars in England Begun in the Year 1641*, ed. William D. Macray (6 vols, Oxford, 1888), iv, 259.

[18] John Fell, 'The Life of the Most Learned, Reverend, and Pious Dr. Henry Hammond', in *The Miscellaneous Theological Works of Henry Hammond...* ed. Nicholas Pocock, (3 vols in 4, 3rd edn. Oxford, 1847–50), i, pp. xlii–iii; idem, *The Life of Richard Allestree* (London, 1848), 9.

[19] Peter Barwick, *The Life of the Reverend Dr. John Barwick*, ed. and trans. Hilkiah Bedford (London, 1724), 30, 32.

[20] *Sermons and Discourses upon Several Occasions by G. Stradling*, preface,

[21] Joseph Taylor's Latin history of the college, drawn up after the Restoration, described Cheynell as 'non tantum fanaticus sed et furiosus' (quoted in William H. Hutton, *S. John Baptist College* (London, 1898), 160).

Restoration president of Trinity, Oxford, and vice-chancellor of the university, produced a vindication of his conduct during the Interregnum since he felt sure that some would think he was 'chargeable with temporary compliance, in retaining his fellowship'.[22] Other authors were equally explicit that they wrote to rebut accusations of collaboration. A biography of John Harris, warden of New College's sister foundation Winchester College, was drafted in the knowledge that 'some are ready to Censure both him and the fellows that they would designe to keep their places in such times'.[23] The decision to stay *in situ* was so damaging because so many had left their posts on the grounds of conscience and endured hardships as a result.[24] Much like the anger towards conformist clergy after the Restoration, conformist scholars were faced with a similar level of dislike from those who felt that their conduct was worthy of criticism.[25] Ralph Rawson, who had suffered 'great hardship' after losing his fellowship at Brasenose in 1648, attempted to block the promotion of Robert South to a doctorate of divinity in 1663 precisely because of such sentiments. South had spent the 1650s at Christ Church College and Rawson was outraged that South might be fast-tracked thanks to the influence of his patron, the earl of Clarendon, despite having 'not at all suffered for his majesty's cause, but rather that he had preached against it' when the political climate was different.[26]

Although an in-depth discussion of the authorship of the texts is beyond the scope of this article, the biographies ought also to be considered within the context of other post-Restoration publications. As the work of Neufeld and Peters has highlighted, the later Stuart state exercised enormous influence over publishing thanks to the passage of the 1662 Licensing Act and the establishment of the Surveyor of the Post the following year.[27] Although the Act of Oblivion theoretically barred acrimonious

---

[22] Thomas Warton, *The Life and Literary Remains of Ralph Bathurst*... (London, 1761), 204.
[23] Winchester College Archives (hereafter WCA), 447.
[24] Beeton, 'The Rump Parliament and Places of Learning, 1649–53', 212–13.
[25] See also Christopher Haigh, 'Where was the Church of England, 1646–1660', *HJ*, 62:1 (2019), 127–147, 137–42.
[26] Anthony Wood, *Athenae Oxoniensis*..., ed. Philip Bliss (4 vols, London, 1813–20), iv, 634–5. South had plenty to regret following the Restoration, including the contribution of a poem to a 1654 collection in celebration of Oliver Cromwell (*Musarum Oxoniensum*... (Oxford, 1654), 40). Both South and his biographer would later attempt to refashion his earlier years as a time of brave royalism, including making 'himself remarkable... by Reading the Latin Prayers' at his school 'on the Day of King *Charles* the Ist's Martyrdom, and praying for his Majesty by Name' (*Memoirs of the Life of the Late Reverend Dr South*... (2nd edn. London, 1721), 4. See also Robert South, *Twelve Sermons and Discourses on Several Subjects and Occasions* (London, 1717), v, 47–8).
[27] Neufeld, *Public Remembering*, 21; Peters, *Commemoration and Oblivion*, 26.

discussions of the past, Neufeld has pointed out that many of the historical texts published after 1660 'did not advance the agenda of oblivion'.[28] The biographies discussed below, which dredged up the past in often partisan terms, may be characterised in a similar way. They also should be considered within the corpus of later Stuart histories of the revolution which were intended to 'disseminate a memory of the civil wars and Interregnum that vindicated an exclusively Anglican confessional polity'. Propagation of such memories, it has been argued, was intended to stabilise the political nation by building allegiance to this 'confessional polity' and to justify legislation such as the Act of Uniformity which excluded nonconformist ministers from the church.[29] As already suggested, the biographies largely presented an image of unlearned sectarians destroying order and learning, in the process associating peaceful education and lawful authority with the exclusive episcopalian Church of England which emerged after the Restoration. The question therefore arises of what possible motivations supposedly anti-learning parliamentarians could have in university reform.

II

Parliament's motivations for university reform have long been understood to be underwhelming and largely driven by political expediency. As discussed above, many historians have agreed with the contemporary Oxford scholar John Hall's analysis that the educational reforms of the Long Parliament 'reached no further then Politicall aimes', such as the purge of royalist personnel, and 'medled not at all with a view or reformation of those fundamental constitutions'.[30] In recent decades, more generous descriptions have emerged.[31] One example of this, associated with a 1980s article by John Twigg, has argued that Parliament's deep reverence for the existing university structure guided their reform efforts and influenced their decision-making.[32] Notably, the possible implications of Twigg's insight have not been fully realised by later historians. It is also striking

---

[28] Neufeld, *Public Remembering*, 54.
[29] Ibid., 5; see also Sarah Ward Clavier, 'The Restoration Episcopate and the Interregnum: Autobiography, Suffering and Professions of Faith', in Elliot Vernon and Hunter Powell (eds), *Church Polity and Politics in the British Atlantic world, c 1635–66* (Manchester, 2020), 242–59; White, 'Episcopalian Conformity'.
[30] J[ohn]. H[all]., *An Humble Motion to the Parliament of England Concerning the Advancement of Learning, and Reformation of the Universities, by J.H.* (London, 1649), 5.
[31] For an overview of the historiography of this issue, see Beeton, 'The Rump Parliament and Places of Learning', 10–26.
[32] John Twigg, 'The Limits of 'Reform': Some Aspects of the Debate on University Education During the English Revolution', in *History of Universities*, 4 (1984), 99–114.

how long it took for a positive analysis of parliamentary action to emerge and challenge the mid-twentieth century belief that Parliament's defence of the universities was due to social conservatism.[33] One possible reason for this lengthy wait has been the influence of memories of university reform. These did not often discuss the aims of parliamentary reform in detail and instead were intended to defend the conduct of the biographical subject. However, as will be explained, their attempts to justify the conduct of individuals often involved presenting Parliament as opposed to university customs and the education of the ministry. The effect of such rhetoric is to push historians away from considering likely motivations of reform and so to buttress the idea that Parliament's aims were limited to political expediency.

Where possible, Restoration biographers wished to demonstrate that remaining inside Oxford and Cambridge could be a rational choice. As William White's excellent work on memories of episcopalian conformity has exemplified, many clerics who had continued in their parochial positions during the 1640s and 1650s 'chose to present their conduct in the 1650s as an expression, rather than a betrayal, of their loyalist allegiances' by arguing that their decisions had been 'motivated by a determination to achieve some great, longer-term good for king or Church'.[34] A similar phenomenon can be seen in the memories of Interregnum educational establishments. These remembrances stressed how individuals had used their positions to uphold the royalist or episcopalian causes at their lowest. The warden and fellows of Winchester College, for instance, were defended after the Restoration for remaining in their positions in a comparable way. As an exculpatory biography of the warden, John Harris, stated, although some criticised Harris's actions for staying in his post, 'wiser men and such as were no lesse affected to the interest of the K[ing]. and Church highly applauded their designe' since 'it [Winchester] was the onely publique or considerable schoole that was not infected with the Venime of the Times'.[35] Similarly, biographies of those like Lightfoot and Rainbow lingered on the defiant adherence to the Church of England shown by both men while acting as Cambridge college masters: Lightfoot by using the Book of Common Prayer in the university church and Rainbow by producing a thesis for his doctorate of divinity in which he defended the idea that the Church of England held all that was necessary for salvation.[36] Joseph Glanvill went as far as to argue that his time spent first as a student

---

[33] See Beeton, 'The Rump Parliament and Places of Learning', 15–17.
[34] White, 'Episcopalian Conformity'.   [35] WCA, 447.
[36] Jonathan Banks, *The Life of the Right Reverend Father in God, Edw. Rainbow...* (London, 1688), 41; *The Works of the Reverend and Learned John Lightfoot D.D....*, rev. by George Bright, (2 vols, London, 1684), i, preface.

in Interregnum Oxford and then as chaplain to the MP Francis Rous had given him an insight into the mentality of rebels and the ability to better refute them. As he wrote, thanks to being 'educated in bad times' he had a 'great advantage for providing, and applying the Remedies, and Confutations that were proper and effectual'.[37]

Alongside these sweeping claims about having served the king and church, more specific arguments for the usefulness of having stayed in university positions also emerged after the Restoration. It is important to emphasise that these justifications utilised issues which had been of great significance during the Interregnum. An awareness of this fact helps us to understand the genealogy of beliefs surrounding Parliament's approach to Oxford and Cambridge which have become rooted in modern historiography. One justification offered by Restoration authors for scholars they sought to defend concerned the university customs. The mass ejections and intrusions which Parliament carried out during the 1640s were frequently accompanied by the threat of violence and were often legally dubious. Thomas Reinhart, for example, has calculated that five-eighths of all Oxford fellows who refused to submit to the parliamentary visitation did so on the grounds that to do so would contravene oaths they had already sworn.[38] Among these Oxonians were the fellows of New College who argued that to submit would be in contradiction of the college statute 'De Visitatione Collegii' which stated that the college was not to be visited by any who were members of the university (which some of the parliamentary visitors were).[39] Such arguments received little sympathy from parliamentarians and the methods employed to remove truculent fellows were often harsh, with several colleges being violently entered and threats made to hang as spies those who remained.[40] Although Charles I exaggerated when he said that the Oxford scholars had been 'men of eminent learning and Piety... ejected for observing the Statutes', there was a grain of truth in his remark; his words endorsed the idea of the parliamentarians as a threat to the statutes and to the more general traditions of the universities.[41]

---

[37] Joseph Glanvill, *Essays on Several Important Subjects in Philosophy and Religion...* (London, 1676), 16.
[38] Reinhart, 'Oxford', 385.
[39] *The Register of the Visitors of the University of Oxford, from A.D. 1647 to A.D. 1658*, ed., Montagu Burrows, Camden Society, 133 (London, 1881), 53–9; WCA, 809a ('The Case of Roger Heigham').
[40] Even the generally sympathetic Philip Henry noted 'that milder methods might have done better' in the visitation (Henry Matthew, *An Account of the Life and Death of Mr Philip Henry* (London, 1698), 19).
[41] Reinhart, 'Oxford', 419.

This perception was only strengthened by parliamentary rule of the universities. Many college fellowships were traditionally filled in ways specified by their statutes, such as by county or the length of time in which a degree had been held. These rules, partly because of the rapid turnover of fellows during the 1640s, were often overlooked. To give a few examples: at Corpus Christi, Oxford, the committee for the regulating of the universities ordered Thomas Wight to be put into the college's Durham scholarship as if he had been born in that area.[42] A fellow of Peterhouse noted that five fellows had been put into the college by the same committee despite not having yet attained the degree of MA.[43] If the handling of appointments invited condemnation, so too did the frequent discussion of statute reform and criticism of university customs which took place under parliamentary rule. Statutes and university traditions were perceived by their critics as tied to medieval Catholicism, or to beliefs that ought to have no place in Interregnum England. As William Dell, master of Gonville and Caius, put it, 'the self-same Statutes of the Universities and Colledges still remain with them in force, which were at first given to them by their Popish Founders, through the help of Antichrist' with many 'outwards and Antichristian forms and follies still remain[ing]' such as 'their Hoods, Caps, Scarlet Robes, Doctoral Ring, Kiss, Gloves, their Doctoral Dinner and Musique'.[44] As has been discussed by several historians, neither university statute reform nor attacks on customs amounted to much during the Interregnum, despite intermittent interest.[45] Yet, it was easy for both contemporaries and later authors to combine the attacks on institutional customs with the management of ejections and, on the basis of that combination, to label Parliament as an enemy to the traditional running of the institutions.

In such a context, it was possible for biographers to defend their subject on the basis that they had defended the traditions and customs of the universities at a time when they had been threatened. One beneficiary of this line of argument was the aforementioned John Harris, warden of Winchester College, as a detailed discussion of his case reveals.

---

[42] Bodl., MS J. Walker c.8, fol. 243r.

[43] Charles Hotham, *The Petition and Argument of Mr. Hotham...* (London, 1651), 'To the Hounourable, the Committee for Reformation of the Universities'.

[44] William Dell, *The Tryal of Spirits...* (London, 1653), epistle to '[T]he Truely Faithful'. See also, Christopher Hill, 'The Radical Critics of Oxford and Cambridge in the 1650s', in, John W. Baldwin and Richard A. Goldthwaite (eds), *Universities and Politics, Case Studies from the Late Middle Ages and Early Modern Period* (London, 1972), 107–132, esp. 117.

[45] Reinhart, 'Oxford', 442–5, John Twigg, *The University of Cambridge and the English Revolution, 1625-1688* (Woodbridge, 1990), 129–130, 172; Blair Worden, 'Politics, Piety, and Learning: Cromwellian Oxford', in his *God's Instruments, Political Conduct in the England of Oliver Cromwell* (Oxford, 2012), 129–33, 156–7.

The biography of Harris appears on the backs of the warden's letters along with several other small, related documents such as a comparison of Harris to Titus Pomponius Atticus, the learned friend of Cicero, and a discussion of his education.[46] The biography itself is evidently unfinished and is closer to a series of preliminary notes and justifications of Harris's conduct during the 1640s and 1650s than a conventional life of the warden. It was possibly written by the Harris's son, Thomas, to whom the warden's papers had been bequeathed and may have been compiled in the 1670s as one of the biographical passages appears on the back of a letter from the 1640s endorsed 'N[icholas] Love about the Visitation w[i]th my Observ[ations]. 1679'.[47] Whether motivated by filial loyalty or not, the self-confessed aim of the biographical musings was to exonerate Harris and the other fellows of the college from the 'Censure' some had placed on them after the Restoration.

Whoever wrote the biography had access to Harris's documents and appears to have had influence over what materials were kept by Winchester College. It is noticeable that the biographical passages tend to have their claims confirmed by individual documents surviving in the archive rather than from a mixture of surviving materials, memory, and lost sources. For example, in an effort to clear Harris of the charge of pluralism, to which he was liable having kept a living in the Hampshire village of Meonstoke alongside his position at Winchester, the biographer notes other examples of university college heads holding positions distant from a church living, such as Lightfoot holding 'a living att least 40 miles distant from the University together with his headship'. This fact was 'certifyed from Mr Needler Clerk of the Com[m]ittee for the Reformation of the Universityes'; Needler's paper, endorsed 'Examples of Pluralityes kept by Parliamentary Ministers with approba[ti]on', has survived in Winchester College Archives.[48] It appears that the archival documents have been retained as proof to support the arguments the biographer wishes to make, a suspicion strengthened by what documents have been lost. It is clear that Harris was in regular correspondence with a number of regional parliamentarians yet almost all of these letters are missing and the few which have been retained show Harris in a good light, for example a letter sent from Robert Reynolds, MP for Hindon in Wiltshire, beseeching Reynolds to prevent the unstatutable intrusion of personnel into New College and to favour the petition of Roger Heigham, an ejected New College member and relative of

---

[46] WCA, 424, 426–8, 445, 447, 452.   [47] TNA, PROB 11/280/411; WCA, 445.
[48] WCA, 419.

Harris.[49] As the historian of archives Simon Fowler has written, '[s]ources and archives are neither neutral nor natural. They are created. It is this that is the reason for so many silences.'[50] The biography of Harris would seem to bear this point out as it appears plausible that the biographer has formed the archive as much as the archive has determined the biography.

Because of this, the biography of Harris and the contents of the Winchester College Archives offer a revealing glimpse into what those writing after the Restoration considered to be sound ground for defending those accused of serving the times in Interregnum places of learning. Noticeably, it is clear that Harris's biographer staked the reputation of his subject on the latter's defence of the statutes of Winchester and New College. Winchester acted as a feeder school for New College, both establishments sharing William of Wykeham as a founder. Each year elections were held to determine which scholars would progress from the school to the university college. However, the usual order was threatened during the Interregnum. New College was one of the last Oxford colleges to be purged and in 1649 a wave of ejections took place, much to the alarm of Harris who was unhappy with the changes of personnel and concerned that the rights of the Winchester scholars to those places would be filled in an unstatutable manner.[51] One such case occurred in 1651 when a college fellow named William Hiccocks resigned. A form of corruption, common to New and All Souls at the time, was for fellows to hand in their resignations to a friend or associate who would then fill the position.[52] Technically this was against the statutes of New, which specified that resignations were to be handed into the warden and fellows of the college, thus preventing such underhand dealings. Hiccock's resignation was not handed to the college authorities, however, and instead appears to have been given to William Staughton. In turn, Staughton appears to have gone to the committee for regulating the universities armed with the document and received an order to fill the vacancy.[53]

The entire affair appears to be of little significance, yet it was over this and subsequent events that Harris's biographer chose to dwell. Staughton's appointment not only contravened New College's statutes but also stole the fellowship from a Winchester scholar named James Sacheverell to

---

[49] WCA, 424. See also Alex Beeton, "That pack horse-roade of private sollicitations': Educational Reform, Parliamentary Committees, and the Visitation of Winchester College, 1649–1650', *Parliamentary History* (forthcoming).
[50] Simon Fowler, 'Enforced Silences', in Simon Fowler, Valerie Johnson, and David Thomas, *The Silence of the Archive* (London, 2017), 1–40, 1.
[51] WCA, 424, 447, 452, 891.
[52] Hastings Rashdall and Robert S. Rait, *New College* (London, 1998), 178–9.
[53] WCA, 402.

whom it belonged by right as 'the next in order' of the elected scholars.[54] Harris and Sacheverell seem to have collaborated to organise a campaign to have the committee rescind their decision and to appoint Sacheverell to fill Hiccock's place. Via petition, they complained to the committee and to Oliver Cromwell, the chancellor of Oxford, that Staughton's appointment was against the statutes of both New and Winchester as the fellowship of the former was supposed to be filled by those educated at the latter.[55] Not only did they press for the earlier decision to be annulled, but Harris called for the committee to prevent such unstatutable activities happening in the future, likely being the driving force behind an order passed by the committee in January 1652 to desist filling spaces at either university for a month after resignations and to ensure there was no skullduggery in the business.[56] He was certainly the inspiration for the order of February 1652 that all fellows of New College were to hand resignations into the warden and fellows of New College according to statutes, in order to protect the rights of the annually elected scholars of Winchester.[57] These orders, along with Sacheverell gaining his wish and matriculating at New College in May 1652, were the fruits of Harris's labour and represented an impressive victory on the behalf of statutable rule.[58]

Harris's biographer appears to have recognised the possibilities of using these events to defend his subject. He wrote how

> Dr Harris his prudence in his last times after the unhappy overthrow of the K[ing']s army was cheifely exercised in his endeavors to pr[e]serve his owne Colledge and if possible New Colledge in Oxon also from the Violent purges of the prevailing party and the intrusion of such persons as were not statuteably qualified for those places. Being well assured as the history of that time may sufficiently prove and the event did evidence that no person statuteably qualified would accept of a fellowship in eyther Colledge by way of intrusion. For no person was qualifyed for those places w[i]thout having been educated att Winchester, And besides those that had been expelled Winchester Coll: for debauchery there was but one single person found that would accept a place voided by that reformation, and I know that very person did it upon the violent perswasion of some of his neere relations not w[i]thout scruple and reluctance in his owne minde...[59]

The author intended to praise Harris as a defender of institutional statutes and customs, going on to note 'that his [Harris's] requests were allwayes very reputeable being onely in the behalfe of the locall statutes'.[60] The biographer, understandably given the background to the issue in the 1640s

---

[54] WCA, 407. [55] WCA, 403, 407. [56] WCA, 401. See also WCA, 405.
[57] WCA, 404, 423. [58] *Alumni Oxonienses*, iv, 1297.
[59] WCA, 445. [60] WCA, 445.

and 1650s, believed that Harris's defence of statutes was so valuable a service to the cause of learning, and that statutes had been so threatened by Parliament in the Interregnum, that Harris's championing of both New and Winchester College's customs would be proof of the service he had performed by staying in post. With this and the earlier comments about the retention of documents by the biographer in mind, it is noticeable that the documents relating to the Sacheverell business form a surprisingly large portion of surviving materials from Harris's tenure given the relative insignificance of what occurred.

The case of Harris suggests that showing how perceptions of university reform were formed involves delving into the examples authors chose to make their case and investigating the knock-on consequences of those choices on readers. Additionally, given its arguments, the biography of Harris might be seen as an example of how the post-Restoration biographies have affected later perceptions of university reform. Harris's biography is part of a memorialisation of the Interregnum which has deterred scholarly interest by painting Parliament as anti-institutional and opposed to university customs; in the process the topic has been reduced to an uninspiring binary question of whether Parliament was an institution-wrecker or not. Yet, as Twigg has suggested, Parliament's attitude to the existing educational structure of England was more complex than simply rigid conservatism or destruction. Instead, there are paths for further study of the topic beyond the concealing fog spread by Restoration memories.

The biographies have also concealed other motivations for university reform. One of the most important and frequently cited examples of valuable service to the Church and royalist cause offered by biographers concerned the issue of the learned ministry. This was a potentially rich area in which to find justification due to its significance during the Interregnum. During that period, the learned-minister controversy occurred. This debate, which overlapped substantially with the 'ordination controversy', was fought over the question of what qualifications were necessary for preaching.[61] By the 1640s it was widely accepted that both university degrees and ordination were required to be a minister. However, the destruction of the Caroline ecclesiastical establishment with the Civil Wars led to these traditional assumptions coming under assault. Some

---

[61] Richard L Greaves, 'The Ordination Controversy and the Spirit of Reform in Puritan England', *JEH*, 31:3, (1970), 225–41; Barbara Lewalski, 'Milton on Learning and the Learned-Ministry Controversy', *HLQ*, 24:4 (1961), 267–81; James F. Maclear, 'Popular Anticlericalism in the Puritan Revolution', *Journal of the History of Ideas*, 17:4 (1956), 443–70; Richard Schlatter, 'The Higher Learning in Puritan England', *Historical Magazine of the Protestant Episcopal Church*, 2 (1954), 167–87; Leo Solt, 'Anti-Intellectualism in the Puritan Revolution', *Church History*, 25:4 (1956), 306–16; Twigg, *Cambridge*, 206–33.

pamphleteers began to suggest that 'the Spirit of Christ... is sufficient [to preach], and doth teach them those things of which the Humanists are ignorant'.[62] Others insisted that 'in the Common-wealth of Saints there is no such distinction of Laity and Clergy'.[63] Still others took aim at the link between universities and the ministry with Roger Williams, the minister and founder of Rhode Island, referring to Oxford and Cambridge as 'the pretended Seed-plots and Seminaries for the Ministry'.[64] Critics such as Williams argued that ministers needed to be neither learned nor ordained to preach; similar views were found inside the universities themselves with the intruded master of Gonville and Caius, William Dell, asserting that only the 'Unction' of the Spirit was necessary for would-be ministers.[65] Such opinions enjoyed their apotheosis during the Nominated Assembly of 1653 when significant elements of the government seemed sympathetic to the critics of the universities, prompting what Blair Worden termed a 'scare' among the scholars.[66]

The attacks on the learned ministry could be utilised in the Restoration biographies as a reason for their subject to stay in the universities in order to protect the cause of an orthodox learned clergy when it had been imperilled. Just such an argument was made by the biographer of John Lightfoot, John Strype. Strype argued that Lightfoot's conduct ought to be commended:

> For when in those unjust and Violent times wherein so much malice was exercised against *Religion*, no wonder its handmaid *Learning* was designed for ruine: nothing then was talked of so much, and so much intended, and almost come to a final resolution, as the seizing the possessions and revenues of the University, and turning out the Scholars to shift for themselves.[67]

Lightfoot's service to orthodoxy in this time had been to preach 'up the necessity of humane Learning, and exploded the Enthusiasm which had at that time gotten a great possession of the minds of unstable Men'.[68] Robert Harris, one of the Oxford visitors appointed president of Trinity at the suggestion of a '*Noble man*', would be praised along similar lines in a biography published in 1660.[69] William Durham, Harris's biographer,

---

[62] Thomas Collier, *The Pulpit-Guard Routed*...(London, 1651), 41.
[63] William Hartley, *The Prerogative Priests Passing-Bell*...(London, 1651), epistle to Thomas Hall.
[64] Roger Williams, *The Hireling Ministry*...(London, 1652), 14.
[65] William Dell, *The Stumbling Stone*...(London, 1653), 23.
[66] Worden, 'Cromwellian Oxford', 127.
[67] John Strype, 'Some Account of the Life of John Lightfoot', in *The Works of the Reverend and Learned John Lightfoot*, i, p. xxvii.
[68] Strype, 'Life of John Lightfoot', p. vi.
[69] W[illiam]. D[urham]., *The Life and Death of... Robert Harris* (London, 1660), 40.

presented Harris as an earnest believer in the necessity of a learned clergy, revealing that Harris had complained that 'the liberty of Prophecying ... was abused to meer licentiousness, and confusion' and 'did very much bewail the so much sleighting of solemn *Ordination of Ministers*'.[70] Durham continued on to show that Harris had possessed exacting standards for a minister's learning with the college head lamenting that few in Oxford 'could bee called constant Students' since 'most made a short work of it, and posted into the Pulpit before they understood their grounds'.[71] Harris, like Lightfoot, had protected the need for a learned clergy when it had seemed most threatened. Given Harris's connections to the regimes of the Interregnum, Durham needed ammunition for a defence of the college head and believed he had found it in his attitude to the ministerial qualifications.

As has been discussed elsewhere, there are good reasons to think that the desire to produce a learned ministry was one of Parliament's central goals for university reform during the 1640s and 1650s.[72] With ecclesiastical uncertainty and disagreements over ordination, it appears that greater emphasis was placed on ministers possessing a university degree as a qualification for preaching. This is a rich topic for further discussion which may reveal much about parliamentary attitudes to education and the ministry in the revolutionary era. However, as with the issue of institutional traditions, the texts discussed here can divert historians away from considering this motivation. In their efforts to justify the decisions of some during the Interregnum, these biographies present a Parliament guided by crudely political and destructive aims. It is notable, however, that this image of university reform has had largely indirect consequences for the historiography of university reform. Much excellent recent work has examined the ways in which regimes and private individuals attempted to mould the remembering of the mid-century conflicts. Historians have discussed the efforts of the Interregnum governments 'to craft a version of past events', or the 'conscious attempt[s]' of the Restoration regimes to mould memories of the wars, or the same government's 'sanctioned histories', or even similarly intentional remembering of the past by individuals and small communities such as civilian petitioners, the family of Oliver Cromwell, or John Toland's partisan editorship of Edmund Ludlow's memoirs to support the Whig interest.[73] To these seminal works may be added an awareness of the

---

[70] Ibid., 96.   [71] Ibid.
[72] Beeton, 'The Rump Parliament and Places of Learning', 124–38.
[73] David Farr, *Oliver Cromwell's Kin, 1643–1726: The Private and Public Worlds of the English Revolution and Restoration* (Abingdon, 2024), esp. 243–56, 261–78, 301–22; Neufeld, *Public Remembering*, 54; Imogen Peck, 'Civilian Memories of the British Civil Wars, 1642–1660', in Bowen and Stoyle, *Remembering the English Civil Wars*, 24–42; Peck,

unintentional effects these texts have had on later historiography. The primary aim of the texts outlined here was to serve as apologias; they were not intended to provide a detailed analysis of parliamentary ambitions for Oxford and Cambridge. Because their influence on how later scholars have depicted university reform has so often been inadvertent it has been easy to miss and has required so detailed a deconstruction. The remembering of the Interregnum has the same misleading consequences for understanding the shape of university reform.

III

In similar patterns to those outlined above, the *Lives* of Interregnum scholars have prevented historians from appreciating the importance of parliamentary structures in shaping university reform. This point may be seen by considering the removal and intrusion of individuals and the role of parliamentary committees in overseeing these processes. Although such groups as the committee for the university of Oxford or the committee for the regulating of the universities did not regularly intervene in the lives of the scholars, they did play decisive roles in these particular issues. This point can be explained by utilising the lessons of recent academic work on the parliamentary state and the functioning of committees. As the studies of Jason Peacey, David Scott, Lloyd Bowen, and Chris Kyle have demonstrated, parliamentary committees were often malleable.[74] Due to small quorum sizes and a lack of central supervision, committees could be hijacked by vested interests who possessed the necessary means to gain the help of a group sitting at the committee. Access, information, and inducements were critical factors to getting business done at Westminster. Peregrine Pelham, the MP for Hull whose interests he frequently promoted, boasted to the mayor and aldermen of the town that 'I am confident you neede not feare any committee to doe you any p[re]iudice.

Recollection in the Republics, 13; Peters, *Commemoration and Oblivion*, 23; Worden, *Roundhead Reputations*, 65–121.

[74] Chris R. Kyle and Jason Peacey (eds), *Parliament at Work: Parliamentary Committees, Political Power and Public Access in Early Modern England* (Woodbridge, 2002); David Scott, "Particular Businesses' in the Long Parliament: The Hull Letters 1644–1648', in Chris R. Kyle (ed.), *Parliament, Politics and Elections, 1604–1648* (Cambridge, 2001), 273–341; Lloyd Bowen, 'Faction, Connection and Politics in the Civil Wars: Pembrokeshire, 1640–1649', *EHR*, 138:590–1 (2023), 92–131; Jason Peacey, "Written according to my usual way': Political Communication and the Rise of the Agent in Seventeenth-Century England', in Chris R. Kyle and Jason Peacey (eds), *Connecting Centre and Locality Political Communication in Early Modern England* (Manchester, 2021), 94–11.

I doe not spend £500 p[er] ann[um] here for nothing'.⁷⁵ As Pelham's comments suggest, the mechanisms of parliamentary rule mattered and shaped how it was implemented. If this is the case, then it might be expected that committees and the framework of parliamentary governance influenced the treatment of the universities.

That this was the case may be seen when examining the issue of academic ejections. It is clear that many royalist scholars who survived the parliamentary visitations did so because they were able to influence the committees. Colleges during the Interregnum and those within them often possessed connections to influential patrons of politicians at Westminster, sometimes including those at the top of political tree. For example, in 1651, Brasenose sent a gift costing £03.07.06 to John Bradshawe, president of the Council of State, to thank him for the favour he 'shew'd uppon sev[er]all addresses made unto him by the College'.⁷⁶ Connections were put to use during the visitations of the universities by scholars seeking to avoid expulsion, though most of the relevant evidence has since been lost. However, small glimpses of this process do emerge. George Stradling's correspondence from 1648 contains several letters in which he thanks anonymous correspondents, likely the MPs Michael Oldisworth or Edmund Ludlowe for reasons discussed below, for their role in ensuring that he could 'write to you from a Coll[ege] wherein I still p[re]serve an interest' and he appears to have taken on the task of tutoring his nephew, Edmund Thomas of Wenvoe, who was both the stepson of Oldisworth and brother-in-law of Ludlowe, in Latin, possibly as a form of thanks.⁷⁷ Stradling's colleague at All Souls Timothy Baldwin along with

---

⁷⁵ Scott, 'Particular Businesses in the Long Parliament', 279.

⁷⁶ Brasenose Oxford College Archives, A 2.43–44 (Senior Bursar's accounts for 1647, 1648, 1651, and 1650–1, sections titled 'Dona et Regarda').

⁷⁷ Oldisworth had married Stradling's sister, Jane. Jane had two children, Edmund and Elizabeth, by her first husband, William Thomas of Wenvoe. Elizabeth married Ludlowe (Thomas Wotton, *The English Baronets...* (London, 1727), 7–8; *Burke's Genealogical and Heraldic History of the Peerage and Knightage*, ed. Peter Townend, (103ʳᵈ edn, London, 1963), 2395). For the letters see Bodl., MS Add. B 109, fols. 114v–115/129v–30, 120r–1/135r–6, 129r–32/144r–7, 134v–6/149v–51. Stradling urged Edmund to practice writing Latin frequently in order to acquire fluency in it and gave feedback on the quality of his Latin letters (Bodl., MS Add. B 109, fols. 114v–5/129v–30). That this was a favour to repay his parliamentarian relations rather than purely altruistic is hinted by a letter to a 'D. N.', presumably his 'Dear Neece', Elizabeth, with whom he corresponded elsewhere. In the letter in question, written around the time Elizabeth married Ludlow, Stradling thanked the recipient and her husband for their 'unalterable custome of obliging' and concluded the letter by saying 'For the yong gentlem[a]n you mention, I thinke my selfe very happy to heare of his forwardnes, towards whose improvem[en]t how willingly sh[oul]d contribute the utmost of my endeav[ou]rs' (Bodl., MS Add. B 109, fols. 120r–1/135r–6). Stradling, whose knowledge of the Latin language was famous, presumably aided the ongoing pedagogical efforts of

John Houghton of Brasenose and Thomas Barlow of Queen's managed to gain the favour of Colonel Thomas Kelsey, deputy-governor of Oxford, by presenting Kelsey's wife with 'certain gifts' and there were doubtless more cases of scholars buying protection which are now impossible to discover.[78] The universities were places where scholars and their colleges possessed the means and contacts to make things happen. It would have been strange had those seeking to avoid ejection not made use of these resources.

However, the importance of the parliamentary state's framework in university reform does not shine through the biographical texts. The reason is partly one of perspective. For many scholars, the most visible, and odious, symbols of parliamentary rule were not distant committees but the visitors and the members of their colleges whom they intruded. The opprobrium given to Francis Cheynell in later accounts as 'hot and furious' and 'hated and abused by' the scholars reflected his very prominent role in the mass ejections of Oxford royalists in 1648.[79] By contrast, Francis Rous, one of the chairmen of, first, the committee for the university of Oxford and, later, the committee for regulating the universities is an invisible presence in such accounts for the understandable reason that most scholars had little direct interaction with him. Indeed, in 1671 Joseph Glanvill, who became Rous's chaplain after studying at Oxford in the mid-1650s, claimed that at the time of his appointment he had 'never heard' that his 'Patron' had been a member of the Rump Parliament and knew nothing more 'of that Gentleman, but that he was a very *grave* and Learned Man'.[80]

Alongside issues of perspective, biographers often ignored parliamentary authorities and focussed on individuals as part of the aforementioned desire to defend otherwise embarrassing conduct. The texts wished to both exculpate the royalists from any suggestion of being guilty of association with Parliament and to remain true to a worldview in which Parliament was the enemy of royalism. It therefore suited their aims to represent reprieves as the result of luck and personal connections.

Georg Horn, Edmund's German-born tutor (*Sermons and Discourses upon Several Occasions by G. Stradling*, preface; Stephen K. Roberts (ed.), *The History of Parliament, The House of Commons 1640–1660* (9 vols, Woodbridge, 2023), ix, 1).

[78] *Athenae Oxonienses*, iv, 334. Houghton went on to play an important role in the governance of Brasenose, despite mocking the new master, Daniel Greenwood, and fellows as 'Moses and his Myrmidons' (Brasenose Oxford College Archives, GOV 6 B1 (Folder 21), letters of John Houghton to Thomas Yates, 1649–50. The quote is from the letter dated 11 January 1650).

[79] Bodl., MS J. Walker c.8, fol. 247v; Anthony Wood, *The History and Antiquities of the University of Oxford...*, ed. John Gutch (2 vols, Oxford, 1792–6), ii, 618.

[80] Joseph Glanvill, *A Further Discovery of M. Stubbe...* (London, 1671), 31.

Walter Pope's *Life* of Seth Ward is a useful example with which to explain this argument since it is a text which emphasises the miraculous nature of Ward's survival in visitation-era Oxford. Ward, later bishop of Salisbury, had been Cambridge's mathematical lecturer before being ejected from his fellowship at Sidney Sussex College for refusing to swear the Solemn League and Covenant in 1644. As Pope wrote, Edward Greaves, the incumbent Savilian professor of astronomy at Oxford, met Ward by chance in 1649 outside the Bear Inn in Oxford. Greaves, knowing he was soon to be ejected, urged Ward to take over his position lest Parliament gave 'it to some Cobler of their Party who never heard the name of Euclid.'[81] Ward was able to take the position and survive thanks to 'the means of Sir John Trevor, who tho' of the Parliament Party, was a great lover of Learning... Sir John had great Interest in the Committee which dispos'd of the Places of those who were ejected.'[82]

Pope's account highlights several features which recur in other biographies of those who survived the ejections. He highlights the fortune behind Ward's new position, but also the rareness of finding a parliamentarian interested in saving royalist scholars. In Pope's version of the story, Ward's position in Oxford was down to a chance encounter and one benevolent MP. Within the context of committee culture during the Interregnum, it is an unlikely tale. As is well-known, bending committees to favour an individual or cause usually required deep pockets and the ability to get a number of the committeemen on side. The efforts of Lady Mary Verney to have the sequestration of her husband's estate of Claydon removed in 1647–8 were drawn out because it took time and money to secure the support of enough members of the committee of sequestrations to conclude the business in her favour.[83] The notion that one MP speaking for Ward was enough to save him is not impossible, but it ought not to be accepted uncritically. Yet, many other biographies made similar claims of lives being shaped by the intervention of one or two parliamentarians. Anthony Wood claimed to be saved by his mother's friendship with the visitor of Oxford, Sir Nathaniel Brent.[84] George Stradling survived at All Souls thanks to his family ties to the MPs and committeemen Michael Oldisworth and Edmund Ludlowe. Philip Henry was not removed from his position at Christ Church College, despite making only a limited submission to the visitors, 'by the Favour of the Earl of Pembroke'.[85]

---

[81] Walter Pope, *The Life of Seth Ward...* (London, 1697), 20.   [82] Ibid.
[83] Samuel R. Gardiner, *History of the Great Civil War, 1642–1649* (4 vols, repr. London, 1987), iv, 70–8.
[84] *The Life and Times of Anthony Wood, Antiquary of Oxford, 1632–1695*, ed. Andrew Clark (5 vols, Oxford, 1891–1900), i, 144.
[85] Matthew, *Philip Henry*, 18.

Edward Rainbow, his biographer claimed, was able to keep his position as master of Magdalene College, Cambridge, until 1650 'by the intercession of his Noble Friends'.[86] Benjamin Whichcote, provost of King's College, Cambridge, managed to avoid taking the Solemn League and Covenant and protect most of his college's fellows from expulsion thanks to his 'particular friendship and interest which he had in some of the chief *Visitours*'.[87] Gerard Langbaine was similarly reputed to have protected the fellows of Queen's College, Oxford, from ejection thanks to his 'favour and interest' with John Selden, the MP for Oxford University.[88]

As this list of examples illustrates, the idea of individuals managing to avoid ejection thanks to their friendship with one person or a few individuals appeared often in the corpus of biographical works. Yet, if the trope is scrutinised further, the influence of the royalist motivations behind these claims quickly becomes apparent. It was in the interests of biographers to emphasise the individual, lucky, or personal circumstances behind their subjects' survival because a key motivation of the biographies was to defend those who stayed in Parliament-controlled places of learning during the Interregnum. This could be advanced by removing any suggestion that they had been tainted by association with parliamentarians while simultaneously maintaining the idea of parliamentarians as uniformly opposed to royalists. Symon Patrick's discussion of how he avoided ejection from Cambridge without taking the Solemn League and Covenant emphasised how, luckily, he had been left unblemished: 'But God so directed me, that I, telling them my age, was dismissed [from taking the Covenant], and never heard more of it'.[89] The biographer of Stradling, by crediting Oldisworth and Ludlow with protecting him, absolved his subject from any suspicion of retaining his place dishonourably. Benefitting from the kindly actions of family relations could not be criticised. Nor could the biographer be accused of deviating from the general idea of Parliament as malevolent. Ludlow and Oldisworth's benevolence was in no way emblematic of a wider parliamentarian leniency in much the same way as John Selden or Sir John Trevor were not usual parliamentarians in the eyes of the sources. Trevor, in Pope's words, was a 'great lover of learning' despite being of the 'Parliament Party', not because of it. Those writing after the Restoration were not discussing the structure of Parliament's governance, but they have still strongly affected how historians think of its relevance to university reform.

[86] Banks, *Rainbow*, 45.
[87] John Tillotson, *A Sermon Preached at the Funeral of the Reverend Benjamin Whichcot* (London, 1683), 23.
[88] Bodl., MS J. Walker c.8, fol. 257r.
[89] *The Works of Symon Patrick, D.D. Sometime Bishop of Ely Including his Autobiography*, ed. Alexander Taylor (9 vols, Oxford, 1858), ix, 415.

For the biographers, luck was everything in determining those who stayed and those who left the universities. The reality, which likely involved intensive lobbying by scholars worried about their positions, was probably very different and is waiting to be uncovered.

IV

Memories of the Interregnum have also moulded how the consequences of university reform are perceived. This point can be shown through the representations of intra-university divisions which were made after the Restoration. Many of the *Lives* produced at that time depicted fierce boundaries along the lines of the First Civil War, with surviving royalists faced by hostile, newly intruded personnel. That colleges were, to an extent, often split over 1640s loyalties is well attested. Wood noted how during the Interregnum Presbyterians and Independents in the universities might bicker, but they could still combine to attack royalists 'whom they stiled the com[m]on enimy'.[90] Likewise, Henry Newcome remembered his time at St John's, Cambridge, as one dominated by a 'bitter feud between the old Fellows and the new'.[91] However, even if there were animosities between supporters of the king and supporters of the Parliament, two points ought to be considered. The first is that new concerns emerged after the visitations which cut across existing rivalries. The second is that the Restoration emphasis on enmity was intended to serve a specific purpose. Taken together, these arguments lead to the conclusion that the memory of what set scholars apart during the Interregnum could differ from the reality.

There were issues during the Interregnum which transcended old political loyalties in the universities. Indeed, in some ways, the previous divisions between royalists and parliamentarians became less relevant as the political context changed. This argument can be supported by the example of the Engagement, the effort to impose a promise of loyalty to the new kingless Commonwealth regime which followed the Regicide in 1649.[92]

---

[90] Bodl., MS Wood F. 31, fol. 13v.
[91] *The Autobiography of Henry Newcome, M.A.*, ed. Richard Parkinson (2 vols, Manchester, 1852), i, 7. See also, Twigg, *Cambridge*, 120.
[92] For the Engagement see especially Glenn Burgess, 'Usurpation, Obligation and Obedience in the Thought of the Engagement Controversy', *HJ*, 29:3 (1986), 515–36; Quentin Skinner, 'Conquest and Consent: Thomas Hobbes and the Engagement Controversy', in Gerald Aylmer (ed.), *The Interregnum: The Quest for Settlement, 1646–1660* (London, 1972), 79–98; Amos Tubb, 'The Engagement Controversy: A Victory for the English Republic', *Historical Research*, 89:243 (2016), 42–61; Blair Worden, *The Rump Parliament* (Cambridge, 1974), 226–32.

The implementation of the Engagement was not a case of parliamentarians against royalists, but of supporters of the new Commonwealth government against royalists, Presbyterians who felt the Engagement was a breach of the earlier Solemn League and Covenant, and some Independents who were uneasy about the prospect of further ejections in the only recently purged universities.[93] Opposition to the rigid implementation of the Engagement came from as varied a cast as a royalist like George Stradling, the Independent Oliver Cromwell, and Francis Cheynell, the Presbyterian visitor, master of St John's Oxford, and Lady Margaret lecturer in divinity.[94] Cheynell, articulating the fears that many Presbyterians held, beseeched the chairman of the committee overseeing the Engagement in the universities to consider why Presbyterians who 'are ready to perform all lawfull things required of them for the defence and preservation of the true Religion and publique Liberties' could not be maintained in their places.[95] Cheynell was eventually removed, though it is unclear whether it was due to the Engagement or his possession of a church living which clashed with his university duties.[96] However, very few others at either university were forced out and the lacklustre implementation of the Engagement was understood at the time as a result of collusion and closely aligned interest between a variety of parties which cut across the former binary division of parliamentarians and royalists.[97] As one royalist noted, '[t]he truth is, they [the Presbyterian authorities in Oxford] would not subscribe themselves, and so neither would they require us'.[98]

---

[93] See the general studies of the Engagement cited above, but also see the contemporary comments of Charles Hotham, a fellow of Peterhouse, who noted that some royalists, 'even those most disaffected to the Common-wealth', were happy to take the Engagement insincerely (Charles Hotham, *A True State of the Case of Mr. Hotham. Late Fellow of Peter-House* (London, 1651), 31).

[94] Stradling 'I fear lest that new obligation will be very little to our taste; since the land was made Independent, we have expected liberty, we have found chains' ('Sed vereor ne nova ista obligatio parum futura sit nobis ad gustum; ex quo orbis factus est Indepens, expectavimus libertatem, invenimus vincula') (Bodl., MS Add. B 109, fol. 135v/150v). For Cromwell, see *Memorials of the Great Civil War in England from 1646–1652*, ii, 224 and Worden, 'Cromwellian Oxford', 113–14.

[95] Francis Cheynell, *The Divine Trinity...* (London, 1650), epistle to Francis Rous. For the order for the Engagement to be taken in the universities and for its implementation to be overseen by the committee for the regulating of the universities, see *CJ*, vi, 307.

[96] Bodl., MS J. Walker c.8, fol. 247v; St John's Oxford College Archives, ADM I.A.3, 430–1; Worden, 'Cromwellian Oxford', 106.

[97] Edmund Calamy, *A Continuation of the Account of the Ministers...* (2 vols, London, 1727), i, 113; Hartlib Papers, 9/11/19A (The Hartlib Papers (dhi.ac.uk) accessed 13/1/2023); *Historical Manuscripts Commission, Report on the Manuscripts of the Right Honorable Viscount De L'Isle... Volume VI: Sidney Papers, 1626-1698*, ed. G. Dyfnallt Owen (London, 1966), 472; Reinhart, 'Oxford', 453; Twigg, *Cambridge*, 162.

[98] Worden, 'Cromwellian Oxford', 104.

In addition to reconfigurations of loyalties in response to the national context, those inside the universities often found that adherence to institutional interests overcame former political divisions. Blair Worden and John Twigg's work has shown how old and new members of the universities worked together after 1649 to protect the universities from sectarian critics of the learned ministry and attempts to create a new university at Durham.[99] Another instructive example of a similar occasion can be seen in an effort by Oxford in late 1648 to protect the university's financial security. At the time, Parliament was discussing the act for abolishing dean and chapter lands.[100] This act had the potential to badly affect the universities' revenue stream and Oxford's members were eager to secure exemptions. As is known from correspondence at the time, the Oxford group pursuing favourable treatment was a cross-section of the newly modelled university with Richard Zouche travelling to London to further their efforts via lobbying. Zouche had displayed royalist sympathies during the 1640s and had helped to draft the reasons given by the university for rejecting the Solemn League and Covenant.[101] Although he appears to have reached some accommodation with the visitors, he was still branded a 'cavalier' in the 1650s by John Wallis and supported by royalists in an unsuccessful attempt to win the post of keeper of the university's archives.[102] His participation is striking when it is considered that he was working not only with the MP for the university John Selden, but also the newly installed Presbyterian vice-chancellor, Edward Reynolds, the sometime chair of the committee for regulating the university of Oxford, Francis Rous, and two of the most notorious members of the Oxford visitation: Francis Cheynell and Henry Wilkinson of Magdalen Hall. Zouche reported that, after discussing the situation, Rous had recommended the university send either Cheynell or Wilkinson to plead their case since the committee for Oxford were familiar with both men and more likely to give them a favourable reception.[103]

However, stories of cooperation did not fit easily into the schema of royalist biographies. Instead, some of the biographies sought to show that their subjects had not been tainted by any association with the parliamentary regimes. To prove this, several authors suggested that royalist members of the universities were able to exist, at least for a time, as an isolated community. Bathurst, for example, discussed how he had spent much of

[99] Ibid., 155–6, 165–74.
[100] This act was eventually passed in April 1649 with both universities and their colleges exempted (*Acts and Ordinances of the Interregnum, 1642–60*, ed. Charles H. Firth and Robert S. Rait (3 vols, London, 1911), ii, 81–104).
[101] Peter Stein, 'Richard Zouche', *ODNB*.
[102] *Athenae Oxonienses*, iii, 1074–5.
[103] Bodl., MS Tanner 456, fols 3r, 5r. A letter related to these efforts was written by Reynolds to Selden and is in the British Library (BL, Add. MS 32093, fol. 266r). See also Calamy, *A Continuation of the Account*, i, 96–7.

the Interregnum in the company of Oxford's remaining royalists 'with whom, and such like, I had my constant converse, and scarce knew, or was knowne to, any of the other party, for some years after'.[104] Other authors went so far as to suggest that royalists had spent the Interregnum conversing with no one. It was said that, 'Archimedes *like*', the Cambridge Platonist Henry More had been '*so busie in his Chamber, with his* Pen *and* Lines, *as not to mind much the Bustles and Affaires of the World that were without*'.[105] His contemporary John Lightfoot was similarly described as having been 'more concerned about what was done in *Judea* many Centuries since, than what was transacted in his own Native Country'[106] Such claims of scholarly disengagement with the real world were of a piece with Bathurst's argument of royalist purity. The biographers of More and Lightfoot were aware that engagement with parliamentarians could be interpreted as collaboration and could tarnish the reputations of the two men. By arguing they had remained locked in their studies, it was implied that they had remained politically immaculate. Walter Pope, the biographer of Seth Ward, would attempt to make this argument on a grand scale for not one person but for many when he spoke of:

> all the Antediluvian Cavaliers, I mean Fellows of Colleges, who had the good fortune to survive the Flood of the Visitation, and keep their Places, and who had ever since that liv'd retir'd in their Cells, never medling with Public Affairs in the University.[107]

As mentioned above, there was certainly hostility within the universities between their old and new members following the visitations. However, Pope's emphasis on the separation between different parts of the universities' membership is significant. One way in which authors could counter accusations of collaboration was to argue that sufficiently strong barriers existed within Oxford and Cambridge to separate royalists and parliamentarians. Indeed, if those like Pope are to be believed, the political walls thrown up by the Interregnum kept those antipathetic to the regime imprisoned in their studies with only their books for company.

CONCLUSION

In their efforts to defend those who had been in the Interregnum universities from censure, biographers mispresented life during that period. In some cases, the gaps between memory and reality can be identified and

---

[104] Warton, *Bathurst*, 205.
[105] Richard Ward, *The Life of the Learned and Pious Dr. Henry More* (London, 1710), 191.
[106] *The Works of the Reverend and Learned John Lightfoot,* preface to the reader.
[107] Pope, *Ward*, 40.

explained relatively easily as efforts to embroider otherwise potentially embarrassing activities from the 1650s or to vilify Parliament. However, in other cases, the differences are more complex and their consequences less obvious. As this piece has argued, when discussing the effects of the English Civil Wars' memorialisation it is important to pay close attention to unintentional outcomes as well as the deliberate construction of the past on which recent historians have dwelt. The primary focus of the biographical literature produced after the Restoration was not to analyse Parliament's rule of Oxford and Cambridge, yet its consequences for how parliamentary university reform has been perceived by later historiography are vast.

These remembrances have concealed the role and aims of the parliamentary state and the formative influence of parliamentary structure on educational reform. Instead, they have helped to establish a misleading image of life inside Oxford and Cambridge as one riven by divisions along the political battlelines of the 1640s. By charting what biographers wrote and why, including the use of Interregnum controversies, historians can gain a clearer view of the reality of Oxford and Cambridge under the Interregnum regimes. With such a vantage point, new research pathways into relatively underexplored areas of university reform during the important decades of the mid-seventeenth century are revealed. The goals, achievements, and failures of Parliament's handling of the universities may yet be better understood. The biographical literature discussed in this piece will continue to be an important source for future projects, but their claims must receive the wariness with which some sceptics met them at the time. When the eighteenth-century antiquarian and Church of England minister John Walker compiled materials for his *Sufferings of the Clergy*, a correspondent wrote to him about three fellows of St John's, Cambridge, elected before the Revolution and ejected over the Engagement. The trio at the time of their election had been 'esteemed orthodox and loyall'. When they returned to their positions after the Restoration, they 'were then likewise so reputed'. 'What they were at the time of their ejectment,' the correspondent concluded, 'I cannot say'.[108]

History of Parliament Trust
18 Bloomsbury Square
London
WC1A 2NS

---

[108] Bodl., MS J. Walker c.4, fol. 44v.

Revisioning John Sherman's *A Greek in the Temple*

Teaching apologetic responses to pagan religion as confessionalised polemic at Cambridge University, c.1627–1641

S. F. M. Head*

Studying seventeenth century university theology teaching and the educational materials it produced bears directly on the history of religion, since divinity lecturers and the institutions they belonged to were integral to post-Reformation confession-building.[1] The influence that university tutors had on future clerics – and hence wider religious belief – in this period is an underexplored subject, however. In light of the need to interrogate the relationship between pedagogy and confessionalisation further, this article discusses a set of common-places delivered by the Cambridge Fellow John Sherman in Trinity College's chapel. Originating from the 1630s and published as *A Greek in the Temple* (1641), Sherman's common-places expound on a passage from Paul's address to the Athenians at the

---

* I am much obliged to Adam C. Green (Archivist at Trinity College, Cambridge) for his advice and support regarding records pertaining to John Sherman's tenure as a Fellow. I would also like to thank Dr Eloise Davies and Dr Alex Beeton for their helpful comments on earlier versions of this article. Additionally, I am grateful to Professor Sarah Mortimer and Professor Jon Parkin for the numerous conversations that have developed my thinking about this subject. Lastly, I would like to express my thanks to the journal's editors and the two anonymous reviewers who provided substantial support and constructive feedback.

[1] For a discussion of confessionalisation and the universities see Dmitri Levitin, 'Introduction: Confessionalisation and Erudition in Early Modern Europe: A Comparative Overview of a Neglected Episode in the History of the Humanities', in *Confessionalisation and Erudition in Early Modern Europe: An Episode in the History of the Humanities* (Oxford, 2019), eds. Nicholas Hardy and Dmitri Levitin, 1–94.

Areopagus.[2] Whilst teaching about Christian apologetics and pagan religion in these lectures, Sherman continually emphasised the confessional implications of his insights. This paper revises previous interpretations of Sherman's thought by reading *A Greek in the Temple* in relation to both its pedagogical and polemical contexts. What becomes clear is that the lectures' historical significance lies not in their content's originality but rather in what they reveal about their genre and its confessional applications.

Sherman describes his lectures alternatively as 'common-places' or 'morning exercises'.[3] College chapel 'common-places' were an important element of a Cambridge University student's education in the 1600s.[4] The genre's quotidian nature is attested to in the diary of a near-contemporary of Sherman's at Cambridge – the Emmanuel College Fellow John Worthington.[5] Given that what students were taught could influence their future attitudes when holding positions of power, the lack of attention paid to this genre by intellectual historians is surprising.[6] Moreover it confirms Dmitri Levitin's observation that 'university theological pedagogy is one of the great lacunae of... English religious and intellectual history'.[7] Expanding on an exegesis of Acts 17:28b, Sherman's commonplaces reference Bible commentaries, humanist erudition, patristic apologetic, medieval scholastic texts, and sermons. Therefore, revisioning *A Greek in the Temple* involves discussing its contents and genre in relation to contemporary developments in the history of scholarship.[8] Whilst Sherman's lectures do not demonstrate scholarly originality there is evidence of an awareness of recent developments in biblical criticism and erudition. However, Sherman typically resorts to apologetic arguments that predate the seventeenth century. Acknowledging this tendency with

---

[2] John Sherman, *A Greek in the Temple* (Cambridge, 1641), Title page.
[3] Sherman, *A Greek in the Temple*, ¶2.
[4] Other examples of the genre include Caleb Dalechamp, *Christian hospitalitie handled common-place-wise in the chappel of Trinity Colledge in Cambridge: : whereunto is added, a short but honourable narration of the life and death of Mr Harrison, the late hospital vice-master of that royal and magnificent societie* (Cambridge, 1632); Nathaniel Culverwell, *An Elegant and Learned Discourse of the Light of Nature* (Toronto, 1971), eds. Robert A. Greene and Hugh MacCallum, 1–170. For a discussion of the genre see Greene's 'Introduction' to that edition, xlix–liii.
[5] *The diary and correspondence of Dr John Worthington*, 2 Vols. (Manchester, 1847–86), eds. Richard Copley Christie and James Crossley, I, 7–10.
[6] Dmitri Levitin, 'Teaching Political Thought in the Restoration Divinity Faculty: Avant-Garde Episcopacy, the Two Kingdoms and Christian Liberty', in *Politics, Religion and Ideas in Seventeenth- and Eighteenth-Century Britain: Essays in Honour of Mark Goldie* (Woodbridge, 2019), eds. John Coffey, Justin Champion, Tim Harris et al., 39.
[7] Levitin, 'Teaching Political Thought', 39–40.
[8] For an overview of these changes see Dmitri Levitin, *The kingdom of darkness: Bayle, Newton, and the emancipation of the European mind from philosophy* (Cambridge, 2022), esp. 120–223.

a tongue-in-cheek remark, Sherman described himself as a 'man of yesterday' who was not a 'learned critic' trained in philology.[9] Here, the importance of genre as context emerges. It is inappropriate to read *A Greek in the Temple* as a 'treatise' and to expect it to expand the frontiers of knowledge.[10] One should not demand novelty or the inclusion of innovative scholarship in a text whose function was primarily didactic. *A Greek in the Temple*'s *raison d'être* was to equip future clerics with tried and tested arguments that had an immediate confessional application when they addressed lay congregations beyond the college's walls. Thus, Sherman's lectures and the genre they belong to offer historians an insight into how divinity teachers controlled the ideas that their students (and in turn the young clerics' future congregations) encountered. Additionally, Sherman consulted a wide-range of commentaries, sermons, and treatises. Recognising the presence of these types of sources and their role within the common-place genre affords insights as to the relationship between pedagogy, scholarship, and ministration in a confessionalised age.

This article begins by updating and clarifying Sherman's biography with information gleaned from previously unnoted records. Secondly, there is a critical discussion of the existing scholarship. Thirdly, the paper illustrates the relationship between *A Greek in the Temple*'s content, genre, and context through a survey of Sherman's exegesis, his discussion of Christian apologetics and pagan religion, and his confessionally barbed conclusions. Sherman uses Paul's speech as a prompt for educating his audience about apologetics and doctrine. Crucially however he always does this with an eye to the present. At each turn Sherman offers edifying advice or orientates his conclusions towards anti-Catholic polemic (and occasionally offers implicit critiques of religious developments closer to home). Finally, the discussion examines Sherman's use throughout *A Greek in the Temple* of arguments reliant upon textual criticism in relation to two topics: the handling of theological texts by Catholic scholars, and reading Acts 17:28b in relation to Genesis. Sherman uses these themes to explain Paul's words but also to derive polemical, doctrinal, or edifying conclusions.

[9] 'I might take a rise unto a generall treating, in way of reprehension, of the Abuse of authours, contrary to our Apostles practice: And then I might note who, and how, and wherein, and who most, and how farre they have proceeded in this most disingenuous injury unto writers deceased or living. But this would be a theme for some grave Aristarchus and learned Critick, not for a man of yesterday.' (Aristarchus of Samothrace was an ancient Greek grammarian. He was also the head librarian of the Library of Alexandria.). In Sherman, *Greek in the Temple*, 48. Sherman's quaintness is noted in Joseph M. Levine, 'Latitudinarians, neoplatonists, and the ancient wisdom', in *Philosophy, Science, and Religion in England 1640–1700* (Cambridge, 1992), eds. Perez Zagorin, Richard Ashcraft, and Richard Kroll, 88.

[10] Eric Parker, 'Cambridge Platonism(s): John Sherman and Peter Sterry', in *Revisioning Cambridge Platonism* (Cham, 2019), eds. Douglas Hedley and David Leech, 31.

II

The *Alumni Cantabrigiensis* records that Sherman came from Dedham, Essex, and started out at 'the Free-School in Charter House' (London).[11] It appears that he filled a vacancy as a scholar at the school thanks to the intervention of the Lord Privy Seal, Edward Somerset (4th Earl of Worcester).[12] Sherman then proceeded to Cambridge University, possibly enjoying an Exhibitioner's scholarship courtesy of his *alma mater*, and matriculated at Trinity College as a sizar (1626) and then as a scholar in Michaelmas Term, 1627.[13] He proceeded B.A. (1629–30) and became a Fellow in 1632.[14] Sherman received his M.A. in 1633 before becoming an 'under reader' (college lecturer) teaching Logic in November, 1634.[15] In 1636 he became a college tutor; a post he held until 1644.[16] It was around this time that *A Greek in the Temple* was likely delivered. Sherman claimed that despite 'much time, and years' elapsing between the lectures' delivery and their printing in 1641 he had resisted the urge to edit the text.[17] Furthermore, he indicated that these printed lectures recorded only the second theological common-places he gave. Both *A Greek in the Temple*

---

[11] John Archibald Venn, *Alumni cantabrigiensis; a biographical list of all known students, graduates and holders of office at the University of Cambridge, from the earliest times to 1900* (Cambridge, 1922–54), I, iv, 62. Sherman's lectures are dedicated to the governors of Charter House and were printed with a foreword addressed to them. See Sherman, *Greek in the Temple*, 2¶–3¶v. For a general sense of Sherman's school days and the patronage system exercised by the governors that he may have benefited from, see Anthony Quick, *Charterhouse: a history of the school* (London, 1990), 7–18. Note especially p.15 which provides details of the Oxbridge Exhibition Scholarships that free-school scholars like Sherman competed for annually. Sherman bequeathed £5 for the purchase of books to both of the free schools in Dedham and Charter House in his Will. See *The New England Historical and Genealogical Register, Volume L* (Boston, 1896), ed. John Ward Dean, 395.

[12] Each of the Foundation's sixteen governors could nominate a boy for entry according to the *Alumni Carthusiani* (London, 1913), eds. Bower Marsh and Frederick A. Crisp, v. Sherman's nomination is recorded under the entry for 11th December, 1617. Ibid, 4.

[13] Venn, *Alumni cantabrigiensis*, I, iv, 62; *Admissions to Trinity College, Cambridge Volume II* (London, 1913), eds. W. W. Rouse Ball and John Archibald Venn, 314.

[14] Venn, *Alumni cantabrigiensis*, I, iv, 62.

[15] Trinity College Archive, *Admission Book 1560–1760*, 39. Entry reads 'Johannes Sherman praelector tertiae† [*sic*] classis Novembris 6°.' Note that 'tertiae' is an error in the original M.S. and should read 'secundae'.

[16] *Admissions to Trinity College*, 314.

[17] It is unclear how many 'morning Exercises' made up the 'small bundle' that became *A Greek in the Temple* as Roger Daniel (the official Cambridge University printer) published them as continuous prose. Additionally, J. B. Mullinger claims that Sherman could not make the revisions he would have liked to the printed text, but this is a misreading. See James Bass Mullinger, *The University of Cambridge. Volume 3, From the Election of Buckingham to the Chancellorship in 1626 to the Decline of the Platonist Movement* (Cambridge, 1911), 588. Cf. Sherman, *Greek in the Temple*, 2¶–3¶.

and an earlier sequence Sherman referenced took Gospel episodes involving Paul as their subject. Sherman wrote: 'I have formerly spoken of him [Paul] upon another text: but he deserveth second and third thoughts. Surely never can be said enough of so devout, so seraphicall, so industrious, so eloquent, so learned an Apostle'.[18] One of the three decorative poems prefacing *A Greek in the Temple* provides information on one of his associates during this period. Each verse lauds Sherman or his subject-matter and two are anonymous. However, the third belonged to Sherman's Trinity contemporary, James Duport.[19] 'An eminent scholar and author' Duport held the Regius Professorship of Greek between 1639–1654. He later occupied other senior posts including Master of Magdalene College (Cambridge) and King's Chaplain to Charles II.[20] During September 1637, Sherman was ordained priest at Peterborough and proceeded BD in 1640.[21] In March, 1643, he began as a college preacher.[22] Yet only a year later he suffered during the Earl of Manchester's purge of Cambridge University and was ejected alongside forty-eight other Trinity Fellows, including the College's head Thomas Comber.[23]

---

[18] Sherman, *Greek in the Temple*, 3.
[19] The title of the first poem (in order of printing) translates as 'To the most excellent & accomplished man, Mr John Sherman, concerning his most learned and devout treatise, *of prophecy*.' ['Ad virum optimum & integerrimum, Mʳ Johannem Shermannum, de eruditissimo hoc suo pientissimóque tractatu, προφητικὸν(?)']. A printing blemish partially obscures the Greek text, which compromises its legibility. However, 'prophecy' seems correct as a signpost to a key theme in *A Greek in the Temple*. i.e 17–21. The title of the second poem translates as 'To the reader in praise of the work and the author.' [Ad Lectorem in laudem Operis & Autoris]. See Sherman, *Greek in the Temple*, 4¶ (my pagination following the previous pages' pattern, the print edition is blank). Also, Venn, *Alumni Cantabrigiensis*, I, ii, 76. These and all other translations contained in this article are my own unless otherwise attributed.
[20] Venn, *Alumni Cantabrigiensis*, I, ii, 76. Duport appears in the College's Senior Bursar's Audit Book – see fn.23.
[21] Venn, *Alumni cantabrigiensis*, I, iv, 62.
[22] Trinity College Archive, *Admission Book 1560–1760*, 111. Entry reads "Johannes Sherman concionator electus Martii 21º, 1642'.
[23] Venn, *Alumni Cantabrigiensis*, I, iv, 62; David Lloyd, *Memoires of the lives, actions, sufferings & deaths of those noble, reverend, and excellent personages…* (London, 1677), 449. Regarding the purge see John Twigg, 'The Parliamentary Visitation of the University of Cambridge, 1644–45', *The English Historical Review* 98:388 (1983), 522. Also, John Twigg, *The University of Cambridge and the English revolution, 1625–1688* (Woodbridge, 1990), 91–103. College records provide additional illumination regarding this period. They indicate Sherman's quarterly salary as a Fellow in 1637 stood at 13s. 4d. rising to 20s. by the end of 1640. The college did not pay Sherman as a Fellow after 1646. This was likely due to his ejection. Payments resume however in 1648 until 1651 – it is not clear why. Information on Sherman's stipend can be found in Trinity College Archive, Senior Bursar's Audit Book, 1637, fols. 5r–5v; Ibid, 1640, fols. 3v–4r; Ibid, 1642, fols. 5v–6r; Ibid, 1643, fols. 4r–4v; 1644, fols. 4r–5r; Ibid, 1645; 1646, fols. 5r–5v; Ibid, 1648, fols. 6v–7r; Ibid, 1649, fols. 3v–4r; Ibid, 1650, fols. 5v–6r; 1651, fols. 6v–7r.

Previously, little evidence pertaining to Sherman's life between 1644 and 1660 has been uncovered. Several unnoted records suggest, however, that this period was one of mixed fortunes for him. The royalist hagiographer David Lloyd's *Memoirs* described Sherman as 'a very learned, sober, and charitable man in the worst times' and confirmd that he was ejected from Cambridge for refusing to conform to the Solemn League and Covenant.[24] Lloyd attributed two other works to Sherman's pen besides *A Greek in the Temple*: *White Salt* (1653), and the posthumously published *The infallibility of the Holy Scripture asserted, and the pretended infallibility of the Church of Rome refuted* (1663).[25] Lloyd also credited Sherman with having assisted in collecting contributions to Brian Walton's *Polyglot Bible* (1657).[26]

It appears that during the Interregnum Sherman came into the possession of property and land in Ubbeston, Suffolk.[27] Lloyd described it as a 'small estate' that 'derived to him by providence'.[28] Acquiring this property alongside his place of residence in Christchurch, Norwich, evidently improved Sherman's material standing and softened the blow of losing his university post.[29] So much so that following the Restoration Sherman declined an offer to return to his Fellowship at Trinity College.[30] Nonetheless, Sherman received his D. D. from the university *per Literas Regias* [by Royal Decree] in 1660.[31] In August of that year, the position of Archdeacon was vacant in the see of Norwich and Gilbert Sheldon recommended that Sherman be granted the role by His Majesty's gift.[32] What became of this initiative is unclear, however.

---

[24] Lloyd, *Memoires*, 419.

[25] Lloyd, *Memoires*, 619. John Sherman, *White salt: or, A sober correction of a mad world in some wel-wishes to goodness* (London, 1653); John Sherman, *The infallibility of the Holy Scripture asserted, and the pretended infallibility of the Church of Rome refuted in answer to two papers and two treatises of Father Johnson, a Romanist, about the ground thereof* (London, 1664). The attribution of *White Salt* to Sherman is also noted in D. W. Dockrill, '"No Other Name": The Problem of the Salvation of Pagans in Mid-Seventeenth Century Cambridge', in *The idea of salvation: papers from the Conference on the Idea of Salvation, Sacred and Secular* (Auckland, 1988), 128.

[26] Lloyd, *Memoires*, 449.

[27] Sherman bequeathed his Suffolk holdings to his brother Henry in his will. See *The New England Historical and Genealogical Register*, 395.

[28] Lloyd, *Memoires*, 619.

[29] Sherman's connection to Christchurch, Norwich, is indicated in his will where he bequeathed 10 shillings apiece to the elderly poor. In *The New England Historical and Genealogical Register*, 395.

[30] Lloyd, *Memoires*, 619.   [31] *Admissions to Trinity College*, 314.

[32] Calendar of State Papers, Domestic Series, of the Reign of Charles II: 1660–61 (London, 1860), ed. Mary Anne Everett Green, 219.

Regardless, the Norwich Consistory Court proved Sherman's will in 1661 indicating that death intervened.[33]

III

The discussion of pagan religion in *A Greek in the Temple* has previously led historians to emphasise Sherman's references to neo-platonic philosophical ideas and to connect him with the 'Cambridge Platonist' movement.[34] The nineteenth-century historian of religion John Tulloch portrayed 'Cambridge Platonism' as a philosophical turn in England's mid-seventeenth century.[35] Tulloch identified its champions as a group of scholar-divines that, he claimed, reacted against Calvinist orthodoxy and constructed the foundations of a more liberal theology using neo-platonic thought. The Platonists' "latitudinarian" students, such as John Tillotson, who served in the Restoration Church, supposedly promulgated this post-Calvinist theological alternative. James Bass Mullinger linked Sherman to Tulloch's narrative by identifying commonalities between *A Greek in the Temple* and texts belonging to the so-called Cambridge Platonists Benjamin

---

[33] Venn, *Alumni cantabrigiensis,* I, iv, 62; *The New England Historical and Genealogical Register,* 395. In Levine, 'Latitudinarians', 102, there is confusion concerning Sherman's biography. Levine claims Sherman matriculated at Queen's College and was a Fellow there. This pertains to a different John Sherman however who died in 1671, having arrived at Queen's in 1645. See Venn, *Alumni Cantabrigiensis,* I, iv, 62.

[34] Parker, 'Cambridge Platonism(s)', 31, 44; Mullinger, *The University of Cambridge,* 588–9; Levine, 'Latitudinarians', 86–8. Cambridge Platonism has generated much scholarship and only a limited discussion is feasible here. For a revised defence of the category, see Douglas Hedley and David Leech, 'Introduction' in *Revisioning Cambridge Platonism: Sources and Legacy* (Cham, 2019), eds. Douglas Hedley and David Leech, 1–12. Those scholars who employ the term currently tend, *pace* Mullinger, to describe the Cambridge Platonists as an intellectual circle united by familial and tutorial connections rather than as a monolithic intellectual body. See for example Marilyn Lewis, 'The educational influence of cambridge platonism: tutorial relationships and student networks at christ's college, cambridge, 1641–1688', Ph.D. thesis (Birkbeck University of London, 2010). A recent critique of the category's historical validity, alongside a discussion of the relationship between political and intellectual change in the seventeenth century, is present in Dmitri Levitin, *Ancient wisdom in the age of the new science: histories of philosophy in England, c. 1640–1700* (Cambridge, 2015), 16, 126–138, 546.

[35] John Tulloch, *Rational Theology and Christian Philosophy in England in the seventeenth century, Vol. II* (London, 1872), *passim*. Tulloch drew on a comment in Bishop Gilbert Burnet's history: '... if a new set of men had not appeared of another stamp, the Church had quite lost her esteem over the Nation. These were generally of *Cambridge*, formed under some divines, the chief of whom were Drs. *Whichcot, Cudworth, Wilkins, More,* and *Worthington.*' See Gilbert Burnet, *Burnet's History of my own time. Part 1: The reign of Charles the Second* (Oxford, 1900), ed. Osmund Airy, 186. For a critique of Tulloch's narrative see Levitin, *Ancient Wisdom,* 16. Also, John Spurr, '"Latitudinarianism" and the Restoration Church', *The Historical Journal* 31/1 (1988): 61–82.

Whichcote and Henry More.[36] Furthermore, Mullinger nominated Sherman as the pioneer due to his work appearing in print before the others'.[37] More recent contributions to discussions of Sherman have continued in this vein. According to Joseph Levine 'Sherman's little work anticipates... the neoplatonists'.[38] Meanwhile Eric Parker describes Sherman's 'platonism'.[39]

There are several reasons why this is an unsatisfactory account of Sherman's thought and its place in seventeenth-century Cambridge's intellectual history, however. Beginning with Mullinger's comparison, the similarities he identifies in the scholars' works are typical of the period's erudition in general. Allusions to Greek philosophy reflect a 'classically orientated culture' rather than the emergence of a new school of Platonist thought.[40] That Sherman, Whichcote, and More discuss Aristotle's treatises, theories of the soul, and supposedly accept versions of a *prisca theologia* (a postulated universal theology based on myth-histories of archaic Judeo-Grecian interaction) neither proves Sherman's originality nor his role in forming a Platonist movement at Cambridge.[41] Indeed, Mullinger fails to substantiate his proposal that Sherman's 'printed discourses... contributed, to a far greater degree than is on record, to aid the movement the origin of which has generally been attributed to Whichcote's unprinted discourses alone'.[42] Recently scholars have analysed the scholarship produced by individuals traditionally associated with 'Cambridge Platonism' including Whichcote, More, and Ralph Cudworth. This work has called into question the appropriateness of the collectivising term 'Cambridge Platonism' by revealing considerable variations in the content and methodology underpinning the scholarship of Whichcote, More, and the others.[43]

---

[36] Mullinger, *The University of Cambridge*, 588–9. A similar reading of Sherman appears in Dockrill, 'The Problem of the Salvation of Pagans', 127–8.
[37] Mullinger, *The University of Cambridge*, 589.
[38] Levine, 'Latitudinarians', 88.   [39] Parker, 'Cambridge Platonism(s)', 32.
[40] Dockrill, 'The Problem of the Salvation of the Pagans', 125; Levitin, *Ancient Wisdom*, 546.
[41] Mullinger, *University of Cambridge*, 589. Recent scholarship shows that regarding Henry More, *'prisca theologia'* is an inaccurate description of his approach to scriptural exegesis and philosophy. See Levitin, *Ancient wisdom*, 130–1.
[42] Mullinger, *University of Cambridge*, 589. A remark on the lack of evidence behind Mullinger's theory appears in Parker, 'Cambridge Platonism(s)', 32. See also the comment in James Deontis Roberts, *From puritanism to platonism in seventeenth century England* (The Hague, 1968), 208.
[43] See the discussion of Benjamin Whichcote and Nathaniel Culverwell in Jon Parkin, *Science, religion, and politics in Restoration England: Richard Cumberland's De legibus naturae* (Woodbridge, 1999), 75–85. Also, the discussion of Henry More and Ralph Cudworth in Levitin, *Ancient Wisdom*, 16, 126–38, 171–80.

Moreover, if an anti-Calvinist theological outlook indicates membership of the Cambridge Platonist circle, there are strong grounds for doubting that Sherman was a fellow-traveller with Whichcote, More, or Cudworth. Not least because the narrative of a Platonic revival associated with the rise of anti-Calvinist theology in mid-seventeenth century Cambridge, which historians have thus far implicated Sherman in, rests upon assumptions that have been radically revised. Andrew Ollerton's recent study of English Arminianism argues that it was during the Civil Wars and Interregnum, and not the era of the Laudian Church, that anti-Calvinist synergistic theories of salvation were increasingly popular.[44] If Ollerton's thesis stands then not only was Sherman mostly absent from Cambridge at this crucial juncture but the suggestion that so-called Cambridge Platonism followed a pre-Civil War turn away from Calvinism is brought into question.[45] Additionally, Cambridge University's complex seventeenth-century intellectual landscape is irreducible to monolithic 'Calvinist' and 'Anti-Calvinist' blocs.[46] A similar point could be made about seventeenth-century England more generally where, as Ollerton amongst others has argued, individuals often held different combinations of positions on theological issues that do not map onto consistent binary divisions.[47]

---

[44] Andrew Ollerton, *Crisis of Calvinism in revolutionary England, 1640–1660: Arminian theologies of predestination and grace* (Woodbridge, 2023), 1–2.

[45] In 1668, Ralph Cudworth remarked in a letter to Philipp van Limborch that in 1653 he marked his turn away from the Calvinist doctrine of predestination by defending a realist (as opposed to voluntarist) conception of good and evil in public disputations at university. Cudworth wrote that, 'Sed cum res ethicas attentius consideraerem et evidenter perciperem boni et mali moralis naturas esse prorsus immutabiles, nec revera ab ipsius Dei arbitrio pendere (cum hoc discrimen honestorum et turpium potius ab immutabili natura Dei derivandum sit), non poteram Deo adscribere horrenda ista decreta, quibus ex mere beneplacito homines insontes vel ad culpas et peccata aeternis cruciatibus leunda inevitabiliter damnaret' [when I attentively considered ethical matters and clearly perceived that the natures of moral good and evil were entirely immutable, and not truly dependent on the arbitrary will of God (since this distinction of good and evil must rather be derived from the unchangeable nature of God), I could not attribute to God those dreadful decrees by which He would inevitably damn innocent people to eternal torments or sins and transgressions]. This exemplifies Ollerton's thesis of a rise in Arminianism in the 1650s, which occurred during Sherman's absence from Cambridge. See Georg Freiherrn von Hertling, *John Locke und Die Schule Von Cambridge* (Freiburg, 1892), 164n.

[46] See Peter Lake, *On Laudianism: Piety, Polemic and Politics During the Personal Rule of Charles I* (Cambridge, 2023), 492–517; David Hoyle, *Reformation and religious identity in Cambridge, 1590–1644* (Woodbridge, 2007), 161–95; Margo Todd, ' "All One with Tom Thumb": Arminianism, Popery, and the Story of the Reformation in Early Stuart Cambridge', *Church History* 64/4 (1995), 563–579. For Trinity College in particular, see also W. W. Rouse Ball, *Notes on the history of Trinity College, Cambridge* (London, 1899), 88–9.

[47] Ollerton, *Crisis of Calvinism, passim*. A similar logic governs a recent work on the reception of Dutch Remonstrant theology by theologians within the established Church of England post-Restoration, a study that compels us to re-evaluate the relationships between so called 'Anglicans', 'Calvinists', and 'Socinians'. See Samuel Fornecker, *Bisschop's Bench:*

Sherman's academic environment featured religious disagreements that permeated the University as a whole and individual colleges too. Yet friendships could bridge such divides.[48] Furthermore, bringing these theologically grounded controversies into the classroom risked incurring the wrath of senior University figures.[49] Nothing in *A Greek in the Temple*'s contents suggests that Sherman took an unorthodox view on the Reformed doctrines of predestination and original sin. In fact, Sherman struck a Reformed note throughout *A Greek in the Temple* on topics such as justification and sacred scripture's primacy.[50] Moreover, his lectures ooze anti-Catholic polemic. When combined these points compromise both Parker's reading of Sherman as 'radically different' from his 'Calvinist' contemporaries and the suggestion that Sherman instigated an anti-Calvinist Cambridge Platonist movement.[51] Whether 'Cambridge Platonism' can be said to have existed is clearly debatable, but even if it did Sherman did not participate in it.

* * *

The association of Sherman with 'Cambridge Platonism' also fails to account for the contents and purpose of *A Greek in the Temple* and the broader pedagogical and scholarly context that surrounded it. Contextualising Sherman's thought requires recognising that *A Greek in the Temple* belongs to a genre designed for particular purposes. John Sherman was not a philosopher penning a treatise, but a theologian instructing a class who used philosophical references to inform his exegesis.[52] Sherman's lectures dissected Acts 17:28b and Paul's address to the Athenians at the Areopagus more broadly. Acts 17:28b provided Christian apologists with an *ur*-text for disputing with pagans.[53] Sherman's lecture opens with a discussion of

Contours of Arminian Conformity in the Church of England, c.1674–1742 (Oxford, 2023), *passim*.

[48] The treatment of the future High-Church Tory Bishop William Sancroft Jnr. by his Puritan Calvinist contemporaries at Emmanuel College Cambridge during the English Civil Wars is a touching example. See Twigg, *Cambridge and the English Revolution*, 153. See also a letter to Sancroft from one such colleague that reveals their friendship. In Dillingham to Sancroft, Cambridge, 6 June 1642, Bodl., Tanner MS 63, fol. 43.
[49] A point repeatedly evinced in the works by Lake, Hoyle, and Todd cited in fn. 12.
[50] On justification, 'God first accepteth Abels person, then his offering' in Sherman, *Greek in the Temple*, 6. On the importance of scripture and Catholic abuse of it, 'This unfaithfull and sacrilegious dealing with sacred Scripture hinteth me to the next particle in our text...', ibid, 43.
[51] Parker, 'Cambridge Platonism(s), 31.
[52] For the methodological significance of considering what a writer is doing as well as saying, see Quentin Skinner, *Visions of Politics: Volume 1 Regarding Method* (Cambridge, 2002), 82.
[53] David Haines, *Natural theology: a biblical and historical introduction and defense* (Landrum, 2021), 33–5. For other examples of how similar apologetics used Paul's Address

conversion strategies, which signals his focus on apologetic and ties *A Greek in the Temple* to the traditional use of Acts 17:28b.[54] In the verse, Paul references a line belonging to the pagan poet Aratus: 'as certain also of your own poets have said, "For we are also his offspring" '. Implied here is a common-ground between Christian teaching and pagan wisdom. Claiming certain pagan religions as similar to (because derived from) Christian teaching, dubbed the 'patristic paradigm' by Levitin, underpinned apologetic strategy from the Church Fathers to the early modern era.[55] Different approaches for explaining such similarities existed but most relied upon historical claims about Judeo-Christian interaction, or natural theology, to explain the transmission of sacred knowledge.[56] There was nothing original in Sherman alerting his audience to the potential synergies between neo-Platonic philosophy and Christianity.

Sherman's lectures regularly reference Christian apologetic tropes and invoke the tradition's arguments whilst discussing pagan religion and its 'similarity' to Christianity. Sherman cites St Augustine's works, other Church Fathers, and later medieval theologians during his discussion.[57] However, he also referenced early modern apologists who observed the existence of similarities between Christianity and pagan religions that demonstrated knowledge of God's existence, elite monotheist worship, and an awareness of idolatry as mistaken.[58] *A Greek in the Temple* sits firmly within this Christian apologetic tradition. In addition, Parker and Levine's studies raise Sherman's debt to the Italian Reformed Scholastic Girolamo Zanchi.[59] Yet Parker's deduction that Sherman anticipated a Cambridge 'platonist' movement involves implying that Sherman read Zanchi as a 'Platonist' rather than as a Reformed Scholastic who was indebted to Aristotle and many other authorities besides Plato.[60] If one instead studies how Sherman cited Zanchi one sees that he utilised the scholastic as a Christian apologist not as a Platonist philosopher.

Sherman summarised passages from Zanchi's treatise 'On the Soul' from *De Operibus Dei* [Of the works of God] (1591) when describing theories of the soul's creation.[61] Elsewhere in the text, Sherman cited Zanchi only

---

to the Athenians, see Levitin, *Kingdom of Darkness*, 176, 185–6, 189–90. It was certainly not Sherman's choice of scripture or discussion of apologetic strategy that made the text '…so unusual' – Sherman, *Greek in the Temple*, ¶3.

[54] Sherman, *Greek in the Temple*, 1. [55] Levitin, *Kingdom of Darkness*, 167–171.
[56] Levitin, *Kingdom of Darkness*, 178. [57] Sherman, *Greek in the Temple*, i.e 69.
[58] Sherman, *Greek in the Temple*, 30.
[59] Parker, 'Cambridge Platonism(s)', 32–40; Levine, 'Latitudinarians', 87.
[60] At times Parker also acknowledges Zanchi's Aristotelianism, however. See Parker, 'Cambridge Platonism(s)', 40.
[61] Parker, 'Cambridge Platonism(s)', 35 and Sherman, *Greek in the Temple*, 63–76. Trinity College's Library catalogue lists a copy of Girolamo Zanchi, *Hieronymi Zanchii Tractationvm*

three times and the context in which he did so is significant. Twice Sherman invoked Zanchi's authority to confirm the age-old apologetic argument that certain pagan ideas' similarity to holy scripture was due to Plato and several other gentiles accessing revealed truths either directly from God or via the Israelites.[62] *Pace* Parker and Levine, Sherman was not arguing '…for a pious reception of pagan wisdom…' or '…to defend the pagan writers against their critics' (who Levine elsewhere identifies as 'radical Puritans') any more than Christian apologists had done for centuries.[63]

That the 'patristic paradigm' of Christian apologetic crumbled during the late sixteenth and seventeenth century under philological pressure is irrelevant here.[64] Sherman saw value in the 'similarity' method for his students in their future role as ministers. *A Greek in the Temple* was a set of common-places designed to teach future clergymen practical strategies for defending their faith and Church. It was not an original 'treatise' on ancient philosophy and religion.[65] Failure to acknowledge *A Greek in the Temple*'s genre explains Parker and Levine's overemphasis on Sherman's positivity towards pagan thought. Moreover, misquotations from the lectures compound Parker and Levine's misinterpretations. Levine suggests that Sherman believed pagan poets' works complemented antediluvian scriptural sacred history: 'To Sherman, it seemed a shame, for example, to give up the pagan poets whose admittedly fabulous histories nevertheless supplies some useful "allusions into real things before the flood, as if in a manner they would redeeme the losse of the history of the world"'.[66] This quote is incomplete however and hides Sherman's sarcasm. He actually wrote the following: 'To omit many fictions of the Poets, which are little else then fabulous histories, allusions unto reall things before the floud, *as if* in a manner they would redeem the losse of the history of the old world'.[67]

Secondly, Parker claims that 'Sherman also hints that one might give a "very favourable and charitable" conclusion concerning the "eternall state

---

theologicarvm volvmen librvm de operibvs creatinionis…(Neostadii Palatinatvs, 1597) – a possible reference text for Sherman. Philip Gaskell, *Trinity College Library. The First 150 Years: The Sandars Lectures 1978–9* (Cambridge, 1980), Appendix A (Catalogue of Trinity College Library, c.1600) does not list this work, however. For the publication history of Zanchi's 'Of the Works of God' see Christopher J. Burchill, 'Girolamo Zanchi: Portrait of a Reformed Theologian and His Work', *The Sixteenth Century Journal* 15/2 (1984), 203, n101.

[62] Sherman, *Greek in the Temple*, 13, 30. The other citation of Zanchi is on a point of detail regarding the heterodox doctrine against external forms of worship pursued by the central European Schwenkfeldian sect, Ibid, 61.

[63] Parker, 'Cambridge Platonism(s)', 32; Levine, 'Latitudinarians', 86.
[64] Levitin, *Kingdom of Darkness*, 174–207.
[65] Parker, 'Cambridge Platonism(s)', 31.   [66] Levine, 'Latitudinarians', 87.
[67] Sherman, *Greek in the Temple*, 25 (italic emphasis my own).

and condition of those Heathens"'.[68] This is incorrect. In fact, Sherman arrives at the opposite conclusion subsequent to the line Parker paraphrases.

> But suppose we now that all these places quoted out of them were absolutely theirs, and not deduced from any higher doctrine, and not revealed by a supernaturall way; and suppose we [sic] a great many more of such divine passages in them: what then? Happily it is expected now that from this little survey of their knowledge some conclusion should arise towards the eternall state and condition of those Heathens; and *a conclusion also very favourable and charitable:* as if by the small posie we have gathered and made up of the best flowers in Natures garden, we might collect that their knowledge and goodnesse and virtues and education were means likely able to put them not only into a saveable estate, but also into a hopefull condition. For this I answer, I am not engaged any way by the text to speak at all, much lesse definitively, touching the finall end of the Gentiles. *But he that thinketh too well of them, understandeth not sufficiently the priviledge of the Gospel…*[69]

At best, Sherman's views on heathen salvation are doubtful and inconclusive. 'These Philosophers then and Poets are not acknowledged here to be of the Church visible: and whether they or any of them be members of the Church invisible, of the Church triumphant, now, God knoweth. I am not here engaged to speak definitively of their eternall condition…'.[70]

Effusing Reformed orthodoxy, Sherman's lectures acknowledged the monergistic nature of salvation and the role of divine grace.[71] It was also grace, he pointed out, which enlightened both Christian and Pagan natural reason. 'God, I see, respecteth not excellencie of learning where there is no measure of grace: but he respecteth the least degree of grace in whatsoever person'.[72] *A Greek in the Temple* testifies that for Sherman and his colleagues the presence of common grace amongst the ancient pagans explained the more sublime aspects of their thought and rendered their insights useful to students. 'Wit and Eloquence, and Erudition are Gods creatures; yet doth he not vouchsafe them a power to move his delight, unlesse they be exercised to his glory'.[73] With shades of Colossians 2:8, Sherman reminded his students that 'proud philosophy' is not an alternative to faith, a message he

---

[68] Parker, 'Cambridge Platonism(s)', 32. Interestingly the debate about the salvation of the pagans had recently been re-invigorated by the publication of several arguments in favour of the possibility, including the Catholic Francesco Collio's *De animabus paganorum libri quinque* (Milan, 1621), and on the Protestant side Edward Herbert's *De Veritate* (Paris, 1624) and the second edition of John Selden's *De Diis Syris* (Leiden, 1629). This was a niche view to take regardless of confessional outlook however and Sherman is far from joining them. For relevant discussions in the secondary literature see Levitin, *Kingdom of Darkness*, 184. Also G. J. Toomer, *John Selden: a life in scholarship, Vol. I* (Oxford, 2009), 220–1, 252–4.
[69] Sherman, *Greek in the Temple*, 30–1 (italic emphasis my own).
[70] Sherman, *Greek in the Temple*, 24–5.   [71] Sherman, *Greek in the Temple*, 47.
[72] Sherman, *Greek in the Temple*, 15.   [73] Sherman, *Greek in the Temple*, 17.

brought home resoundingly at the end of the lectures when he stated that 'All our learning is soon refuted with one black [spot], which understanding us not, snappeth us unrespectively without any distinction, and putteth at once a period to our reading..'.[74] That Sherman's lectures conform to apologetic tradition and balance the usefulness of pagan knowledge against its limitations is also indicated on the title-page of *A Greek in the Temple*, which is discussed in what follows.

IV

Previous treatments of Sherman's lectures have not discussed the Greek-Latin quotation adorning *A Greek in the Temple*'s front page. Yet the text is no mere decoration since it introduces the reader to an important theme in the lectures.[75] The passage is an excerpt from the *Address to Young Men, on How They Might Derive Benefit from Greek Literature* penned by the Church Father Basil of Caesarea.

'Εἰ μὲν οὖν ἐστί τις οἰκειότης πρὸς ἀλλήλους τοῖς λόγοις, προὔργου ἂν ἡμῖν αὐτῶν ἡ γνῶσις γένοιτο· εἰ δὲ μή, ἀλλὰ τό γε παράλληλα θέντας καταμαθεῖν τὸ διάφορον, οὐ μικρὸν εἰς βεβαίωσιν τοῦ βελτίονος. BASIL, in *Homilia, Ad Juvenes quomodo è Graecis utilitatem caperent'*.[76]

In the *Address*, Basil, who was immersed in classical learning, contends that young students not yet mature enough to handle Holy Scripture's profundity can benefit from aspects of pagan literature as a propaedeutic.[77] Basil instructs his students that when they find pagan poets, historians, and philosophers describing virtuous thoughts and deeds they ought to take note.[78] Scriptural justification for this could be found in Exodus and the story of Moses who grew up amongst the Egyptians before

---

[74] Quotation translated from Latin in the original text. See Sherman, *Greek in the Temple*, 17, 80. Cf. Colossians 2:8 (KJV): 'Beware lest any man spoil you through philosophy and vain deceit, after the tradition of men, after the rudiments of the world, and not after Christ.'
[75] Sherman, *Greek in the Temple*, Title page.
[76] 'Now if there is some affinity between the two bodies of teachings, knowledge of them should be useful to us; but if not, at least the fact that by setting them side by side we can discover the difference between them, is of no small importance for strengthening the position of the better.' This translation is by Roy J. Defarrari and Martin R. P. McGuire in Basil, 'Address To Young Men on Reading Greek Literature', in *Letters, Volume IV* (London, 1934), 384–5. Sherman's own title page accidentally omits γένοιτο from this quotation.
[77] Basil, 'Address To Young Men', 383–5. See also the preface, 368.
[78] Basil, 'Address To Young Men', 385–7.

contemplating the true God.[79] However, Basil's students must never forget that studying the classics is but preparation. Their '...hopes lead...forward to a more distant time, and everything we do is by way of preparation for the other life. What, therefore, contributes to that life, we say must be loved and pursued with all our strength; but what does not conduce to that must be passed over...to that other life the Holy Scriptures lead the way'.[80]

The passage that Sherman chose from Basil's *Address* captures the ambiguous relationship of pagan learning to Christianity. On the one hand, apologists could not dismiss certain religious insights contained within classical thought since they were apologetically useful, as Paul's use of Aratus showed. But on the other hand, they had to use pagan wisdom with caution and not allow it to supplant theology; as Sherman noted, 'Humane learning' must always 'carrieth the candle to Divinity'.[81] That this view was taken for granted in the 1630s at Cambridge University was signalled by Sherman during his lecture.

> so if it should be asked, Whether [*sic*] humane knowledge were usefull, it might be answered, It is an illiterate question. Certainly there is some good to be gotten in the study of Greek authours...I might now tell you Nicephorus his arguments for the point, and that *Basil hath wrote a book to this purpose*...and how learned the Fathers were, and that S. Paul after conversion did not burn his books nor parchments: *But it is an errour to bring this into question in an Universitie*. In lieu of all arguments this may serve, that in this dispute of S. Paul, where he useth both Philosophy and Poets, a woman, Damaris, and many others...were converted.[82]

Sherman's exposition on Acts 17:28b was not an attempt to emulate Basil and to justify the study of pagan learning. As the passage quoted demonstrates, the value of the classics was indisputable in scholastic university curricula at this time.[83] Rather, the lectures' purpose was to explain how the Christian apologetic tradition incorporated pagan learning. Christian teaching could exploit apparent similarities between Greek philosophy and Christianity in order to educate students about the latter. Meanwhile, any differences reinforced the superiority of true religion.

* * *

Early in *A Greek in the Temple*, Sherman ponders why Paul intimated that 'certain of your own poets have said, For we are also his offspring' and

---

[79] Basil, 'Address To Young Men', 387. Sherman copies the Moses allusion, in *Greek in the Temple*, 4. See also the early verses of Exodus 2.
[80] Basil, 'Address To Young Men', 381–3.   [81] Sherman, *Greek in the Temple*, ¶3.
[82] Sherman, *Greek in the Temple*, 20–1 (italic emphasis my own).
[83] William T. Costello, *The Scholastic Curriculum at Early Seventeenth-Century Cambridge* (Cambridge MA, 2013), 10.

yet only quoted one of them?[84] He reminds his students that Paul was learned and that whilst scholarship is a 'rush-candle' in comparison to 'the glorious... holy Scriptures...' yet 'some light is given'.[85] It was not lack of knowledge that prevented Paul from referring to pagan poets other than Aratus, then. The answer instead, Sherman explains, is that Paul was a skilled orator who demonstrated modesty and an understanding of his audience.[86] Tapping into his students' prior learning, Sherman takes the opportunity to use Acts 17:28b to discuss the art of rhetoric. He suggests that Paul cited one poet rather than several so that he did not appear to show off his knowledge.[87] Paul ingratiated himself with the Athenians by moderating his speech and thereby took 'off from himself the envie of much reading'.[88] Sherman praises this move since 'It is none of the least things which belong unto the facultie of eloquence, respectively to take notice of the auditours understandingnesse in the present matter'.[89] Paul showed discretion in limiting his allusions to one poet.[90] He did not assume his audience was as learned as he and recognised that 'Mixt assemblies require at least mixt discourses'.[91] This part of *A Greek in the Temple* is overtly pedagogical, but its tail carried a confessional sting.

Sherman interprets Paul's use of one rather than many quotations belonging to pagan poets as proof that it is not the quantity of voices that proves something to be true.[92] The misplaced assumption that volume is all, notes Sherman, is the basis for Roman Catholic boasting 'that she hath ever had a world of authoritie for her religion, multitudes of Professours;' meanwhile 'little petty England thrust up into a corner of the world, enterteineth a religion which now hath not so great a number of followers'.[93] Such confidence is misplaced however, according to Sherman, and Paul's speech proved it. After all, *'certain* are sufficient to make an evidence'.[94] Sherman remarks that 'in every century since Christ we have had some or other, more or fewer, who have maintained the greatest parts of the Protestants most important and fundamentall opinions, whatsoever Campian prattleth'.[95] His mocking reference to Edmund Campion, a Jesuit priest martyred at Tyburn in 1581 for treasonous missionary work, typifies the anti-Catholic tone of the lectures as a whole.[96] As does Sherman's

---

[84] Sherman, *Greek in the Temple*, 5.
[85] Sherman, *Greek in the Temple*, 3–4.
[86] Sherman, *Greek in the Temple*, 6–10.
[87] Sherman, *Greek in the Temple*, 7.
[88] Sherman, *Greek in the Temple*, 8.
[89] Sherman, *Greek in the Temple*, 8.
[90] Sherman, *Greek in the Temple*, 9.
[91] Sherman, *Greek in the Temple*, 10.
[92] Sherman, *Greek in the Temple*, 10.
[93] Sherman, *Greek in the Temple*, 5.
[94] Sherman, *Greek in the Temple*, 10 (italic emphasis my own).
[95] Sherman, *Greek in the Temple*, 11.
[96] For details about Campion, see Michael A. R. Graves, 'Campion, Edmund [St Edmund Campion] (1540–1581)', *ODNB*.

identifying of Rome with the 'Antichrist'.[97] In the 1630s, this assertion was an intra-confessional weather-gauge within the Church of England. Whilst most Reformed English theologians maintained that the Pope was indeed the Antichrist, certain more *avant-garde* conformist figures including Richard Hooker had previously dissented. Hooker argued that if this were true then pre-Reformation congregants were damned unreasonably.[98] By the late 1620s the 'Antichrist' question had boiled over into a pamphlet war with the Laudian Bishop Richard Montagu declaring that Rome was a true (though errant) Church.[99] It is certain, therefore, that Sherman's audience would have grasped his reference's significance.

The next question Sherman turns to is why Paul cited Aratus during his Address at the Areopagus but did not name the poet explicitly?[100] The lecturer's response is lengthy and digressive. The common-place's pedagogical purpose once more comes to the fore as Sherman leads his audience through protracted discussions about the absence of notable pagan names from the Bible, the lowly condition of human knowledge without divine grace, different attitudes towards poetry amongst heathen philosophers, and the resemblance between the role of the pagan poet and the figure of the Old Testament prophet.[101] Sherman's teaching style is expansive and digressive; his discussions jump between topics and are filled with references and rhetorical flourishes that model declamatory style for his students.[102] Yet Sherman's arguments arrive at a telling conclusion. He announces that Paul cites but does not name his pagan source in order to demonstrate the importance of meditating on what is said rather than who is saying it: 'the Teacher of the Gentiles instructeth us Christians not to disembrace goodnesse in any, nor truth in any... Let us not consider so much who saith, as what is said; who doeth, as what is done. Let not the authority of the teacher tempt thee to erre... the errours of the Fathers were temptations to the Church'.[103] The reference to the 'errours of the Fathers' is loaded given that the Laudian Church placed much greater emphasis on early Church authorities than had previously been the case and downplayed continental Reformed theologians in comparison.[104]

---

[97] Sherman, *Greek in the Temple*, 11.
[98] Anthony Milton, *Catholic and Reformed: the Roman and Protestant churches in English Protestant thought, 1600–1640* (Cambridge, 1995), 146, 162.
[99] Milton, *Catholic and Reformed*, 128.   [100] Sherman, *A Greek in the Temple*, 12.
[101] Sherman, *A Greek in the Temple*, 12–21.
[102] For a survey of the seventeenth-century Cambridge curriculum, see Costello, *The Scholastic Curriculum at Early Seventeenth-Century Cambridge*, passim.
[103] Sherman, *A Greek in the Temple*, 21.
[104] Jean-Louis Quantin, *The Church of England and Christian Antiquity: The Construction of a Confessional Identity in the 17th Century* (Oxford, 2009), 155–202.

Though he does not say so explicitly, Sherman is hinting at another Protestant principle here – private judgement. He alludes positively to the 'noble' Bereans who 'received the word with all readiness of mind, and searched the scriptures daily, whether those things were so'.[105] Sherman's reference (taken from Acts 17:11) was a popular proof-text used by Protestant divines to justify the tenet of *sola scriptura* in the face of Catholic criticism.[106] Protestant exegetes often concluded that the Bereans were nobler than the Thessalonians because they were willing to listen to Paul but did not take him at his word. Nor did they rely upon 'records from antiquity'.[107] Instead, they consulted the scriptures to see if the things themselves were true. It was a standard move in Catholic polemic to argue that the Protestant Churches' reliance upon scripture alone was inevitably schismatic and that only the authority of the Roman Church could resolve exegetical questions and provide the unity Christendom required.[108] The Protestant retaliation involved painting the papacy as an arbitrary tyrant that encouraged believers to blindly hold a 'colliers fayth' rather than think for themselves whilst inspired by the Holy Spirit.[109] Moreover, Protestants criticised the Catholic emphasis on antique ecclesiastical tradition by denying its foundation in scripture. Sherman's argument against authority, derived from Paul's words, belongs to this Protestant line of attack and it carried both pedagogical and confessional implications. Paul had been circumspect in his use of one particular pagan poet and Basil had warned his young students to sift the classical sources carefully. Here Sherman encouraged a similar criticality in his auditors. Moreover, given Sherman's reference to the 'Antichrist' it may also be the case that he was encouraging his students to question certain voices within the contemporary Laudian Church of England.

There are also less controversial theological and pedagogical conclusions to draw from Sherman's comments. The lecturer points out that Paul says '*your* own poets'.[110] He interprets this to mean that Paul makes apologetical use of Aratus' words but rejects his person. Generalising the point Sherman remarks that 'he (Paul) approveth what they (certain poets) say, but he owneth not them'.[111] The lessons Sherman derives from this reading are firstly that 'Word and Work are two things' and secondly that one

---

[105] Sherman, *A Greek in the Temple*, 15–16.
[106] i.e Culverwell, *Light of Nature*, 129.   [107] Sherman, *A Greek in the Temple*, 16.
[108] For example, see Edward Knott, *Mercy and Truth, Or Charity Maintain'd by Catholiques* (St Omer, 1634), I, ii.
[109] For instance, see Culverwell, *Light of Nature*, 131. Also M. Hanmer, *The Iesuites Banner* (London, 1584), X, xiv.
[110] Sherman, *Greek in the Temple*, 21.   [111] Sherman, *Greek in the Temple*, 22.

should 'give everyone his due'.[112] The message to the audience is the importance of leading holy lives, acting justly, and fulfilling Christ's instruction to keep his commandments in word *and deed*, since 'We are in a mighty errour and in a deep ignorance, if we think… to be saved for our knowing or speaking only the truth'.[113]

* * *

The middle third of *A Greek in the Temple* discusses pagan religion and the problem of idolatry. As has been noted already, an essential feature of patristic apologetics that descended to the seventeenth century was proving the similarity of the pagan mind to the Christian.[114] The argument was that this would make Christianity more appealing to possible converts.[115] Arguing for 'similarity' required explaining how pagans had come to know something of the true religion. There were three standard explanations. Either insights from universal reason (natural theology), or the plagiarising of Jewish sources, or certain pagans had access to divinely revealed truths via the universal *logos*.[116] This last explanation involved a neo-platonic conception of the human soul as naturally capable of participating with the eternal divine.[117] In his extended discussion, Sherman explores all of these options whilst reiterating pagan religion's limitations. At the opening of this part of *A Greek in the Temple* Sherman declares that

> it is not amisse to see what the twilight of humane reason can see of God, and towards God, and what analogy there is betwixt some of their speeches and some of Scripture. And by this discourse, we finding in it no mention of the formall object of Christianity, may perceive how little knowledge they had of it.[118]

Pagan religion had no knowledge of Christ nor of the Fall and the necessity of a saviour.[119] This theological reality put a hard-stop on pagan wisdom accruing too much credit amongst Christians. Certainly, nothing Sherman goes on to say encourages an overly positive reading of pagan writers or strays beyond Calvinist Reformed positions on grace and revelation.

Sherman relied upon a common though not uncriticised explanation for how certain pagan writers came to have Judeo-Christian-like insights.[120] The Renaissance rediscovery of texts belonging to the Church Fathers had enabled sixteenth-century apologists such as Agostino Steuco to access

---

[112] Sherman, *Greek in the Temple*, 23–4. [113] Sherman, *Greek in the Temple*, 24.
[114] Levitin, *Kingdom of Darkness*, 167–71. [115] Levitin, *Kingdom of Darkness*, 167.
[116] Levitin, *Kingdom of Darkness*, 169. [117] Levitin, *Kingdom of Darkness*, 169.
[118] Sherman, *Greek in the Temple*, 25. [119] Sherman, *Greek in the Temple*, 28, 31.
[120] Sherman, *A Greek in the Temple*, 28–30.

patristic arguments for pagan religion's similarity to Christianity.[121] Steuco's *De perenni philosophia* (1540) publicised the syncretic *logos* theology thesis and the work became recommended reading for divinity students.[122] In contrast, the Huguenot Philipe Du Plessis Mornay's widely-read apologetic work *Traité de la vérité de la religion chrétienne* (1581) invoked the plagiarism theory.[123] Throughout this section of *A Greek in the Temple* Sherman does not commit to either the 'positive' theory that pagans independently attained religious wisdom or the 'negative' theory that they relied upon Jewish sources. Both elements are present in his writing.[124] Regardless of the preferred explanation, early moderns including Steuco, Zanchi, and Sherman pointed to the writings of the pagan Sibylline Oracles and the Hermetic Corpus attributed to Hermes Trismegistus as evidence that various heathens had accessed the truths of Christianity. This claim had immense apologetic value.

However, as far back as St Augustine these 'Christians amongst Heathens' were criticised.[125] The Bishop of Hippo had suggested that they were diabolically inspired.[126] Furthermore, by the late sixteenth-century Isaac Casaubon's philological scholarship had proved that the Oracles and the Corpus were pious Christian forgeries.[127] Interestingly, Sherman demonstrates an awareness of this scholarly development but refutes the suggestion that the texts were fake. He claims that the mention of the Sibylline Oracles in Cicero's *De natura Deorum* is proof of their legitimacy.[128] Moreover, he cites the work of the German Catholic scholar Johann Reuchlin as a defence of Trismegistus' existence.[129] The apologetic value of the 'similarity thesis' which relied upon syncretism was too appealing for Sherman to drop even when confronted with philological insights that disproved it.

---

[121] Levitin, *Kingdom of Darkness*, 170.
[122] Agostino Steuco, *De perenni philosophia libri X* (Lyon, 1540). Also, Levitin, *Kingdom of Darkness*, 170.
[123] Philippe de Mornay, *De la verité de la religion chrestienne* (Paris, 1585), 67–93, *passim*. Mornay is referenced by Sherman in *A Greek in the Temple*, 75.
[124] Sherman, *Greek in the Temple*, cf. 29 and 30.
[125] St Augustine, 'The City of God', in *Nicene and Post-Nicene Fathers, First Series, Vol. 2* (New York, 1887), trans. Marcus Dods, Book VIII, Ch. xiii; Sherman, *Greek in the Temple*, 31.
[126] Sherman's in-text citation reads 'as Augustine thinketh De Civit. Dei, viii. 13'. Marcus Dods translates the lines of Augustine Sherman refers to as 'Is he not verily compelled by divine influence, on the one hand, to reveal the past error of his forefathers, and by a diabolical influence, on the other hand, to bewail the future punishment of demons?' See Augustine, 'City of God', VIII, xxiv.
[127] Anthony Grafton, *Defenders of the Text: The Traditions of Scholarship in an Age of Science, 1450–1800* (Cambridge MA, 1991), 162–77; Nicholas Hardy, *Criticism and Confession: the Bible in the seventeenth century republic of letters* (Oxford, 2017), 122–7.
[128] Sherman, *Greek in the Temple*, 29. See also Marcus Tullius Cicero, *The Nature of the Gods* (London, 1972), 127, 194–5.
[129] Sherman, *Greek in the Temple*, 29.

The first discussion of pagan natural theology in *A Greek in the Temple* is brief and rehearses standard apologetic arguments. Sherman states that the pagans (as created beings) could know 'God Creatour' by one of three ways: negation, causality, or eminence.[130] This is a rehearsal of Thomas Aquina's three *viae* [ways of knowing God exists by analogy] that derived from the writings of Pseudo-Dionysius.[131] A common-place of medieval natural theology, the presence of Aquina's three *viae* reinforces modern historians' arguments for the persistence of Catholic Scholastic theology within seventeenth-century Reformed teaching.[132] However, Sherman goes no deeper into scholastic natural theology debates here and pauses only to observe that this 'rationall knowledge' could not bring the pagans to see the use or possibility of a Messiah.[133] Sherman's unwillingness to explore natural religion further is suggestive given that he dedicates considerably more time to questions of revelation and tradition.[134] Appealing to reason was a necessary aspect of Reformed preaching and conversion strategy but it was not held to be enough on its own; the infusion of an external regenerating grace was a prerequisite to learning in spiritual matters.[135] Sherman reinforces this point by stating that

> suppose we now that all these places quoted out of them [pagan writers] were absolutely theirs, and not deduced from any higher doctrine, and not revealed by a supernaturall way; and suppose we a great many more of such divine passages in them: what then?... God who is best able to judge, accounted the times of Paganisme before Christ, for all their knowledge, even *times of ignorance*; and accordingly he respected them, as our Apostle in the second verse unto our text, *And the times of this ignorance God winked at*;... which we may expound of a neglect; as if God *looked over* or *beyond* those times, and had respect onely unto the times of Christianity.[136]

Sherman's exegesis conforms with his Reformed theological perspective and places strict limits on the value of pagan natural knowledge.

---

[130] Sherman, *Greek in the Temple*, 31.
[131] Thomas Aquinas, *Summa Contra Gentiles* I, xiii; Idem *Summa Theologica* I q. 2 a. 3. See also Levitin, *Kingdom of Darkness*, 177.
[132] A point made with reference to other sources in Levitin, *Kingdom of Darkness*, 178. See also Richard Muller, 'Not Scotist', *Reformation & Renaissance Review* 14/2 (2012): 127–50.
[133] Sherman, *Greek in the Temple*, 31–2.
[134] Sherman, *Greek in the Temple*, 28–31.
[135] John Philip Morgan, *Godly learning: Puritan attitudes towards reason, learning, and education, 1560–1640* (Cambridge, 1986), 54–6. See also Richard Muller, *Post-Reformation Reformed Dogmatics, Vol. I* (Grand Rapids, 1987), 270–310.
[136] Sherman, *Greek in the Temple*, 30–1.

Later on Sherman returns to the theme of the 'cognoscibility of God by humane understanding without any supernaturall doctrine'.[137] He again draws upon the Catholic scholastic tradition by referencing Distinction III in Book One of Peter Lombard's *Sentences*, which handles natural theological ways to know that God exists.[138] However, Sherman also references the early Christian apologist Arnobius's work *adversùs Gentes* and its contention that within pagan religion there was an acknowledgement of the true God.[139] Thirdly, Sherman draws upon Varro (whom he found in St Augustine and Cicero) and his tripartite distinction of pagan religions into poetical, civil, and philosophical.[140] Varro's argument implied that learned pagan philosophers understood the deities worshipped within civil religion not to be the true God but human inventions.[141] Sherman combined these classical and patristic references with an exegesis of Romans 1:18–21; in these verses Paul declares that the ungodly are without excuse given that they possess a natural knowledge of God's existence. This passage from Paul's Epistle was a *locus classicus* for discussions of natural theology as it provided scriptural justification for knowledge of God via creation and through an innate idea of the deity.[142] Referencing Calvin's commentary on Romans, Sherman conventionally explains that the Gentiles had a natural knowledge of God but they failed to worship him properly and thus descended into idolatry.[143]

From the beginning of the Christian apologetic tradition there was an awareness of pagan idolatry and the challenges it posed to claims of 'similarity'. Indeed, Paul's address at the Areopagus criticised the Athenians' superstitious practices and their objectification of the divine. However, Church Fathers such as Justin Martyr circumvented the problem of pagan idolatry by distinguishing between vulgar pagan polytheism and 'correct' elite pagan monotheists, who relied upon Jewish knowledge of true religion.[144] Whilst the pagan masses had indeed been idolatrous, Martyr held that there were a select few who acknowledged this to be wrong. In his discussion of the problem of pagan idolatry Sherman follows this argumentative strategy.

---

[137] Sherman, *Greek in the Temple*, 36–7.
[138] Sherman, *Greek in the Temple*, 37. See Peter Lombard, *Sentences* (Toronto, 2007), trans. Giulio Silano, 18–27.
[139] Sherman, *Greek in the Temple*, 37. See *The Seven Books of Arnobius Adversùs Gentes* (Edinburgh, 1871), trans. Hamilton Bryce and Hugh Campbell, 2.
[140] Sherman, *Greek in the Temple*, 38–9. Cf. Augustine, 'City of God', VI, v.
[141] Augustine, 'City of God', VI, iv.   [142] Haines, *Natural Theology*, 36–40.
[143] Sherman, *Greek in the Temple*, 39. See also John Calvin, *Commentary upon the Epistle of Saint Paul to the Romans* (Edinburgh, 1844), 30.
[144] Justin Martyr, *Dialogue with Trypho* (Oxford, 1755), 56–8.

> Though the sillier of the Heathen might think them to be the onely Gods, yet the more learned and intelligent of them did not firmly believe their absolute Divinities... That the learneder sort of the Gentiles, some more clearly, some more indistinctly, according to the measure of common illumination from God, and light of their own reason, did ultimately aim at a true Divinity, even amongst their false ones.[145]

An earlier verse in Paul's address to the Athenians (Acts 17:23) provided a convenient scriptural basis for the suggestion that the learned pagans practiced an imperfect yet correctly directed monotheistic worship. The 'altar...TO THE UNKNOWN GOD' symptomised an ignorant objectification of the supreme monotheist God of Jewish and Christian religion. The argument that Acts 17:23 lent biblical sanction to the claim that elite pagans practised monotheism was put forward by the English Member of Parliament Jurist, and Hebraic scholar John Selden in his work on comparative religion, entitled *De Diis Syris*.[146] The same argument appeared in the Dutch theologian G. J. Vossius' *De theologia gentili* (1695–1701) and the work of Selden's compatriot Edward Herbert (Lord Herbert of Cherbury).[147] Though Sherman does not reiterate this exegetical argument in *A Greek in the Temple*, his distinction between vulgar pagan idolatry and an elite pagan monotheism drew upon a particular apologetic argument that was clearly in circulation when his lectures were first delivered. Moreover, Sherman's conclusion that the learned pagan's religious insight was not enough to enable them to 'Glorifie him...in the right manner' reiterates heathen religion's impotency and the necessity of Christ's revelation.[148] In the next part of the lecture, Sherman explained the relationship between pagan religion (vulgar and learned) and idolatry before developing this into another attack on Catholicism.

* * *

Sherman resorted to regular scholastic arguments drawn from natural theology to establish that all men were capable of recognising the existence of God and of knowing to worship this divinity alone. According to him, man owed homage to God by dint of the latter's 'sovereigne Power' and 'Goodnesse'.[149] Sherman's explanation as to how this natural religion corrupted and became idolatrous was also not original. In *De Diis Syris*,

---

[145] Sherman, *Greek in the Temple*, 34–6.
[146] Selden, *De Diis Syris*, lxi–lxii, 112,114.
[147] G. J. Vossius, 'De theologia gentili', in *Opera omnia, 6 vols* (Amsterdam, 1695–1701), v. 5b–6a; Edward Herbert, *De religione gentilium* (Amstelodamum, 1700), 162. Whether or not Sherman had consulted these texts is unclear. His reference in the dedicatory preface to the 'raritie of the subject' contained therein, his description of his lectures as 'so unusual', and his claim that 'Few such texts there are; this, to my knowledge, not touched before' would imply that he had not. See Sherman, *Greek in the Temple*, ¶3.
[148] Sherman, *Greek in the Temple*, 39.   [149] Sherman, *Greek in the Temple*, 40.

Selden had argued that idolatry originated from two primitive practices: worshipping the heavenly bodies and deifying the dead.[150] Echoing these points, Sherman claimed that

> Now since in a Divine essence there is considered so much majesty and glory that they [the pagans] might think it an impudent presumption to make an immediate addresse unto this great God, therefore they might think they should do God service in shewing their honour of him by the doing honour *unto his glorious creatures, the Sunne, the Moon, and the like, and in making great men after death as mediatours betwixt him [God] and them*...[151]

Turning to his copy of Augustine's *City of God*, Sherman interprets Varro's argument contained therein as claiming that the making of images for worship was wrong because it takes away man's fear of the Lord.[152] This was also why, according to Sherman, God never appeared to the Israelites in corporeal form.[153] Nonetheless, according to Sherman over time the 'common sort' fell into idolatry; they esteemed mediatory images and objects 'as complete Gods'.[154]

Sherman uses the term 'idolatry' to denote the worship of an image and thus explains that 'the more intelligent of them [the pagans]' avoided resorting to idolatry.[155] Yet this is a sleight-of-hand since Sherman admits that the learned pagans still worshipped God 'by mediation and image'.[156] In relation to this claim, Sherman quoted Arnobius, whom he found mentioned in a sermon given by the Primate of Ireland James Ussher before the House of Commons in 1620, voicing the heathen claim that 'We worship the Gods by the images'.[157] In other words, the learned pagans aimed at the true God '...through or by those false Gods'.[158] Drawing also on Diogenes Laertius' *Lives of eminent Philosophers*, Sherman pointed out that the pre-Socratic philosopher Thales had 'looked further at 'God the Ancient of dayes'.[159] Sherman also claimed that Socrates was martyred for his monotheism.[160] In light of this, contended Sherman, one can understand why Paul felt able to quote Aratus. The latter 'through *Jupiter*

---

[150] Selden, *De Diis Syris*, xxvi–xxxviii.
[151] Sherman, *Greek in the Temple*, 40–1 (italic emphasis my own).
[152] Augustine, 'City of God', IV, ix, xxxi; VII, v.
[153] Sherman, *Greek in the Temple*, 41–2.
[154] Sherman, *Greek in the Temple*, 41.   [155] Sherman, *Greek in the Temple*, 41.
[156] Sherman, *Greek in the Temple*, 41.
[157] Sherman, *Greek in the Temple*, 40. See also James Ussher 'A sermon, preached before the Commons House of Parliament, in St. Margaret's Church, at Westminster, the 18th of February, 1620', in *The Whole Works of the Most Rev. James Ussher, Vol. 2* (Ireland, 1864), 442
[158] Sherman, *Greek in the Temple*, 40.
[159] Sherman, *Greek in the Temple*, 41. See also Diogenes Laertius, *Lives of eminent Philosophers* (Cambridge, 2020), trans. Stephen White, 47, ln.357-8.
[160] Sherman, *Greek in the Temple*, 35.

meaneth GOD'.[161] Nevertheless, as Sherman stated this imperfect elite pagan monotheism was still false worship.[162] Clearly then, Sherman is not engaged in an attempt to salvage heathen religion from Christian condemnation. In fact, his distinguishing of pagan idolatry as vulgar image worship versus learned worshipping of God via an image had a far more immediate and confessionally driven polemical purpose.

A clue as to what Sherman was doing in drawing the distinction outlined above exists in the Ussher sermon he referenced. Taking 1 Corinthians 10:17 as its scriptural *locus*, Ussher's sermon embarked on a tirade against idolatry and the need for the truly faithful to separate themselves from wicked practices in worship.[163] During the course of his address, Ussher charged Roman Catholicism with breaching scriptural commands by committing idolatry (defined as using images 'set up for religious adoration').[164] Ussher voiced two Catholic counter-arguments to the accusation of idolatry: that their images are not the same as pagan idols and that scripture's instructions about idolatry do not apply to their practices. On this second point, Catholic theologians claimed that the Bible forbade the idolatry of the errant Old Testament Israelites and pagans because it involved holding 'images themselves' to be God, which Catholics did not.[165] Ussher responded by contending that this was not the case however since some pagans understood that they were worshipping God *through* such images, as Arnobius had claimed.[166] In other words, Ussher contended that the distinction that Catholics drew between their worship and ancient pagan practices was a false one since not all heathens worshipped images as gods. A learned minority worshipped God through images just like Roman Catholics.

Here lies the explanation for why Sherman laboured the distinction between vulgar and learned pagan worship. It is in this section of the primate's sermon that Sherman found the reference to Arnobius and he uses the apologist's words in precisely the same manner that Ussher had previously.[167] By arguing that some pagans worshipped God through images and not merely the images themselves, Sherman (following Ussher) set a trap to undermine Catholic defences of their use of images during worship. In case Sherman's audience had any doubts as to what he was up to, the lecturer laid bare his intentions and begged the question:

> Now by this, though hasty and short discourse of the Gentile worship occasioned by S. Pauls expression, we may in some manner calculate and decipher

---

[161] Sherman, *Greek in the Temple*, 41. [162] Sherman, *Greek in the Temple*, 41.
[163] Ussher, 'A sermon', 417. [164] Ussher, 'A sermon', 440.
[165] Ussher, 'A sermon', 440, 444. [166] Ussher, 'A sermon', 442.
[167] Cf. Ussher, 'A sermon', 442 and Sherman, *Greek in the Temple*, 40.

the difference betwixt the false worship of Rome Pagane and Rome Christian, of Gentiles and of Papists, which difference in a Pontifician eye is so wide and mighty.[168]

Sherman then proceeded to elide the distinction between learned pagan worship and contemporary Catholic practices for the purpose of confessional point scoring. Gilded throughout with humour and sarcasm, Sherman's lectures substantiated the comparison made by Ussher between pagan and Catholic worship by deriding the latter's angelology and doctrine of intercession.[169] Christian Rome, said Sherman, 'worshippeth God by men-saints (besides by Angels) and some of those Saints happily as bad for Christians as the other were for Heathens'. He continued

> The sillier of the Heathen might worship the men for true Gods: the best of Rome Christian give a kind of Divine worship to Saints. The sillier of the Heathen might worship the Images of their feigned Gods: the sillier of the Papists distinguish not betwixt the Image of the Saint and the Saint... the Heathen worshipped by a multitude of Gods: but the Papists by more Saints and Angels. The Heathen had for every occasion a severall Tutelar Mediatour: the Papists likewise have a severall Saint, beside their particular Angel.

According to Sherman, Catholics and pagans alike were either guilty of vulgar idolatry or of worshipping God through something made by human hands. Paul's address to the Athenians forbade both actions.[170] Sherman's conventional survey of pagan idolatry emerges, then, as a strategy for generating anti-Catholic confessional polemic.

Before concluding this discussion, it is important to note that Sherman's words, inspired by Ussher's sermon, touched a nerve closer to home too. Ussher addressed the House of Commons at St Margaret's church, Westminster. Amongst his opening words the Archbishop reminded his audience that 'The special cause of your assembling at this time is, first, that you, who profess the same truth, may join in one body, and partake together of the same blessed communion: and then, that such as adhere unto false worship, may be discovered and avoided'.[171] The occasion of Communion provided Ussher with an opportunity to discuss 'false worship' in 1620; a time when a faction within the Church of England, led by Bishop Lancelot Andrewes, were pushing for a more beautified and ceremonial form of worship.[172] By the time that Sherman came to reiterate Ussher's sentiments in the 1630s the *avant-garde* conformist agenda had been brought into the open by William Laud and his followers.

---

[168] Sherman, *Greek in the Temple*, 42.   [169] Sherman, *Greek in the Temple*, 42–3.
[170] Acts 17:25, 29.   [171] Ussher, 'A sermon', 417.
[172] Nicholas Tyacke, 'Archbishop Laud', in *The early Stuart Church, 1603–1642* (London, 1993), ed. Kenneth Fincham, 64.

As Peter Lake's recent study of their project has shown, the Laudians sought to change the terms of the debate by achieving 'a full-scale remaking, a true reformation, of the English church, based on a coherent vision of what the church ought to look like and of what the salvific mission of the visible church was…'.[173] This included an emphasis on the 'beauty of holiness' and an outward aesthetic in worship that the Laudianism's opponents regarded as nothing less than idolatry reborn.[174] If Ussher's sermon constituted a warning against what was stirring, then Sherman's lecture was a critical commentary of contemporary practice now that Laud '…was actually in the saddle'.[175] Thus, Sherman's anti-Catholic polemic provided a stalking-horse for targeting an opponent closer to home. Ironically, Sherman delivered *A Greek in the Chapel* in a space that had been recently (or was about to be) redecorated in line with Laudian requirements.[176]

The Laudian context may also account for the delay between the delivery of Sherman's lectures in the 1630s and their printing in 1641. One explanation is the change in England's religious and political landscape that occurred in this period. This article has claimed that Sherman was implicitly critical of aspects of Laudian ideology. To take such a line in the mid-1630s involved walking a dangerous tight-rope and required subtlety. By 1641 however the Long Parliament had begun and the Laudian project was collapsing following the Archbishop's arrest.[177] It is possible that Sherman's lectures were released then because they suited this changed environment. Nonetheless, Sherman remained cautious. In the dedicatory preface to the print edition of *A Greek in the Temple*, Sherman suggested that the print edition was not intended for a wide audience but only Charter House's governors.[178]

V

The common-place genre's flexibility allowed Sherman to depart from a narrow exegesis of Acts 17:28b and to discuss a wide range of themes with a view to their contemporary confessional or edificatory relevance. As a result, his lectures canvassed a range of sources from alternative periods and genres. Sherman's use of these authorities involved synthesising texts

---

[173] Lake, *On Laudianism*, 1.   [174] Lake, *On Laudianism*, 257–60.
[175] Tyacke, 'Archbishop Laud', 62.
[176] Hoyle, *Reformation and religious identity*, 165.
[177] Anthony Milton, *England's second Reformation: the battle for the Church of England 1625–1662* (Cambridge, 2021), 66–7.
[178] He writes 'But I mean not that the world shall see it…' in Sherman, *Greek in the Temple*, ¶3.

not commonly consulted by intellectual historians, such as Bible commentaries.[179] This is demonstrated in the last third of *A Greek in the Temple* where Sherman discusses Acts 17:28b in relation to exegeses on Genesis.[180] Firstly however, earlier in *A Greek in the Temple* Sherman relies upon textual criticism to attack the Catholic handling of scripture and other theological works.

Sherman ponders why Paul quoted Aratus verbatim rather than paraphrasing the poet and exercising the same liberty to expand on texts that the Apostle deployed with regards to Old Testament scripture.[181] The answer, Sherman suggests, is that although it did not add to his argument Paul did not want to give the Athenians any excuse to complain that he was arguing disingenuously.[182] As with other parts of *A Greek in the Temple* that have already been discussed, it is not Sherman's answer here that is significant so much as the inference he draws from it: 'we have from hence a divine rule and example, or a rule divine by example, concerning an honest and faithfull and ingenuous citing of authours'.[183] Paul, Sherman claims, had gone *ad fontes* and read Aratus in the original.[184] Expanding on this humanist motif, Sherman exclaims

> let me reade the authour and the originall; let me reade them my self. The quotations of others which they make of authours may be false, and therefore will deceive. The connexion, the interpunction, the accent, the sense of the term in the writers time, may turn the sense of the place; and so what I reade of an authour at the second hand may seem to be the authours, but peradventure it is the quoters: therefore let me reade the authour, or at least

---

[179] Multiple scholars have studied Bible commentaries more recently in a Dutch context. See Anthony Ossa-Richardson, 'The Naked Truth of Scripture: André Rivet between Bellarmine and Grotius', in *Scriptural Authority and Biblical Criticism in the Dutch Golden Age: God's Word Questioned* (Oxford, 2017), eds. Henk Nellen, Dirk van Miert, Piet Steenbakkers et al, 109–30; Dirk van Miert, 'Grotius's Annotations on the Bible (1619–1645)', in *Scriptural Authority and Biblical Criticism in the Dutch Golden Age: God's Word Questioned* (Oxford, 2017), eds. Henk Nellen, Dirk van Miert, Piet Steenbakkers et al, 133–69. Also relevant is Debora K. Shuger, *The Renaissance Bible: scholarship, sacrifice, and subjectivity* (Berkely, 1994).
[180] Sherman, *Greek in the Temple*, 53–80. Sherman's lectures conformed to a standard feature of early seventeenth century English sermons in that they ended by offering practical conclusions to the audience. Bishop Gilbert Burnet described the structure of early seventeenth century sermons: '... (the) way of preaching... a great mixture of quotations from fathers and ancient writers, a long opening of a text with the concordance of every word in it, and a giving all the different expositions with the grounds of them, and the entring into some parts of controversy, and *all concluding in some, but very short, practical applications, according to the subject or the occasion.*' (italic emphasis my own). In Burnet, *History of my own time. Part I*, 191.
[181] Sherman, *Greek in the Temple*, 45–8.
[182] Sherman, *Greek in the Temple*, 47.
[183] Sherman, *Greek in the Temple*, 47.
[184] Sherman, *Greek in the Temple*, 48.

quote the quoter. Let me reade the originall: Translations may vary. They may be either false or slender, inexpressive, obscure, obscurer sometimes then the Text.[185]

Sherman's purpose here was not simply to advise his students on good scholarly practice, however. In line with his strategy throughout the lecture he turned this argument into confessional polemic by claiming that Catholic scholiasts are counterfeiters.[186]

Sherman begins coyly by suggesting that 'I might take a rise unto a generall treating, in way of reprehension, of the Abuse of authours, contrary to our Apostles practice: And then I might note who, and how, and wherein, and who most, and how farre they have proceeded in this most disingenuous injury unto writers deceased or living'.[187] Swiftly though he clarifies whom he has in mind. Sherman accuses two Catholics, Cardinal Robert Bellarmine and the Polish priest Wacław Grodziecki [Grodecius], of the 'false interpretation of authors'.[188] Additionally, he suggests that the Catholics are guilty of 'false printing' through either the addition, the subtraction, or the alteration of texts.[189] Sherman offers examples of each kind of error including: the changing of the word '*imagines*' for '*idola*' in Vatablus' scholia on Psalm 107; the deleting of a letter from Book One of Athanasius' writings; and adding marginalia such as '*Autor est damnatus*' [the author is condemned] next to controversial passages.[190] Throughout this part of the lecture Sherman continually references the *Index Librorum Prohibitorum* [Index of Forbidden Books] as proof of Roman Catholic censoriousness.[191] In strengthening his polemic with additional examples of Catholic malpractice, Sherman also demonstrates an awareness of contemporary scholarly book culture and the circulation of different editions of the same works. For example, he claims that

> Ferus, one of their own, yet in many points of our religion ours, (as appeareth by their dealing towards him) in his comment upon the first epistle of S. John, in fifty leaves is falsified thrice fifty times, as is exactly observed. In thrice fifty places doth the Romane Edition of him, which came out 1577. differ in the former wayes, either adding or taking away or altering from the Antwerp-edition, which came out 1556. And not

---

[185] Sherman, *Greek in the Temple*, 48.
[186] Sherman, *Greek in the Temple*, 85–88 [sic] (49–52; pages 49–56 of Sherman's book are erroneously numbered 85–92).
[187] Sherman, *Greek in the Temple*, 48.
[188] Sherman, *Greek in the Temple*, 85 [sic] (49).
[189] Sherman, *Greek in the Temple*, 85 [sic] (49).
[190] Sherman, *Greek in the Temple*, 85–6 [sic] (49–50).
[191] Sherman, *Greek in the Temple*, 85–6 [sic] (49–50).

onely Ferus, but Fulbert also Bishop of Chartres, who lived in the eleventh centurie, is falsified by addition.[192]

Sherman claims that Catholic interlocutors edited Fulbert's writing and released a Parisian edition in 1608 that altered the sense of his argument concerning the Eucharist, in order to make it seem that he explicitly defended transubstantiation when in fact Fulbert had not.[193] Sherman concludes the discussion with a lengthy stream of anti-Catholic sentiment including a witty remark in relation to their supposed doctoring of texts: 'It seemeth where Peters keyes cannot open the difficulty, his sword must cut the knot'.[194]

Elsewhere in *A Greek in the Temple*, Sherman deploys the same strategy of enlisting critical scholarship in order to attack Catholicism. This time, however, he makes an argument with domestic resonances too. Sherman notes that the final verse of Acts 17 names one of the Athenians who heard Paul speak – Dionysius the Areopagite.[195] Previously, Sherman posits, some Catholics have mistakenly elevated this individual by suggesting that he organised the building of the Altar to the unknown God and that he wrote several texts (known as the *Corpus Dionysiacum*) that elucidated Christian teaching.[196] Sherman brusquely dismisses the former suggestion and draws upon the humanist scholars Lorenzo Valla and Desiderius Erasmus in order to counter these latter claims:

> concerning the books which the Pontificians father upon his name, *De caelesti hierarchia*, *De ecclesiastica hierarchia*, *De Divinis nominibus*, it were not very difficult to determine them not to be his. For Hierome in his Catalogue of Ecclesiastick writers maketh no mention of them. Valla and Erasmus have proved by many arguments that they are none of his, as Chemnitius [Martin Chemnitz] relateth.[197]

Furthermore, Sherman contends that the references to Temples, Altars, and Monks in the texts prove that Dionysius the Areopagite could not have written them in Paul's time.[198]

In the context of 1630s England, this argument carried a confessional edge. The veneration of the altar as the site of the sacrament was a keystone of Laudian ideology.[199] A physical manifestation of this was the removing of the communion table from the church floor by elevating it and railing it off from the rest of the church in the chancel. A controversial alteration

---

[192] Sherman, *Greek in the Temple*, 86–7 [sic] (51–2).
[193] Sherman, *Greek in the Temple*, 87 [sic] (52).
[194] Sherman, *Greek in the Temple*, 88 [sic] (53).
[195] Sherman, *Greek in the Temple*, 14.   [196] Sherman, *Greek in the Temple*, 14.
[197] Sherman, *Greek in the Temple*, 14.   [198] Sherman, *Greek in the Temple*, 14.
[199] Lake, *On Laudianism*, 179–88.

that changed the configuration of England's churches and chapels.[200] Laudian sympathisers went in search of arguments to defend this policy and turned to the practices of the primitive Church and the Jewish temples before them.[201] Indeed they went further by excavating the early sacred history narrated in Genesis. For instance, Peter Heylyn argued in his *Parable of the Tares* that not only did Cain and Abel worship at an altar and perform sacrifices but that their father Adam and younger brother Seth began the line of the priesthood.[202] Opponents of Laudianism denied that the term 'altar' had such a venerable history and referred instead to the 'communion table' so as to avoid the alternative.[203] Sherman's argument that the appearance of the term 'altar' in the Pseudo-Dionysian corpus rules out it having been written in the time of Paul communicates an anti-Laudian sentiment to his students:

> Where the Altar is and the Priest the Temple may be supposed. Now settled temples in Dionysius his time, almost certain it is, there were none: Questionlesse no Monks, the order whereof was instituted first by Paul the Hermite some two hundred and seven years after the conversion of Dionysius, as the Chronologer hath it. Dionysius then who is named in Scripture was no very learned scholar, for ought we know.

* * *

The final third of *A Greek in the Temple* discusses what Paul meant in applying Aratus' phrase 'For we are also his [God's] off-spring' to a Christian context.[204] Sherman builds his answer to this question through an interrogation of Man's relationship to God via his body, his soul, and then his body-and-soul in union.[205] The result of his discussion is to draw out the practical implications of the lectures for his students' spiritual lives.[206] This conclusion to *A Greek in the Temple* serves to highlight another purpose of the common-place genre, which was to edify its audience. Whilst it is not as aggressively polemical as earlier parts of the lectures, Sherman's discussion here still hints at theological anxieties. In particular, the need to reconcile man's Fall with the fact that God made

---

[200] Lake, *On Laudianism*, 184. For a discussion of this in relation to Cambridge University's chapels see Twigg, *Cambridge and the English Revolution*, 35.
[201] Lake, *On Laudianism*, 196.
[202] Lake, *On Laudianism*, 197. Cf. Peter Heylyn, *Parable of the Tares* (London, 1659), 9.
[203] For an example of this response see Thomas Morton, *Of the Institution of the Sacrament of the Blessed Body and Blood of Christ* (London, 1631), Second Pagination, 50. See also Stephen Hampton, *Grace and conformity: the reformed conformist tradition and the early Stuart Church of England* (Oxford, 2021), 207–36.
[204] Sherman, *Greek in the Temple*, 53–80.
[205] Sherman, *Greek in the Temple*, 53, 62, 76.
[206] Sherman, *Greek in the Temple*, 78–80.

him in his image – without making the Almighty the author of sin. The passage as a whole illustrates Sherman's reliance upon biblical commentaries when composing his lectures and his methodological blending of positive and scholastic theology.[207]

Sherman explicitly connects Acts 17:28b to the book of Genesis by explaining the word 'off-spring' in relation to God's creation of Man's body and soul.[208] To begin with, Sherman draws on the account of Adam and Eve's creation to argue that God is the efficient cause of Man's being and that, whilst humans thereafter were naturally procreated, God is their father.[209] Drawing on early Christian sources including Montanus and Theoderet's comments on Genesis and Augustine's *Confessions*, Sherman raises a routine natural theological argument for God's existence.[210] He remarks upon the mystery of Man's body being so well designed and quotes the supposed writings of Trismegist on this subject.[211] According to Sherman, the implication of this revelation that Man is God's offspring, in terms of his body, is that he owes it to God to act purely. He calls upon his audience to not 'dishonour this temple of the holy Ghost by uncleannesse, by fornication, by adultery, or any such turpitude'.[212] The paramount manner in which to acknowledge that 'we are God's off-spring' in terms of our bodies, Sherman suggested, was the physical act of worship.[213]

Sherman's examination of how Man is God's offspring in terms of his soul occasions a lengthy survey of theories of the soul's creation that relies once again upon the work of Zanchi.[214] Whilst the questions of when the soul is created, with what materials, and by whom may seem abstract, it transpires that they are pivotal to Sherman's doctrinal concerns. For example, at that time one explanation for the creation of the soul was that it grew in the womb (traducianism) whilst the alternative thesis was that God creates all souls *ex nihilo* and infuses them into the individual's body during gestation. If one took the latter view, it was difficult to explain how Man partook in original sin without suggesting that God was the creator of evil. Yet, Reformed doctrines of total depravity and imputed sin relied upon this principle of shared guilt. In order to address this pressing question Sherman turned once more to biblical scholarship.

---

[207] For a discussion of the rise of positive theology and its relationship to scholastic theology in the seventeenth century see Levitin, *Kingdom of God*, 120–64.

[208] Earlier in the lectures Sherman references events in Genesis – including the story of Abel's sacrifice and the dispersion of Man after the Tower of Babel – in passing. See Sherman, *Greek in the Temple*, 8, 16.

[209] Sherman, *Greek in the Temple*, 91–2 [sic] (55–56).
[210] Sherman, *Greek in the Temple*, 92–57 [sic] (56–7), 61.
[211] Sherman, *Greek in the Temple*, 92–59 [sic] (56–9).
[212] Sherman, *Greek in the Temple*, 60.   [213] Sherman, *Greek in the Temple*, 62.
[214] See note 52 above.

Sherman enters into the debate by referencing Exodus 21:22, which concerns God's decree regarding the accidental striking of a woman – who is with child – by brawling men.[215] If the woman miscarries as a result and the foetus is 'not shaped' then the penalty is a fine. If, however, the foetus is fully formed then the punishment is death, since this act constitutes murder.[216] This legal issue hinged on whether or not God infused the soul into the foetus whilst it is in the womb. Sherman highlights that the possibility that the foetus can exist prior to the creation of the soul, meaning that abortion is possible without committing murder, tells against the traducean theory of the soul's development.[217] Sherman's interpretation of Exodus 21:22 relied upon the Septuagint translation and the Greek Fathers' reading of the relevant passage. This was because the Hebrew rendering of Exodus 21:22 does not detail stages of foetal formation. Sherman admitted that

> we must reade the Scripture in the Septuagints translation; and then two things are to be granted: first, that we have the right and true translation of the Septuagint; and secondly, that this translation is true, which indeed great Ecclesiastick writers have followed... Yet since the originall [Hebrew] (which our English translation followeth) maketh not at all for our purpose, we will passe over this place without any urging of it, and without any observation how the Interpreters, and in how many respects, were here mistaken... we have here the judgement of the Septuagint delivered in favour of our cause, and also the judgement of the Greek Fathers, and others who use their interpretation of Scripture... That he is not a murtherer who maketh an abortive before the infusion of the soul.[218]

This use of a specific biblical translation within Sherman's common-place not only demonstrates a connection between the common-place genre and biblical philology but also a strategy of exploiting differences between the Greek Septuagint and the Hebrew scriptures.[219]

Sherman references Genesis, Augustine's commentary on it, and a range of authorities to defend his position that souls are created by God *ex nihilo*.[220] These include Zanchi, David Paraeus, and Catholic figures including the school-man Gabriel Biel and Bible commentator Santes Pagninus.[221] He also draws upon arguments from reason and the

---

[215] Sherman, *Greek in the Temple*, 66.
[216] Sherman, *Greek in the Temple*, 66–7.
[217] Sherman, *Greek in the Temple*, 67.
[218] Sherman, *Greek in the Temple*, 67.
[219] On this point, see Nicholas Hardy, 'The Septuagint and the Transformation of Biblical Scholarship in England, from the King James Bible (1611) to the London Polyglot (1657)', in *The Oxford Handbook of the Bible in Early Modern England, c. 1530–1700* (Oxford, 2015), eds. K. Killeen, H. Smith, and R. Willie, 117–30.
[220] Sherman, *Greek in the Temple*, 68.
[221] Sherman, *Greek in the Temple*, 69–71.

authority of pagan writers for the same purpose.[222] Yet, no answer to the thorny question regarding the transmission of Adam's guilt is offered. Sherman simply remarks that 'although the soul be created, yet there is a way conceiveable for the intromission of originall sinne without any danger of making God any way the Authour of sinne. This Zanchie maketh good'.[223] Asserting the incorporeal, immortal, and created nature of the soul is vital, Sherman reminded his audience, in order to defend key Christian tenets such as resurrection after death; a doctrine which had an earthly application in encouraging moral uprightness under the threat of eternal punishment.[224] Whilst the principle of the immortal soul is necessary, Sherman admits that one's view on the origin of the rational soul is not critical for salvation.[225]

Drawing together his extended discussions of Man's body and soul in relation to God, Sherman completed his lecture with a list of edifying practical rules for his audience. Since Man is God's offspring by virtue of his body and soul 'in union' he ought to do the following: worship God, love his neighbour, respect his created body and soul, show humility, trust in God's providence, and not commit idolatry.[226] With this last note Sherman returns to the excerpt from Paul's address with which he began. He reminds his students not to think of God, who created them in his own image, in corporeal terms; this was the error the heathens made. Yet even here Sherman could not resist one last barb directed at his Catholic adversaries. On the subject of worship, Sherman urged his students to consider 'what is due from hence to him that made thee a man, not a beast; what piety, what devotion, what obedience, what rationall service, what a *rationall* or *reasonable sacrifice*'.[227] The term 'sacrifice' was theologically divisive during the Reformation. Amongst the Reformed, personal ethical acts such as worship or charity could indeed be classed as sacrifices in the manner Sherman suggests. Amongst post-Tridentine Catholics, however, sacrifice was intimately connected with liturgical ritual and particularly with the Eucharist and the miracle of transubstantiation overseen by the priest. This far more restricted definition of 'sacrifice' underpinned some Catholics' arguments for the authority of the Roman Church in uniting a commonwealth through public religious ritual.[228] In talking of individual sacrifices, Sherman ended *A Greek in the Temple* in a markedly Reformed manner.

---

[222] Sherman, *Greek in the Temple*, 71–5.
[223] Sherman, *Greek in the Temple*, 70.   [224] Sherman, *Greek in the Temple*, 72.
[225] Sherman, *Greek in the Temple*, 76.
[226] Sherman, *Greek in the Temple*, 79–80.
[227] Sherman, *Greek in the Temple*, 79. Italics are the author's own emphases.
[228] Sarah Mortimer, 'Sacrifice and the limits of sovereignty 1589–1613', *History of European Ideas* 49/8 (2023), 1309–11.

VI

This article has denied John Sherman his place in Cambridge University's intellectual history as the genius behind so-called 'Cambridge Platonism'. In fact, the paper has repeatedly highlighted the lack of originality in *A Greek in the Temple*'s contents. However, with this study's central claim borne in mind, neither point ought to be surprising; one must situate the lectures in the context of their genre and their purpose. Sherman's task in delivering these 'morning exercises' was not to be a setter forth of strange or original ideas.[229] What Sherman was in fact doing in *A Greek in the Temple* was drawing out the contemporary relevance of Christian apologetic responses to pagan religion; these conclusions are either edificatory in that they encourage the audience to reflect upon their spiritual lives or they are weapons for confessionally orientated polemic. In the case of the latter, the article has accumulated examples throughout the lectures of where Sherman either explicitly or implicitly critiqued inter and intraconfessional opponents using his analysis of Acts 17:28b, and the Christian apologetic tradition's responses to pagan religion that were inspired by Paul's address to the Athenians.

The conventional character of *A Greek in the Temple* and Sherman's unoriginal use of neo-platonic sources suggests the need for an alternative narrative concerning theological pedagogy in 1630s Cambridge, to replace that of an innovative 'Cambridge Platonism'. Anthony Milton and Stephen Hampton's scholarship has revealed that a lively Reformed tradition persisted in England during the Caroline era.[230] The traditional liberties of the university and its tendency to resist external interference provided an environment in which divinity lecturers, who were critical of the Laudian programme, could continue to teach in the tradition historically associated with Cambridge Puritanism.[231] Sherman's thought, expressed through confessionally edged remarks in *A Greek in the Temple*, fits this Reformed profile. Indeed, reading Sherman's lectures in their contemporary pedagogical context avoids projecting later post-Calvinist developments in English theology back on to them.

From a wider perspective, Sherman's common-places afford an opportunity to study the convergence of pedagogical and confessional demands

---

[229] This is a reference to Acts 17:18 where-in several Stoic and Epicurean poets encounter St Paul preaching: 'And some said, What will this babbler say? other some, He seemeth to be a setter forth of strange gods'.
[230] Milton, *England's Second Reformation*, 68–100; Hampton, *Grace and Conformity*, passim.
[231] Twigg, *Cambridge and the English Revolution*, 6–9.

upon a seventeenth-century lecturer at Cambridge University and the way that they combined within a set of common-place lectures, a traditionally overlooked genre. In particular, this paper's discussion of *A Greek in the Temple* confirms the close relationship that existed in daily university teaching between the curriculum and wider religious debates. In light of this, college chapel common-places would reward further consideration by intellectual historians. Just as certain Athenians received Paul's message and promised to 'hear thee again of this matter', it is hoped that this article's discussion of Sherman's common-places encourages further study of seventeenth-century theological pedagogy and its confessional context.[232]

Wolfson College, University of Oxford
Oxford, United Kingdom, OX2 6UD
samuel.head@wolfson.ox.ac.uk
https://orcid.org/0009-0007-9980-1893

---

[232] Acts 17:32 (KJV).

Anthony Tuckney's Anti-Socinian Lecture on the Divinity of Christ

Sergiej Slavinski[*]

EDITORIAL INTRODUCTION TO ANTHONY TUCKNEY'S LECTURE ON JOHN 17:3

In 1656, Anthony Tuckney (1599–1670), a leading Presbyterian of the Westminster Assembly, delivered his probationary lecture on John 17:3 ('And this is eternal life, that they may know you, the only true God, and Jesus Christ whom you have sent') for the regius chair of divinity at Cambridge University.[1] In his Latin lecture, Tuckney defended the divinity of Christ against Socinianism, an anti-Trinitarian movement that used John 17:3 to argue that only God the Father is the 'true God', thereby excluding Christ and the Spirit from the Godhead. According to Tuckney, the Socinians made John 17:3 'their chief weapon and place it at the front of their battle line'.[2] Jonathan Tuckney, Tuckney's son, published his lecture in *Praelectiones theologicae* (1679), a four-volume collection of Tuckney's Latin works, including 'lectures, determinations, and other theological exercises'.[3] The volume was published for readers 'to learn, use,

---

[*] I am thankful for Simon Burton for reading an earlier draft of the introduction. I am also grateful for Carolinne White for polishing my translation. Lastly, I would like to thank the anonymous readers for their comments.

[1] Johnathan Tuckney, 'Praefatiuncula ad lectorem', in Anthony Tuckney, *Praelectiones theologicae, nec non determinationes quaestionum variarum insignium in Scholis Academicis Cantabrigiensibus habitate; quibus accedunt exercitia pro gradibus capessendis* (Amsterdam: 1679) (Wing T3217A), sig. A1^{r-v}. Tuckney was elected to the regius chair 'by the unanimous consent of the electors'. The electors were Thomas Dillingham, Benjamin Whichcote, Ralph Cudworth, James Duport, and 'two senior fellows of that college'. Thomas Baker, *History of the College of St. John the Evangelist, Cambridge*, vol. 1 (Cambridge: 1869), 231.

[2] Page 5 of translation.

[3] Tuckney, 'Praefatiuncula', sig. A1^{r}: '…Praelectiones, Determinationes, reliquáque exercitia Theologica'.

[and] enjoy'.[4] This article presents the first English translation of Tuckney's lecture along with a commentary.

The polemical exchanges of mid-seventeenth-century England cannot be understood without recognising the centrality of the doctrine of the Trinity in matters of biblical exegesis, ecclesiology, and advances in philosophy.[5] Indeed, linguistic confusion over 'nature' and 'person' with respect to God and humans, radical divergence in biblical interpretations of God, and religious and political turmoil due to the Civil War, Interregnum, and Restoration all contributed to a 'heightened sense of crisis over the doctrine of the Trinity'.[6]

Tuckney was renowned for his 1651 debate with the Platonist tendencies of Benjamin Whichcote, then vice-chancellor of the University of Cambridge;[7] his lecture, however, showcases the graver threat of Socinian exegesis to Trinitarian orthodoxy due to its hermeneutic of literalism and pan-European influence. The denial of Christ's divinity was characteristic of Socinian exegesis. After all, the collapse of state censorship during the Civil War coincided with the outbreak of Socinian views, chiefly espoused by the Puritan[8] biblicists Paul Best and John Biddle. Biddle's literary activities in particular were instrumental in the 1650s assault on Christ's divinity.[9] Tuckney's lecture serves as a lens through which we can understand better the polemical context of diverging theologies, including diverging applications of *sola Scriptura*, surrounding the Trinitarian controversies of mid-seventeenth-century England.

---

[4] Tuckney, 'Praefatiuncula', sig. A1ʳ: '...percipere, uti, frui'.

[5] See Paul C. H. Lim, *Mystery Unveiled: The Crisis of the Trinity in Early Modern England* (Oxford: Oxford University Press, 2012); Ariel Hessayon and Nicholas Keene (eds.) *Scripture and Scholarship in Early Modern England* (New York: Ashgate, 2006); Sarah Mortimer, *Reason and Religion in the English Revolution: The Challenge of Socinianism* (Cambridge: Cambridge University Press, 2010); Richard A. Muller, *Post-Reformation Reformed Dogmatics: The Rise and Development of Reformed Orthodoxy, ca. 1520 to ca. 1725*, 2nd edn, vol. 4, The Triunity of God (Grand Rapids: Baker, 2003). Hereafter *PRRD*.

[6] Lim, *Mystery Unveiled*, 67–8.

[7] See Youngchun Cho, *Anthony Tuckney (1599–1670): Theologian of the Westminster Assembly* (Grand Rapids: Reformation Heritage Books, 2017), 29–32; Patrick Collinson, 'Tuckney, Anthony: (1599–1670)', *Oxford Dictionary of National Biography*. Hereafter *ODNB*.

[8] Best and Biddle were 'radical Puritans', with 'Puritanism' referring here to 'a set of positions' on the spectrum of the English Church, a spectrum that ranged from church papists and high churchmen, through conformist Calvinists, to moderate Puritans and radical Puritans'. John Coffey and Paul C. H. Lim (eds.) 'Introduction', in *The Cambridge Companion to Puritanism* (Cambridge: Cambridge University Press, 2008), 5. Indeed, 'the porous membrane of Puritan radical religion and *theologia pectoris* was a difference of degrees, not of kind'. Lim, *Mystery Unveiled*, 39.

[9] Lim, *Mystery Unveiled*, ch 1.

Tuckney's lecture is significant as it elucidates why John's Gospel 'became *the* major arsenal for both sides of the trinitarian divide'.[10] His lecture confirms that, to Tuckney's mind, John 17:3 was the chief Socinian text against the divinity of Christ and indeed the doctrine of the Trinity.[11] Tuckney justified the length of his lecture on this very basis, explaining that John 17:3 was the Achilles heel of the Socinians. Francis Cheynell, Westminster divine and Lady Margaret professor of divinity at Oxford University, also argued that the Socinians 'lay most weight upon' John 17:3 in support of their 'invincible argument to prove that God the Father alone is God'.[12] Tuckney explicitly said that John 17:3 'has become the most troubled text' in the Trinitarian debates, which underscores the importance of his lecture in understanding how Reformed Trinitarians like Tuckney answered Socinian Johannine exegesis. His exegesis of John 17:3 also reflects the Protestant Trinitarian effort to reconcile Trinitarian doctrine with a biblical text that appears to challenge this doctrine. Tuckney's lecture underlines how the early modern reception of John's Gospel fueled divergent interpretations of Scripture, church history, and Christian forms of worship.[13]

In the historiography of English religious controversy, there is a tendency to focus on the response of Oxford, not Cambridge, to Socinianism in the 1650s.[14] The result is a somewhat skewed picture of how both

---

[10] Lim, *Mystery Unveiled*, 14. See also Paul Cefalu, *The Johannine Renaissance in Early Modern English Literature and Theology* (Oxford: Oxford University Press, 2016).

[11] It is important to clarify that, according to Tuckney's lecture, John 17:3 was not *the* key text supporting the doctrine of the Trinity. Rather, Tuckney considered it the most contentious text, as the Socinians exploited it to refute Christ's divinity. Yet, as Tuckney's lecture pointed out, once John 17:3 is read in line with the *analogia fidei* concerning Christ's divinity, the text in question supports Trinitarian doctrine.

[12] Francis Cheynell, *The Divine Trinity of the Father, Son, and Holy Spirit* (London: 1650) (Wing C3811), 43. See Sergiej S. Slavinski, '*Solus Verus Deus*: Francis Cheynell and the Johannine Trinity', *Reformation & Renaissance Review* 23.1 (2021): 68–91; Sergiej Slavinski, *Francis Cheynell: Polemic and Piety in the Divine Trinity of the Father, Son, and Holy Spirit (1650)* (Leiden: Brill, 2024).

[13] Page 6 of translation.

[14] See, for example, Nicholas Tyacke, *Aspects of English Protestantism, c. 1530–1700* (Manchester: Manchester University Press, 2001), 290; Blair Worden, 'Cromwellian Oxford', in Nicholas Tyacke (ed.) *The History of the University of Oxford: Volume IV, Seventeenth-Century Oxford* (Oxford: Oxford University Press, 1997), 754. The following book omits reference to Socinianism but discusses the usual controversy of Cambridge Platonism: Victor Morgan, *A History of the University of Cambridge: Volume II, 1546–1750* (Cambridge: Cambridge University Press, 2004). John David Twigg relegates Socinianism to a footnote in *The University of Cambridge and the English Revolution, 1625–1688* (Woodbridge: Boydell Press, 1990). The following learned works discuss Oxford but overlook Tuckney and Cambridge's response to Socinianism: Mortimer's *Reason and Religion*, Lim's *Mystery Unveiled*, and Philip Dixon, *Nice and Hot Disputes: The Doctrine of the Trinity in the Seventeenth Century* (London: T&T Clark, 2003). On debates about the Trinity in post-Restoration Cambridge, see Dmitri Levitin and Scott Mandelbrote, 'Becoming

universities responded to the nationwide challenge of Socinianism. Tuckney's anti-Socinian lecture not only emphasises the presence of Reformed teaching in 1650s Cambridge,[15] but also aligns Cambridge with Oxford in opposing Socinianism. This also sheds new light on the theological transition, indeed continuity, of Cambridge from the Interregnum into the Restoration, for recent scholarship has convincingly shown the enduring presence of Reformed theology in the post-Restoration established Church.[16]

Tuckney was vice chancellor of the University of Cambridge from 1648, master of Emanuel College, Cambridge, between 1645 and 1653, and master of St John's from 1653.[17] The 1656 appointment of Tuckney to regius professor at Cambridge was facilitated by the prominent Presbyterians Edmund Calamy, Stephen Marshall, and Simeon Ash.[18] According to Patrick Collinson, this appointment demonstrates Tuckney's 'lingering influence' at Cambridge.[19] Tuckney's lecture offers firsthand insight into the theological impact of his influence. After all, as regius professor, Tuckney was responsible for overseeing the entire theological curriculum.[20]

Tuckney's lecture must be placed against the backdrop of the politics of heresy and the growing spectre of Socinianism. According to Blair Worden, '[n]o heresy was harder to tolerate than anti-Trinitarianism'.[21] In response to the perceived threat of anti-Trinitarianism, Parliament drafted an ordinance against 'heresy' and 'blasphemy' in 1646. This was followed by the Presbyterians' Blasphemy ordinance of 1648, making the advocacy of Socinianism a capital crime. Although the penal sanctions of this heresy legislation were not enforced, it also reflected debates about religious toleration and partly represented the Presbyterian ideology of religious uniformity, aiming to legalise a Presbyterian state church and stigmatise

Heterodox in 17th-Century Cambridge: The Case of Isaac Newton', in Nicholas Hardy and Dimitri Levitin (eds.) *Confessionalisation and Erudition in Early Modern Europe: An Episode in the History of the Humanities* (Oxford: Oxford University Press, 2019), 301–94.

[15] See Tyacke, *Aspects*, 288.

[16] See, for example, Jake Griesel, *Retaining the Old Episcopal Divinity: John Edwards of Cambridge and Reformed Orthodoxy in the Later Stuart Church* (Oxford: Oxford University Press, 2022); Samuel D. Fornecker, *Bisschop's Bench: Contours of Arminian Conformity in the Church of England, c. 1674–1742* (Oxford: Oxford University Press, 2022); Stephen Hampton, *Anti-Arminians: The Anglican Reformed Tradition from Charles II to George I* (Oxford: Oxford University Press, 2008).

[17] Cho, *Anthony Tuckney*, 28–9.

[18] Collinson, 'Tuckney', *ODNB*, referring to Johnian Henry Paman's comment about Tuckney's promotion.

[19] Collinson, 'Tuckney', *ODNB*.

[20] George Peacock, *Observations on the Statutes of the University of Cambridge* (London: J.W. Parker, 1841), 169.

[21] Blair Worden, *God's Instruments: Political Conduct in the England of Oliver Cromwell* (Oxford: Oxford University Press, 2012), 66.

non-conformists as heretics.[22] By the 1650s, as Sarah Mortimer has shown, English theology was in flux, as those who were disenchanted with Reformed theology sought inspiration from Remonstrant and Socinian theology.[23] This was an obvious concern for Reformed theologians like John Owen who spearheaded a 1650s crackdown on Socinianism, specifically against the 1652 publication of the Socinian confession of faith, *The Racovian Catechism*.[24] In the same year, votes of Parliament ordered that all copies of the Socinian work be burnt.[25] Under Cromwell, there were also efforts to hammer out the fundamental articles of the faith in opposition to anti- and non-Trinitarian ideas. For instance, the *Instrument of Government* (1653), the constitutional basis of the Cromwellian government, set the parameters of religious orthodoxy, yet failed to proscribe anti-Trinitarianism. In response, a group of Presbyterians and Independents under Parliament's approval produced *A New Confession of Faith, of The First Principles of the Christian Religion* (1654). The document broadly targeted Socinians, Ranters, Quakers, and Arminians, although Parliament never adopted it given its concern to protect religious liberty.[26]

The question of heresy and religious liberty surfaces in Tuckney's volume. In his preface to *Praelectiones theologicae*, William Dillingham, Tuckney's successor as master of Emmanuel College, Cambridge, noted that Tuckney championed 'true' doctrine in opposition to the leniency of those in power who purportedly helped to generate 'monstrous opinions and a vast army of errors'.[27] Dillingham doubtless had in mind debates about religious toleration and the Cromwellian government. For example, Biddle's anti-Trinitarian publication of *Twofold Catechism* (1654) resulted in his imprisonment. In 1655, pro-Biddle tolerationists petitioned the Cromwellian government for his release. But Biddle's subsequent release and exile to the Isle of Scilly in 1656 was perceived by London Presbyterians as a lenient punishment by Cromwell towards anti-Trinitarians. As Paul C. H. Lim observes, the 'genuine Presbyterian fear' was that

---

[22] Youngkwon Chung, 'Parliament, the Heresy Ordinance of 1648, and Religious Toleration in Civil War England', *Journal of Church and State* 57.1 (2015): 123. See Robert Florida, 'British Law and Socinianism in the 17th and 18th centuries', in Lec Szczucki (ed.) *Socinianism and its Role in the Culture of the XVIth to XVIIth Centuries* (Warsaw: Polish Scientific Publisher, 1983), 201.
[23] Mortimer, *Reason and Religion*, 206. [24] Lim, *Mystery Unveiled*, 44–5.
[25] *Votes of Parliament Touching the Book commonly called The Racovian Catechism* (London: 1652).
[26] Crawford Gribben, *John Owen and English Puritanism: Experiences of Defeat* (Oxford: Oxford University Press, 2017), 153–4.
[27] William Dillingham, 'Praefatio', in Tuckney, *Praelectiones*, sig. A2ʳ: '…mirum quot opinionum monstra, et quantum errorum exercitum progenuerit'.

'Cromwell's sincere desire for protection of tender conscience would prove to be the Trojan horse of the antitrinitarians' devising'.[28]

Part of the significance of Tuckney's lecture is due to its survival, which contributes to our knowledge of Reformed scholastic texts.[29] His lecture is scholastic, with scholasticism referring here to 'a *methodology* characterized by the use of a system of definitions, distinctions, argumentative techniques and styles of disputation'.[30] For example, he adopted the medieval *quaestio* method to resolve Socinian arguments against Christ's divinity. He also utilised Aristotelian causality to postulate that eternal life depends on the 'knowledge of faith' as an efficient cause.[31] Of course, his scholasticism was refracted through *both* educational developments during the Renaissance and post-Reformation periods *and* the polemics of his day.[32] Tuckney's Reformed scholasticism aided precision in theological discourse, and his lecture demonstrates Renaissance humanist education.[33] Indeed, a philological feature of Tuckney's text is his sustained analysis of the grammar and syntax of the original Greek text of John's Gospel. Another humanist example is Tuckney's appropriation of Johannine exegetes of the patristic, medieval, and late scholastic periods.[34]

Tuckney's defence of scholastic systematisation was a hallmark of his teaching at Cambridge. According to Dmitri Levitin, 'Tuckney not only made full use of the most elaborate Reformed scholastic arguments in his teaching [at Cambridge], but also offered a full methodological defence of 'systems of divinity' and the use of logical extrapolation in scriptural exegesis that drew heavily on [Gisbertus] Voetius', professor of theology at Utrecht.[35] In standard Reformed fashion, Tuckney interpreted difficult

---

[28] Lim, *Mystery Unveiled*, 66.

[29] Most extant theological lectures are still in Latin, such as John Prideaux's *Lectiones novem de totidem religionis capitibus* (1625) or Thomas Barlow's *Exercitationes aliquot metaphysicae de Deo* (1637). See Stephen Hampton, *Grace and Conformity: The Reformed Conformist Tradition and The Early Stuart Church of England* (Oxford: Oxford University Press, 2021), cha. i; Tyacke, *Aspects*, 323–4.

[30] Dolf te Velde (ed.) *Synopsis Purioris Theologiae/Synopsis of a Purer Theology: Latin Text and English Translation*, vol. 1, disputations 1–23 (Leiden: Brill, 2014), 3.

[31] Page 4 of translation.

[32] See Richard A. Muller, *Post-Reformation Reformed Dogmatics: Prolegomena to Theology*, 2nd edn, vol. 1, Grand Rapids 2003, 74–8.

[33] On the interconnected relationship between scholasticism and humanism, see Paul Oskar Kristeller, *Renaissance Thought and its Sources*, ed. Michael Mooney (New York: Columbia University Press, 1979); Richard A. Muller, *After Calvin: Studies in the Development of a Theological Tradition* (Oxford: Oxford University Press, 2003), ch. v.

[34] On the invocation of patristic authority in seventeenth-century England, see Jean-Louis Quantin, *The Church of England and Christian Antiquity: The Construction of Confessional Identity in the 17th Century* (Oxford: Oxford University Press, 2009).

[35] Dmitri Levitin, *The Kingdom of Darkness: Bayle, Newton, and the Emancipation of the European Mind from Philosophy* (Cambridge: Cambridge University Press, 2022), 150.

passages in light of the *analogia fidei*; that is, the overall theological meaning of Scripture. This systematic approach characterises the Westminster Confession of Faith. In 'To the Christian Reader' of the second edition of *The Confession of Faith* (1658), Tuckney was described as 'a learned Divine of this age' who spoke about 'compendiary systems'.[36] This was in reference to his sermon on 2 Timothy 1:13, delivered on 30 June 1650 at Great St Mary's Church, Cambridge. There, Tuckney encouraged the use of

> *Summes, Institutions, Systems, Syntagmes, Synopses*, or by what ever other name you call such Modells of Divinity, as orderly lay down together such divine truths as are scattered up and down in the Scripture, or explain such as there seem to be something obscure, so present them, in a full and clear distinct view, for the better help, especially of a weaker eye against the *fascinations of jugling Imposters*.[37]

Tuckney also spoke about the importance of adhering to the

> *words of this life* [Acts 5:20]; what ever therefore either they expressely affirm, or is from them soundly and directly gathered and commended to us, whether by whole Churches, or particular Persons, although they be not expressed wholly in Scripture words, yet if according to the Analogy of faith, for the further clearing of Scripture sense, and the better discovering of errors and heresies as they arise, we willingly accept, and carefully hold fast.[38]

Tuckney's Reformed approach to Scripture stood in a positive relationship with a late sixteenth and early seventeenth-century Reformed theological method at Cambridge, akin to the method of William Whitaker, regius professor of divinity at Cambridge who argued that Scripture is its own interpreter.[39] Between c.1520–1620, Cambridge theological pedagogy emphasised the study of continental Reformed divinity.[40] But Whitaker's successor, John Overall, along with other Cambridge divines such as Matthew Wren, John Cosin, and Jerome Beale, all contributed significantly to redirecting Cambridge theology towards emphasising the role of history in theology.[41] This shift was symptomatic of wider European debates in patristic authority that influenced the English Church to

---

[36] 'To the Christian Reader', in *The Confession of Faith, Together with the Larger and Lesser Catechisms* (London: 1658), sig. [A4]ᴿ. See Levitin, *The Kingdom of Darkness*, 150.

[37] Anthony Tuckney, *A Good Day Well Improved* (London: 1656), 248.

[38] Tuckney, *A Good Day Well Improved*, 279.

[39] William Whitaker, *Disputatio de Sacra Scriptura* (Cambridge: 1588), 200: 'Summa nostrae sententiae est, esse Scripturam αὐτόπιστον, id est, ex se suam omnem authoritatem & fidem habere'.

[40] Levitin and Mandelbrote, 'Becoming Heterodox in 17th-Century Cambridge', 308.

[41] Levitin and Mandelbrote, 'Becoming Heterodox in 17th-Century Cambridge', 313–19.

establish its confessional identity in the early church.[42] Tuckney's teaching at Cambridge, however, contrasted this pre-Civil War pedagogical system that foregrounded historical and philological methodology while downplaying the utility of modern Reformed divinity. This is not to imply that Tuckney devalued such an approach to theology. After all, his lecture on John 17:3 engaged extensively with patristic figures and exemplified philological erudition. Tuckney's Cambridge lectures, though, contrasted an overly historical approach to divinity, and instead reasserted Reformed theology.[43]

This background on Cambridge theology and Tuckney's Reformed theological method in particular is helpful in elucidating his method of argumentation in his lecture on John 17:3. His lecture shows that his exegetical method could adapt under the polemical pressure of Socinian exegesis. Indeed, Tuckney appeared to defend the legitimacy of the 'orthodox' making distinct (perhaps even 'innovative') theological arguments, while rejecting such latitude to the Socinians. He argued that, in exegeting John 17:3, 'right is rather on the side of the orthodox than the heretics' who, in 'an act of arrogance', had reinterpreted Scripture in a manner that diverged from both the overall meaning of Scripture and long-standing beliefs.[44] Yet, Tuckney commended theologians who defend 'the orthodox catholic faith' by interpreting Scripture in harmony with the *analogia fidei*, even if the grammatical construction of a biblical text suggests an alternative reading.[45] 'Despite the grammatical construction of the words, it [John 17:3] can be understood differently. Indeed, the truth of the matter and the analogy of faith urge us, indeed compel us to do so'.[46] Tuckney interpreted John 17:3, then, in light of the *analogia fidei*, affirming Christ as the true God within a Trinitarian framework. Accordingly, he argued that the copulative conjunction 'and' in John 17:3 connects 'only true God' and 'Jesus Christ'. The conjunction distinguishes the person of the Father from the person of the Son without separating them, and, as such, 'does not separate the nature and does not take away the divinity'.[47]

We can get another sense of Tuckney's Reformed scholasticism by considering the type of literature that he was reading in his polemic with Socinianism. The presence of Catholic biblical exegesis in Tuckney's lecture indicates the positive reception of Catholic literature in Reformed theology. This is not surprising given the fact that both Catholics and Protestants affirmed the doctrine of the Trinity. It is also unsurprising since

---

[42] See Quantin, *The Church of England and Christian Antiquity*, chap. 4.
[43] Levitin and Mandelbrote, 'Becoming Heterodox in 17th-Century Cambridge', 319–321. See Tuckney, *Praelectiones*, 28–9.
[44] Page 7 of translation.   [45] Page 7 of translation.
[46] Page 8 of translation.   [47] Page 8 of translation.

Catholic scholarship played a leading role in critical exegesis during the late sixteenth and early seventeenth centuries.[48] A leading exponent of Catholic exegesis was the Jesuit Juan Maldonatus, who appears frequently throughout Tuckney's lecture. Maldonatus' commentaries on the four Gospels 'surpass all preceding ones in erudition, critical diligence, and exegetical perspicacity'.[49] Tuckney's engagement with Maldonatus' commentary on John, besides Maldonatus' exegetical prowess, can be seen as a response to the Socinian Johannes Crell, who had positively appropriated Maldonatus in his anti-Trinitarian exegesis of John 17:3. According to Crell, Maldonatus was 'a most accurate and learned popish Interpreter'.[50] Still, Maldonatus' commentary was useful for Tuckney in shaping his fourfold response (noted below) to Socinian Johannine exegesis.[51]

Tuckney's use of Maldonatus' work does not imply that he regarded his authority above others. Tuckney actually relied on a broad range of literature, and he was clear that the content of his lecture owed much to Johannine scholarship.[52] For instance, Tuckney cited the Leuven and Catholic scholar Francis Lucas 'of Bruges' to explain that Christ in John 17 prayed according to his divine and human natures. Additionally, Tuckney positively cited the German-born Swiss reformer Johann Oecolampadius in pointing out that the Trinity can be understood under the name 'Father' in John 17:3. Tuckney also agreed with the German Lutheran Johann Gerhard in equating Christ's prayer in John 17 with Hebrews 5:7. Here, Tuckney disagreed with the twelfth-century Benedictine scholar Rupert of Deutz who thought Christ's prayer in John 17 was his Gethsemane prayer. Of course, he also engaged with Reformed continental thinkers like Girolamo Zanchi and Johann Heinrich Bisterfeld, both of whom defended the doctrine of the Trinity against anti-Trinitarianism. It is clear that Tuckney stayed informed about leading humanistic exegesis, irrespective of its confessional orientation.

It is helpful to outline briefly the Socinian argument against the divinity of Christ based on John 17:3, for Tuckney's lecture consists of a fourfold response to this argument. According to Tuckney, the Socinians argued from John 17:3 that 'Christ asserts that the Father is the only true God and distinguishes himself from the Father. He therefore rejects that divinity

---

[48] Marius Reiser, 'History of Catholic Exegesis, 1600–1800', in Richard A. Muller, A. G. Roeber, and Ulrich L. Lehner (eds.) *The Oxford Handbook of Early Modern Theology, 1600–1800* (Oxford: Oxford University Press, 2016), 76–7.
[49] Reiser, 'History of Catholic Exegesis, 1600–1800', 77.
[50] Crell, *Two Books*, 12.
[51] I have noted instances where Tuckney drew upon Maldonatus in the annotated text below.
[52] Page 6 of translation.

which we falsely ascribe to him'.[53] Tuckney's lecture underscores the ambiguities of early modern interpretations of John 17:3, and it was Socinian renderings of John 17:3 that exercised him throughout much of his lecture. According to Zanchi, whom Tuckney often cited, 'all interpreters translate it [John 17:3] in this way: "that they may know you, the only true God, etc." But the interpretation is different'.[54]

Socinianism was named after the Italians Laelius Socinus and his nephew, Faustus Socinus.[55] The latter argued that 'only true God' applies to the Father, yet he also added that John 17:3 primarily means knowing and obeying the will of both the Father and Christ.[56] Following Desiderius Erasmus, Socinus interpreted John 17:3 as 'you who are that only true God', although Erasmus was clear that the word 'only' does not exclude the Son but distinguishes the 'true God' from the gods of the Gentiles.[57]

In his lecture, Tuckney provided evidence of the supposed chief Socinian argument by citing the heavyweight Socinians Valentinus Smalcius and Johannes Crell. Smalcius, along with Hieronymus Moskorzowski and Johannes Völkel, were associates of Socinus. After Socinus' death in 1604, they co-authored the *Racovian Catechism* (Polish: 1605; German: 1608; Latin: 1609). Tuckney had the *Racovian Catechism* in mind when referring to Smalcius, who translated it into German. The *Racovian Catechism* denied that

> the words 'this is the true God' refer to the Son of God:—Not that I deny that Christ is, in his sense of terms, a true God, but that he is that true God

---

[53] Page 6 of translation.
[54] Girolamo Zanchi, *De Tribus Elohim, Aeterno Patre, Filio, Et Spiritu Sancto, Uno Eodemque Iehova* (Frankfurt: 1573), liber 4, chap. 10, 142: 'Omnes interpretes sic vertunt: ut cognoscant te solum verum Deum, &c. Interpreatio verò diversa'.
[55] On Socinianism, see Herbert J. McLachlan, *Socinianism: In Seventeenth-Century England* (Oxford: Oxford University Press, 1951); Earl M. Wilbur, *A History of Unitarianism*, 2 vols. (Cambridge: Harvard University Press, 1945–1952); Stanisław Kot, Socinianism in Poland: *The Social and Political Ideas of the Polish Antitrinitarians in the Sixteenth and Seventeenth Centuries*, trans. Earl Morse Wilbur (Boston: Star King Press, 1957); Martin Mulsow and Jan Rohls (eds.) *Socinianism and Arminianism: Antitrinitarians, Calvinists, and Cultural Exchange in Seventeenth-Century Europe* (Leiden: Brill, 2005); Lim, *Mystery Unveiled*.
[56] Faustus Socinus, 'Tractatus de Ecclesia', in Socinus, *Opera omnia in duos tomos distincta*, 2 vols. (Amsterdam: 1656), 1:345.
[57] Socinus, 'Tractatus de Ecclesia', 1:345: 'Adde, quod etiamsi ex Christi verbis illis intelligendum esset, cognosci debere quod Christi ipsius pater sit ille solus verus Deus; Id quod nullo modo mihi videtur, quippe qui verba illa, *illum solum verum* Deum, ut modo indicavi, per appositionem legenda omnio censeam; ut perinde sit, ac si dictum fuisset, *qui es ille solus verus Deus*, non autem, ut Theodoro Bezae placet, *solum esse verum Deum*, possemque interpretationem meam, immo & Erasmi & aliorum quorundam, firmis rationibus, ex ipsis Graecis verbis eorumque propria significatione petitis, comprobare'. See Desiderius Erasmus, *In Novum Testamentum Annotationes* (Basil, 1527), 251; Theodore Beza, *Annotationes Majores in Novum Dn. Nostri Jesu Christi Testamentum*, 2 vols. (1594), 1:431–2.

who is spoken of in this passage [1 John 5:20]. Because Christ is in no instance styled absolutely God (ὁ Θεος) with the article, or the true God; and in this very passage, as also in like manner in John xvii.3, he is clearly distinguished from the only true God.[58]

Socinian exegesis of John 17:3 assumed an interchangeable identity of 'nature' and 'personhood', resulting in a denial of both Chalcedonian orthodoxy and the belief that Christ possessed the divine nature. For 'as the divine nature, by itself, constitutes a person, so also must the human nature, by itself, constitute a person; since it is a primary or single intelligent substance'.[59] According to the *Racovian Catechism*, then, 'Jesus Christ is a man; which itself deprives him of the divine nature that would render him the supreme God'.[60]

Furthermore, Crell translated John 17:3 as: 'This is Life eternal, that they might know thee (Father) the Onely true God, and whom thou has sent, Jesus Christ'.[61] Crell equated 'true God' with the 'most high God', reasoning that 'since Christ describeth the Father, as to call him the Onely true God, it is understood that onely the Father of Christ is the most High God'.[62] Similar to Socinus, Crell also observed that the words 'the only true God' are in apposition to the subject, meaning 'Who onely art the True God: And therefore the article set before the word *onely* in the Greek, sheweth that the same thing is again described'.[63] Of course, in Crell's metaphysics, 'person' and 'substance' are indistinct, unlike in traditional Trinitarian theology. Since Christ is distinguished from the person of the Father, Crell believed, he is distinguished from the substance of the Father;

---

[58] *The Racovian Catechism*, trans. Thomas Rees (London: 1818), 79.
See Ariel Hessayon and Diego Lucci, 'The Supposed Burning of the Racovian Catechism in 1614: A Historiographical Myth Exposed', *History* 107(374) (2021): 25–50. See also Johan Volkel, *De vera religione* (Racow: 1630), liber v, cap. ix, 419.

[59] *Racovian Catechism*, 57.

[60] *Racovian Catechism*, 57. It is important to note that Socinian theology harboured a metaphysical materialism, which also formed the basis of its rejection of the belief in three divine persons subsisting in one essence. Sascha Salatowsky has argued that the Socinians promoted their 'own confessional physics which is characterised by a materialistic understanding of the Aristotelian philosophy combined with a rational reading of the Bible'. Sascha Salatowsky, 'God in Time and Space. Socinian Physics and its Opponents', in Pietro Daniel Omodeo and Volkhard Wels (eds.) *Natural Knowledge and Aristotelianism at Early Modern Protestant Universities* (Wiesbaden: Harrassowitz Verlag, 2019), 52. See also Sascha Salatowsky, *Die Philosophie der Sozinianer: Transformationen zwischen Renaissance-Aristotelismus und Frühaufklärung* (Stuttgart-Bad Cannstatt: Frommann-Holzboog, 2015).

[61] Johannes Crell, *The Two Books of John Crellius Francus, touching one God the Father* (London: 1665) (Wing C6880), 1. Italics removed.

[62] Crell, *Two Books*, 1.

[63] Crell, *Two Books*, 9. Italics removed. See Socinus, 'Tractatus de Ecclesia', 1:345.

consequently, Christ, by virtue of his words in John 17:3, is 'excluded from that true and most high Godhead'.[64]

Turning to Tuckney's fourfold response (or rather the 'orthodox' response, as Tuckney stated) to Socinian exegesis of John 17:3, his first response was rooted in patristic thought and argued that the words 'only true God' apply to both the Father and Son by way of the conjunction 'and'. It is conceivable that Tuckney derived this first response from Maldonatus.[65] Tuckney had admitted that this response was the same as his initial argument based on the *analogia fidei*.[66] Grounding his second response in both patristic and medieval thought, Tuckney reasoned that the word 'only' excludes not the Son and Spirit but created things and false gods. The third response was derived from the Franciscan exegete Nicholas of Lyra. It held that the word 'only' does not define the pronoun 'you' in that only the Father is God, but that the name 'God' refers to the only true Godhead common to the Father and Son. The final and most compelling response, according to Tuckney, was that Christ said the words of John 17:3 as Mediator and High Priest.

Tuckney established his fourth response in the Reformed understanding of the Chalcedonian Christological tradition. The 'genuine meaning' of John 17:3 is: 'When it is a question of eternal life, this comes to us by the Father through Christ, from the Father, the Son and the Spirit, the Triune and only true God, through the merits and obedience of our Mediator Jesus Christ, whom he sent'.[67] His response carried salvific implications: denial of Christ's divinity undermined his redemptive role as the Mediator between God and humans based on his divine and human natures.[68] Tuckney also explained that the other Socinian arguments outlined in his lecture are easily resolved by understanding the twofold nature of Christ. His lecture emphasised John 17:3 as 'the sum of heavenly doctrine'[69] and 'the essence of all theology'.[70]

Overall, Tuckney's lecture is a vital source in understanding the Reformed reaction to Socinianism that was gaining popularity due to the 'theological accessibility' and 'unadorned prose' of English Socinianism.[71] It offers fresh insight into how the Reformed read John's Gospel and paints a fuller picture of 1650s Cambridge theology.

---

[64] Crell, *Two Books*, 4.
[65] See the first response of the 'orthodox' on page 8 of the translation and the note on Maldonatus.
[66] Page 8 of translation.
[67] Page 13 of translation.
[68] See Cho, *Anthony*, 71.
[69] Page 2 of translation.
[70] Page 13 of translation.
[71] Lim, *Mystery Unveiled*, 126.

ANTHONY TUCKNEY'S PROBATIONARY LECTURE AT THE UNIVERSITY OF CAMBRIDGE

[Page 1][72] Probationary Lecture, etc.

With the help of God.

Eternal God, most loving Father of both mercies and lights in Jesus Christ grant, we beseech you, repentance to miserable sinners, so that you may grant forgiveness to those who are repentant. In addition, shine forth upon us wretches who crawl here in darkness, and (after having removed the veil still covering our hearts) reveal the wonders of the Law and the great deeds of the Gospel, so that we, who can do nothing without you, may finally by your help understand the truth and do what is right, and may at last be able to attain that eternal happiness stored up for us in heaven through Jesus Christ your Son, our only Saviour. Amen.

That which is currently proposed to me to discuss is found in the Gospel according to St. John chapter 17, verse 3, in the following words:

'And this is eternal life, that they may know you, the only true God, and Jesus Christ whom you have sent'.[73]

---

[72] Bracketed pagination corresponds to the original text.

[73] Tuckney's Latin reads as: 'Haec est autem vita aeterna, ut cognoscant Te solum verum Deum, & quem misisti Jesum Christum'. John 17:3 was variously rendered in the early modern period. For example, the famous London Polyglot Bible presented a Syriac, Arabic, Ethiopic, and Persian version of John 17:3 with a corresponding Latin translation. The Latin Syriac version is: 'Haec est autem vita aeterna, ut cognoscant te esse Deum Veritatis solum, & quem misisti, Jesum Christum'. The Latin Arabic version is: 'Haec autem est vita aeterna, ut cognoscant te unum esse solum Deum verum, & quem misisti Jesum Christum'. The Ethiopian Latin version is: 'Et haec est vita aeterna, ut cognoscant te unum, qui verè es Deus, & quem misisti Dúm Jesum Christum'. The Persian Latin version is: 'Haec autem est vita ia [or possibly 'in'?] aeternum, ut te cognoscant, quod tu es Deus in veritate solus, & ille quem misisti, Jesus Christus'. It also included the Latin Vulgate version of John 17:3: 'Haec est autem vita aeterna: Ut cognoscant te, solùm Deum verum, & quem misisti Jesum Christum'. 'Brian Walton (ed.) *Biblia Sacra Polyglotta: Complectentia Textus Originales, Hebraicum, cum Pentateucho Samaritano, Chaldaicum, Graecum*, vol. 5 (London: 1657), 490–1. Within Protestantism, two English Bible translations are worth noting given their popularity. First, the Geneva Bible, first printed in 1560, was arguably 'the most widely distributed book in the English Renaissance'. William H. Sherman, *Used Books: Marking Readers in Renaissance England* (Philadelphia: University of Pennsylvania Press, 2007), 166. The 1560 version translated John 17:3 as: 'And this is life eternal, that they knowe thee to be the onely verie God, and whome thou hast sent, Iesus Christ'. *The Bible and the Holy Scriptures conteyned in the Olde and Newe Testament* (Geneva: 1560), 51ᵛ. The Geneva marginal annotation clarified that eternal life is bound up with acknowledging both the Father and Son as 'verie God'. Second, although lacking marginal annotations, the 'King James' Bible (1611) rendered the verse as: 'And this is life eternall, that they might know thee the onely true God, and Jesus Christ whom thou hast sent'. *The Holy Bible, Conteyning the Old Testament and the New* (London: 1611), 'S. Iohn, Chap. xvii,' unpaginated.

First of all, academic gentlemen, I thank the most prudent moderators of the matter currently being discussed, for the assignment of this most pleasant passage of Holy Scripture. Although they have sent me here to work today, it is, however, to a vineyard where I cannot so much labour to the point of exhaustion as drink a full cup of comforting wine. Even though (to exaggerate somewhat) they have sentenced me to the mines, it is at least a gold mine to which I am sent. For this passage among others—or indeed above all others—is the field in which the treasure is hidden and from which the precious pearl must be excavated. [Note: Matt. 13:44][74] Look! Here everything is of gold and precious stones,[75] in comparison with which 'the gold has grown dim and the pure gold is changed', if I may use the Prophet's words [Note: Lamentations 4:1]; all else that is considered most valuable is filthy dross and worthless.[76] Enter, for here are the Gods,[77] or rather behold here the one true God; and behold the one whom he sent, Jesus Christ. Here is salvific knowledge of this same one. Indeed, behold the eternal life that follows hereafter. So, it was not so much Maldonatus[78] who spoke truly when he said that each one of the previous words contains its own problems, but rather Calvin,[79] who said that each of these words has its own weight. Did he say weight? Indeed, who

---

[74] All bracketed notes correspond to marginal notes in the original text.
[75] This is an allusion to 1 Corinthians 3:12.
[76] This is an allusion to Philippians 3:7–8.
[77] The plural form 'Gods' in Tuckney's view does not imply two separate Gods, such as Father and Son, but rather emphasises their shared divine essence or their distinct ways of possessing the divine essence. Tuckney immediately qualified that there is 'one true God', a Trinitarian title, according to Tuckney, that is appropriately applied to both the Father and Son essentially rather than personally and exclusively to the Father. Throughout his lecture, Tuckney taught that John 17:3 teaches unity and distinction within the one Godhead.
[78] Juan De Maldonado (John Maldonatus) (1533–83) was a Spanish Jesuit who published a commentary on the Four Gospels. See Maldonatus, *Commentarii in quatuor Evangelistas*, 2 vols. (Mussiponti: Typographica Stephani Mercatoris, 1596–7); Maldonatus, *Joannis Maldonati, Societatis Jesu Theologi, Commentarii in Quatuor Evangelistas ad optimorum librorum fidem accuratissime recudi curavit Franciscus Sausen*, Tomus V (Moguntiae: Sumptibus Kirchhemii, Schotti & Thielmanni, 1844), 503–7.
[79] In his commentary on John, the French Reformer John Calvin (1509–64) said: 'Almost every one of the words has its weight; for it is not every kind of knowledge that is here described, but that knowledge which forms us anew into the image of God from faith to faith, or rather, which is the same with faith, by which, having been engrafted into the body of Christ, we are made partakers of the Divine adoption, and heirs of heaven'. John Calvin, *Commentary on the Gospel According to John*, 2 vols. trans. William Pringle (Edinburgh: Calvin Translation Society, 1847), 2:166. Calvin's commentary on John was originally published in 1553, entitled: *In Evangelium Secundum Iohannem Commentarius*. See Barbara Pitkin, 'Calvin as Commentator on the Gospel of John', in Donald K. McKim (ed.) *Calvin and the Bible* (Cambridge: Cambridge University Press, 2006), 164–98. Tuckney recognised the words of John 17:3 as both exegetically complex and 'weighty' (Latin: *pondus*). According to Tuckney, this 'weightiness' pertains to salvific knowledge of the one true God.

(although he might be a second Atlas)[80] would not be overpowered and completely crushed by the infinite majesty of the one true God, the inaccessible light[81] of Jesus Christ (as long as we are outside him), the sun of righteousness,[82] and indeed the rays of his most splendid knowledge that teach, console, and bless us most fortunately in the meantime? So what he said about the whole of this most blessed prayer of the Saviour, recited in this chapter, [Note: Gerhardus][83] we can rightly say about this verse of his, or should I say this summit, [Page 2] namely that it is undoubtedly the sum of heavenly doctrine, a treasury of life-giving consolation, the most precious treasure of the church, a most effective remedy for all diseases, and thus most worthy of constant reading, meditation, and our keen inquiry and your attention.

But now it is not a question of giving a sermon to the people; instead, we must deal with the matter as is appropriate in the schools.

Christ the Lord, when he became our High Priest, wanted to fulfil all righteousness and thus the entire office[84] of the High Priest. [Note: Matt. 3:15] This office was in fact threefold, namely to teach, to pray and to offer, all of which, as noted by Zanchius[85] and others, he himself fully,

---

[80] In Greek mythology, Atlas was a Titan god who was condemned by the Greek god Zeus to bear the weight of the heavens upon his shoulders.

[81] This is an allusion to 1 Timothy 6:16. Tuckney applied 'inaccessible light' here to Christ, not God the Father. This is not to imply that 'inaccessible light' did not apply to the Father in Tuckney's thought, for 'inaccessible light' and 'one true God' are connected in Tuckney's text. According to Maldonatus' commentary on John, which Tuckney was reading when he wrote his lecture, 1 Timothy 6:16 applies to the Father, not Christ. Yet, Maldonatus understood that 1 Timothy 6:16 applies to Christ in view of the fact that Christ spoke of himself as 'life' and 'light'. See Maldonatus, *Joannis Maldonati*, 506.

[82] This is an allusion to Malachi 4:2.

[83] Johann Gerhard (1582–1637) was a Lutheran theologian whose *Loci Theologici* (9 vols., 1610–22) became the standard dogmatic work of Lutheran orthodoxy. Gerhard also completed Martin Chemnitz and Polycarp Lyser's work on the harmony of the Gospels. The specific reference to Gerhard is unclear in Tuckney's text. On Gerhard's exegesis of John 17:3, see Johann Gerhard, *On the Nature of God and On the Most Holy Mystery of the Trinity*, ed. Benjamin T. G. Mayes, trans. Richard J. Dinda (St. Louis: Concordia Publishing House, 2007), chap. 6, sec. 100. For the Latin text, see Johann Gerhard, *Loci Theologici*, ed. Ed. Preuss, vol. 1 (Berlin: Gustav Schlawitz, 1863). See also Gerhard, *Harmonia quatuor evangelistarum*, 2 vols. (Frankfurt am Main: Hertel, 1652); Henk Jan de Jonge, 'Sixteenth-century Gospel Harmonies: Chemnitz and Mercator', in Irena Backus and Francis Higman (eds.) *Théorie et pratique de l'exégèse: Actes du 3me colloque international sur l'histoire de l'exégèse biblique au XVme siècle* (Geneva: Droz, 1990), 155–66.

[84] This relates to the threefold office of the Mediator as prophet, priest, and king. See 'Mediator' and 'munus triplex' in Richard A. Muller, *Dictionary of Latin and Greek Theological Terms: Drawn Principally from Protestant Scholastic Theology* (Grand Rapids: Baker Book House, 1985).

[85] Girolamo Zanchi (1516–90) was an Italian thinker who made significant contributions to the development of early modern Reformed theology. Zanchi's influential work, *De Tribus Elohim* (1572), interpreted the Hebrew word *Elohim* in an exegetically Trinitarian manner. Tuckney cited Zanchi's exposition of John 17:3 where he presented arguments for

indeed abundantly, accomplished as was shown quite clearly by the Evangelist. [Note: *On the Triune Elohim*, Book 4, chapter 10]

In the preceding chapters,[86] he[87] taught. In the remaining chapters,[88] he offered himself as a sacrifice to God in a sweet-smelling aroma. Here,[89] he prays to the Father, first for himself and then for the Apostles, and finally for the whole church. And so the entire chapter can rightly be termed the Lord's Prayer.

However, it is not that Lord's Prayer which he himself taught us in Matthew 6,[90] where he told us to ask for forgiveness of sins, sins which he himself totally lacked. Nor is it that one, in Matthew 26 and Luke 22, which he poured out to the Father alone in the garden, as Rupert[91] believes.

---

the divinity of Christ. Zanchi noted, 'Triplex enim erat in lege pontificis officium: Docere, orare, offerre. Docere: nempe populum legem, & voluntatem domini. Orare nimirum pro populo: & pro se. Postremò, sacrificia offerre pro peccatis; tam suis, quàm totius populi'. Zanchi, *De Tribus Elohim*, Liber 4, chap. 10, 138. See Benjamin R. Merkle, *Defending the Trinity in the Reformed Palatinate: The Elohistae* (Oxford: Oxford University Press, 2015); Luca Baschera and Christian Moser, *Girolamo Zanchi, De religione Christiana fides – Confession of Christian Religion*, 2 vols. (Leiden: Brill, 2007).

[86] That is, in the chapters prior to John 17.
[87] The 'he' throughout this paragraph refers to Jesus.
[88] That is, in the chapters after John 17.   [89] This refers to John 17.
[90] In the 1640s and 1650s, the use of the Lord's Prayer was contested between Presbyterians and Independents. The Westminster *Directory* was flexible in its instructions, explaining that the Lord's Prayer was 'not only a Patern of Prayer, but it self a most comprehensive Prayer'. *A Directory for the Publique Worship of God* (London: 1645), 18–19. This ministerial flexibility conceded the Independent perspective that considers the Lord's Prayer as an example of prayer rather than a strict liturgy to be recited. On June 18, 1647, Tuckney, as chairman of the Westminster committee for the Larger Catechism, made a report concerning the Lord's Prayer. The Assembly resolved the following question about prayer: 'What Rule hath God given for our direction in the duty of prayer? A: The whole word of God is of use to direct us in praying, but especially the rule of Direction is that forme of prayer (commonly called the Lords Prayer) which our saviour Christ taught his Disciples'. Chad Van Dixhoorn and David F. Wright (eds.) *The Minutes and Papers of the Westminster Assembly 1643–1652*, 5 vols. (Oxford: OUP, 2012), 4:602 (Sess. 865). In the 1650s, the decline in the use of the Lord's Prayer partly reflected 'an enduring commitment to extemporary worship in presbyterian confessional culture'. Alasdair Raffe, *The Culture of Controversy: Religious Arguments in Scotland, 1660–1714* (Woodbridge: The Boydell Press, 2012), 135. See also Michael Ramsey, *The English Prayer Book, 1549–1662* (London: S.P.C.K., 1963); Ian Green, *The Christian's ABC: Catechisms and Catechizing in England c. 1530–1740* (Oxford: Clarendon Press, 1996), chap. 11.
[91] Tuckney was referring to the Benedictine biblical commentator Rupert of Deutz (Rupertus Tuitiensis) (c. 1075–1129). Rupert's *De sancta trinitate et operibus eius* examined the works of the Father, Son, and Holy Spirit throughout biblical history. He also commentated on numerous biblical books, including the Gospel of John. Tuckney referred to Rupert's commentary on John. See Rupert of Deutz, *Ruperti Abbatis Monasterii Tuitiensis... Commentaria in Evangelium Joannis, Libri XIIII* (Leuven: 1564), Liber XII, cap. XVI, 275. According to Edward Leigh, 'He was esteemed one of the most learned men of his age. The many Volumes which he hath left written, do testifie the eminency of his Learning. Some of his Works are mentioned in *Oxford* Catalogue'. Edward Leigh, *A Treatise*

But rather (as is clear from the first verse of the following chapter) it is the one that he offered up with a loud cry and tears in the presence of all the disciples who were listening in the upper room (Heb. 5:7). Some people, indeed the most learned, want this passage to apply to the prayer of the Saviour contained in this chapter. [Note: Gerhardus][92]

But first and foremost, the only thing (in the first five verses) that he asks should be granted to him by the Father is that the Father should be willing to glorify him immediately after he has been shamefully defiled by his passion; he urges this with a twofold argument:

1. That he may in turn glorify the Father, in the first verse.
2. That he may bring about the salvation of the elect, namely that he might give eternal life to those whom the Father has given him, in the second verse.

The reason for this is given in this verse, and that eternal life (which he mentioned in the preceding verses) is described more clearly. Namely, that it is based on the knowledge of the only true God and Jesus Christ whom he sent. And just as he previously made a close connection between both his own and his Father's glorification, so here he closely connected the knowledge of both. 'This, then, is eternal life, that they may know you, the only true God, and Jesus Christ whom you have sent'.

But in order for us to shed some light on the following discussion, let us begin with a brief explanation of the words.

First, the predicate of the proposition, 'eternal life', occurs here.

For since we had died in sin, he mentioned life.

Also, since the physical life that we lead here is of a day, rather than long-lasting, mortal, perishable and transitory, the life that he speaks of here he calls eternal in contrast, because it will never pass away, neither in this age nor the age to come.

---

of Religion & Learning and of Religious and Learned Men (London: 1656) (Wing L1013), 312. See Rupert of Deutz. *De sancta trinitate et operibus eius*, 4 vols., ed. Hrabanus Haacke CCCM 21–4 (Turnhout: Brepols, 1971–1972); Rita Copeland and Ineke Sluiter (eds.) 'Rupert of Deutz, *De sancta trinitate et operibus eius*, 1112–1116: Grammar and Rhetoric', in Copeland and Sluiter, *Medieval Grammar and Rhetoric: Language Arts and Literary Theory, AD 300–1475* (Oxford: Oxford University Press, 2012), 390–404; John H. Van Engen, *Rupert of Deutz* (Berkeley: University of California Press, 1983).

[92] In his popular book, *Enchiridion Consolatorium* (1611), Gerhard seemed to assume that the prayer of Hebrews 5:7 is part of the prayer of John 17. See Johann Gerhard, 'Dubitatio de perseverantia', in *Enchiridion Consolatorium Morti Ac Tentationibus in Agone Mortis Opponendum* (Jena: 1611), fol. H[7ᵛ]. For the English translation, see Johann Gerhard, *Handbook of Consolations: For the Fears and Trials That Oppress Us in the Struggle with Death*, trans. Carl L. Beckwith (Eugene: Wipf & Stock, 2009), chap. 29.

However, there is no agreement among interpreters as to what this 'eternal life' means. Is it eternal life in heaven, as Augustine[93] believed [Note: *Tractate* 105 on the Gospel of John; *On the Trinity*, Book 1, chapter 8],[94] as well as other ancient writers who often try to show that this heavenly happiness lies in the beatific vision?[95] Or is it rather the life of grace and of faith in this age, an idea approved by many, both ancient and modern, [Page 3] because, since believers are elsewhere said to have eternal life already [Note: John 3:36; 1 John 5:12–13], therefore in the whole prayer that follows Christ speaks as if he had already given them this eternal life?

As for me, I have always judged that the safest way of interpreting Scripture is the one that most properly respects its inexhaustible richness, which (provided that the context and analogy of faith[96] allow) is so extensive. And so here, it is the one that includes both these lives, namely the glory in heaven that is called preeminent (Matt. 25:46), as well as this grace on earth which will never disappear completely but will reach perfection, of which it is indeed the foretaste and gateway and the pledge and the firstfruits, or if we want to use the words of Cyril[97], 'the root, the mother, and the bridesmaid'.[98] This much is certain: this eternal life that Christ

---

[93] On the early modern reception of Augustine in Catholic and Protestant thought, see *PRRD* 4:19–20, 72–4; Jean-Louis Quantin, 'The Fathers in Seventeenth Century Roman Catholic Theology', in Irena Backus (ed.) *The Reception of the Church Fathers in the West: From the Carolingians to the Maurists*, 2 vols. (Leiden: Brill, 1997), 2:951–86; Quantin, *The Church of England and Christian Antiquity*; Arnoud S. Q. Visser, *Reading Augustine in the Reformation: The Flexibility of Intellectual Authority in Europe, 1500–1620* (Oxford: Oxford University Press, 2011).

[94] See *Tractate* 105 in Augustine, *Tractates on the Gospel of John, 55–11*, trans. John W. Rettig, vol. 4 (Washington, D.C.: Catholic University of America, 1994), 258–9; Augustine, *The Trinity*, trans. Edmund Hill (Brooklyn: New City Press, 1991), 94, 96, 176–7, 213.

[95] In *De trinitate* 1, Augustine discussed the 'beatific vision' (or the blessed vision of God) in which the saints shall behold God's unchanging being or contemplate the three divine persons. See Augustine, *The Trinity*, 76–86. For a helpful account of the beatific vision in church tradition, including the Puritans' perspective, see Hans Boersma, *Seeing God: The Beatific Vision in Christian Tradition* (Grand Rapids: Eerdmans, 2018). See also Lewis Ayres, *Augustine and the Trinity* (Cambridge: Cambridge University Press, 2010).

[96] In contrast to the analogy of Scripture, which compares unclear biblical passages with a collation of clear passages, the analogy of faith here 'presupposes a sense of the theological meaning of Scripture'. Muller, *Dictionary*, 33.

[97] Cyril of Alexandria was born in the last quarter of the fourth century and died in 444. As a Greek Church Father, Cyril became a leading authority for Eastern Orthodox Christology. He played a crucial role in the fifth-century Christological controversy, opposing the teaching of Nestorius, Bishop of Constantinople, who was condemned by the Council of Ephesus. See John A. McGuckin, *St. Cyril of Alexandria: The Christological Controversy. Its History, Theology, and Texts* (Leiden: Brill, 1994).

[98] Cyril authored his *Commentary on John* between 425 and 428, just before the Nestorian controversy erupted in 428. On John 17:3, he wrote: 'He defines faith as the mother of eternal life and says that the power of the true knowledge of God will cause us to remain forever in incorruption and blessedness and holiness'. He also noted that 'Our Lord Jesus Christ...says that it is "eternal life" in that it is the mother and nurse of eternal life because it is pregnant, as it were, in its own power and nature with those things that cause

speaks of in this text is the same eternal life that he had said in the previous verses that he would grant to the elect, and both are given by him and both are understood here.

In the subject of this statement, the particle ἵνα[99] appears first, which (as Beza[100] rightly comments) should be taken specifically, not ultimately; it denotes not the end but the thing itself as is claimed in John 15:8, 12.

'That they may know'. First, not by means of the knowledge that is inherent in our nature (which, as regards God, is obscure and faint, but of God in Christ is non-existent.) Second, this knowledge is not acquired by natural means or infused by ordinary illumination, since this obtains among the most wicked men or demons themselves (James 2:19). But according to the custom of the Hebrews (among whom words of sense and knowledge express affection and action), knowledge does not include merely a bare notion of the mind but also assent in the will and confidence in the heart. In fact, it is the same as faith itself, which ingrafts us into the body of Christ, whereby we become members of divine adoption and eventually heirs of heaven. For just as we have both kinds of eternal life in the subject of the proposition, so too we do not doubt that both these forms of knowledge, inchoate here through faith, are contained in the predicate and consummated in the intuitive and beatific vision of God. The fact that someone objects that this vision is indicated by another word, namely θεωρέω,[101] in verse 24 of this chapter, in no way means that it cannot be expressed here by this word γινώσκω,[102] in 1 Cor. 13:12 and frequently elsewhere.

Regarding 'you'. First of all, [this refers] not only to your will but also to your nature. Second, it certainly refers to 'you the Father', as proven by the first verse, but is it taken as referring to personhood? This is what the Socinians[103] argue, as Zanchius claims,[104] and I agree with this, provided

---

life and lead to it'. Cyril of Alexandria, *Commentary on John*, 2 vols. trans. David R. Maxwell, ed. Joel C. Elowsky (Downers Grove: InterVarsity Press, 2013–15), 2:273–4.

[99] The Greek word ἵνα means 'that'.

[100] The French Protestant Theodore Beza (1519–1605) was a disciple and successor of John Calvin at the Genevan church. Among his theological works was his annotated Greek New Testament (1556), which was later followed by his Greek-Latin New Testament (1565). These works underwent subsequent editions. Beza's pan-European influence partly coincided with his *Annotationes* (1594). Tuckney was referring to Beza's comments on John 17:3 in his *Annotationes* here. See Beza, *Annotationes*, 1:431–2.

[101] The Greek word θεωρέω means 'I see'.

[102] The Greek word γινώσκω means 'I know'.

[103] Although Tuckney was attacking the anti-Trinitarianism of Socinianism, the word 'Socinian' was polemically linked to individuals whose opinions were directly or indirectly associated with Socinianism, as well as those who emphasised the use of reason in religion.

[104] See Zanchi, *De Tribus Elohim*, Liber 4, chap. 10, 142–3. Zanchi here reported an interpretation that the name 'Father' is not restricted to the person of the Father but could be understood as referring to the Trinity.

that it is explained correctly, in such a way that under the name of the Father, the whole divine essence, which is common to all the persons of the Holy Trinity, is understood.[105] I will explain this later.

'You, the only true God', in contrast to the gods of the Gentiles, who were not only numerous but also false.

And 'whom you sent', first in the incarnation, second to fulfil the office of the Mediator; about which we will also speak more when we get to the disputation.

'Jesus Christ', though the sweetest of names, will not be explained at this point.

Rather, attention should be directed towards drawing out the meaning of this sentence: just as in verse 2, Christ had said that 'power was granted to him over all flesh', which was usually divided into both Gentiles and Jews; so here, he provides the most appropriate cure, with the twofold object of his salvific knowledge, for both Jews and Gentiles, each suffering from their own diseases, and these being deadly. He opposes God to the atheism of the Gentiles, a single God to their polytheism, [Page 4] for μόνος means singleness, as μονάς signifies oneness. But in contrast to their idolatrous practices, which undoubtedly involved the worship of idols that were worthless, false, and non-existent gods, or were entirely nothing or at least had nothing of the true God, he places the true God in contrast, whom they must know and recognise if they want to share in eternal life.

But with regard to the Jews, even though they had eventually been taught better during the Babylonian captivity and then renounced their ancestral polytheism and idolatry and worshipped the only true God according to their own custom, yet they were so far from believing that Jesus Christ was either sent by God or the only true Saviour and Messiah, that they considered him a slave to the Devil, the most accursed of all humans. In order to apply a remedy to their wound, Christ clearly proclaims that knowledge of himself as well as of the Father is necessary for eternal life.

We have said more than enough about the subject and predicate. Only the copula 'is' remains, that they may know you, etc. is eternal life.

Concerning the meaning of this, people hold different opinions, but they can all be brought back to this point.

If the proposition is understood to refer to intuitive knowledge and the happy life in heaven, this knowledge is formally eternal life, in which that happiness principally consists.

---

[105] Reformed orthodox theologians distinguished between the essential (as applied to the Godhead) and personal (as applied to the Father alone) uses of the name 'Father'. See *PRRD* 4:246–51.

Anthony Tuckney's Anti-Socinian Lecture on the Divinity of Christ 141

But if it is taken as the knowledge of faith,[106] then similarly (at least in part) it is formally spiritual life which we live here now, inasmuch as it is its principal part, and can be partly called eternal life as an efficient cause,[107] to the extent that (at least of its own kind) it is not only the cause of this spiritual life which flows forth from faith now, but also of that eternal life in heaven. Knowledge of faith is the way, the manner, and the means of attaining this eternal life.

To summarise briefly: the copula 'is', seeing that it can be applied to different things, either means that eternal life is, with respect to its formal nature, contained in that knowledge or depends on that knowledge as from a cause, either specifically from an efficient cause or which at least promotes it in some way.

So, in this explanation of the aforementioned words, an abundant crop appears, to which a labourer may apply his sickle, and it is certain that he who called this verse (as we saw earlier) the sum of heavenly doctrine is not wrong, for the following reasons:

1. If it is called 'life', this means that outside of Christ we are entirely dead in our sins, contrary to the [beliefs of the] Catholics, Arminians, Socinians, and others.[108]
2. Since life is eternal, or is understood to be the life of grace, against the above opponents it asserts permanence that is not subject to impairment.

---

[106] The Latin here is *cognitione fidei*.

[107] Tuckney employed the Aristotelian theory of fourfold causation (efficient, material, formal, and final) as a philosophical method for theological elaboration. He posited that the knowledge of faith serves as the agent, source, or cause of eternal life.

[108] The notion of dead in sin reflects Tuckney's Reformed belief in the spiritual impotence of unregenerate sinners who cannot hope in Christ until God efficaciously draws them to himself and justifies them based on Christ's merits. Underlying this is the concept of original sin, which has by the result of the fall completely defected human nature as regards saving activities. See *peccatum originalis* in Muller, *Dictionary*; Westminster Confession of Faith VI.4; Stephen Hampton, 'Sin, Grace, and Free Choice in Post-Reformation Reformed Theology', in Ulrich L. Lehner (ed.) *The Oxford Handbook of Early Modern Theology, 1600–1800* (Oxford: Oxford University Press, 214), 228–41. For Catholicism, the Council of Trent's 1547 Decree on Justification taught that original sin did not completely corrupt human nature after the fall, but merely weakened it. According to Jacob Harmenszoon (Arminius) (1559–1609), divine grace in salvation is resistible. He stressed 'deprivation [of original righteousness] more than depravation'. Keith D. Stanglin and Thomas H. Hall, *Jacob Arminius: Theologian of Grace* (Oxford: Oxford University Press, 2012). On Arminius and post-Arminian Remonstrant theology, see Keith D. Stanglin, 'Arminian, Remonstrant, and Early Methodist Theologies', in Lehner, *Oxford Handbook of Early Modern Theology*, 387–401. Socinianism denied the concept of original sin, for 'the equity and justice or rectitude of God will not allow that he should deprive man of the will and power of acting rightly'. *Racovian Catechism*, 325. Furthermore, like the word 'Socinian', the polemically charged labels 'Arminian' and 'Catholic' were directly or indirectly associated with Arminius or Rome respectively.

142 *History of Universities*

3. Or if this is the life of glory, it also confirms its eternity, against certain innovators among us who are atheists.
4. When the verse says that eternal life is stored in knowledge, it produces a compelling argument against the Catholics, specifically Bellarmine,[109] who thought that faith should rather be defined by ignorance than understanding.
5. Furthermore, this verse presents an opportunity for investigating whether the eternal happiness of the saints in heaven consists in the beatific vision of God or intuitive knowledge, as some of the Fathers claim here.
6. If knowledge is of God, it confounds the atheists.
7. If it is of the one God, this confounds recent Tritheists and all Polytheists.
8. If it is of the true God, it confounds idolaters.
9. If knowledge is of Jesus Christ, it confounds the Jews.
[Page 5] 10. Since eternal life is to know not only the true God but also Jesus Christ, two other things can be asked and discussed as a result.

Namely, 1. whether it was possible for eternal life to be obtained from the first covenant entered into by Adam.[110]

2. Whether some people who are completely ignorant of Jesus Christ can currently be partakers of eternal life under the covenant of grace.

But actually, those words 'whom you have sent' require more to be said concerning the sending of Christ, as also of the Holy Spirit.

However, I will pass over these things now. My main concern here is with the Arians, Photinians, and Socinians.[111] For as the bee sucks honey

---

[109] In his time, Robert Bellarmine (1542–1621) was a highly influential Catholic theologian and a staunch adversary of Protestantism. He was born in Montepulciano, Tuscany, and joined the Jesuit Order in 1560. In 1569, the Jesuit Order sent Bellarmine to the University of Louvain, where he was appointed to a chair of theology. In 1576, Bellarmine was appointed to the chair of controversial theology at the Roman College. He was a leading architect behind the Council of Trent (1545–63) or the Counter-Reformation. His three-volume work, *Disputationes de controversiis Christianae fidei adversus hujus temporis haereticos*, was published in 1586–93. The full quote that Tuckney had in mind is: 'Igitur mysteria fidei, quae rationem superant, credimus, non intelligimus, ac per hoc fides distinguitur contra scientiam, et melius per ignorantiam, quam per notitiam definitur'. Robert Bellarmine 'Controversiarum de Justificatione, Qui est de Fide Justificante', in *Opera Omnia*, 12 vols. (Paris: Vivès, 1870–84), 6:1.7.

[110] Tuckney had in mind the covenant of works, a Reformed concept popular in seventeenth-century Britain and Holland. The concept refers to the first covenant made between God and humanity before the fall, when humans were capable of perfect obedience. This contrasts the covenant of grace in which God graciously promises salvation apart from any human merit. See *foedus operum* and *foedus gratiae* in Muller, *Dictionary*.

[111] The grouping of 'Arians, Photinians, and Socinians' stems from the fact that each historically denied that the Son is of the same substance with the Father. Tuckney used these

from the same flower as the spider sucks venom, so it is with this verse (which is altogether honey): all faithful and orthodox believers correctly conclude from this verse that, since knowledge of both Jesus Christ and the Father is spoken of here as eternal life, he is truly God, one with the Father; on the other hand, the ancient Arians and modern Socinians try to carve out more here so that they can, as far as possible, remove Christ from the verse by way of trickeries here and blasphemies there, and divest him of all the glory of his Godhead. For although they harp on about the divinity of Christ, they still completely deny his true divinity. Indeed, Smalcius,[112] so as to fill cunningly an incautious reader of his work[113] with flattery, painstakingly proves in his preliminary arguments that Christ is the true God, and even the rest of his herd willingly admit that Christ is the true God, yet not God by nature, as the Apostle says in Galatians 4:8. They want him to be not God by nature, not eternal, not consubstantial with the Father, but a created God, that is, in reality a fictitious God. They do not regard him as a mere man, since he was adorned with surpassing qualities as well as offices, raised high above the ordinary, and indeed raised to the highest status among other humans, a man who is deified, or, as they like to put it, a divine man. But with respect to his own nature, they consider this to be only human, and for this reason they argue fiercely that he is a mere man.

Moreover, while they attempt to extract this interpretation from various other passages of Holy Scripture which have been adduced against their will, they do so in particular from this verse, which was therefore considered the Achilles heel of the ancient Arians. And so with malicious intent and with lines of arguments arrayed against the true eternal divinity of Christ,

---

religious labels as epithets of abuse, reflecting the religious polemics of his time. But he saw Socinianism as a contemporary revival of Arianism and Photinianism.

[112] Valentinus Smalcius (1572–1622) was a German Socinian and the chief editor of the Socinian publishing house in Raków, Poland. He was also one of the authors of the *Racovian Catechism* (1605) and translated it into German as *Der Kleine Catechismus, zur Uebung der Kinder in dem Christlichen Gottesdienste* (1608). Compiled and published after Faustus Socinus' death, the *Racovian Catechism* summarised the essential tenets of Socinian thought. Translated into various languages, the work underwent numerous revisions until its final form in 1680, which later appeared in Thomas Rees' 1818 English translation. On the list of editions of the *Racovian Catechism*, see Piotr Wilczek, *Polonia Reformata: Essays on the Polish Reformation(s)* (Göttingen: Vandenhoeck & Ruprecht, 2016), 64–8. Since Tuckney identified Smalcius as the author of the *Racovian Catechism*, see *Racovian Catechism*, 79, where it affirms that Christ is 'a true God', not *the* true God. See also Martin Schmeisser, *Sozinianische Bekenntnisschriften: Der Rakower Katechismus des Valentin Schmalz (1608) und der sogenannte Soner-Katechismus* (Berlin: Akademie Verlag, 2012).

[113] Tuckney was likely referring to the *Racovian Catechism*.

Smalcius, in his *Racovian Catechism*, and Crellius,[114] in his works on *The One God the Father*, make this verse their chief weapon and place it at the front of their battle line. But what is the damage? What weapons have they taken from their well-stocked arsenal against the Father and the Son? These are their arguments:

1. Because he prays to the Father in verse 1.[115]
2. Because he asks to be glorified by the Father, both of which things (as they definitely believe) imply that he is human as they are unworthy of God.
3. Because in this verse he admits that he is sent by God.
4. And this is the greatest argument: because he recognises that the Father is the only true God in the first part of the verse, 'That they know you, the only true God', but in the latter part of the verse, 'And Jesus Christ whom you have sent', he clearly distinguishes himself from the Father and completely renounces any sharing of all the divinity proper to the Father alone.

These are doubtless the props, with which the Socinians support the damnable cause that will be destroyed in eternity. These are battering rams with which to attempt to undermine with great audacity the eternal divinity of our Lord Christ. But although these weapons made of reeds [Page 6] may strike against this rock of eternity (עוֹלָמִים צוּר) [Note: Isa. 26:4; Tzur Gnolamin],[116] they will not shatter it.

If you like, we will first call the final argument for examination, as it is of special importance. It goes as follows:

Christ asserts that the Father is the only true God and distinguishes himself from the Father. He therefore rejects that divinity which we falsely ascribe to him.

I have many things to oppose to this, although most of them are not my own. For while this is the sweetest text, providing us with the gentlest peace of consciences, since it has become the most troubled text as the result of the blasphemous impudence of both ancient and modern heretics, it has exercised the piety, zeal, and ingenuity of both ancient and modern orthodox Christians in such a way that hardly anything remains to be said now that has not been said already. Hence it has come about that later

---

[114] Johannes Crell (1590–1633) was a highly influential German Socinian and Rector of the Socinian Academy in Raków. His *Liber duo de uno Deo Patre* (1631) argued that the Father alone is God. It was translated into English as *The two books of John Crellius Francus, touching one God, the Father* (1665).
[115] This is John 17:1.
[116] 'Tzur Gnolamin' is Tuckney's Latinised transliteration of the Hebrew עוֹלָמִים צוּר.

writers have mostly just copied the works of earlier writers. Just as the cow follows the cow, so an author follows an author, as the illustrious Scultetus[117] does elegantly in Book 1, chapter 3 of his *Evangelical Exercises*, in that very chapter where he copied almost everything from Cunaeus.[118] In the same way, Arnoldus[119] had recently borrowed almost everything that he has on this text verbatim from someone else. [Note: Gerhardo][120] For this reason, it would be fruitless for a diligent person to say more after so many and such great people have written about this. But since, according to the nature of this text and work, I must say something here on the orders of the most learned men, now that the die is cast, we must test to see whether we must attempt to explain what has been said by others in some way, or at least add our own weight (although it is certainly lighter) on some points.

1. And the first thing that I would like to say is with reference to the men, namely the Socinians: if only they were consistent with themselves and their own opinions, they could not pull out like a twisted cord from this verse a different nature of Christ from the Father, but rather reveal their own insanity. For nothing is attributed to the Father here according to what is literally said that they do not also at length and of their own accord bestow on Christ himself. Certainly, according to their own opinion, Christ is the 'true God', which is affirmed here of the Father. Therefore, not only the Father is the true God, though there is a fierce dispute among them regarding this matter; thus, they cut their own throats, as long as they continue to dare to fight against the divinity of Christ.

In fact, they say that Christ was a true God, which they willingly admit, but he is not the supreme God, who is to be understood in this verse. The 'true God' or 'the supreme God' as paraphrased by Crellius[121]—that is good. Consequently, they need another passage on which to base their

---

[117] Abraham Scultetus (1566–1624) was a Reformed German professor of theology at the University of Heidelberg and Advisor of Frederick V, King of Bohemia. He wrote *Exercitationes Evangelicae*. 2 vols. (Amsterdam: 1624). Tuckney was probably referring to Scultetus, *Exercitationes*, Liber 1, cap. 3, 13. There, Scultetus wrote: 'Confutatur autem ab eruditissimo viro Petro Cunaeo, libellis commentariis de Repub. Ebraeorum: ubi docet, excellentiam alicujus tribus non esse notam indubitatam sceptri sive regni'.

[118] Tuckney was referring to Petrus Cunaeus (1586–1638), professor of Latin at Leiden University and author of the bestselling book *De Republica Hebraeorum* (Leiden: 1617).

[119] Tuckney likely had in mind Nicolaus Arnoldi (1618–80), the Polish Reformed theologian who was professor of theology at Franeker University. Arnoldi refuted Socinianism in his *Religio Sociniana: seu Catechesis Racoviana major publicis disputationibus... refutata* (Franeker: 1654). On John 17:3, see Arnoldi, *Religio Sociniana*, 115–21.

[120] See Gerhard, *On the Nature of God*, chap. 6, sec. 100.

[121] See Johannes Crell, *De Uno Deo Patre Libri Duo* (Racoviae: 1631), Lib. I, sect. I, cap. I.

own opinion, in which the word 'supreme' occurs, which is not found in this verse.

But this is understood, and I admit and willingly recognise that it is implied by the emphatic article τόν (τόν μόνον ἀληθῖνόν θεόν). But I consider that the Socinians do not deserve that we should grant them this interpretation, since according to their construction of the sense and wording, according to the expression of their thoughts, that article (τόν) has nothing emphatic about it, and it is purely relative.[122] [Note: see Bisterfeld][123]

In the meantime, it needs to be established that whoever (not in a figurative or improper way) is called 'true God', to him true divine worship should be given (which is customarily done and defended by the majority of the Socinians in their adoration of Christ), and it will be blasphemy to deny him the majesty of the highest God.

But setting aside these men and their concessions, let us approach the matter itself more closely.

2. There is a second thing that I would like to put down as a foundation, namely, that which is [Page 7] very clearly asserted in many other texts in Scripture is not contradicted here (for the Holy Spirit is very consistent and the differences in the Scriptures are always amicable; if only the same could be said of our writings.) [Note: 'There is nothing contradictory in the writings of the Holy Scripture'. Chrysostom,[124] Homily 10 on Genesis,

---

[122] Tuckney rejected the idea that the article τόν (the) in John 17:3 is not emphatic but purely relative in that it is connected to the subject rather than the predicate of the sentence. The Socinian Johannes Crell, for example, translated John 17:3 as: 'Haec est vita aeterna, ut cognoscant te (Pater) solum verum Deum'. Crell, *De Uno Deo Patre Libri Duo*, Lib. I, sect. I, cap. I. According to Crell, the predicate of the sentence is 'true God', not 'the only true God', such that the words 'the' and 'only' refer to the subject, namely, the Father.

[123] Johann Heinrich Bisterfeld (1605–65) was a Reformed theologian and professor of theology and philosophy at Herborn. He was also the son-in-law of Johan Heinrich Alsted (1588–1638). Among his works is his *De uno Deo, Patre, Filio, ac Spiritu Sancto, mysterium pietatis, contra Iohannis Crelli, Franci, de uno Deo Patre, libri duos, breviter defendum* (Leiden: 1639). Tuckney was directly reading Bisterfeld's response to Crell's argument that John 17:3 proves that the Father of the Lord Jesus Christ alone is the 'supreme God'. Bisterfeld noted: 'For if the word "only" is to be referred immediately to the term "you," the article loses all its emphasis and only has a relative and connecting force, standing for the word "who"'. Bisterfeld, *De uno Deo*, Lib. I, cap. 1, 3–4: 'Nam si vox *solus* immediatè est referenda ad vocem *Te*, omnem suam emphasin amittit articulus, ac tantum habet vim relativam ac conectentem, & ponitur pro voculâ *qui*'.

[124] Born in Antioch, Syria, John Chrysostom (347–407) was one of the most significant Church Fathers of the East, alongside Basil the Great, Gregory of Nazianzus, and Gregory of Nyssa. He wrote sixty-seven homilies on the book of Genesis. Tuckney quoted Chrysostom's Homily 10, in which Chrysostom clarified that God's rest on the seventh day does not contradict John 5:17 ('my father is at work up until now and I am at work'). The former means that God 'ceased creating and bringing from non-being into being', whereas the latter speaks of God's 'unceasing care for us'. Saint John Chrysostom, *Homilies on*

p. 63, edit. Savil.]¹²⁵ But that Jesus Christ is God, and true God, and indeed the highest God, is proved by the most brilliant testimonies of Holy Scripture, indeed affirmed word for word. 'The Word was God', namely the Word who was made flesh (according to John Chrysostom's Commentary 14)[126] is Jesus Christ. Behold! Christ is God!

In the first Epistle of John, chapter 5, verse 20: 'We know that the Son of God has come and given us understanding, so that we may know him who is true, and we are in him who is true, that is, Jesus Christ; he is the true God and eternal life'. The same Apostolic author copies almost all the same words there, which here compose almost the entire sentence that we now have here in our hands. He certainly looked back to that text; he is the interpreter of those words. What the Socinians here wish to attribute particularly to the Father alone, the Apostle attributes to Jesus Christ there, that he is the true God. Behold, Christ is the true God in the second instance.

Behold, he is also the highest God. Romans 9:5: 'Christ, who is God over all, blessed forever.' I admit they apply all their efforts in doing this and they turn in every direction so as to introduce, by means of their deceptions, darkness into these most clear testimonies and others regarding the divinity of Christ—and some of these they themselves are now ashamed of. For these [testimonies] are inscribed as much in the Scriptures as in the hearts of the faithful like the rays of the sun, as a solemn means of escape for them. It seems that these testimonies can be understood in a different way, and passages like these will never prevent it being established undeniably that Christ Jesus is the true highest God. Unless the Holy Spirit contradicts himself, nothing here can contradict this fact.

3. Indeed, I say that there is no appearance nor shadow of a contradiction, at least for slightly more discerning eyes.

The aforementioned approved testimonies clearly and distinctly declare that Christ is the true highest God. Here, we have eternal life, 'that they may know you' (namely, the Father) 'to be the only true God, and Jesus Christ whom you have sent'. What kind of contradiction, I ask, is there here?

Can it then be rightly concluded from this that the Father is the only true God in such a way that Christ is excluded from sharing this true

---

Genesis, 1–17, trans. Robert C. Hill (Washington, D.C.: The Catholic University of America, 1986), 139.

[125] Henry Savile (1549–1622) published an eight-volume edition (Eton, 1611–12) of Chrysostom's works in Greek.

[126] 'Commentary 14' likely refers to John 1:14. See Saint John Chrysostom, *Commentary on Saint John the Apostle and Evangelist, Homilies 1–47*, trans. Sister Thomas Aquinas Goggin, S.C.H. (Washington, D.C.: The Catholic University of America, 1957), 103–10.

divinity? Certainly not. Rather, it can and ought to be understood in a different way.

First of all, I say that it can be understood differently, and no one should in the meantime fault me for responding with the means of escape that I have just noted. Accordingly, in this matter there is greater liberty, and right is rather on the side of the orthodox than the heretics; so that the more the heretics overturn what is solidly founded in the Scriptures, clearly transmitted and always firmly believed everywhere in the entire church, it seems they declare more often that it can be understood differently (by the heretical mind, cunning and deceitful). This is an act of arrogance in no way to be tolerated, but it should be tolerated and praised in a theologian who is fighting on behalf of the orthodox catholic faith, so as to blunt the heretics' shameless behaviour. First, then, I say that this can be understood differently, namely that the conjunction 'and', so far from creating a separation, actually creates a stronger connection and this conjunction enables Jesus Christ to share in this statement 'only true God'. Nor does it follow from this that the words of Christ by themselves do not prevent the attribution of the same predicate to countless other subjects, [Page 8] as Crellius argues [Note: Book 1, chapter 1], since there is a vast difference between the essence of Christ and all creatures. Certainly, I understand that Crellius also rather arrogantly bursts out with these words, namely, 'It should be proved that anyone can speak correctly in this way with a suitable example, either sacred or profane. They will not put forward an example from the sacred writings: the common people are not accustomed to speak in this way. But Christ spoke in a common way'.[127] [Note: Ibid.] However, with all due respect to him, I would prefer to say that both Holy Scripture and the common people are accustomed to speak in this way. With respect to the common people, that which Athanasius[128] considers in his disputation with Arius[129] at the Council of Nicaea is of particular relevance here. Thus, in that place, 'If someone says that I know Constantine to be the only emperor of land and sea, and his son

---

[127] See Crell, *Two Books*, 8–9.
[128] Born in the 290s and died in 373, Athanasius, Bishop of Alexandria, was mentored by Alexander of Alexandria (250–328). In 325, he served as a secretary to Alexander at the Council of Nicaea. Athanasius was a powerful defender of pro-Nicene orthodoxy and wrote an anti-Arian work between 356 and 360 entitled: *Four Discourses against the Arians*.
[129] Arius of Alexandria (256–336) was a Libyan presbyter whose denial of the eternal generation of the Son had led to the Council of Nicaea, which condemned Arius. On Arius and the fourth-century Arian controversy, see Rowan Williams, *Arius: Heresy and Tradition* (London: SCM, 2001); Lewis Ayres, *Nicaea and its Legacy: An Approach to Fourth-Century Trinitarian Theology* (Oxford: Oxford University Press, 2004).

Constantius, the son is not separated from imperial partnership, but rather he is joined to it'.[130]

Neither is it uncommon to find this manner of speaking in Holy Scripture [Note: Deut. 1:36; 1 Kings 22:20; Mark 6:47]. Our theologians have collected many examples of it. I will bring forward only two, and indeed ones that are quite widely known. The first is John 8:9 where it is written as follows: 'And Jesus was left alone, and the woman standing before him'. In that passage, Christ is said to be left alone there, but since 'and the woman' is added, it is to be understood that she stayed or remained along with Christ. And therefore, just as 'μόνος'[131] excludes the rest who were standing there previously, but not the woman, similarly, in the case of 'the only true God', it excludes other gods, foreign gods, false gods, but not Jesus Christ who, together with the Father, is true God. The second example (which is Chrysostom's Homily 80 on John) is found in 1 Cor. 9:6, where the Apostle says the following: 'Or is it only I and Barnabas who do not have the power of not working?' On this passage, Chrysostom says the following: 'When Paul says, "Only I and Barnabas," does this exclude Barnabas? Not at all'.[132] In the same way as when Paul says, 'Only I and Barnabas', he does not exclude Barnabas. Similarly, when Christ says here, 'You the only true God and Jesus Christ whom you have sent', he is not excluding himself, indeed he rather includes himself. And so we have accomplished the first thing, namely to show that this can be understood differently from how the Socinians intend it.

Second, it must in fact be understood differently. Despite the grammatical construction of the words, it can be understood differently. Indeed, the truth of the matter and the analogy of faith urge us, indeed compel us to do so. For since Christ (as we have proven earlier) is clearly and forcefully called true God in Holy Scripture, this copulative conjunction 'and' connects 'only true God' and 'Jesus Christ'. Of course, it makes a distinction, but it does not separate. It distinguishes the person but does not separate the nature and does not take away the divinity. This now leads me directly to the well-articulated responses of the orthodox to this Socinian

---

[130] Tuckney might have lifted this quote from Gerhard. See Gerhard, 'On the Unity of the Divine Essence', chap. 6, sec. 100. Tuckney was referring to the pseudo-Athanasian text *Disputatio Contra Arium in Concilio Nicaeno*. The text states: 'Certo cognoscas velim, solum Caesarem Constantinum Imperatorem terrae & maris esse, Constantius eius filius esse, is né ea confessione patri filium coniungit, an non?'. Pseudo-Athanasius, *B. Athanasii Archiepiscopi Alexandrini: Operae Quae Reperiuntur Omnia, in Duos Tomos Tributa*, vol. 1 (Heidelberg: 1601), 93.

[131] The Greek word μόνος means 'only'.

[132] See Saint John Chrysostom, *Commentary on Saint John the Apostle and Evangelist: Homilies 48–88*, trans. Sister Thomas Aquinas Goggin, S.C.H. (New York: The Catholic University of America, 1960), 371.

argument which still need to be considered. Since there are many of them, I will present their four chief responses, setting aside the rest, and I will attempt to the best of my ability to explain or confirm them.

1. The first response is that of Tertullian,[133] Athanasius, Nazianzus,[134] Hilary,[135] Ambrose,[136] and Augustine, and this is the same as the one I have just mentioned. For they say that those three words 'only true God' are attributed not only to the Father but also to the Son by way of that conjunction 'and'.[137] Thus, Tertullian (or rather Novatian)[138] says in chapter 24 of his book *On the Trinity*, 'if he did not want to be understood by God why add, "And Jesus Christ whom you have sent," unless it was because he wished to be received as God as well. He joined himself to God, as he wanted to be understood as God, as he is, by way of this conjunction'.[139] Similarly, Athanasius [Page 9] (in the text just mentioned) responded to Arius.[140] And Arius did not have any counterargument against his response. Nazianzus' opinion on this matter is skilfully expressed: 'For he would not have added "and Jesus Christ whom you have sent," if "the only true God" were contrasted with him, and the sentence did not proceed according to a shared Godhead'.[141] [Note: Fourth Theological Oration]

---

[133] Tertullian (160–225) was a Christian apologist who wrote against Gnosticism and Marcion. He was the first Church Father to write prolifically in Latin until Augustine.

[134] Gregory of Nazianzus (329–89) was one of the Cappadocian fathers and chaired the Council of Constantinople (381). His five *Theological Orations* defended Nicene theology, delivered in 380 at his church called the Anastasia.

[135] Hilary of Poitiers, born in the 300/310s and died in 367/368, was Bishop of Poitiers and confessor of the Church for his defence of Nicene orthodoxy. His famous works are *De synodis* and *De trinitate*, the latter opposing 'Arianism'.

[136] Born in Trier to a Christian family, Ambrose of Milan (339–97) was bishop of Milan, succeeding the 'Homoian' bishop, Auxentius. He was a prominent defender of Nicene theology and opponent of 'Arianism'. Among his works are *De fide* and *De Spiritu Sancto*. The term 'Homoian' designates those who thought the Son was *homoiousios* (similar in essence) with the Father.

[137] Tuckney likely followed Maldonatus here in pointing out that the three words 'only true God' are applied to the Son by way of the conjunction 'and'. See Maldonatus, *Joannis Maldonati*, 505–506.

[138] Novatian (c. 200–58) was a Roman presbyter whose *De Trinitate* (c. 250) was attributed to Tertullian in the medieval period. For the Latin text of Novatian's *De Trinitate*, see *Corpus Christianorum: Series Latina*, vol. 4.

[139] See Novatian, *The Trinity; The Spectacle; Jewish Foods; In Praise of Purity; Letters*, trans. Russell J. DeSimone, O.S.A. (Washington, D.C.: The Catholic University of America Press, 1974), 62. Novatian's quote also appears in Maldonatus' text. See Maldonatus, *Joannis Maldonati*, 505.

[140] Tuckney was thinking of *Disputatio Contra Arium in Concilio Nicaeno*, a pseudo-Athanasian text. See Pseudo-Athanasius, *B. Athanasii Archiepiscopi Alexandrini*, 93.

[141] See The Fourth Theological Oration (Oration 30) in St Gregory of Nazianzus, *On God and Christ: The Five Theological Orations and Two Letters to Cledonius*, ed. John Behr (New York: St Vladimir's Seminary Press, 2002), 104.

Hilary[142] and Ambrose,[143] along with others, hold the same opinion. It is only Augustine who does not hesitate to affirm that the order of these words is, 'that they may know you and Jesus Christ whom you have sent as the only true God'.[144] [Note: *Tractate* 105 on the Gospel of John. Among the words of Augustine in the statement of Prosper. 371] And indeed, at least on this point, I agree with Maldonatus[145] when he writes about the matter as follows: 'I do not know whether this interpretation can be refuted by those who disagree. For I cannot find any reason'. Neither can I. For although Gerhardus' statement is true, that 'this coordination of words cannot win against an obstinate adversary',[146] we do not pay attention to their obstinacy. For there is nothing so clear in Scripture and, as it were, written with the rays of the sun, that it cannot be questioned by minds sophistical and hardened in unbelief (as with many of the Socinians). As far as I am concerned, let them protest noisily, then, as much as they want, provided they do not have anything with which to refute it. But what Calvin asserts to the contrary does not have this effect, namely, that the same question will be raised about the Holy Spirit.[147] For not all things must be said at once and together. The divinity of the Holy Spirit is clear from other texts, but there was no controversy about it here nor was there even any occasion for it to be mentioned. Here, Christ prays to the Father, asks for the manifestation of his glory, which necessarily had already been diminished by his death. He mentions eternal life, of which he himself was the sole Mediator. He had no need to make mention of the Holy Spirit, whose perfect knowledge had not yet even been handed down, for it became fully known later, by means of the outpouring upon the Apostles. But even if the whole divine essence, common to each of the persons (as will become clear later) is understood under the name 'Father' in this verse, the Holy Spirit is not included. This was the first response of the ancient Fathers.

---

[142] See Saint Hilary of Poitiers, *The Trinity*, in *The Fathers of the Church*, trans. Stephen McKenna, vol. 25 (Washington D.C.: Catholic University of America Press, 2002), Book 9, sec. 32–6, 353–6.

[143] See Ambrose *De Fide* V, 1, 16–27 in *Sancti Ambrosii Opera Pars VIII: De Fide [Ad Gratianum Augustum]*, ed. Otto Faller, *Corpus Scriptorum Ecclesiasticorum Latinorum* 78 (Vienna: Hölder-Pichler-Tempsky, 1962).

[144] According to Augustine, 'the order of the words is: "that you and Jesus Christ, whom you have sent, they may know as the only true God" '. Augustine, *Tractates on the Gospel of John*, 258.

[145] This further confirms that Tuckney was closely reading Maldonatus here. Maldonatus said: 'Nescio, an haec interpretatio ab iis, quibus non placet, refutari possit; ego enim, qua ratione possit, non invenio. Maldonatus, *Joannis Maldonati*, 505.

[146] It is unclear where this exact quote is found in Gerhard's works.

[147] See Calvin, *Commentary on the Gospel According to John*, 2:167.

The second response was that of Basil,[148] Chrysostom, Theophylact,[149] and even Nazianzus[150] and others, namely that, by this word 'only', the Son or Holy Spirit, who have the same nature as the Father and therefore the same divinity, are not excluded but created things are excluded. [Note: 'That is said in opposition to polytheism', so says Epiphanius,[151] *Against Heresies*, 69. See also James Ussher[152] on Ignatius' Epistles, chapter 12, page 88. Epistle 141.][153] According to Augustine, the gods and idols of the Gentiles especially were excluded, which were either nothing (1 Cor. 10:20) or of no value; at least they were infinitely distant from the infinite majesty of the true God, 'which either have no nature or not the same nature as that of God the Father', as Brugensis[154] rightly says. According to Basil, 'It [the word 'only'] is not used in contradistinction to the Son or Holy Spirit, but in contrast to those who are not gods, yet are falsely so

[148] Basil 'the Great' (330–79) was one of the Cappadocian fathers, bishop of Caesarea, Cappadocia, and promoted Nicene orthodoxy.
[149] Theophylact of Ohrid (1050–1108), Byzantine Archbishop of Ohrid (Bulgaria), famously wrote an entire commentary on the New Testament.
[150] See Oration 30 in Nazianzus, *On God and Christ*, 104.
[151] Born in Palestine at Besanduc between 310 and 320 and died in 403, Epiphanius of Salamis was Bishop of Salamis on Cyprus and attacked the Arians and Origenism. According to Epiphanius' *Against Heresies* (also known as *Panarion*), written in the 370s, 'the only true' was written 'to refute the notion of those who talk mythology and believe in polytheism'. Epiphanius, *The Panarion of Epiphanius of Salamis: Book 1 (Sects 1–46)*, trans. Frank Williams, vol. 63 (Leiden: Brill, 2009), 88.
[152] James Ussher (1581–1656) was Archbishop of Armagh, Ireland, and professor of Theological Controversies at Trinity College, Dublin. In 1644, he published two treatises on the epistles of Ignatius of Antioch. Tuckney was referring to Ussher's comments on John 17:3. Ussher wrote: 'Qui enim *verus* Deus est, ut *solus* Deus agnoscatur necesse est: quum in primo *ente* illud *unum* & *verum* primarium habere locum Metaphysici; & in divinae essentiae attributis, particulam illam *solum*, personarum nullam in unâ & indivisâ illâ naturâ subsistentium, sed creaturas tantùm, & idola, & quicquid ab infinitâ illâ essentiâ est diversum excludere, nos doceant Theologi'. Ussher, 'De Diaboli ignorantiâ, & persona Filii Dei, doctrina Pseudo Clementis Constitutionibus & Pseudo-Ignatii epistolâ ad Philippenses tradita, proponitur & expenditure', in *In Polycarpianam epistolarum Ignatianarum syllogen annotationes* (Oxford: 1644), chap. 12, unpaginated. See also Alan Ford, 'Ussher, James (1581–1656)', *ODNB*.
[153] Ignatius, Bishop of Antioch (35–107), was one of the Apostolic Fathers and known for writing seven letters during his journey as a prisoner en route to Rome, where he faced execution on account of his beliefs.
[154] This refers to Francis Lucas 'of Bruges' (1548/49–1619), a Flemish, Catholic theologian whose *Notationes in Sacra Biblia* (1580) examined textual issues in the Vulgate. Tuckney was reading his commentary on John. There, Lucas wrote: 'Non ergo persona excluditur, sed natura, id est, creatura omnis & quidquid est alterius quomodocumque naturae: docetur enim sola una numero esse credenda divina natura (tametsi communis tribus personis) & unus solus Deus, in quo tamen tres personae contineantur. Quocircà deos idoláque gentium signanter excludit dictiuncula *solus*, quibus vel nulla vel non illa natura est quae est Deo Patri'. Franciscus Lucas Brugensis, *In Sacrosancta Quatuor Iesu Christi Evangelia*, vol. 4 (Antwerp: 1616), 158. See Antonio Gerace, 'Francis Lucas 'of Bruges' and Textual Criticism of the Vulgate Before and After the Sixto-Clementine (1592)', *Journal of Early Modern Christianity* 3.2 (2016): 201–37.

called'.¹⁵⁵ Chrysostom concurs: 'To distinguish him from those who are not true gods'.¹⁵⁶ Theophylact (as usual) follows him: 'By distinguishing him from the false gods among the Gentiles, he does not separate himself from the Father. Far from it!'¹⁵⁷ But citation from the Fathers is useless when we address the Socinians, who simultaneously repudiate the ancient Fathers and the ancient faith. Let us see, then, whether we are able to achieve something in this matter by means of reason (which is their Helena¹⁵⁸) and seek it from Holy Scripture. Indeed, this seems to prove the true meaning of these words.

1. From a very similar text (1 Thessalonians 1:9) where the Apostle says, 'And how you turned to God from idols (or as Beza puts it, 'leaving idols')¹⁵⁹ to serve the living and true God'. There as well as here, 'true God' occurs. But if a reason is sought as to why he is called 'true God', what is kept silent here is clearly explained in that passage, namely that he is contrasted with idols, to whom they had given their letter of divorce as soon as they turned to God, [Page 10] who is, therefore, called living and true, because all their gods were false and most of them were dead. On this text, Theodoretus¹⁶⁰ comments as follows: 'Comparing him not with the Son but with those who are not gods, he called him who is, living and true, living inasmuch as they are not living, while true inasmuch as they are falsely called gods'.¹⁶¹

2. The reason that proves this can be taken from this very verse that we have in our hands, namely from its purpose and context here. In the previous verse, Christ had asserted that 'all authority had been given to him over all flesh', that is, not only over Jews but also over Gentiles. Of these the Jews had completely rejected Christ as the only way to eternal life but the latter were indeed devoted to the full-scale

---

¹⁵⁵ This quote comes from Basil's Letter 8. See Saint Basil, *Letters: Volume I (1–185)*, in *The Fathers of the Church*, trans. Sister Agnes Clare Way C.D.P., vol. 13 (Washington, D.C.: The Catholic University of America Press, 1981), 25–6.
¹⁵⁶ Chrysostom noted: 'He said "the only true God" to differentiate Him from the gods that do not exist. And He did so because He was about to send them to the Gentiles'. Chrysostom, *Commentary on Saint John the Apostle and Evangelist: Homilies 48–88*, 371.
¹⁵⁷ This quotation can be found here: Theophylact, *Theophylacti Archiepiscopi Bulgariae: Commentarii in Quator Evangelia* (Paris: 1635), 796.
¹⁵⁸ In Greek mythology, Helen of Troy was the exemplar of female beauty. Tuckney compared the Socinian perspective of the faculty of reason to the cherished woman.
¹⁵⁹ See Beza, *Annotationes*, 2:423.
¹⁶⁰ Born in Antioch, Theodoret of Cyrus (393–457) played a pivotal role in the Christological debates of the fifth century, representing the Antiochene party. He was partly behind the production of the Chalcedonian Definition.
¹⁶¹ See Theodoret, *Beati Theodoreti, Cyprensis Episcopi, Theologi Vertustissimi, Operum*, vol. 2 (Cologne: 1573), 141.

worship of many of their false gods. Christ provides healing for both groups (as I said earlier). For the Jews, it is in recognition of Jesus Christ whom they had thus far rejected. But for the Gentiles, it is in saving knowledge and worship of the only true God, leaving behind their many false gods whom they previously worshipped in a remarkable state of blindness. Even Crellius himself does not deny that this provides the reason for these words.[162] Hence it is quite evident from the genuine meaning of the verse that this word 'only' is contrasted with many gods, whereas the word 'true' is contrasted with false gods, and thus these are either exclusively or chiefly excluded. Or, to take it more broadly, creatures, or all things, or their images that are not the true God are excluded. However, the Son is never excluded, who is in the Father (John 14:10), one with the Father (John 10:30), and who is God (John 1:1). For 'only' is one who is not with another. But what prevents him from being able to be with himself? But the very same God the Father is with the Son. With respect to 'person', 'another' is the word used in John 5:32. 'Another' is he who testifies about me. With respect to 'nature', God is entirely the same or if by some other reasoning he can be called 'only', yet in this sense (that is, with respect to divinity), he will never be alone. Therefore, from the fact that the Father is called the 'only true God', it no more follows that the Son is not likewise the 'true God' than, conversely, from the fact that the Son is said to be the true Light in John 1:9, it can be inferred that the Father is not the Light nor the true Light. As Theophylact rightly says, 'So is the Father, then, false light? Far from it'.[163] In that passage, what is said about the Son alone is shared with the Father. Here, on account of the communion of the same nature, what is solely attributed to the Father is shared equally by the Son. This is true here and also frequently elsewhere. In Romans 16:27, 'the only wise God' is mentioned. But Christ will not as a result be unwise, he who is the very Wisdom of God. Also, God alone is said to have immortality (1 Tim. 6:16).[164] Shall Christ, then, still be subject to death, when he testifies about himself thus: 'I am the living one, but I was dead, and behold, I am alive for evermore, Amen'? Away with these blasphemous absurdities. 'Truly, these things are preposterous', as Theophylact comments very piously.[165]

---

[162] See Crell, *Two Books*, 7.
[163] See Theophylact, *Theophylacti Archiepiscopi Bulgariae*, 797.
[164] Tuckney was likely reading Maldonatus here. Cf. Maldonatus, *Joannis Maldonati*, 506.
[165] See Theophylact, *Theophylacti Archiepiscopi Bulgariae*, 797.

What therefore oppresses the Socinians, what their Smalcius and his followers have conceded and declared, is that when the word 'only' and the particles signifying the same thing are spoken about God, they never exclude those who are subordinate to God.[166] Oh good people, does that which does not exclude those who are subordinate to God ever exclude Christ the Son? Although Christ is subordinate to God, insofar as he is a man, insofar as he is the Son (something which the Socinians blaspheme against) he existed from eternity and will be consubstantial and ὁμοούσιος [of the same substance][167] with the Father into eternity.

[Page 11] In fact, this is what Oecolampadius[168] intended when he said that in this verse the whole Trinity is understood under the name Father, and I am of pretty much the same view. For although (as I said earlier) I readily concede that the pronoun 'you' in this verse is understood of the Father, and that the name 'Father' in the first verse should be taken personally (as Zanchius[169] and others wish it to be), yet I would like it to be understood in such a way that the Son and Holy Spirit are not excluded, since they have one and the same nature, essence and shared divinity.

Objection

Nor does that which the adversaries are accustomed to object, do anything to the contrary; namely, that by this reasoning, Christ is praying to himself.

---

[166] It is very likely that Tuckney derived this observation from Gerhard, who in turn quoted Socinians: 'Socinus, *Miscell.*, p. 273: "When the word 'only' and the words meaning the same thing are said with reference to God, they never exclude those who are subordinate to Him". In his response to part 1 of Smiglecki, c. 2, p. 14, Schmalz writes as follows about Matt. 4:10: "Christ is not excluding Himself when He cites these words from the Law: 'You shall serve God alone' ". Socinus, *Epist. Ad Radecc.*, p. 149: "When the word 'only' and the words meaning the same thing are spoken concerning God, they never exclude those who are subordinate to Him" '. Gerhard, 'On the Unity of the Divine Essence', chap. 6, sec. 100. See also Crell, *Two Books*, 4.

[167] The word ὁμοούσιος (*homoousios*) or consubstantial was the term used by Athanasius against Arius at the Council of Nicaea. Its Nicene usage meant the equality of the Father and Son. See 'homoousios' in Muller, *Dictionary*.

[168] Johannes Oecolampadius (1482–1531) was a German theologian and leading Reformer of the Swiss Reformation. Oecolampadius believed that, according to John 17:3, the name 'Father' refers not simply to the person of the Father but the Godhead of the Father, Son, and Spirit: 'Loquitur hic ut Paulus in salutationibus suis, qui dixit: Gratia nobis & pax &c. Coniungit dominum Iesum patri. Quid sibi autem velit Scriptura, scitote: nomine scilicet patris primum Deum ipsum cōmendari, non solum nomen personae, sed pro ipso Deo toto, qualiscunq; est. Unde, oratio quae hic sit, dirigitur ad totam divinitatem, quae est una, & in tribus personis subsistit: nam filium & Spiritum Sanctum quamvis ponamus in trinitate, nō tamen tres Deos dicimus esse'. Oecolampadius, *Annotationes piae ac doctae in Evangelium Ioannis* (Basel: 1553), fols. 310ʳ–311ʳ.

[169] See Zanchi, *De Tribus Elohim*, Liber 4, chap. 10, 142–3.

Solution

For here he does not pray as God, but either as a man (as many commentators believe) or rather insofar as he was our Mediator and High Priest (as some more sensible commentators believe). And so, when he addresses the Father, he includes all the persons of the Holy Trinity, who share one and the same common nature.

The sum of everything goes back to this: the word 'only' excludes idols, fictitious gods, and all creatures in general but not Jesus Christ, not the Son, nor any person of the Holy Trinity who is consubstantial with the Father. And this was the second response of the ancients, and this is particularly consistent with the piety, truth, and meaning of this verse.

The third response is mostly from recent scholars, namely, that this exclusive word 'only' does not define the pronoun 'you', with the sense being that only the Father is God. But rather the sense is that the name 'God' is the only true divinity, which is in the Father, from which the Son is not excluded, since he is consubstantial with the Father. This is the opinion of Lyra.[170]

This response should be given all the more attention because not only is it that of those scholars who are trained in the more elegant literature and languages, but also those who are well-versed in both Greek and Latin and their idioms. Among these, some say the following about that verse: 'The sense is not, "that they may know you who alone is the true God," but, 'that they may know you, who is that God, who alone is true.' [Note: Maldonatus][171]

The learned Beza speaks in a similar way. This sentence can be perverted, as if the Father alone were said to be the true God, so that the particle μόνον is constructed from the preceding part with the substantive verb necessarily implied, while the article τὸν placed before the particle indicates that this should be connected to the latter part with the verb, so that

---

[170] Nicholas of Lyra (1270–1349) was a Franciscan exegete whose *Postillae* (written between 1322–31) on the entire Bible was highly successful. It was printed with the *Glossa Ordinaria* (a twelfth-century glossed Bible) numerous times from the fifth century onwards. Tuckney was referring to Lyra's *Postilla* on John's Gospel. According to Lyra, the word 'only' does not determine that only the Father is God but that the Father is God. 'True divinity' is in both the Father and Son: 'Per hoc.n.non [*sic*] habetur, quod solus Pater sit Deus, & filius sit creatura, ut dicebat Arrius, quia haec dictio exclusiva solus, non determinat ly. te, ut sit sensus, quod solus pater sit Deus, sed determinat ly Deū. Et sensus, quod illa est sola deitas vera q̃ est in patre, & sicab ea nō excludit filius, sed magis includitur, qa una est deitas in utroq̃'. *Bibliorum Sacrorum cum Glossa Ordinaria*, 6 vols. (Venice, 1603), 5:1285. On the Glossa Ordinaria, see Lesley Smith, *The Glossa Ordinaria: The Making of a Medieval Bible Commentary* (Leiden: Brill, 2009).

[171] According to Maldonatus, *Joannis Maldonati*, 506, 'Non enim est sensus: *Ut cognoscant Te*, qui solus es verus Deus, *sed ut cognoscant Te*, qui es ille Deus, qui solus verus est'.

the Father is said to be the true God, who alone is, because he is one and utterly singular.[172] Similarly, the same article is also constructed with the same particle in Romans 16:27 and 1 Timothy 1:17, so that it is not 'you only' are the true God, but that 'you' are the only true God, that is, 'you are the one who is the only true God', as the Syriac interpreter[173] also translated it.

I realise, however, that this seems unconvincing to Calvin.[174] But with all due respect to such a great man,[175] it seems to have a good deal of substance to it. For these two propositions, 'You alone are the true God' and 'You are the only true God', differ greatly from each other.

1. Regarding the manner of the statement. In the former, the word 'alone' pertains to the subject of the proposition, whereas in the latter it pertains to the predicate of the proposition. This is immediately evident to anyone, as the article (τὸν) placed between σὲ[176] and μόνον ἀληθινὸν θεὸν[177] plainly indicates. For Christ does not say 'that they may know you only as the true God' but 'that they may know you the only true God'.

2. Regarding the meaning of the words. For if only the Father, taken personally, is called [Page 12] God, this would indeed have excluded the Son from the Godhead, according to the opinion of the Socinians. But since the Father is called the only true God, this just means that the Godhead, which is only true, is applicable to the Father. Yet, Christ is neither excluded from the truth of the matter nor by the manner of expression; for this reason, he is called 'my

---

[172] Tuckney derived this from Beza. See Beza, *Annotationes*, 1:432.

[173] The Renaissance resurgence in languages such as Chaldean, Aramaic, and Syriac influenced the Protestant use of non-biblical Jewish writings to understand the biblical text. See Henry M. Knapp, 'Revealing the Mind of God: Exegetical Method in the Seventeenth Century', in Jordan J. Ballor, David S. Sytsma, and Jason Zuidema (eds.) *Church and School in Early Modern Protestantism: Studies in Honor of Richard. A. Muller on Maturation of a Theological Tradition* (Leiden: Brill, 2013), 533–49.

[174] On 'the only true God', Calvin said: 'Some explain it, *That they may know thee, who alone art God*; but this is a poor interpretation. The meaning therefore is, *That they may know thee alone to be the true God*'. Calvin, *Commentary on the Gospel According to John*, 2:166–7.

[175] Although Tuckney referred to Calvin very positively throughout his lecture, this is evidence that Calvin was not normative for seventeenth-century Reformed figures. Indeed, pluriformity marks early modern Reformed theology. See Bruce Gordon and Carl R. Trueman, 'Introduction', in Gordon and Trueman (eds.) *The Oxford Handbook of Calvin and Calvinism* (Oxford: Oxford University Press, 2021), 1–25.

[176] The Greek word σὲ means 'you'.

[177] The Greek words μόνον ἀληθινὸν θεὸν mean 'only true God'.

partner' (יתי גֶּבֶר צָמ)[178] [Note: Geber Gnamithi][179] in Zechariah [1]3:7, as Piscator[180] translated very accurately, following Pagninus.[181] And by that expression he[182] means to imply the equality of Christ with God the Father, which Vatablus[183] also believes when he renders it as 'a man equal to me', and as the Chaldaean[184] interpreter

[178] This is how the Hebrew appears in Tuckney's text. It is likely a misspelling, intended to say: גֶּבֶר עֲמִיתִי. The intended spelling is confirmed by comparing a Hebrew text published in the same year as when Tuckney delivered his lecture. Brian Walton was arguably 'the greatest linguistic scholar of the age' and edited the London Polyglot Bible, printed between 1653 and 1657. Muller, *After Calvin*, 152. Walton's 1656 polyglot edition rendered the Hebrew of Zechariah 13:7 as: גֶּבֶר עֲמִיתִי. Brian Walton (ed.) *Biblia Sacra Polyglotta: Complectentia Textus Originales, Hebraicum, cum Pentateucho Samaritano, Chaldaicum, Graecum*, vol. 3 (London: Thomas Roycroft, 1656), 136.

[179] This is Tuckney's Latinised transliteration of the Hebrew.

[180] Born in Strasbourg, Johannes Piscator (1546–1625) was a Reformed theologian who taught in the exegetical department at the Academy in Herborn. Among his works is his *Aphorismi doctrinae christianae ex Instituione Calvini excerpti* (1589). He also translated the Bible into German and wrote Latin commentaries on the Old and New Testaments. His biblical commentaries reached 'the furthest corners of the Reformed world'. Howard Hotson, *Commonplace Learning: Ramism and Its German Ramifications, 1543–1630* (Oxford: Oxford University Press, 2007), 119. Commenting on Zechariah 13:7, Piscator noted that 'my neighbour' (*proximum meum*) or 'my partner' (*socium meum*) signifies the equality of Christ with the Father. Johannes Piscator, *Commentariorum in Omnes Libros Veteris Testamenti*. Tomus Quartus (Herbornae Nassoviorum, 1645), 505. On Piscator's exegetical methodology of the Old Testament, particularly of Zechariah, see G. Sujin Pak, *The Reformation of Prophecy: Early Modern Interpretations of the Prophet & Old Testament Prophecy* (Oxford: Oxford University Press, 2018), chap. 8.

[181] This refers to Santes Pagninus (1470–1541), a Dominican known for his Hebrew proficiency. His *Veteris et Novi Testamenti nova translatio* (1528) was widely successful, particularly among Protestants like Calvin and anti-Trinitarians like Michael Servetus. Pagninus focused on the text and grammar of Scripture, heavily engaged in rabbinical commentary, and translated the Bible literally. He used the same expression 'my partner' (*socium meum*) in Santes Pagninus, *Biblia Veteris ac Noui Testamenti* (Basileae: Per Thomam Guarinum, 1564), 685. On Pagninus, see Arjo Vanderjagt, 'Ad fontes! The Early Humanist Concern for the Hebraica veritas', in Magne Sæbø (ed.) *Hebrew Bible/Old Testament: The History of Its Interpretation*, vol. 2 (Göttingen: Vandenhoeck & Ruprecht, 2008), 185–9.

[182] Tuckney was referring to Piscator. See Piscator, *Commentariorum*, 505.

[183] This refers to Francis Vatablus (c. 1485–1547), the French regius professor of Old Testament at the Royal College of Paris. Tuckney might have been referring to the 1584 edition of the 'Vatable' Bible', in which 'socium meũ' ought to be understood as 'cōsubstātiāle'. That is to say, according to the 1584 annotation, 'my partner' implies the consubstantiality or co-equality of the Father and Son. *Biblia sacra cum duplici translatione, & scholijs Francisci Vatabli* (Salmanticae: Apud Gasparem à Portonariis suis & Guilielmi Rouillii, Benedictique; Boierii expensis, 1584), 211[b]. In 1545, Robert Estienne or Stephanus published a Latin Bible, containing the Vulgate text and annotations (or lecture notes as recorded by his students) by Vatablus. Estienne's second edition (1557) included the Old Testament translation by Pagninus with annotations by Vatablus, along with Theodore Beza's Latin translation of the New Testament. Published in Salamanca, the third edition (1584) was a revised version of Vatablus' annotations. See Alice Philena Hubbard, 'The Bible of Vatable', *Journal of Biblical Literature* 66.2 (1947): 197–209.

[184] The Chaldaean interpreter refers here to a Targum on Zechariah. In the seventeenth century, the two main Targums were Jonathan and Onkelos. See Stephen G. Burnett,

previously rendered as 'a similar partner' or as the Vulgate,[185] 'a man who cleaves to me',[186] that is, according to the divinity he is consubstantial with the Father, whereas according to his humanity he is closely related and very similar to him, given that he is intimately joined to God, given their hypostatic union.

But if I may return to the point from which I have digressed somewhat, I venture to affirm boldly that these two propositions, 'only the Father is the true God' and 'the Father is the only true God', differ greatly from each other. Certainly, I do not deny that propositions of this kind, based on the common subject matter and with a less accurate method of speaking, collapse and convey the same meaning. For instance, if I say, 'You only are my heir' and 'You are my only heir', I perhaps mean the same thing in both cases. But examples can be given in which such propositions differ greatly from each other. For example, when a small piece of some pure gold is shown, if I say, 'This only is pure gold', it can be the same as if I had said, 'This piece alone contains in itself all that exists of pure gold anywhere'. But if I say the following, 'This is the only pure gold', I only mean that this small piece, by its nature and shape, is true pure gold, which exists along with the other small pieces of its kind. In exactly the same way, the Father is here called the only true God, because without doubt he possesses in himself the only true Godhead, although it is shared with the Son and the Holy Spirit.

But in order for me to finally complete this third response, I will add another point of importance: if the particles τὸν μόνον do not refer to the words that follow, but to the words that precede:

1. This article τὸν would be inserted inappropriately. Indeed, if it had been written in this way, 'that they may know you only', the verse would flow very neatly and quite smoothly. However, if it were as follows, 'that they may know you the only', as the Socinians prefer, the construction of the words would actually be displeasing to the ears, or at least poorly adapted to Greek usage.

'The Targum in Christian Scholarship to 1800', in Alberdina Houtman, Eveline van Staalduine-Sulman, and Hans-Martin Kim (eds.) *A Jewish Targum in a Christian World* (Leiden: Brill, 2014), 250–65.

[185] The Vulgate Bible is a Latin translation of the Bible, compiled by Saint Jerome (347–420) in the late fourth to early fifth centuries. The Council of Trent sanctioned the Latin Vulgate as the authoritative Bible.

[186] According to the 1598 Clementine Vulgate, Zechariah 13:7 reads as: 'Framea, suscitare super pastorem meum, et super *virum cohaerentem mihi*, dicit Dominus exercituum: percute pastorem, et dispergentur oves: et convertam manum meam ad parvulos'. *Biblia Sacra juxta Vulgatam Clementinam*, Editio Electronica, ed. Michaele Tweedale (Londoni, 2005), 1197. Emphasis added.

2. Considering this reasoning, just as the place of the article would not be sufficiently correct, so the article itself would be less emphatic, which, however, the Socinians are very much in favour of, as it would denote the highest (their favourite term) God. But if it refers to the previous words, it would be merely relative, and it would have nothing emphatic in itself. That is enough about the third response.

[Note: See Catop. on 2 Peter 1:2. Masius on John 6:2, page 101–2.[187] Also, see Calvin, *Institutes*, Book 1, chapter 13, section 26.[188] It designates the Father as the creator but to be known salvifically in Christ the Redeemer. See Calvin, *Institutes*, Book 2, chapter 6, section 1.][189] The fourth response, and the final and most genuine of all (as far as I can understand), and the most suitable for this verse and many others (especially in the Epistles of St. Paul) is this, namely, that Christ said this not precisely as God, but either as man or as our Mediator and High Priest. In this sense, he certainly distinguishes himself from God, but does not disunite himself, or even separate himself. For as regards eternal life or happiness, with which we are here concerned, two things in particular ought to be noted: the end, in which there will finally be rest, and the means by which that end must be reached. The end [Page 13] is God, according to the words of the Apostle (1 Cor. 15:28), where it is said that after Christ has handed over his kingdom to the Father, God will be all in all. But the means by which we make our way to that place and finally reach that end is Christ, the Mediator, or, to use his own testimony, 'I am the way and the truth and the life. No one comes to the Father except through me' (John 14:6). Christ clearly distinguishes these two things here. The Father, together with the Son and the Holy Spirit, is the only true God, whom we delight in as our end. Jesus

---

[187] The Latin reads as: 'Vide Catop. in 2 Per. 1. 2. Masium in Joh. 6. 2. pag. 101. 102'. It is unclear what or who 'Catop.' and 'Masium' refer to here.

[188] On John 17:3, Calvin said: '[W]hen a comparison of one person is made with another, the name of God is not to be taken without particularization, but restricted to the Father, seeing that he is the beginning of deity, not in the bestowing of essence, as fanatics babble, but by reason of order. In this sense is to be understood that saying of Christ to the Father [in John 17:3]...For speaking in the person of the Mediator, he holds a middle rank between God and man; yet his majesty is not on this account diminished. For even though he emptied himself [Phil. 2. 2:7], he lost not his glory with the Father which was hidden to the world...Moreover, I wonder what these makers of new gods mean when, having confessed Christ as true God, they immediately exclude him from the deity of the Father. As if he could be true God and not be one God, and as if a divinity transfused were anything but a newfangled fiction'. John Calvin, *Institutes of the Christian Religion*, ed. John T. McNeill, trans. and indexed by Ford Lewis Battles, 2 vols. (Louisville: WJK, 1960; reissued 2006), book 1, chap. 13, sec. 26.

[189] Calvin argued here the idea that all knowledge of God the Creator would be useless without faith in Christ the Redeemer. See Calvin, *Institutes of the Christian Religion*, book 2, chap. 6, sec. 1.

Christ as Mediator is the only means by which we are led to the true God and thus to eternal life. It is in accordance with this economy of the Mediator that (if at all) he here distinguishes himself from the true God. This is also abundantly clear from those inserted words 'whom you have sent'. For the mission of Christ pertains to the work of the Mediator, and it is this work for which he was sent. Granted, then, that God is in the God-man, and Christ as Mediator is true God according to his other nature, with regard to this mission and both the office and the work of the Mediator, he distinguishes himself from God considered absolutely and simply in himself. As I understand it, here is the genuine meaning of these words. 'And this is eternal life, that they may know you, the only true God, and Jesus Christ whom you have sent'. These words contain the essence of all theology, namely that all our happiness is based on this, that we may know the only true God by true faith, but only through Jesus Christ, our only Mediator.

In exactly the same way, Paul often distinguishes Christ from the Father and from God, while joining them together, specifically with regard to the dispensation of the Mediator. Thus, 'there is one God and one Mediator between God and men, the man Jesus Christ' (1 Tim. 2:5). 'There is one God, the Father, and one Lord, Jesus Christ' (1 Cor. 8:6). 'The kingdom of Christ and God' (Eph. 5:5). And there are many other similar texts. All these texts certainly do not prove that the Son is not God, but that Christ is God manifested in the flesh, our Mediator and High Priest, who emptied himself for our salvation, and died for us, removing the sins and penalties of us all by taking them upon himself. And so he is the only means, the only way through which access to the Father, to heaven, and to eternal life is open to us.

To summarise: When it is a question of eternal life, this comes to us by the Father through Christ, from the Father, the Son and the Spirit, the Triune and only true God, through the merits and obedience of our Mediator Jesus Christ, whom he sent. Thus, it seems to me and to others along with me, that this is the genuine meaning of this verse. It is necessary, therefore, to believe in the true God, which relates to faith in divinity. It is also necessary to believe in Jesus Christ, which relates to faith in the dispensation, according to Cardinal Toletus.[190] But the eminent Calvin

---

[190] The Jesuit Cardinal Toletus (1532–96) taught theology and philosophy at the Roman College. According to Toletus, '*Haec est autem vita aeterna*, non formalem sensum, sed causalem facit, nempe haec est causa vitae aeternae, & hac sola vita consequenda est; nempe fide divinitatis, & mysterio dispensationis, ut credatur Deus, & credatur Christus: articuli enim fidei ad haec duo reducuntur ad vertitatem divinitatis, & ad mysterium incarnationis Christi, per quam redemptio perfecta est: sine qua fide nemo vitam habet aeternam'. Toletus, *In Sacrosanctum Joannis Evangelium* (Rome: 1588), 313–14.

states this beautifully, as usual: 'It must always be remembered what character Christ represents in this verse. We must not consider his eternal divinity alone (which he establishes, however, in the next verse when he speaks about the glory that he had with the Father before the world existed), because he speaks here as God manifested in the flesh and according to his office as Mediator'.[191] This is what Calvin says. Certainly, according to the divine economy, he makes a distinction here between himself and the Father, and indeed elsewhere he recognises that the Father is greater than himself (John 14:28). He prays to the Father here and elsewhere, and he refers everything that he has received to the Father (John 10:28–9). Without the Father he says that he can do nothing (John 5:19). He receives the Father's orders (John. 5:36). He is ordered (John 14:31), taught (John 8:28), sanctified and sent (John 10:36) by the Father. Many other examples also occur in different places, similar to these. [Page 14] It is not implied in any of these passages that, as the Son, he was not the same God as the Father, but that he, as our Mediator according to the mutual plan entered into between them from eternity, undertook and accomplished everything that pertains to the office of sponsor, to the illumination of God's glory, and to the aim of reconciling divine love to us. It was for this purpose that he submitted himself to the Father, always speaking about the Father with respect and about himself with true modesty. And that is why in this verse (as Maldonatus notes)[192] he spoke in the third person. He attributes all things to the glory of the Father (that is, to God), ascribing everything, both doctrine and signs (as Euthymius[193] says), to him. And so no one should be surprised that he draws a distinction between himself and the Father here in some respect (that is, to this extent), if he even does do so. Some people do not agree with this.

On the other hand, there are indeed others who have attempted something more, in that they want Christ here not only as the true Mediator but also as the eternal Son of God to be distinct from the Father. [Note:

---

[191] See Calvin, *Commentary on the Gospel According to John*, 2:165.

[192] Maldonatus underscored Christ's modesty in how he addressed his Father as God while refraining from calling himself God. Christ did not say 'that they may know you and me' (*Ut cognoscant Te et me*), but 'that they may know you, and Jesus Christ whom you have sent' (*Ut cognoscant Te et, quem misisti, Jesum*). Maldonatus added that Christ's use of the third person here demonstrates greater modesty compared to the first person. Maldonatus, *Joannis Maldonati*, 506: '…per tertiam personam de se ipso loquens, quod majoris modestiae, quam se ipsum, cum de rebus agitur honorificis, qualis haec erat, nominare'. Crell also cited Maldonatus' point here about Christ's modesty in not calling himself God to support his anti-Trinitarian interpretation of John 17:3. See Crell, *Two Books*, 12.

[193] Born in Melitene, Armenia, Euthymius the Great (377–473) was a monk and priest, and supported Chalcedonian orthodoxy.

Theodorus, Heracleon[194]] For they think that the Father is also understood personally and, as such, can be called 'only true' because of a particular attribute or in relation to the Son and Holy Spirit, namely, because of his unbegottenness, that he is not born, neither generated nor proceeding from any other person. On the contrary, among the persons of the Holy Trinity, he is the fountain of divinity, and to him that fontal divinity belongs, as some like to term it. Maldonatus believes that this interpretation is rather bold, and perhaps not without cause.[195] Certainly, Gerhard[196] considers it to be dangerous, as on account of the order of the persons alone, only the Father is called the true God, since it either conflicts with the truth of the matter or at least appears to conflict with the consubstantiality of the persons. As far as I am concerned, I admit that this is certainly rather difficult and less consistent with the analogy of faith. Also, I do not deny (as he fears) that it could be misleading, at least for the less well-educated and the less discerning regarding the consubstantiality of the most sacred persons. I will therefore pass over this, namely (to say the bare minimum), as it is by no means necessary for the interpretation of this verse, and I am also afraid that it is completely unrelated to it. For it does not deny that Jesus Christ as the Son of the Father is the true God, but it says that as Mediator he is sent by the Father, and to that extent, he is distinct from him. Calvin, in whose footsteps I prefer to follow, speaks about this beautifully, and it is with his words that I will conclude everything on this point: 'Because God is not known except in the face of Christ, who is the living and express image of the Father, for this reason it is said, "that they may know you and Christ, whom you have sent" '.[197] And elsewhere Calvin says: 'The explanation is easy: Christ, appearing in the form of a man, makes known under the person of the Father the power, essence, and glory of God. There is, then, one true God, the Father of Christ, that is that God who promised long ago a Redeemer for the world. But in Christ the unity and truth of the Godhead is found. Christ was

---

[194] This is a reference to Theodore, Bishop of Heraclea (c. 328–55), a non-Nicene figure whose commentary on John's Gospel exists in fragments. Probably by consulting Maldonatus' commentary on John, Tuckney referred to the surviving fragment on John 17:3. Here, Theodore noted: 'Ἀληθινὸν θεὸν λέγει τὸν πατέρα ὡς ἀγέννητον, οὐ μὴν ἑαυτὸν ἐκβάλλει τοῦ εἶναι θεόν· θεὸς γὰρ καὶ ὁ μονογενής, ἀλλὰ γεννηθεὶς ἐκ θεοῦ. τοῦτο δὲ εἰπὼν τὸ τῆς ἀληθείας ἡμᾶς ἐδίδαξε δόγμα'. *Fragmenta in Joannem*, no. 331, in Joseph Reuss, *Johannes-Kommentare aus der griechischen Kirche*, TU 89 (Berlin: Akademie Verlag, 1966), 152. See also Matthew R. Crawford, 'On the Diversity and Influence of the Eusebian Alliance: The Case of Theodore of Heraclea', *Journal of Ecclesiastical History* 64.2 (2013): 227–57.
[195] See Maldonatus, *Joannis Maldonati*, 505.
[196] See Johann Gerhard, 'Deo Deo Patre et Aeterno ejus Filio', in *Locorum Theologicorum... Tomus Primus* (Jena: 1610), 421–2.
[197] See Calvin, *Commentary on the Gospel According to John*, 2:166.

humbled so that he might raise us on high. When we reach that point, then his divine majesty displays itself. Then it is perceived that he is wholly in the Father and that the Father is wholly in him. In summary, he who separates Christ from the divinity of the Father does not yet acknowledge him who is the only true God, but rather creates for himself a foreign god'.[198]

And thus, we finally complete the fourfold response to the Socinian argument against the divinity of Christ, although drawn unwillingly from this verse. Since this argument is the chief one and, as they believe, an Achilles heel, we wanted to refute it at greater length. The remaining arguments are lightly armoured soldiers and easy to refute. These were the three arguments that seem (at least to the Socinians) to fight against the divinity of Christ in this verse.

[Page 15] 1. Because he prays to God the Father

2. Because he asks that he be glorified by the Father; in the previous verses.

3. Because in this passage he confesses that he was sent by the Father.

All of which (as they determine) speak of a man or a creature, denying that he is God.

But if these points are made and understood according to the economy, as will soon be clear, how, I ask, will they damage the divinity of Christ in the end?

Let us deal with each point separately, and do so briefly.

1. He prays humbly to the Father. But if he prays as a man, and that in a state of humiliation, are we to deny that he is God by virtue of him being a man and acting in a manner appropriate for a man, when we believe that he is the God-man, that he is both truly God and truly human. But the beloved and bosom disciple of Christ taught us better, who, when he was [leaning] on the bosom of Christ, got to know and explained very well what was in him, when he united these two distinct natures, even though they were indissolubly opposed to each other. 'The Word became flesh and dwelt among us, and we have seen his glory, glory as of the only begotten from the Father, full of grace and truth' (John 1:14). And this word 'as' (*quasi*) means the Caph of 'truth' (אמת),[199] as the Hebrews usually express it.

---

[198] See Calvin, *Commentary on the Gospel According to John*, 2:167.

[199] The Hebrew letter Caph or Kaph denotes the meaning of likeness or resemblance. This is known as the *kaph veritatis*. See Bruce K. Waltke and Michael Patrick O'Connor (eds.) *An Introduction to Biblical Hebrew Syntax* (Winona Lake: Eisenbrauns, 1990), 202–3. Sometimes the letter 'is used in partic. to compare an object with the *class* to which it belongs, and express its correspondence with the idea which it ought to realize'. Francis Brown, Samuel Rolles Driver, and Charles Augustus Briggs (eds.) *A Hebrew and English*

As Chrysostom very rightly says, 'The word 'as' does not imply resemblance or similarity, but confirmation'.[200] It affirms not just that he is similar to the only-begotten of the Father but that he is the very only-begotten of the Father himself. If, however, he prayed not only as a man but (as I rather believe), as our Mediator and High Priest, will this divine economy detract from his divinity? Certainly not. For it was part of the office of the Priest not only to pray, but also to sacrifice, and to expiate the sins of the people through sacrifice. Although he could have prayed as a mere man, yet in order to expiate our sins and satisfy divine justice by the sacrifice of his death, divinity was certainly required. Hence it is necessary that our High Priest both prays and atones as the God-man, as both truly human and truly God. The human and divine natures are truly bound up together, and the prayer is composed by both, as Cyril correctly notes on this matter.[201] [Note: [Cyril] on John, Book 11, chapter 17.] For just as there is a twofold nature in the Mediator, so there is in the prayer that which indicates both natures. The humble aspects and the submission towards the Father that are present in this prayer belong to Christ according to his human nature. However, there are other higher and magnificent aspects that reveal the divine nature. To die is characteristic of a human, but to die for humanity is characteristic of the Mediator, who is both human and God. So, 'to pray' smacks of a human, but what he prays to obtain is the clearest evidence of divinity. Pouring forth requests sounds humble, but making those requests as one who mediates, reconciles, and obtains declares that he is God. And so it is that even though the Socinians consider it paradoxical for Christ himself to pray, yet orthodox Fathers believe that there is nothing absurd about Christ both requesting and granting the same thing, according to one nature and then another. [Note: Athanasius, *Orations Against the Arians*. 'It is marvelous that what the Son [gives] with

---

Lexicon of the Old Testament: With an Appendix Containing the Biblical Aramaic, Based on the Lexicon of Wilhelm Gesenius as translated by Edward Robinson (Boston: Houghton Mifflin, 1906), 454. See also Antoon Schoors, *The Preacher Sought to Find Pleasing Words: A Study of the Language of Qoheleth* (Leuven: Peeters, 1992), 110; Edward Robinson (ed.) *A Hebrew and English Lexicon of the Old Testament: Including the Biblical Chaldee*, 4th edn. (Boston: Crocker and Brewster, 1850), 441.

[200] Chrysostom explained that 'the word "as" in this context does not express likeness or comparison, but affirms and unmistakably defines, as if he said: "We saw glory such as it was fitting and probable for Him to have who is the only-begotten and true Son of God, the King of all things"'. Chrysostom, *Commentary on Saint John the Apostle and Evangelist, Homilies 1–47*, 112.

[201] On John 17:4–5, Cyril noted: 'Once again he combines the human with the divine, and his statement sort of mixes them together, looking at both, neither raising the person of the speaker to the full authority and glory of God, nor allowing it to stay completely within the confines of human nature. No, he mixes both into one, which is foreign to nothing in the statement'. Cyril, *Commentary on John*, 2:274–5.

the Father, he also receives from himself'.]²⁰² 'What the Son of God in the form of a servant received from the Father, he himself also gave in the form of God'.²⁰³ This is what Leo²⁰⁴ says in Epistle 41. 'Just as the man received by grace from the Godhead that which he naturally possesses as God, so too he himself, as man, receives from himself as from God'. This is what Cyril says in his *Thesaurus*, Book 8, chapter 1.²⁰⁵ To this one may add Bernard's²⁰⁶ Sermon 76 on the Song of Songs: 'What is in the power of the petitioner to receive is freely sought. Therefore, the petition of the Son is dispensatory, not necessary, for he gives with the Father whatever he receives from the Father'.²⁰⁷ The fact that he prays to God as a man, as Mediator, in no way detracts from his divinity, for the very thing that he prays for as Mediator, as the God-man, he has earned and, insofar as he is God, he has given it. This was the first point.

[Page 16] The second point was that he prayed to be glorified by the Father. But this concerns us less. For if the prayer does not diminish his divinity, much less does glorification diminish his divinity. 1. To be glorified does not diminish his divinity and 2. to be glorified by the Father does not diminish his divinity.

1. To be glorified does not diminish his divinity. In this there is nothing unworthy of God, to whom all glory is given according to merit. 'Worthy are you, Lord, to receive glory and honour' (Rev. 4:11).

[202] According to Athanasius, 'Δῆλον δέ, καὶ οὐκ ἂν ἀμφιβάλοι τις, ὅτι ἃ δίδωσιν ὁ Πατήρ, διὰ τοῦ Υἱοῦ δίδωσι. Καὶ ἔστι παράδοξον καὶ ἐκπλῆξαι δυνάμενον ἀληθῶς· ἣν γὰρ δίδωσιν ὁ Υἱὸς παρὰ τοῦ Πατρὸς χάριν, ταύτην αὐτὸς ὁ Υἱὸς λέγεται "δέχεσθαι." καὶ τὴν ὕψωσιν, ἣν ὁ Υἱὸς παρὰ τοῦ Πατρὸς ποιεῖ, ταύτην ὡς αὐτὸς ὑψούμενός' ἐστιν ὁ Υἱός'. Saint Athanasius, *The Orations of St. Athanasius Against the Arians according to the Benedictine Text: With an Account of his Life by William Bright* (Oxford: Clarendon Press, 1873), Oration 1.45, 47.

[203] This quote can be found here: Pope Leo, 'Ad Episcopos per Palestinam constitutos, epistola', in *D. Leonis Papae, huius nominis primi, qui merito summo Magni cognomē iam olim obtinet, Epistolae decretales ac familiares, quae quidem hactenus reperirii potuerunt omnes* (Cologne: 1548), chap. lxxxiii.

[204] Leo the Great (400–61) was Bishop of Rome and opposed Eutyches and Nestorius. His Christology is encapsulated in his *Tome* (449), a letter whose content was accepted by the Council of Chalcedon (451).

[205] According to a sixteenth-century Latin publication, Cyril wrote: 'Ut homo igitur per gratiā à deitate accipit ut homo, quae ut Deus naturaliter habet. Quare à se quoque ipso ut à Deo ipsemet accipit ut homo'. Cyril of Alexandria, *Thesaurus adversus haereticos*, in *Divi Cyrilliar Chiepiscopi Alexandrini Operum... Tomus Secundus* (Cologne: 1546), Lib. 8, chap. 1.

[206] Bernard of Clairvaux (1090–1153) was a Cistercian monk who opposed the Trinitarian theology of Peter Abelard in 1141 and Gilbert de la Porrée in 1148. He is also known for his sermons on the Song of Songs.

[207] See Sermon 76 in Saint Bernard, *Cantica Canticorum: Eighty-six Sermons on the Song of Solomon*, trans. Samuel J. Eales (London: Paternoster, 1895), 469.

This may be said without specific reference. But let us treat it more specifically. This glorification, as it is understood here, says two things, and includes the thing itself and knowledge of it; in other words, the true bestowal of glory and, furthermore, its manifestation. Christ asks for both here, but he asks for one according to one nature and the other according to his other nature. [Note: Brugensis][208]

With respect to his human nature, he asks for the true bestowal of glory. For while he was still 'a worm and not a man, the reproach of men and the contempt of the people' [Note: Psalm 22:6; Isa. 53], and his own ignominious death was approaching, all that was left of the little spark of glory was to be completely extinguished, so to speak. He prays that by support in death, resurrection from the dead after death, and ascension to heaven, there will be true granting of glory for the human nature that was so despised. But how does this detract from his divinity or his essential glory? For it is the same Christ who, 'being put to death in the flesh, was made alive in the spirit' [Note: 1 Peter 3:18], and who, with respect to the human nature, was 'the most abject of men', according to the Prophet (Isaiah 53:3). With respect to this divine nature, according to the Apostle, he may most deservedly be understood as 'the Lord of glory' (1 Cor. 2:8).

But with regard to his divine nature, he very rightly asks to be glorified, not indeed with respect to a new bestowal of glory, since there can be absolutely no addition to his essential glory for it is already infinite in itself, but in terms of the manifestation of that essential glory, which was actually veiled in his incarnation, and seemed wholly extinguished and buried in the darkness of death. But what is obscured is not immediately and completely lost. It is not the case with the Father's glory so why then with the Son's? He does not deny that the Father is God, who defends his glory from the blasphemous insults of men. Nor does Christ, then, divest himself of the Godhead when he asks that his divine majesty, previously obscured, should at last be made openly manifest. Rather, we must note two things to the contrary from this text.

1. The chief point of Christ (which he was willing to undergo for our sake) was the self-emptying and wonderful descent of the Son of God, so that the glory of his divinity was obscured in such a way that its manifestation was needed. Behold, then, to what point the humility of Christ descended!
2. The ingratitude of the Socinians is utterly detestable, seeing that because the eternal Son of God was made man for us, they wrongly conclude that for that reason he is not God in himself. For they even

---

[208] See Brugensis, *In Sacrosancta Quatuor Iesu Christi Evangelia*, 157–9.

try to strip him of divinity itself because he was willing to hide the highest glory of his divinity under a veil of flesh and death for a while, for the sake of our salvation. Behold, then, to what heights the arrogant shamelessness of ungrateful men ascends!

It is good, however, and it will serve to close their blasphemous mouths forever, that although he asks to be glorified by the Father in verse 1, which leads them to dare to deny that he is God, he still wants to be glorified with the glory that he had with the Father before the world existed (verse 5), which (as will be clear later) declares him to be the eternal God. There is nothing, therefore, in the fact that he is glorified that detracts from his glorious divinity, which was the first point.

[Page 17] 2. But does the fact that he asks to be glorified by the Father express some inferiority, thereby detracting from his divinity?

Certainly not. For if we consider the phraseology of Scripture as well as common usage, not only can someone superior glorify someone, but an equal can also glorify an equal, a person can glorify himself and indeed an inferior can glorify a superior.

The Holy Spirit glorifies the Son (John 16:14), but this text does not imply that the Spirit is superior to the Son, even according to the Socinians.

The Son also glorifies the Father, as in that passage when he said at first, 'Father, glorify your Son' (John 17:1), and immediately added, 'that the Son may glorify you'. And again in verse 4: 'I have glorified you on earth' (John 17:4). But even according to their interpretation, this would not imply that the Father is inferior to the Son.

Indeed, we, the lowest of all, can and ought to glorify the supreme God. Therefore, 'let your light shine before people, so that they may see your good works and glorify your Father who is in heaven' (Matt. 5:16). But from this verse an earthly person will not be able to equal, let alone ever surpass the heavenly Father.

But perhaps some may say that, although the syntax or manner of speech does not require it, the sense of this verse demands that the Father does not glorify the Son in the same way that we glorify God. We willingly acknowledge that it is not entirely in the same way, and yet it is not dissimilar in every respect.

For inasmuch as glorification is the real bestowal of glory, we are indeed unable to glorify God, in the way the Father glorified Christ, but as a man according to whom we recognise him as inferior to the Father.

But inasmuch as glorification is the manifestation of glory, so we too glorify God, and in that way the Father glorified Christ as man, indeed as God. But the one who reveals the Son to be God does not deny that he is God.

One may also add that just as the Father glorified Christ, so too did Christ glorify himself, certainly not by seizing for himself the highest purity as the man of honour (Heb. 5:5), but by clearly demonstrating that he is the true God by virtue of possessing the highest power as the only begotten Son of God. And so, as the Father raised him (Eph. 1:20), so he raises himself (John 10:18). Similarly, the Father glorified the Son and the Son glorifies himself, because everything that the Father does, the Son does in like manner (John 5:19), establishing that he is the same God with the Father. And these things are relevant to the second point, where he asks to be glorified by the Father.

The third and final point is that he says that he is sent by the Father: 'and Jesus Christ whom you have sent'. According to their opinion, this proves the authority of the Father over him, and his inferiority to the Father, as they put it, thereby denying him to be the supreme God. They also use this argument to argue against the divinity of the Holy Spirit, as they read several times that he was also sent by the Father (John 14:26) and by Christ (John 15:26). We are not discussing the divinity or the sending of the Holy Spirit here. We gratefully acknowledge that Jesus Christ was sent by the Father and, in explanation of this, we say the following:

1. In line with Bonaventure,[209] 'mission' implies manifestation and connotes 'emanation'[210] in the one sent. And hence, although the Father, Son and Spirit are said to send, only the Son and the Spirit are said to be sent, since they are persons who are, so to speak, [Page 18] produced and emanate from the Father who is the source of divinity.
2. Therefore, this mission implies the order of the persons. For it is fitting that the Son sends the Spirit, the second person sends the third, and the first sends the second and third persons.

---

[209] Born in Civita di Bagnoregio, Italy, Bonaventure (1217/1221–74) was Minister General of the Franciscan Order. Among his writings is his commentary on Peter Lombard's Sentences (1250–3). He also provided a synthesis of doctrine in *Breviloquium* (1257). See Bonaventure, *In primum Sententiarum*, in *Opera Omnia*, ed. A. C. Peltier, 15 vols. (Paris: Vivès, 1864–71), vol. 1; Zachary Hayes, 'Bonaventure's Trinitarian Theology', in Jay M. Hammond, Wayne Hellmann, and Jared Goff (eds.) *A Companion to Bonaventure* (Leiden: Brill, 2004), 189–245.

[210] Franciscan Trinitarian theology emphasised 'emanations' to differentiate the divine persons in contrast to the Dominicans that emphasised 'relations'. The late medieval difference here was not an issue for Reformed Trinitarians whose eclectic inheritance of various medieval distinctions served to articulate personal distinction within the Trinity. On medieval Trinitarian theology, see Russell L. Friedman, *Intellectual Traditions at the Medieval University: The Use of Philosophical Psychology in Trinitarian Theology among the Franciscans and Dominicans, 1250–1350*, 2 vols. (Leiden: Brill, 2013). On personal Trinitarian distinctions in Reformed orthodoxy, see *PRRD* 4.

3. Consequently, it also reveals the distinction of the persons. For although one and the same person can send and be sent, just as the will is the same when it moves itself, both as mover and moved, so the Spirit can also be called the sender as he is God, and can be sent, as he is the gift. But when the Father is said to send the Son and the Son is said to send the Spirit, the distinction of the persons is implied.

The question is asked whether it also pertains to essence. The Socinians affirm that it does, while the orthodox deny it. For only then does mission imply a distinction of substance, when it signifies personal authority, such as when God sends an angel, the Lord sends a servant, or Christ sends the Apostles: 'As the Father has sent me, even so I am sending you' (John 20:21). However, although this may express some likeness, it does not express complete correspondence in every way. For the Father did not send the Son in the same way or with the same authority of command as Christ sent the Apostle.

Christ is said to be sent in two ways. First, with respect to the incarnation. In this way, Christ says that he 'came from the Father and has come into the world' (John 16:28). And it is said that the Father 'sent his Son, born of woman' (Gal. 4:4). Second, with respect to the office of Mediator, he is Redeemer, Prophet, King, and Priest of the church. According to the Prophet, 'The Lord has anointed me to preach to the meek, he has set me to bind up the broken-hearted, and to proclaim liberty to the captives' (Isaiah 61:1). For a prophet, anointing, mission, and sending are necessary.

But if these things are understood insofar as he was a man or a Mediator, and thus understood either according to his human nature or to his dispensation as a Mediator, we acknowledge that this mission, strictly speaking, denotes authority and inferiority. But inasmuch as it was the second person who was incarnate and had to take on the office of Mediator, it denotes the order and distinction of the persons. However, in the meantime there is no such distinction either of essence or of personal authority of the sender over the sent, so that both the sender and the sent cannot be the supreme true God. For an equal can send an equal as long as there is mutual consent: one consul can send another by agreement, and in the same way the Father sends the Son. Indeed, the word 'sending' clearly proves this. For the one who is sent already existed before. Thus, Christ was sent by God in his initial incarnation, and before his own incarnation he existed previously. Therefore, he is the true eternal God, manifested in the flesh, according to the Apostle (1 Tim. 3:16). And these points are more or less what the Socinians usually raise against the divinity of Christ, based on these three verses. By contrast, we can present many arguments from this chapter that can establish his divinity, and it will be sufficient merely to name these.

First, that we owe him 'eternal life'. But this expression does not imply that he is human but speaks of the divine, according to 1 John 5:20: 'This is God and eternal life'.

Second, that we owe this eternal life to both Christ and the Father, since it consists equally of knowing Christ and the Father. The same sharing of divine honour with the Father proves that he is the same God. One of these is knowledge of eternal life, their uniter, and one is nature.

[Page 19] Third, that this eternal life is based on the knowledge of Christ, but this knowledge includes trust, which only belongs to God.

Fourth, that the Son is called the preeminent Son of the Father.

1. Namely, only-begotten and essential, which are often not denied in Holy Scripture [and] which are applied to the Father in a special sense.[211]

Fifth, that the ἐξουσια, that is, the authority, power, and armed force, 'is given to him over all flesh' (John 17:2). But this authority is characteristic of God (Numbers 16:22, 27, 16; Jer. 32:27). And the same applies to the words of the Apostle: 'who is God over all, blessed forever' (Rom. 9:5). But if some people object that this is given to him, we can easily follow Cyril[212] in answering that he possesses all things as God, whereas he receives all things as man. Inasmuch as he is the eternal Son of God, just as he has the divine essence, so also he has power naturally communicated in its own way. But inasmuch as he is the Son of Man or the Mediator, it has been freely granted by the Father. Indeed, nothing hinders him from having as God that very thing that he receives as man, or what he received as the Son from the Father with respect to his person, he has the same in himself with respect to nature, as the Son draws divinity from the Father as from a spring, he who is himself nevertheless God from himself.

Sixth, what occurs in verse 5. This verse particularly challenges the adversaries, because he asks to be glorified by the Father 'with the glory that he had with him before the world existed'. These things clearly demonstrate that he is God and that he is eternal. For there was nothing before the beginning of the world, much less did God have glory that was not [before the beginning of the world].

Seventh, let the final point be in verse 10. 'And all mine are yours and yours are mine', not only as the steward who administers all things that are of the Lord, as in Genesis 39:9, nor only as the bride who possesses all things that belong to the bridegroom, or indeed as the bridegroom himself by virtue of the covenant they have entered upon, as in the Song of

---

[211] Tuckney is unclear here. The Latin is: 'Unigenitus scilicet & essentialis, de quo saepiùs in Sacra Pagina non negantur quae Patri tanquam peculariâ accommodantur'.

[212] Commenting on John 17:2, Cyril said, 'Though he possesses everything as God, he says that he receives it as a human being, for whom rule is not essential but given'. Cyril, *Commentary on John*, 2:272.

Solomon 2:16, but as a partaker of the same nature and therefore of the same power.

In opposition to these individual points, I acknowledge that there are many that are commonly presented by the Socinians, and an equal number are put forward by the orthodox to explain and present the same things. However, I now set aside all these things. Since it is quite clear from what has been said already that this verse, so far from undermining the supreme divinity of our Lord Jesus Christ, in fact confirms it very strongly.

Studies at Trinity College, Cambridge, c.1600–c.1750

Richard Serjeantson

It is perhaps a reflection of the tenacious loyalty of members of the University of Oxford that the history of university studies in England between the sixteenth and the eighteenth centuries has been most thoroughly explored there.[1] The nature of learning in the University of Cambridge and its constituent colleges, by contrast, has been less intensively reconnoitred. Cambridge's recent institutional history is less ambitious than that of Oxford, and there has accordingly been less scope to explore the rich printed and, especially, manuscript evidence for the work pursued by its undergraduates and graduates.[2] Furthermore, few single-volume histories of Cambridge colleges have had the scope to focus intensively on the history of the learning that provided the ground-bass against which the events of an institutional history occur.[3] It is only once one enters the eighteenth

---

[1] James McConica, ed., *The History of the University of Oxford*, vol. III: *The Collegiate University* (Oxford, 1986), esp. the chapters on studies by McConica, Fletcher, Lewis, Barton, Greenslade, and Duncan; E. G. W. Bill, *Education at Christ Church, Oxford, 1660–1800* (Oxford, 1988); Nicholas Tyacke, ed. *The History of the University of Oxford*, vol. IV: *Seventeenth-Century Oxford* (Oxford, 1997), esp. the chapters by Feingold, Frank, and Levack; L. S. Sutherland and L. G. Mitchell, *The History of the University of Oxford*, vol. V: *Eighteenth-Century Oxford* (Oxford, 1986), esp. the chapter by Sutherland; William Poole, 'Wadham College Library: The first century', in *John Wilkins (1614–1672): New Essays*, ed. William Poole (Leiden, 2017), 241–84.

[2] See Victor Morgan and Christopher Brooke, *A History of the University of Cambridge*, vol. II: *1546–1750* (Cambridge, 2004), 437–63.

[3] But see John Twigg, *A History of Queens' College, Cambridge, 1448–1986* (Woodbridge, 1987), 98–109, 203–19; Sarah Bendall, Christopher Brooke, Patrick Collinson, *A History of Emmanuel College, Cambridge* (Woodbridge, 1999), 69–79; Quentin Skinner, 'The Generation of John Milton', in *Christ's: A Cambridge College Over Five Centuries* (London, 2004), 55–66; Richard Rex, 'The Sixteenth Century', in *St John's College, Cambridge: A History*, ed. Peter Linehan (Woodbridge, 2011), 41–43; Mark Nicholls, 'The Seventeenth Century', in ibid., 120–23.

century that the shape of learning at Cambridge has been systematically investigated.[4] For seventeenth-century Cambridge, Costello's study of what he called the 'scholastic curriculum' remains fundamental, by virtue of his secure grasp of neo-Latin philosophy and his willingness to immerse himself in the manuscript evidence.[5] But as Feingold has demonstrated in detail for the case of Oxford, the assumption that university learning of this period was inherently 'scholastic' obscures the vital, and perhaps even 'quintessential' place of humanistic studies within the English universities of the period.[6]

The present chapter seeks to address this deficit in the case of the University by undertaking an investigation of the studies pursued in one particular Cambridge college on the basis of contemporary sources. Although the picture that these sources offer is hardly comprehensive, Trinity College was large enough (and certain of its members also became distinguished enough) that a sufficient volume of manuscript (and occasionally also printed) material has been preserved to identify distinctive patterns of exercises, of reading, and of learning in general. From these materials, we will be able to establish not only the shape of learning at Cambridge in general, but also the more specific direction of learning taken at a particular, though not a typical, college. Nonetheless, the leadership that Trinity provided to the University in certain areas of learning – though it contributed rather less to certain others, including (perhaps surprisingly) theology – means that the history of the studies pursued at Trinity in the 'long' seventeenth century will also go some way towards providing a framework for understanding the shape of studies within the University of Cambridge more generally.

Our period sits amidst the arrival in England of the new humanistic learning from Italy and the German-speaking lands in the mid-sixteenth century, and the emergence of newer forms of French-inflected polite learning, and also of mathematics, by the mid-eighteenth century. It witnesses the gradual decline, though by no means the demise, of Latin as the language of instruction and assessment;[7] and it sees an extraordinary

---

[4] Christopher Wordsworth, *Scholae Academicae* (Cambridge, 1877); John Gascoigne, *Cambridge in the Age of the Enlightenment* (Cambridge, 2002).

[5] William T. Costello, SJ, *The Scholastic Curriculum at Early Seventeenth-Century Cambridge* (Cambridge, MA, 1958). Aspects of Costello's work are supplemented by James A. W. Rembert, *Swift and the Dialectical Tradition* (New York, 1988), esp. 198–201 (Appendix 3).

[6] Mordechai Feingold, 'The Humanities', in *Seventeenth-Century Oxford*, 213. This point is also developed by Ian Stewart, '"Fleshy Books": Isaac Barrow and the Oratorical Critique of Cartesian Natural Philosophy', *History of Universities*, 16 (2000), 35–102.

[7] Richard Cumberland, *Memoirs* (London, 1806), 73, an undergraduate at Trinity in the mid-eighteenth century, recalled composing in English on only one occasion as an undergraduate.

expansion in the availability of what became a fundamental instrument of learning, the printed book.[8] But this period also witnesses a narrowing of geographical scope in the horizon of learning in Cambridge, as the pan-European academic world of the sixteenth and earlier-seventeenth centuries slowly gave way to a wilfully insular and sometimes vulgarly triumphalist vision of English intellectual superiority both in philosophy and theology. The studies that were pursued in Trinity in our period by its several thousand undergraduate, graduate, and senior members were undertaken in the context of these large-scale developments.

THE FOUR FACULTIES AND THE WREN LIBRARY

The studies pursued in Cambridge, and at Trinity, before the mid-eighteenth century existed within several frameworks. The first and broadest framework was the institutional one furnished by the four faculties of the medieval and renaissance university: Arts, Medicine, Law, and Theology. This framework has a particular significance for Trinity College, although it is one that has not hitherto been appreciated.

In 1675 the rising young architect and universal genius, Christopher Wren—a graduate of Wadham College, Oxford, who had in the late 1660s designed, to wide acclaim, the Sheldonian Theatre at Oxford—was commissioned by the then Master of Trinity, Isaac Barrow, to design a splendid new library to enclose Thomas Nevile's court to the west of the Hall.[9] To complete his vision, Wren noted that he had given the middle of his 'Frontispeece' certain 'Statues according to ancient example'. Wren's architectural models, such as Sansovino's Marciana library in Venice, or Palladio's drawings, tended to line the entire pediment with figures.[10] Yet the scheme at Trinity has only four, placed centrally overlooking over the court. Wren himself wrote that 'The Statues will be a noble ornament, are supposed of plaister, there are Flemish artists that doe them cheape.' On due reflection, however, a decision was evidently made to use the somewhat more permanent medium of limestone. The four statues were carved by Wren's preferred sculptor, Caius Gabriel

---

[8] David McKitterick, *A History of Cambridge University Press*, 3 vols (Cambridge, 1992–2004), vols. I & II.
[9] David McKitterick, 'Introduction', to *The Making of the Wren Library* (Cambridge, 1995), 1–27. See also the chapters on the Library and its architecture by McKitterick and by Watkin in this volume.
[10] Andrea Palladio, *I quattro libri dell'architettura* (Venice, 1581), lib. II, 9, 19, 17, 23, 31; lib. III, 42, 43. Howard Colvin, 'The Building', in *Making of the Wren Library*, 33.

Fig. 5.1. Representations of (left to right) the Faculties of Divinity, Law, Medicine, and Arts. Wren Library, Trinity College, Cambridge.

Cibber, who received the sum of £80 for the work he and his team had completed in May 1681 (Fig.5. 1).[11]

These four statues clearly convey a symbolic meaning. But what is it?[12] Reading (as was customary in this period) from their right-hand side (but our left) we find, firstly, a veiled female figure looking heavenward, with an eagle at her feet, and holding in her right hand a representation of a codex inscribed with the words *Biblia sacra*. Here, then, we have a representation of theology (*theologia*), who sees darkly the vision of heaven, who has the emblem of the apostle John at her feet, and who carries a copy of the sacred scriptures. Beside her is another female figure, who now looks down at this world rather than up at the next. She has a large pile of books at her feet, and displays in her left hand a scroll bearing the words *iubet et prohibet*. She evidently represents the discipline of law (*jurisprudentia*), the discipline which (in an echo of Cicero's *De legibus*) 'commands and forbids', and whose professors were identified by the learning imparted in their weighty, unreadable, and largely unread books.[13] And to her left again stands a third figure, who is supported by a staff entwined by a snake, and who has a cock at her feet. These are evidently the cock and the staff of Asclepius, the god of healing, and she therefore represents medicine (*medicina*), or, to use the seventeenth-century English term, 'physic'. About the identity of these three statues there is no doubt.

---

[11] Robert Willis, *The Architectural History of the University of Cambridge and of the Colleges of Cambridge and Eton*, ed. John Willis Clark, introd. David Watkin, 3 vols (Cambridge, 1988), ii. 535, 536, 542; Malcolm Baker, 'The Portrait Sculpture', in *The Making of the Wren Library*, 111.

[12] I know of no surviving evidence to identify the designer's intentions. Contrast Queen's College, Oxford, where in 1733–35 the sculptor Henry Cheere was paid £135 to depict 'Law, Physick and Poetry' atop the new building. See J. R. Magrath, *The Queen's College*, 2 vols (Oxford, 1921), ii. 95.

[13] Cicero, *De legibus*, I. vi. 18: 'lex est ratio summa, insita in natura, quae iubet ea quae facienda sunt, prohibetque contraria' (law is the highest reason, implanted in us by nature, which commands what should be done and prohibits the contrary).

Studies at Trinity College, Cambridge, c.1600–c.1750

Fig. 5.2. Representation of the Faculty of Arts, Wren Library, Trinity College, Cambridge.

But what does the statue in the inferior position on the far left represent (Fig.5. 2)? She too has a device at her feet: an open globe-like structure that appears to represent not the terrestrial globe of the earth, but rather the celestial globe of the heavens; an armillary sphere.[14] Furthermore, although this figure is not carrying anything in her hands, she is clearly using them for a particular purpose: she is counting on her fingers. Since the mid-eighteenth century, this figure has accordingly been taken to represent the scholarly discipline most obviously associated with calculation: mathematics. The universal consensus is summarized by Howard Colvin: 'On the parapet stand four stone statues representing Divinity, Law, Medicine and Mathematics.'[15]

[14] I am grateful to Dr Adam Mosley for helpful discussion of this point.
[15] Howard Colvin, 'The Building', in *Making of the Wren Library*, 46. The same attribution is made by Willis and Clark, *Architectural History*, ii. 542; A. B. Cook, *The Rise and Progress of Classical Archaeology* (Cambridge, 1931), 15; André Masson, *Le Décor des bibliothèques du moyen âge à la Révolution* (Geneva, 1972), 115; Baker, 'Portrait Sculpture', 111. Ludmilla Jordanova, *The Look of the Past: Visual and Material Evidence in Historical Practice* (Cambridge, 2012), 40. It is an interpretation which dates back (at least) to Thomas Salmon, *The Foreigner's Companion Through the Universities of Cambridge and Oxford* (London, 1748), 67.

But this is not correct. Ernst Gombrich proposed that iconology—the interpretation of visual meaning—must begin with the study of institutions rather than symbols.[16] And here we have a perfect exemplification of that dictum. It is institutionally implausible that mathematics should stand alongside the higher faculties in late seventeenth-century Cambridge. Mathematics was indeed becoming increasingly important, as we shall see, in the college of Isaac Barrow and Isaac Newton. But it was hardly significant enough in the 1680s to stand alongside such well-established studies as medicine and theology. An institutional reading of these four statutes should tell us, instead, that the statues fronting Wren's library represent the four faculties of the Parisian university system.[17] On this interpretation, therefore, the leftmost statue does not depict mathematics, but instead represents an academic institution like the other three: she is the Faculty of Arts.

The statue's iconography confirms this institutional interpretation. The discipline represented by the counting that she is doing on her fingers is not arithmetic, but logic; she is not calculating figures, but enumerating arguments. A rich iconographic tradition stands behind this point, for since at least the mid-sixteenth century the figure of *Dialectica* had been represented as numbering arguments on her fingers. Maarten de Vos represented her in this fashion in a Flemish engraving of around 1600;[18] Crispijn de Passe did the same thing at some point before 1637;[19] George Glover echoed the same effect in a print published in England at some point after 1625,[20] and so did Francis Cleyn in a London print of 1645 (Fig.5. 3).[21]

The armillary sphere at the figure's feet might be taken to represent astronomy, which in the medieval quadrivium was treated as one of the four mathematical disciplines. But by the seventeenth century this instrument was more usually accompanied representations of natural philosophy. It appears as such on the title-page of a book that was studied in seventeenth-century Trinity, Roderigo de Arriaga's *Cursus Philosophicus*.[22]

---

[16] E. H. Gombrich, 'Aims and Limits of Iconology', in *Symbolic Images* (London, 1972), 21.
[17] On this system, see Richard Tuck, 'The Institutional Setting', in *The Cambridge History of Seventeenth-Century Philosophy*, 2 vols (Cambridge, 1997), i. 15–23.
[18] Maarten de Vos, 'Dialectica' ([Flanders], c. 1600), British Museum (hereafter BM), no. 1868,0612.461.
[19] Crispijn de Passe the elder, 'Dialectica' ([Netherlands], ca. 1590–1637), BM no. D,6.3.
[20] George Glover, 'Dialectica' (London, 1625–35), BM, no. 1870,0514.1239.
[21] Francis Cleyn, 'Dialectica' (London, 1645), Victoria & Albert Museum, no. E.1277-1936.
[22] Roderigo de Arriaga, *Cursus Philosophicus* (Antwerp, 1632). Henry Puckering's copy of the Paris, 1639 edition, is Trinity College, Cambridge (hereafter TCC), shelfmark T. 11. 12.

Fig. 5.3. Francis Cleyn, 'Dialectica' (1645).

And it appears again in this capacity on the title page of another philosophical compendium reprinted in mid-seventeenth century Cambridge, and even more widely read by members of Trinity: Marcus Friedrich Wendelin's *Contemplationes Physicae*.[23]

In short, the leftmost statue is not a composite of the two mathematical disciplines of arithmetic and astronomy, but rather of the two philosophical disciplines of logic and physics. The name we should henceforth assign to her is not *mathematica*, but rather *philosophia*. And the intellectual realm in which she places us is that of the 'arts course'—the undergraduate studies, resulting in the degrees of Bachelor and then Master of Arts, which were a preliminary to the pursuit of learning in the three higher faculties. This undergraduate course in arts was the dominant force shaping studies at Trinity in this period, and will form the focus of this account.

[23] See at n. 144, below.

The four faculties were therefore the fundamental vessels into which the studies pursued at Trinity across our period were poured. They provided the structure for the university's disputations at the four 'Acts' held each summer, at which questions were disputed in Philosophy, Medicine, Law and Theology.[24] Graduation in arts, followed by a further graduation in one of the three 'higher faculties' was the goal of a professional education.

The University statutes fixed the broad structure of studies for these degrees. The course for the Bachelor of Arts degree required four years. The third- and fourth-year students undertaking it were known as junior and senior 'sophisters'. Once it was obtained, a Bachelor was addressed within the university by the venerable clerical title of 'Sir' (*dominus* in Latin), followed by his surname. A further three years were required to elapse before a student could take the Master of Arts degree. Continued residence was not required for this course, though participation in the public examinations remained enforced. A student who passed through this seven-year course was addressed as 'Master', and became eligible to take a degree in one of the higher faculties.

The degree most commonly taken thereafter was that of Bachelor of Divinity (BD), which required that a further seven years again should have elapsed from taking the MA degree. This degree might itself be succeeded after some further time by the degree of Doctor of Divinity (DD), and its recipients were thereafter infallibly addressed by the title of 'Dr'. A very much smaller proportion of students took the degree of Bachelor of Medicine (MB), which might be followed by the doctorate (MD). Edward Browne, son of the physician Sir Thomas Browne, the author of *Religio Medici*, was one of the limited number of students at Trinity who took an MB degree, having spent six years as a member of the College without taking either a BA or MA first.[25] An even small number took the degrees of Bachelor (BCL) and Doctor of Civil Laws (DCL). The modern degree of 'Doctor of Philosophy' did not exist.

The slow timetable set by each of these degrees, and the exercises that were required to obtain them, therefore provided a fundamental framework for the studies undertaken within the Trinity College and in the University as a whole.

---

[24] See J. J. Hall, *Cambridge Act and Tripos Verses, 1565–1894* (Cambridge, 2009), 7–8, and the theses in the four different faculties collected there. Sometimes there was also a Music Act: see 'Extracts from Mr. Buck's Book' (1665), in George Peacock, *Observations on the Statutes of the University of Cambridge* (London, 1841), lxxxvi.

[25] Edward Browne, adm. 1657, MB, 1663 (John Venn and J. A. Venn (eds.), *Alumni Cantabrigienses*, Part I, 4 vols (Cambridge, 1922), i. 232). John Yardley, adm. 1698; MB, 1704, was another (Venn, *Alumni Cantabrigienses*, iv. 487).

CLERICS AND FELLOW COMMONERS

Yet the framework provided by the degrees conferred by the University was only one of the various structures that shaped studies at Trinity. Other, less formal, frameworks also operated. Most notably, there was no requirement upon students to take a degree at all. Many students in this period entered the College for a couple of years of so, and then left, often moving on to spend some more time studying law, and otherwise enjoying life in the capital, at the Inns of Court.

Furthermore, the 'long' seventeenth century was an age that prized the quality of 'general learning'; a broad range of knowledge of the natural, human, and religious realms. It was an ideal laid out a sermon that Isaac Barrow delivered, quite probably in the chapel of Trinity, entitled 'Of Industry in our particular calling, as scholars'. Each part of learning, Barrow wrote, confers 'such a connexion of things' and 'dependence of notions' upon other parts, 'that a man can hardly well understand any thing without knowing divers other things'. A person will be 'a lame scholar, who hath not an insight into many kinds of knowledge', and he 'can hardly be a good scholar, who is not a general one.'[26] The ideal of omniscience was realised in practice in the universal quality of a tutor's teaching and in the rotation of pedagogic offices within the College. Moreover, in the case of some of Trinity's Masters, such as Barrow or his predecessor John Pearson, their appointment genuinely reflected the remarkably broad range of their intellectual interests and achievements.

A different framework within which studies existed was provided by the rank at which students entered the College. The most humble class of student were the 'sizars', who performed certain services in exchange for their teaching and upkeep at Trinity. Other students entered as pensioners, who paid higher fees and lived more comfortably. But the highest rank were the fellow commoners, sons of the nobility and richer gentry, who lived in greater style, paid larger fees still, and had the privilege of dining with the fellows.

It is clear that there was some distinction in the studies that these different ranks received. Fellow commoners were less likely than the other two

---

[26] Isaac Barrow, *Theological Works*, ed. A. Napier, 9 vols (Cambridge, 1859), iii. 434. On Barrow himself as a general scholar, see further Mordechai Feingold, 'Isaac Barrow: Divine, Scholar, Mathematician', in *Before Newton: The Life and Times of Isaac Barrow*, ed. Mordechai Feingold (Cambridge, 1990), 1–104; Anthony Grafton, 'Barrow as a Scholar', in *Before Newton*, 291–302; and Ian Stewart, 'Isaac Barrow: Authorised Reason and Reasonable Authority of a Scholar-Priest' (unpublished Ph.D. diss., University of Cambridge, 1998).

classes to take any sort of degree, except in the case of a few of the most exalted noble status who were permitted to proceed to what was effectively an honorary MA after a mere two years' study.[27] When Francis Willughby, a fellow commoner at Trinity across the 1650s, took not only a BA but also his MA after a full seven years' study, it was a matter for surprised comment by observers.[28] Fellow commoners at Trinity may also have been taught separately from other members of the College by their tutors, as allusions to reading-groups composed of them indicate.[29] Evidence suggests that to some extent fellow commoners also followed less demanding courses of study, reading contemporary books written in English rather than philosophy in Latin or literature in Greek.[30] The Master of Emmanuel College, Richard Holdsworth, identified such 'lighter studies' (*studia leviora*) as being appropriate for 'such as come to the University not with intention to make Scholarship their profession, but only to gett such learning as may serve for delight and ornament'.[31] Many, after all, were destined to live somewhat isolated lives in the country: a good education could help beguile their retirement. Writing the early nineteenth century of his time at Trinity in the 1750s, the sizar Richard Watson remembered having spent a great deal of time in the company of 'idle' fellow commoners.[32]

Yet there are also numerous instances that qualify this potentially pejorative judgment. In the late sixteenth century the University had affirmed at the Act the thesis that it behoved the nobility to be literate more than it did their inferiors.[33] The list of books purchased by James Master, who spent less than two years at Trinity as a fellow commoner in the 1640s, includes some fairly demanding Latin philosophy.[34] Francis Willughby was celebrated for his studiousness as well as for his degrees.[35] John North, who had entered Jesus College as a Fellow Commoner in

---

[27] This order was renewed by Charles II in 1679 with application to baronets and knights: *Statuta Academiæ Cantabrigiensis* (Cambridge, 1785), 307.

[28] Richard Serjeantson, 'The Education of Francis Willughby', in *Virtuoso by Nature: The Scientific Life of Francis Willughby*, ed. Tim Birkhead (Leiden, 2016), 55.

[29] See at n. 211 (Duport) and n. 237 (Pulleyn), below.

[30] Jefferson Looney, 'Undergraduate Education at Early Stuart Cambridge,' *History of Education*, 10 (1981), 1–19.

[31] Richard Holdsworth, 'Directions for a Student in the Universitie', in H. F. Fletcher, *The Intellectual Development of John Milton*, 2 vols (Urbana, Ill., 1961), ii. 647.

[32] Richard Watson, *Anecdotes* (Philadelphia, 1818), 13.

[33] 'Plus interest nobilium literatos esse, quàm hominum inferiori loco positorum', Act verses for *c*.1585–90 (*STC* 4474.7). See Hall, *Act and Tripos Verses*, 106.

[34] Scott Robinson and Matilda Dalison (eds.), 'The Expense-Book of James Master, Esq., A.D. 1646–1676', *Archaeologia Cantiana*, 15 (1883), 163–72.

[35] Serjeantson, 'Education of Willughby', 54–58.

1660, took both arts degrees, became Regius Professor of Greek as a member of Trinity, and was subsequently appointed Master of the College.[36] A contemporary news sheet commented that when a (younger) 'son of the Earl of Salisbury' took his MA in 1656 he had been 'prior opponent in the Philosophie Act and began the dispute with a very elegant Oration.'[37] Fellow commoners were not always merely drones.

By contrast, however, pensioners and *a fortiori* sizars and subsizars, were more likely to regard academic study and the qualifications it conferred as a stepping-stone to a career, whether in the church or elsewhere. A satirical observer felt it mattered less to Francis Bridge that he failed to obtain a fellowship in the year he took his BA, 1659, since he already enjoyed an inheritance of 'an hundred a yeere'.[38] But for those who could not fall back on such resources the stakes of academic success were much higher: it could mean the difference between banishment to teaching in a country school on the one hand, and a remunerative clerical career, with good access to the university, to the capital, and even to the court, on the other.[39]

Studies of colleges other than Trinity have suggested that prospective divines (who were unlikely to be fellow commoners) read more philosophy, and less modern literature, than those whose destiny lay in the Inns of Court.[40] Others, however, have suggested that the distinction was more between the reading of history and geography and the study of Hebrew. In truth (as Stewart has emphasised) the individual relationship that each undergraduate had with his tutor, who could tailor his teaching to a student's interests and abilities, was perhaps as important as the career-path he might propose to take.[41] Although the clerical dominance of the upper levels of the colleges of the English universities may make it appear as if their primary function was the production of future clergy, the fact is that for the first four years of the arts course, at least, secular studies were overwhelmingly more important.

---

[36] C. S. Knighton, 'North, John (1645–1683)', *Oxford Dictionary of National Biography*, Oxford University Press, 2004 onwards (www.oxforddnb.com) (hereafter *ODNB*).

[37] *The Publick Intelligencer*, ed. John Canne (7–14 July 1656), 689 (item for 7 July). The identity of this son is uncertain; Edward Cecil, a Fellow Commoner at Trinity, had already been awarded his MA in March 1654 (CUL, UA Grace Book Eta, p. 118), but there is no other obvious candidate in Venn.

[38] TCC, MS O. 10a. 33, p. 28. But Bridge went on to become a fellow in 1661 and then the vicar of St Michaels, Cambridge (Venn, *Alumni Cantabrigienses*, i. 214).

[39] On this point, see also Stewart, 'Fleshy Books', 47.

[40] Looney, 'Undergraduate Education', 19.

[41] Stewart, 'Isaac Barrow', 57–8 and n. 125

COLLEGE AND UNIVERSITY EXERCISES

A different framework again for a student's studies was provided by the various different scholastic 'exercises' that they were required to undertake in the course of their studies. These exercises were both written and oral in nature. Oral exercises included the handling of philosophical 'problems' in the form of disputations.[42] The disputations themselves have vanished on the wind, but their written residue, in the form of 'problems' and theses, sometimes survive. A significant portion of the life of a 'sophister' – that is, an undergraduate who had not yet obtained his BA degree – was devoted to mastering the skill of handling these philosophical problems decisively, skilfully, and perhaps even eloquently, in the Latin tongue. It was a matter of note in the mid-1640s that an especially demanding Proctor (Charles Hotham, of Peterhouse) required sophisters to deliver their positions 'without book' – that is, from memory.[43] The elaborate 'Rules' that the most energetic tutor in mid-seventeenth-century Trinity, James Duport, wrote for his students makes clear that this was his ideal, as well: he scorned 'that dull, cold, idle, way of reading Syllogismes out of a paper'. The philosophical axioms that grew into favour in mid-seventeenth century Trinity, as in Cambridge more generally, provided 'Logical & Philosophical' rules, 'distinctions' and 'questions' which were faithfully written down, although not always in the 'little pocket-paper-book' that Duport recommended.[44]

Disputations formed the primary means by which the University, in principle at least, tested the learning of its members. At the University's main Commencement in July each year 'Acts' were kept in each of the four Faculties and disputations conducted by the graduating doctors (in the higher faculties) and MAs in the Faculty of Arts.[45] The quadragesimal disputations that took place each year between Ash Wednesday and the fourth Sunday of Lent gathered the 'commencing' Bachelors together with younger sophisters and those who had already gained the degree, and set them disputing against members of other colleges in the University Schools from between one and five o'clock each day, defending two or three theses of their own choosing. 'In this manner'

---

[42] See further Costello, *Scholastic Curriculum*, 14–34; Thomas Hill, 'A Letter to the Seniors', in *The Best and Worst of Paul* (Cambridge, 1648), sig. A3v.

[43] Henry Newcombe, *Autobiography*, ed. Richard Parkinson (Manchester, 1852), 9. Hotham was Proctor in 1646: Richard L. Greaves, 'Hotham, Charles (1615–1672)', *ODBN*.

[44] C. D. Preston and P. H. Oswald, 'James Duport's Rules for his Tutorial Pupils', *Transactions of the Cambridge Bibliographical Society*, 14 (2011), 348, 350. Serjeantson, 'Education of Willughby', 69.

[45] Hall, *Act and Tripos Verses*, 7–8.

wrote a faithful recorder of the University's ceremonial, the Proctors 'will sometimes set 20 or 30 of them to dispute'.[46]

Yet it also seems to be the case that Trinity itself had some responsibility for deciding who should be awarded degrees. In 1659, under the brief Mastership of John Wilkins, a Conclusion was passed enforcing examinations for BA degrees, either 'in the Chapel at the usual time' or in advance by each of the Senior Fellows in their chambers. The same decision also concluded that 'no Batchelors degree shall be conferred by any meeting in *th*e Hall window'; that is, presumably in some less formal fashion.[47]

Examination by disputation remained in force in Cambridge until the mid-nineteenth century.[48] But by 1735 the lengthy schedule of quadragesimal disputations had become shortened, and rather than students disputing against one another, they were being questioned by MAs (on the first two days) and (on the third day) in groups of six by the Moderator, 'as long as he will, and in what science he pleases'.[49] Until the 1760s, however, they did so in classes drawn up by college, rather than by ability, which the Second Wrangler who inaugurated the change, Richard Watson, asserted had allowed for some 'flagrant acts of partiality' on the part of the examiners who drew upon the order of seniority.[50]

A 'respondent' disputing in the schools during the commencement Act composed (or had others compose for him) verses on the subject of his question.[51] These were sometimes distributed on printed broadsheets at the Act, or were otherwise preserved in manuscript, and therefore constitute the fullest surviving record of the disputed questions. Members of Trinity contributed numerous such 'act verses' across the period, and several specimens by Isaac Barrow, in particular, survive.[52]

---

[46] The arrangements (much more elaborate than this summary allows) are fully documented in 'Buck's Book', lxxi–lxxiii.

[47] Archives of Trinity College, Cambridge (hereafter TCA), Conclusions and Admonitions 1607–1673, p. 259 (13 Jan. 1659[/60]). See also James Bass Mullinger, *The University of Cambridge from the Election of Buckingham to the decline of the Platonist Movement* (Cambridge, 1911), 547 n. 2.

[48] See Charles Wesley, *A Guide to Syllogism, Or a Manual of Logic* (London, 1832).

[49] For these points, see John Gascoigne, 'Mathematics and Meritocracy: The Emergence of the Cambridge Mathematical Tripos', *Social Studies of Science*, 14 (1984), 550.

[50] Watson, *Anecdotes*, 19.

[51] John Milton composed Act Verses for others during his time at Cambridge (see Robert Dulgarian, 'Milton's "Naturam non pati senium" and "De Idea Platonica" as Cambridge Act Verses: A reconsideration in light of manuscript evidence', *Review of English Studies*, n.s. 70 (2019), 847–68). So too did Isaac Barrow (Abraham Hill, 'Some Account of the Life of Dr Isaac Barrow', in *Theological Works*, i. xl). Another example is offered by Thomas Carr of Jesus, who composed verses for Samuel Sutton of Peterhouse in 1611 (Durham University Library (hereafter DUL), MS Hunter 31, p. 70).

[52] Verses by Trinity members across the period are thoroughly catalogued in Hall, *Act and Tripos Verses*. For his specimens, see Barrow, *Theological Works*, xi. 429–43.

Yet there is some evidence to suggest that disputations played less of a role in studies at Trinity, at least in the middle years of the seventeenth century, than they did at other colleges. An intriguing observation by John Ray's biographer William Derham (1657–1735) suggests that at the college Ray first entered in 1644, St Catherine's Hall, 'they chiefly addicted themselves to Disputations'; at Trinity, by contrast, to which he moved shortly afterwards, 'the politer Arts and Sciences were principally minded and cultivated'.[53] The safest implication of this late testimony may be that a wider range of studies was pursued at Trinity than at some other colleges, partly because of its size, and partly too, perhaps, because a larger proportion of its members had no intention of entering the church, and therefore had less need of pursuing formal scholastic exercises to the exclusion of other kinds of studies.

Important ceremonial disputations in the Schools were characteristically prefaced by an oration,[54] such as the one Isaac Barrow seems to have delivered in the summer of 1652 at the University commencement at which he obtained his MA.[55] Skill in such declamations was something that college teaching also provided extensive opportunities to hone. Selected students delivered weekly orations before their teachers and peers in the College hall on Saturday evenings.[56] Academic notebooks sometimes record such orations, terminated by the formula *dixi* (I have spoken).[57] Fellows appointed as lecturers (on which see below) might deliver an oration at the outset of the tenure of their office, which would serve both as an encouragement and an example to the students whom their words directly addressed; at least three instances of these survive.[58] In the speech that Isaac Barrow addressed to his audience upon becoming

---

[53] William Derham, 'The Life of Mr. Ray', in *Select Remains of the Learned John Ray* (London, 1760), 2.

[54] Buck, 'Extracts', lxx–lxxi, documents those who might be expected to be permitted to preface their response with an oration. For examples, see Isaac Barrow, 'Præfatio cum opponeret die cinerum' (21 Feb. 1653), in his *Theological Works*, ix. 105–10; John Frost, 'Oratio ante initam disputationem', in *Select Sermons* (Cambridge, 1657), sig. B2v (Frost was a fellow of St John's). See also at n. 38, above.

[55] Isaac Barrow, 'Cartesiana hypothesis de materia & motu haud satisfacit præcipuis naturæ phænomenis', in *Theological Works*, ix. 79–104.' This oration is valuably studied and translated in Stewart, 'Fleshy Books'.

[56] As indicated by TCA, 29 Trinity College 472.

[57] C. J. Cook (ed.), *The Palfrey Notebook* (Cambridge, 2011).

[58] Thomas Plume's Library, Maldon (hereafter PLM), MS MA0079, fols. [2r]–[3v] ('Oratio Mathematici Prælectoris an. 1639', in the hand of Edward Hyde); Isaac Barrow, 'Pro Lectore Humanitatis Oratio [1654]' in *Theological Works*, ix. 128–36 (misdated there to '1659?', but corrected in Whewell, 'Barrow', liii); TCC, MS O. 10A. 33, pp. 33–49 (William Lynnet, 'Oratio...habita in Collegio SStæ & Individuæ Trinit. cum Primarij Lectoris officium exorsus est').

lecturer in 'humanity' (Latin literature) in 1654, he emphasised the importance of students following through an argument in the 'themes' (essentially written orations) that they would compose under his direction. He directed that every part of the oration should be connected by a suitable 'method', confirmed by 'fitting examples', flavoured with 'chaste wit', and embellished with 'sensitive and restrained metaphors'.[59] His own oration distinctly and cleverly exemplifies his precepts.

Trinity had other oratorical traditions as well. The 1560 College Statutes required that declamations 'in the manner prescribed by Quintilian' were to be delivered by the Bachelors of Arts from memory in the chapel every Saturday after supper.[60] In 1650 a number of students petitioned the newly constituted political authorities of the Commonwealth for this timing to be changed, on the grounds that it offered a prejudice to piety, and that a change would mean that 'their thoughts might be at more liberty to præpare for *the* Lords day'. The University Commissioners duly found this to be a 'very pious' request and recommended it to the Master.[61]

There is evidence that, like so many other practices that were altered during the 1640s and 1650s, this statutory practice of Saturday evening declamations was resumed following the Restoration, since Richard Cumberland (BA, 1751; fellow, 1752) recalled reciting carefully-composed Latin declamations publicly in the chapel after evening prayers as an undergraduate.[62] A legacy of the college's oratorical tradition survived (and continues to survive), in the form of the Hooper Declamation Prize, founded by the will of Dr Francis Hooper in 1763, and still competed for (though no longer always in the College chapel) in the twenty-first century.[63]

More specifically, following the shocking events at the opening of Parliament in late 1605 there arose a College tradition of delivering an oration on 5 November each year to commemorate the Gunpowder Plot. A few instances of these again survive.[64] The one that Isaac Barrow delivered in the College hall

---

[59] Barrow, 'Pro Lectore Humanitatis Oratio', 133: 'Totam orationis seriem apta methodus connectat, pulchræ similitudines illustrent, apposita exempla confirment, casti lepores condiant, molles ac modestæ metaphoræ exornent; nullique non flosculi et colores rhetoricae pingant, condecorent, perficiant.'

[60] TCA, 34 Statutes of the College and University 5 (hereafter '1560 Statutes'), p. 53: 'declamationes more ac modo a Quintiliano præscripto [*sic*].' I am most grateful to Adam Green for providing me with his accurate transcription of this document.

[61] TCA, 29 Trinity College 472.

[62] Cumberland, *Memoirs*, 73. As an undergraduate in the 1750s Richard Watson also composed weekly declamations in English and Latin: *Anecdotes*, 14–15.

[63] Wordsworth, *Scholae Academicae*, 89.

[64] Edmund Stubbs' oration from 1617 survives in Gonville and Caius College, Cambridge (hereafter GCC), MS 627/250, pp. 4–7, and SJC, MS S. 18 (unfoliated, copied *c.* 1671); the latter volume also contains a different November 5th oration by Richard Milward, probably delivered in Trinity in *c.*1632. John Ramsey's November 5th oration from 1654 is in TCC, MS O. 10a. 33, pp. 50–73. James Duport also wrote a poem on the event, *Musae subsecivae*, 377–78.

in the politically sensitive year of 1651, two-and-a-half years after the execution of Charles I, led to a justified suspicion of disloyalty to the newly instated Commonwealth, something that may have contributed to him losing the Regius Chair of Greek a few years later.[65] It is possible that a similar tradition arose in the later-seventeenth or early- eighteenth century of delivering an oration commemorating the Restoration of Charles II in 1660.[66]

Then, as now, the best way to learn how to write effective academic prose lay in the imitation of good models. It is this that probably accounts for the habit of keeping and copying exemplars of especially successful speeches. A number of Trinity speeches appear to have circulated in this fashion among interested readers. We have several copies, for instance, of two speeches delivered at Trinity before the exiled Archbishop of Spalato (modern-day Split), Marc'Antonio De Dominis, upon the occasion of his visit to the commencement ceremonies of 1617, at which he received a DD.[67] But the most widely circulated speech by a member of Trinity is certainly the ludic oration that James Duport delivered in his capacity as 'Praevaricator' (licensed jester) before the University of Cambridge in 1631; numerous surviving copies attest to its popularity.[68]

The peak of ceremonial eloquence was the position of Public Orator, 'the finest place in the University, though not the gainfullest', as George Herbert put it. This officer wrote the University's formal letters, made orations to visiting dignitaries, and was so distinguished as to sit above the Proctors themselves in the order of seniority.[69] The Orator's productions were some of the very few academic orations that were committed to print immediately following their delivery. In the early 1620s George Herbert filled this dignified office, and two of his oratorical performances from the period,[70] as well as a number of formal letters written on behalf of the

---

[65] Isaac Barrow, 'Oratio habita quinto nov. anno 1651. in Aula S. Trin. Collegii', in Barrow, *Theological Works*, ix. 48. See further William Whewell, 'Barrow and his Academical Times', in ibid., ix. viii–ix; Hill, 'Some Account', xl.

[66] I am aware of a single specimen of the genre: British Library (hereafter BL), London, MS Harley 7017, fols. 135r–136r, an 'Oratio in Carolum Reducem Habita in Aula Collegij S. S. Trinitatis Cantabr. 29no Maij 1711', by William Dent (BA 1709, MA 1712).

[67] Noel Malcolm, *De Dominis (1560–1624)* (1984), 45. The first speech, beginning 'Salve illustrissime Praesul', is in TCC, MS O. 11A. 5(9) (unfoliated leaf) and BL, MS Add. 44963, fol. 17r (copied by Anthony Scattergood at Trinity in the 1630s). The second speech, by Ralph Goodwin (BA 1612, MA 1615), is in BL, MS Add. 44963, fols. 17v–18r (copied by Scattergood), and SJC, MS S. 18 (unfoliated), probably copied by Richard Berry (St John's College, BA 1668, MA 1671).

[68] See n. 182, below.

[69] George Herbert, *Works*, ed. F. E. Hutchinson (Oxford, 1941), 369–70 (Herbert to Sir John Danvers, Sept. 1619).

[70] George Herbert, *Oratio quae auspicatissimum serenissimi Principis Caroli reditum ex Hispanijs celebravit* (Cambridge, 1623); a translation is in George Herbert, *Complete Works*, ed. A. B. Grossart, 3 vols (London, 1874), iii. 397–417. *True copies of all the Latine orations,*

university, survive.[71] Among these letters is one to a former member of Trinity, Lord Chancellor Bacon, thanking him for the gift of his volume of *Instauratio magna* in 1620.[72] Fellows of Trinity filled this office without intermission between 1594 and 1639, and again in 1696–1726.[73]

The Latin verses by which students introduced their disputations were the most formal way in which the writing of poetry formed part of an undergraduate's studies, yet reading and writing verse more generally seems to have been fairly widespread. James Duport recommended to his students the 'diligent & serious perusall' of the 'divine & heavenly' poems of his former Trinity colleague George Herbert.[74] A few undergraduates published printed volumes of verse during their time at the university; the best-known of these was the precocious fellow-commoner at St John's, John Hall, whose *Poems* were quickly purchased by his Trinity contemporary James Master.[75] At Trinity, the less well-known figure of Nicholas Hookes, a pensioner from Westminster published in 1653 a volume of miscellaneous poems which also included a number of English and Latin poems about Trinity and its members. The collection was dedicated to his former tutor, the Vice-Master, Alexander Akehurst.[76] Among these poems is an 'Inscription, or perspective description of the College of the Most Holy and Undivided Trinity in Cambridge', written in lapidary form, and praising Trinity as 'the sharpest eye of Britain', and the 'brain and *pia mater*' of the Commonwealth of England, and concluding loyally:

Of all the universities which Europe has on offer,
Cambridge is easily the queen.
Of the colleges which most ancient Cambridge claims for its own,
The College of the Most Holy and Undivided Trinity holds the first place.[77]

---

made and pronounced at Cambridge... by the Vice-chancellor and others of the Universitie. In their Entertainment of... Don Charles de Coloma... and... Ferdinand, Baron of Boyscot (London, 1623), sigs. C4r–D1r (Latin) and D1r–v (English).

[71] Herbert, *Works*, ed. Hutchinson, 456–69.

[72] Herbert, *Works*, ed. Hutchinson, 462–63. A translation is offered in Herbert, *Complete Works*, ed. Grosart, iii. 436–38.

[73] Respectively, Robert Naunton (1594–1611), Francis Nethersole (1611–1619), George Herbert (1619–1627), Robert Creighton the elder (1627–1639), and William Ayloffe (1696–1726).

[74] Preston and Oswald, 'Duport's Rules', 335.

[75] John Hall, *Poems* (Cambridge, 1646). Robinson, 'Expense-Book of James Master', 164.

[76] Nathaniel Hookes, *Miscellanea poetica* (London, 1653) (published together with Hookes' longer amorous poem *Amanda*).

[77] Hookes, *Miscellanea poetica*, 137: '*Academiarum* quas *Europa* venditat | Omnium facilè *Regina Cantabrigia* | Collegiorum quæ antiquissima Cantabrigia arrogat | *S. S. & Individuæ Trinitatis Collegium* primas obtinet.' (I thank Philip Hardie for providing me with his translation of this poem.)

Hookes was just a couple of years older than another Westminster and Trinity poet, John Dryden, whose relations with the college were considerably less positive.[78]

But the most public way in which members of Trinity and the wider University displayed their poetic talents were in the volumes of commemorative verse that were produced on the death of major public figures and on other significant occasions. Members of Trinity contributed several verses to the volume that appeared in 1619 representing Cambridge's commemoration of the death of James I's consort Queen Anne.[79] They similarly welcomed the return to health of king Charles in the winter of 1632/3.[80] Trinity members predominate in a volume of verses on the death of Francis Bacon that was edited by Bacon's former chaplain, William Rawley (a former fellow of Corpus, but apparently with good connections to Trinity) in 1626.[81] Trinity is also tolerably well represented in Cambridge's volume of verse celebrating the conclusion of the first Anglo-Dutch war in 1654, and the one lamenting the death of Lord Protector Oliver Cromwell and celebrating the accession to the same office of his son Richard in 1658.[82] At least one of these Trinity authors, John Pratt, then prudently contributed to the volume of verses celebrating the Restoration of Charles II in 1660.[83] This act of expiation was not enough, however, to prevent Pratt from being ejected from his fellowship shortly afterwards.[84] For much of the period in question here there was a formal prejudice in favour of oral modes of teaching and learning. But various forms of written exercise were also pursued, not least because they allowed students to become more effective at their oral examinations. Writing also served to record the successful accomplishment of such exercises, either for the student's own satisfaction, or as a means of demonstrating their prowess to

---

[78] Paul Hammond, 'Dryden and Trinity', *Review of English Studies*, 36 (1985), 35–57.

[79] *Lacrymae Cantabrigienses in obitum Serenissimæ Reginæ Annæ* (Cambridge, 1619).

[80] *Anthologia in Regis exanthemata* (Cambridge, 1632). Among the Trinity contributors are Thomas Comber (the Master); Robert Boreman; James Duport; the future Cromwellian, Dudley Wyatt; the future Master, Henry Ferne; John Cooke, who later contributed to *Justa Eduardo King* (1638); Caesar Williamson; and two sprigs of nobility, Henry Noel and William Williams. See further J. C. T. Oates, 'Cambridge Books of Congratulatory Verses 1603–1640 and their Binders', *Transactions of the Cambridge Bibliographical Society*, 1 (1953), 395–421.

[81] William Rawley (ed.), *Memoriae honoratissimi domini Francisci Baronis de Verulamio, Vice-Comitis Sancti Albani, sacrum* (London, 1626).

[82] *Oliva Pacis* (Cambridge, 1654); *Musarum Cantabrigiensium luctus et gratulatio ille in funere Oliveri* (Cambridge, 1658) (John Pratt's poem is at sigs. A2r–v).

[83] *Academiae Cantabrigiensis Sostra* (Cambridge, 1660) (Pratt's contribution is at sigs. B3v–B4v).

[84] H. McLeod Innes, *Fellows of Trinity College, Cambridge* (Cambridge, 1941), 33.

others.[85] The act of writing itself was also taken seriously. Isaac Barrow reminded his students that it was a mark of cultivation to write clearly and distinctly: 'difficult and inelegant handwriting provokes prejudice and disgust.'[86] Some students employed a writing-master during their time at Trinity. Others may have worn illegibility as a badge of honour.[87] But what is clear is that the experience of being at Trinity itself marked the handwriting of its members. During his schooling at Grantham the young Isaac Newton had learned to write a clear, but rather laboured and by then somewhat old-fashioned 'secretary' script. This had been widely used for writing English for well over a century previously, though it was more usual to use an 'italic' script when writing Latin. Yet the young Newton used his juvenile secretary script for both languages. Shortly after his arrival at Trinity, however, he switched to using the rather more *au courant* italic—even when he was writing English.[88]

The survival of manuscripts arising from students' studies at Trinity, as of any scholastic manuscript from this period, owes as much to chance as to design. In reconstructing the shape of academic studies pursued three or four centuries ago one must work from fragments. The great majority of notebooks maintained by students and their teachers have been lost, either by accident, redeployment (paper was useful in both cookhouse and jakes), or design.[89] Such manuscripts as survive were sometimes kept because of their inherent interest: the survival throughout the eighteenth and nineteenth centuries of the notebook that Anthony Scattergood kept at Trinity in the 1630s probably owes more to the English poems by Caroline authors that he had copied into it than to the Latin orations and theses that it also contains. But this must surely be only the best of several notebooks that Scattergood would have maintained as a student.[90] Although none of the manuscripts survive, an unusually rich collection of Isaac Barrow's eloquent university writings made their way into print in 1687 by virtue of the unusual fact that a stationer had paid Barrow's father

---

[85] For an example of the latter, see DUL, MS Hunter 31, pp. 67–93, written by Thomas Carr for his former tutor in *c.* 1611.

[86] Isaac Barrow, 'Pro Lectore Humanitatis Oratio' [1654] in *Theological Works*, ix. 135.

[87] Serjeantson, 'Education of Francis Willughby', 22.

[88] For his early hand (1659), see TCC, MS R. 4. 48c, fols. 1r–20v. Contrast his hand of the post 1661 period in Cambridge University Library (hereafter CUL), MS Add. 3996, fos. 3r–83v.

[89] Edward King, a fellow of Christ's who died in 1637, required that his executor 'burn all my papers and paper books in which there is any thing written, not reading them himself or suffering any other to do so' (Norman Postlethwaite and Gordon Campbell, 'Edward King, Milton's "Lycidas": Poems and Documents', *Milton Quarterly*, 28 (1994), 95).

[90] BL, MS Add. 44963.

an immense sum to acquire his son's papers, and had a large investment to recoup.[91] It is scarcely conceivable that Barrow himself would have chosen to have published the scholastic compositions of his youth, for in general members of the English universities were exceptionally reluctant to put the fruits of their daily academic work into print. Even works by professors of divinity mostly tended only to appear posthumously.

Thus it is exceptionally rare that we possess the complete manuscript archive of a member of Trinity in our period. We have several that were kept by Edward Hyde, a student and fellow at Trinity between 1625 and 1643, which were preserved by his younger friend Thomas Plume, of Christ's, and later the founder of the Plumeian Professorship of Astronomy.[92] But the triumphant exception to this generalisation is the somewhat special case of Isaac Newton. By virtue both of Newton's immense celebrity at his death in 1727, and also a fair amount of good luck, Newton's entire archive has survived intact (albeit that it is now widely dispersed).[93] Hence in the case of this singular and rather unrepresentative individual it is possible to draw inferences about the full extent of his production as student, fellow, and ultimately Lucasian Professor of Mathematics. From these and other documents that we may set out to reconstruct the studies pursued at Trinity primarily from the actual evidence of surviving manuscript sources, and to test the evidence of practice against more ideal accounts of the pedagogic experience set out in the College statutes and in instructions for students such as Duport's.

ARTS COURSE STUDIES: PHILOSOPHICAL

The studies pursued under the Arts course may broadly be divided into two sorts: formal exercises, and informal studies that were not necessarily examined in any form. To some extent, therefore, this distinction corresponds to one between formally-examined philosophical studies on the one hand, and informal humanistic studies on the other—poetry, drama, history, or what in 1631 the Oxford tutor John Crowther called 'the study of humanity'.[94] A Cambridge author in 1750 noted that 'there are no publick and general

---

[91] Isaac Barrow, *Opuscula* (1687); M. Feingold, 'Barrow, Isaac (1630–1677)', *ODNB*.
[92] Hyde's manuscripts survive in Thomas Plume's Library, Maldon, and are discussed below.
[93] Sarah Dry, *The Newton Papers* (Oxford, 2014).
[94] Nicholas Tyacke, 'An Oxford Education in the Early Seventeenth Century: John Crowther's *Musae faciles* (1631)', *History of Universities*, 27 (2013), 52.

Examinations' in 'Languages', as there were in 'Sciences'.[95] But this distinction should not be taken as a clear-cut one. Philological learning played a significant role in philosophy: writing verses on a philosophical subject was a central part of preparing for the University 'Act', while orations might explore a student's skills in rhetoric but were also focused upon ethical questions.

There is another way of dividing these studies, however, which is according to the time of day in which they were to be pursued. There is firm evidence from both seventeenth-century Cambridge and Oxford that philosophical (and later also mathematical) studies tended to be pursued in the forenoon, while poets, dramatists, and historians were read, after dinner had been taken, in the afternoon.[96] As late as the 1750s the future bishop Richard Watson 'generally studied mathematics in the morning, and classics in the afternoon.'[97]

Let us begin, then, by considering the philosophical studies of the morning. The first and perhaps most intensive of these was logic. To be sure, logic was not always regarded, strictly speaking, as a part of philosophy itself. Writers in the period consistently distinguish between, while also conjoining, 'Logic and Philosophy'. But logic was an essential preparative to philosophy, and indeed to textual interpretation and religious debate; the Trinity lecturer William Lynnet described it as a 'scythe' (*falx*) to use against the rest of the sciences.[98] The evidence indicates that seventeenth-century students at Trinity studied logic intensively for at least the first three years of BA study. For the brief period of its existence between 1620 and 1640 undergraduates might also attend the lectures given by the Maynard reader in logic, delivered on Wednesdays and Fridays in term-time.[99] The 1570 Statutes also mandated the appointment of an annual logic lecturer in the University.

---

[95] Anon., *The Academic* (1750), 25.

[96] This ante-meridional/post-meridional pattern emerges from a number of sources, including Folger Shakespeare Library, MS V. a. 236 (John Crowther, 'Musæ Faciles', 1631; see Tyacke, 'An Oxford Education'); Emmanuel College, Cambridge, MS I. 2. 27 (Richard Holdsworth, 'Directions for a Student in the Universitie', by 1649); Bodeleian Library, Oxford (hereafter OB), MS Tanner 88, fo. 5r (Nathaniel Sterry, 'A direction for a good, & profitable proceeding in study', *c*. 1650).

[97] Watson, *Anecdotes*, 15. But he also adds (p. 22) that the philosophical disputations began in the schools at 2 p.m.

[98] TCC, MS O. 10a. 33, p. 43 (William Lynnet's 'Oratio...habita...cum Primarij Lectoris officium exorsus est').

[99] Maynard's readership, worth £50 per annum, and tenable by a fellow of Maynard's college of St John's, was founded in 1620 following correspondence in 1618 (printed in Heywood and Wright, ii. 297 from BL, MS Sloane 3562, fol. 25r–v). See C. H. Cooper, *Annals of Cambridge*, 5 vols (Cambridge, 1842–1908), iii. 135–36 and v. 356–57. It lapsed following Maynard's death in 1639 (Wordsworth, *Scholae Academicae*, 85). The days on which the reader lectured are documented on the broadsheet by John Scot headed 'The names of all such Noble Persons as have been Chancellours, together with the...Lecturers...' (Cambridge, 1633), *STC* 44897.

194   *History of Universities*

It has been suggested that logic might sometimes have been taught to the higher classes in some grammar schools. I have not found evidence for this in the case of Trinity, and there is countervailing evidence that some students valued their ability at university to leave behind the endless study of the Latin and Greek tongues in favour of the new pastures of philosophy. The future chronologer Edward Simpson (1578–1651), for instance, is said to have rejoiced at leaving behind Homer and Demosthenes when he entered the 'freer air of the Academy' upon his arrival at Trinity from Westminster School in 1596 and to have 'applied himself entirely to studies in Philosophy'.[100]

Detailed evidence for this study is offered by one of the surviving Trinity notebooks of Edward Hyde (1607–1659). Hyde (a kinsman of the future earl of Clarendon) entered Trinity as Pensioner in 1625 and was elected a Westminster Scholar in 1626.[101] The quantity and quality of his surviving notebooks, which survive thanks to their preservation by his younger friend Thomas Plume, indicate that he was a diligent and conscientious scholar. Hyde's academic record confirms this: he took his BA in 1630; was elected to a Fellowship in 1632, and proceeded MA in 1633. (All of these appointments occurred at the standard intervals.) From 1636 Hyde served as a tutor,[102] and in 1640, at the first opportunity (i.e. seven years subsequent to his MA) he took the degree of Bachelor of Divinity. In 1643 Hyde became rector of Brightwell in Berkshire (not a Trinity living), and some of his surviving Cambridge notebooks go on to document his parochial duties there.[103] He was ejected from Brightwell in 1650, and the 'ample estate' he was fortunate enough to possess meant that Parliament controversially exempted his successor, John Ley, from paying the usual fifth part of his tithes to support Hyde's family.[104]

Hyde's studies of logic are documented by two of his surviving notebooks. Neither is dated, but – unless they record his duties as a teacher rather than as a pupil – they were probably compiled at some point before 1630. This may be the case with a well-filled notebook now in Thomas Plume's library in Maldon entitled 'Annotationes Logicæ'. This document contains notes taken from Hyde's reading of the Oxford scholar Edward

---

[100] T. Jones, 'Authoris vita', in Edward Simpson, *Chronicon historiam catholicam complectens* (Oxford, 1652), sig. a5v: 'Philosophiæ studiis gnaviter incumbit.'
[101] W. W. Rouse Ball and J. A. Venn (eds.), *Admissions to Trinity College, Cambridge*, 5 vols (London, 1911–1916), ii. 308; the name of his tutor is not recorded.
[102] Pupils in Hyde's charge included John Riches, Pensioner, adm. 2 July 1636 (Rouse Ball and Venn, *Admissions to Trinity*, ii. 353).
[103] PLM, MS MA0079 (unfoliated), fo. [71]r ('The Heads of some Catechizis at Brightwell').
[104] Richard L. Greaves, 'Ley, John (1584–1662)', *ODNB*.

Brerewood's *Elementa Logicæ*.[105] It follows up with notes on the five mental habits probably derived from a reading of a logic manual by another Oxford scholar, Robert Sanderson.[106] If these document Hyde's reading as a student, a later item in the manuscript may represent his work as a tutor, for it contains a very concise, but efficient, 'Epitome' of logic. We know from the 'Directions for a Student in the University' composed by Richard Holdsworth of St John's in the same period as Hyde was at Trinity, that it was regarded as desirable for students to copy out a logic 'of your Tutors own collecting'.[107] It seems likely that Hyde's epitome represents just this practise—either by his tutor, or by Hyde himself. Hyde's logical studies were not restricted to one notebook alone, however, for a second further document in the Plume collection also contains notes taken from an unidentified treatise headed 'Liber secundus de propositione' (Book Two, on the Proposition). This more detailed and intensive study of the subject of logic may again relate to Hyde's work as a tutor, rather than as a pupil.[108]

Although the evidence of Hyde's notebooks is unusually rich, his studies appear to be entirely representative. The opening chapter of a manuscript 'Synopsis of all Philosophy' that a Bachelor of Arts called Robert Boothe presented to the Master, Thomas Nevile, in around 1607, considers logic, including the natural logic possessed by Adam, as the precondition for *sophia* (wisdom), the object of *philo-sophia*, the love of wisdom.[109] William Ayscough recalled studying Robert Sanderson's *Compendium of the Art of Logic* as soon as he arrived in 1630;[110] one of the first books that Ayscough's nephew Isaac Newton purchased upon his own arrival in 1661 was a copy of the same book, which still survives.[111] Newton also owned a copy of Samuel Smith's *Aditus ad logicam* in the edition of 1613, although its annotations have recently been shown not to be in his hand.[112] Newton

---

[105] PLM, MS MA0087 (unfoliated). 'Annotationes logicæ Ex Brerewood'.

[106] PLM, MS MA0087 (unfoliated). 'De quinque habitus mentis'. Compare Robert Sanderson, *Logicæ artis compendium* (1615), Appendix Posterior, sigs. X5r–Y2v (cap. 1).

[107] Holdsworth, 'Directions', 634.   [108] PLM, MS MA0097 (unfoliated).

[109] BL, MS Harley 5356, fols. 3r–5v.

[110] Richard Westfall, *Never at Rest: A Biography of Isaac Newton* (Cambridge, 1980), 40, persuasively identifies Ayscough as the 'William Askue' who matriculated as a pensioner from Trinity in Lent 1630 and took his BA in 1634 and his MA in 1637 (Venn, *Alumni Cantabrigienses*, i. 48).

[111] King's College, Cambridge (hereafter KCC), MS Keynes 130.10, fol. 2r (transcription from the Newton Papers Project, ed. Rob Iliffe and Scott Mandelbrote, www.newtonproject.sussex.ac.uk); Westfall, *Never at Rest*, 82–3; TCC, Adv. e. 1. 15: Robert Sanderson, *Logicæ artis compendium*, 3rd edn (Oxford, 1631).

[112] Dmitri Levitin, 'Newton and Scholastic Philosophy', *British Journal for the History of Science*, 49 (2016), 53–77 (p. 59). Compare Steffen Ducheyne, *The Main Business of Natural Philosophy: Isaac Newton's Natural-Philosophical Methodology* (Dordrecht, 2012), 16–18.

also seems to have purchased a copy of Franco Burgersdijk's increasingly popular logic as well; a few years earlier, Daniel Foote (BA 1650) had taken notes from the book.[113] Francis Willughby (BA 1656) read a demanding logical treatise by the Polish Jesuit Martin Smiglecius, of which the early eighteenth-century fellow Edward Rud also possessed a copy.[114] In 1661 or so William Davies, a pensioner who took both his degrees and became a scholar, lent 'Ramus his logick' to James Tennant, a sizar who disappears without trace.[115] Both Thomas Millington (BA 1649) and Isaac Newton (BA 1665) took notes from Aristotle's *Organon* and Porphyry's *Isagoge* in their original Greek.[116] Newton also constructed a pictorial representation of the so-called 'Tree of Porphyry', an analysis of all possible types of being in the universe, from substance to 'irrational animals' that flew in the air (bees), walked on the ground, swam in the sea (fish), or slithered on the ground (reptiles).[117] As this suggests, for all that pre-modern logic now possesses a reputation for intellectual aridity, in the long seventeenth century it was regarded as an imperative, indeed, essential, means of comprehending the world in which human beings had been placed, and which it was the goal of the Arts Course to understand. As late as the early nineteenth century Richard Cumberland sternly admonished the readers of his memoirs of the merit of subjecting 'vivacity of imagination' to 'the trammels of a syllogism'.[118]

A portion of that world—the world of action, of passion, and of politics—was subject to human will; the discipline that comprehended these phenomena was moral philosophy, which also included the study of politics. The tenor of pre-modern philosophical study was Aristotelian. The University statutes mandated the works of Aristotle; at Trinity, too, James Duport required of his many students that they must invoke the 'Authority of Aristotle' in 'his owne words, & in his owne language.'[119] And it is clear that what we might think of as the Duport generation at Trinity—those students who studied there between the 1630s and the 1660s—endeavoured to make this a reality. It was not only Aristotle's logical writings that Isaac Newton studied in Greek: he also made a careful

---

[113] TCC, MS R. 4. 48c, fol. 22v (Newton); BL, MS Sloane 600, fols. 24v–43r (Foote). See Mordechai Feingold, 'The Ultimate Pedagogue: Franco Burgersdijk and the English-Speaking Academic Learning', in *Franco Burgersdijk (1590–1635): Neo-Aristotelianism in Leiden*, ed. E. P. Bos and H. A. Krop (Amsterdam: Brill, 1993), 151–65.

[114] Nottingham University Library (hereafter NUL), MS Mi LM 15/1, p. 571. TCC, VI. 11. 57: Martin Smiglecius, *Logica* (Oxford, 1638), Rud's copy.

[115] The loan was recorded by Isaac Newton in TCC, MS R. 4. 48c, fol. 21v.

[116] OB, MS Rawl. D. 1041 item 10, fols. 1r–19r; CUL, MS Add. 3996, fols. 3r–10v.

[117] CUL, MS Add. 3996, fol. 2r.   [118] Cumberland, *Memoirs*, 83.

[119] Preston and Oswald, 'Duport's Rules', 349.

collection of *sententiae* from the Greek text of Aristotle's *Nicomachean Ethics*, with corresponding marginal keywords in Latin. In the course of this work Newton not only learned Aristotle's definitions of virtue and vice, and of specific virtues and vices such as magnanimity and pride; he also learned to incorporate the findings of earlier philosophers into his analysis of Aristotle's Greek text.[120]

Yet it would be a mistake to suppose that Aristotle's Greek was always read in unmediated form. Edward Hyde's notes show that he studied Aristotle through the extensive 'analytical synopses' of his writings that the French scholar Guillaume Du Val prefaced to his edition of Aristotle's *Opera omnia*.[121] Aristotelian moral philosophy was also studied through the medium of contemporary philosophical systems, and in mid-seventeenth century Trinity Aristotle's own text was often supplemented by the ethical portion of the *Summa Philosophiae* by the Cistercian philosopher Eustachius a Sancto Paulo: this book was purchased by James Master, and noted extensively by Daniel Foote in the mid-1640s and by Isaac Newton in the early 1660s.[122] By contrast, in the more self-consciously classical eighteenth century Richard Cumberland recalled that his gouty tutor would occasionally put them both to the trouble of 'a few trifling readings in Tully's Offices' – that is, Cicero's *De officiis* – 'by which I was little edified, and to which I paid little or no attention'.[123]

The philosophical framework of the virtues and vices also provide students with headings for the commonplace books they sometimes kept. These provided opportunities for the collection of moral 'sentences' from a range of authors on set headings. Edward Palmer, a student and then a fellow at Trinity in the 1610s with a reputation as an excellent Greek scholar, kept three massive examples of these across this period, each with a different linguistic and disciplinary focus: Latin, Greek, and theological.[124] Another

---

[120] CUL, MS Add. 3996, fols. 34r–36r; see esp. fo. 34v, on the marks of virtue: 'Golius addit ἐὰν ἡδέως', alluding to Théophile Golius, *Epitome doctrinae moralis* (Strasbourg, 1597), 70.

[121] PLM, MS MA0086 (unfoliated), notes 'ex Duuallo in Aristotelem'. Guillaume Du Val (ed.), *Aristotelis opera omnia quae extant*, 2 vols (Paris, 1629).

[122] Robinson, 'Expense-Book of James Master', 164 (a copy of Eustachius' entire *Summa* for 4s); BL, MS Sloane 586, fols. 2r–23v; BL, MS Sloane 600, fols. 76–80 (Foote). CUL, MS Add. 3996, fols. 38r–40r (Newton). PLM, MS MA0094 (unfoliated) also contains notes from Eustachius' physics, in an unidentified hand.

[123] Cumberland, *Memoirs*, 69. The tutor was William Morgan (BA, 1718; MA, 1722; BD, 1730; DD, 1750), from 1747 vicar of Gainford in Durham, a Trinity living since the College's founding. See John Richard Walbran, *The Antiquities of Gainford in the County of Durham* (Ripon, 1846), 80, 87, 88–89.

[124] TCC, MS R. 16. 6 (Latin moral commonplace-book, predominantly Senecan, signed by Palmer); TCC, MS R. 16. 7 (Greek moral commonplace-book, predominantly from 'Suidas', in Palmer's hand); TCC, MS R. 16. 8 (moral commonplace-book with theological materials, in Palmer's later hand). For Palmer's reputation, see Duport, *Musæ subsecivæ*, 240, 291.

very full surviving commonplace book from seventeenth century Trinity is the one that the fellow commoner Francis Willughby kept during his years at Trinity between 1652 and 1660. In his 'Directions' Richard Holdsworth warned younger students against keeping large folio volumes of this sort, observing that few students 'either continue constant in it, or bring it to any perfection', by virtue of the 'toyle & the interuption' that using them gave rise to.[125] Willughby is a salutary counter-example to this warning. He evidently maintained his commonplace book assiduously, and it provides a remarkable insight into the nature and development of his studies. Characteristically, Willughby acquired his commonplace book at secondhand, with a number of headings already written into it. He sometimes used these and sometimes added to them. For instance, to the inherited heading 'On desire and restraint' (*De libidine et modestia*) he added on separate occasions the further headings 'and beauty' (*et pulchritudine*), 'and nuptials' (*et nuptiis*). The first entry notes the reproving judgment that 'restraint is an uncommon virtue in men' (*modestia in hominibus rara virtus*). But in Willughby's case the sentiments he recorded were not always so morally edifying. A few lines further on he notes from his reading of the French anatomist Jean Riolan the observation that 'circumcision reduces women's pleasure; hence they prefer to have sex with Christians' (*circumcisio minuit voluptatem mulierum ideo malunt congredi Xtianis*).[126]

Willughby's observation was clearly not for public consumption. But a principal function of the moral commonplace book was to provide a wealth of historical and other material that might be deployed in orations and 'problems' in moral philosophy that might be delivered in a formal setting. We do not possess any of these in the case of Willughby, but there is a rich supply of them in the notebook that was carefully maintained by slightly earlier by Anthony Scattergood (1611–1687) during his time at Trinity between 1628 and 1641. These address questions in moral and political philosophy that often have a classical flavour. In one problem, for instance, he asks whether Lycurgus was right to prefer to strike coins from iron rather than gold or silver.[127] In a different one he argued that it was worse for Niobe to have been turned into stone than to have witnessed the death of her fourteen children.[128] Speeches such as these provided their

---

[125] Holdsworth, 'Directions', 651.
[126] NUL, MS Mi LM 15/1, p. 51. Willughby has been reading the extensive discussion of male genitalia in Jean Riolan the younger, *Encheiridium anatomicum et pathologicum* (Paris 1649), 156.
[127] BL, MS Add. 44963, fols. 30v–33r: 'Utrum rectè Lycurgus, qui præ auro & argento ferrum pro nummis excudi maluit.'
[128] BL, MS Add. 44963, fol. 101v: 'Infelicior Niobe in Saxum conversa, quam filijs orbata.'

authors with the opportunity to argue a morally complex case, to demonstrate their knowledge of ancient literature, and to show off their Latinity before an audience upon whose favour they consistently throw themselves at the outset.

The discipline of metaphysics had a rather precarious place in the two English universities following the Reformation, although it received something of a renewed impetus in the second quarter of the earlier seventeenth century, when we find a significant number of questions in metaphysics being collected and briefly analysed by Edward Hyde.[129] Yet Cambridge lacked the stimulus of a figure such as 1630s Oxford possessed in Thomas Barlow, who held that university's lectureship in the subject. In mid-seventeenth century Cambridge, however, and especially in Trinity, a form of metaphysics briefly acquired some prominence in the form of a vogue for the kind of philosophical rules purveyed by the otherwise distinctly minor figure of Daniel Stahl, a professor of logic and metaphysics at the University of Jena.[130] Stahl's *Axiomata philosophica* were printed in Cambridge in 1645 and again in 1651, and it is clear that Trinity undergraduates were set to master his book very seriously.[131] James Master purchased a copy, while Francis Willughby in the early 1650s, and Isaac Newton in the early 1660s, both took extensive notes from it.[132] Stahl's axioms were the kind of 'Logical & Philosophical Rules' that James Duport recommended students should write in a 'little pocket-paper-book' and carry about with them as they 'walke abroade'.[133] Stahl's book gave both of these natural philosophers a facility with contemporary philosophical terminology and with modes of analysis in terms of causation which retained its legacy in their later writings.[134] But it may not merely have

---

[129] PLM, MS MA0086 (unfoliated) contains 128 'Problemata Physica et Metaphysica'. John Milton (Christ's College) also draw extensively upon Francisco Suárez's *Disputationes metaphysicae* (1614) in two student orations; see Robert Dulgarian, 'Milton's Prolusions 4 and 5 as Cambridge Undergraduate Disputation Orations: Sources and contexts', *Milton Quarterly*, 54 (2020), 1–22.

[130] Jacob Schmutz, 'Scholasticon', s.n. 'Stahl, Daniel' (scholasticon.ish-lyon.cnrs.fr).

[131] TCC, T. 9. 108¹: D. Stahl, *Axiomata* (Cambridge, 1651), Henry Puckering's (BA 1657) copy.

[132] Robinson, 'Expense-Book of James Master', 165 (1*s* 8*d*); NUL, MS Mi LM 15/1, pp. 567–71 (Willughby); CUL, MS Add. 3996, fos. 43r–71v (Newton).

[133] Preston and Oswald, 'Duport's Rules', 350.

[134] Serjeantson, 'Education of Willughby', 68–69, 87; J. E. McGuire and Martin Tamny, *Certain Philosophical Questions: Newton's Trinity Notebook* (Cambridge, 1983), 206; Sachiko Kusukawa, 'Nature's Regularity in Some Protestant Natural Philosophy Textbooks, 1530–1630', in *Natural Law and Laws of Nature in Early Modern Europe*, ed. Lorraine Daston and Michael Stolleis (2008), 121; J. Z. Buchwald and Mordechai Feingold, *Newton and the Origin of Civilization* (Princeton, 2013), 14–15. Contrast Richard S. Westfall, 'The Foundations of Newton's Philosophy of Nature', *British Journal for the History of Science*, 1 (1962), 172.

been by virtue of his own idiosyncrasies that the older Newton was polemically hostile to metaphysics.[135] The discipline accordingly seems to have played little role in university exercises by the mid-eighteenth century,[136] but its presence was not entirely negligible, for on his own account Richard Cumberland caused something of a stir when he insisted in about 1750 upon challenging the previous custom of proposing at least one metaphysical question among the mathematical ones he preferred to defend.[137]

Unquestionably the most important philosophical discipline in seventeenth-century undergraduate teaching, therefore, was natural philosophy. The evidence here is clear: whatever else they did, and whether or not they even took a BA degree, undergraduates at Trinity acquired a great deal of philosophical knowledge of the natural world. The 'Synopsis of all Philosophy' that Robert Boothe presented to Nevile carries the subtitle 'and especially Natural Philosophy' (*physiologia*).[138] (Boothe's use of this technical term implies natural knowledge as a whole, not the physiological part of medicine.[139]) Questions in natural philosophy were a staple of the university Acts; these questions in turn reflect the private work that students did to prepare for these public exercises. Even when addressing the French ambassador an orator might draw attention to the natural philosophical question of whether springs had their origin in the sea.[140]

Just as he had composed a system of logic, so Edward Hyde also put together a brief compendium of physics, either in his capacity as a student or (perhaps more likely) as a teacher.[141] Hyde also took a wide variety of other notes relating to physics, including some notes from Franco Burgersdijk's substantial *Collegium Physicum* and Galileo's *Starry Messenger*.[142] James Master bought the former of these in 1647.[143] Francis Willughby studied the *Physical Contemplations* by the Heidelberg

---

[135] Levitin, 'Newton and Scholastic Philosophy'.
[136] So Gascoigne, 'Mathematics and Meritocracy', 553.
[137] Cumberland, *Memoirs*, 77.
[138] BL, MS Harley 5356, fols. 1r–97r ('Synopsis totius Philosophiæ, inprimis verò Physiologia').
[139] Dennis Des Chene, *Physiologia: Natural Philosophy in Late Aristotelian and Cartesian Thought* (Ithaca, NY, 2000).
[140] BL, MS Add. 44963, fols. 26v–28r (Richard Love's 1629 oration to the Chancellor and French Ambassador on the thesis that the 'Origo Fontium est à Mari', copied by Scattergood).
[141] PLM, MS MA0086 (unfoliated) 'Physicæ annotationes breuisculæ', in the hand of Edward Hyde.
[142] PLM, MS MA0086 (unfoliated) notes on natural philosophy, including 128 'Problemata Physica et Metaphysica' in the hand of Edward Hyde.
[143] Robinson, 'Expense-Book of James Master', 166.

philosopher and theologian Marcus Friedrich Wendelin in its recent Cambridge imprint for the BA degree he took in 1656.[144] But one of the principal authorities in natural philosophy at Trinity in the middle years of the seventeenth century was an Aristotelian treatment of physics by the Paduan-educated German philosopher Johannes Magirus, who had taught at the University of Marburg. The first book that the fellow-commoner James Master bought upon arriving at Cambridge in March 1647 was a copy of Magirus' treatise, which had been recently reprinted at Cambridge; Daniel Foote took notes from Magirus in the later 1640s; and Isaac Newton notoriously also did so in the early 1660s.[145] Nor was Magirus the only school natural philosopher Newton read: he also owned a hundred-year old copy of Sebastian Fox Morcillo's book *On the Nature of Philosophy*.[146] Yet Newton does not seem to have been much interested in a different ancient tradition of natural philosophy with which a number of fellows and students had been much taken in the 1650s, that of Stoic natural philosophy—demonstrated, in particular by the ownership and use of copies of the volume *On the Natural Philosophy of the Stoics* by the Flemish neo-Stoic scholar Justus Lipsius.[147]

A significant component of natural philosophy in the seventeenth century concerned the qualities of 'human nature' in respect of the qualities of the human soul and the human body.[148] The *telos* of this portion of natural science was the immortal portion of the human soul, and in the 1630s we duly find the future divine Anthony Scattergood defending the philosophical thesis that 'the rational soul is immortal in its own right' (*anima rationalis est immortalis ab intrinseco*); this was of course conveniently congruent with the theological dogma he would be bound to up

---

[144] NUL, MS Mi LM 15/1, p. 572; Marcus Friedrich Wendelin, *Contemplationum physicarum sectiones tres* (Cambridge, 1648). Serjeantson, 'Education of Willughby', 70. Oliver Heywood, *Autobiography, Diaries, Anecdote and Event Books*, ed. J. H. Turner, 3 vols (Brighouse, 1882–83), i. 162, also mentions neglecting Wendelin (misnamed 'Wendreton') at Trinity in the later 1640s.

[145] Johannes Magirus, *Physiologiæ peripateticæ* (Cambridge, 1642). Robinson, 'Expense-Book of James Master', 164; BL, MS Sloane 586, fols. 24v–43r (Foote); CUL, MS Add. 3996, fols. 16r–27v (Newton). Heywood, *Autobiography*, 162, also mentions neglecting Magirus.

[146] TCC, shelfmark Adv. d. 1. 13: Sebastián Fox Morcillo, *De naturæ philosophia, seu, de Platonis, & Aristotelis consensione libri V* (Paris, 1560), Isaac Newton's copy. In Mordechai Feingold's judgment the annotations in this volume are probably not to be ascribed to Newton.

[147] TCC, shelfmark T. 9. 23²: Justus Lipsius, *Physiologiae Stoicorum* (Paris, 1604) (Puckering family copy; both father and son were at Trinity). Serjeantson, 'Education of Willughby', 71–72.

[148] See e.g. the entries collected under the heading 'Anima. Mens. Ratio', in Edward Hyde's commonplace book, PLM, MS MA0057, p. 60.

hold once he entered holy orders and became a chaplain at Trinity between 1637 and 1641.[149] As late as 1758 Richard Watson was obliged, as an opponent, to find arguments against the question 'the soul is immortal by its nature' (*anima est suâ naturâ immortalis*) when serving as an opponent in the philosophical schools.[150]

Yet an undergraduate did not need to be either a prospective divine nor a prospective physician to take a serious interest in this general subject of human nature, and the future antiquarian and Norroy king of arms, Peter le Neve (1661–1729) did so in 1678 when he read the Latin translation of René Descartes' treatise *L'Homme*.[151] Le Neve did not even take the first degree of BA, and yet his notebook bears witness to the earnestness with which he made notes not only on this work but also on Descartes's *Principles of Philosophy* and on the treatise entitled *Natural Philosophy* by Franco Burgersdijk's student, Adrian Heereboord.[152]

As across Europe, so also at Trinity, a sea-change in the study of nature occurred across the 1640s and '50s. Following his arrival at Trinity from Emmanuel in 1645, the medical fellow John Pratt, and also his student, Daniel Foote, maintained an interest in botany.[153] This tradition probably helped sow the seed for the young John Ray's life-long pursuit of that subject, which began with his expeditions around Cambridge that culminated in the *Catalogue of Plants Growing Around Cambridge* that he published in 1660.[154]

Furthermore, together with his friends among the younger fellows, and also certain students, Ray combined his interests in botany with natural history more generally at Trinity in the later 1650s. Ray's friend Thomas Pockley reported in 1655 from Trinity to the physician Henry Power, formerly a student at Christ's College, on his investigations into the spleen. These included the vivisection of a dog (which survived until Pockley later lost it), and which led him to the conviction that it was 'no meere appendix'. He proposed to further investigate whether the spleen was indeed the 'seate of melancholy' by conducting experiments (unspecified) on the inhabitants of the asylum of Bedlam.[155] Pockley subsequently obtained

---

[149] BL, MS Add. 44963, fols. 118r–119v. Hugh de Quehen, 'Scattergood, Anthony (*bap.* 1611, *d.* 1687)', *ODNB*.

[150] Watson, *Anecdotes*, 17.

[151] Society of Antiquaries of London (hereafter SAL), MS 325, fols. 1r–14v. René Descartes, *De Homine*, trans. F. Schuyl (Amsterdam, 1662).

[152] SAL, MS 325, fols. 15r–25v (notes from Descartes, *Principia philosophiæ*, 1644); fos. 26r–47v (notes from Adrian Heereboord, *Philosophiæ naturalis*, Oxford, 1665 or 1668).

[153] BL, MS Sloane 591 (John Pratt, 'Catalogus plantarum Angliæ').

[154] John Ray, *Cambridge Catalogue*, ed. and trans. C. D. Preston and P. H. Oswald (2011).

[155] BL, MS Sloane 3515, fo. 71r–v (Pockley to Henry Power, 17 Aug. 1655).

three years' leave from Trinity to pursue medicine professionally, and died ministering to the British garrison in Dunkirk in 1661.[156]

Pockley was also present when another friend of Ray's, John Nidd, led an anatomy of four aquatic birds—'a Bittern a Curlew, a Yarwhelp, the fourth was like a duck with a bill hooked at the top, for which we had no name'— whose 'cases' (i.e. stuffed carcasses) he then hung up in the cupboards over his door.[157] The interest that this aspect of natural historical investigation sparked in Francis Willughby, a fellow commoner at Trinity at the time, eventually resulted in his ambitious posthumous *Ornithology* (1676), edited by his friend and client Ray.[158] Willughby's no less thorough passion for what his period generally called insects was also fostered during his time at Trinity, where he kept an 'eruca' (caterpillar), and remembered seeing a specimen of Scolopendra (a long many-legged arthropod) 'in the Cloisters of *Trinity* Colledge in *Cambridge*' in about 1659.[159]

In 1659, John Wilkins briefly became Master of Trinity. When he was courteously removed at the Restoration a year later he went on to found what would become the Royal Society of London for the Advancement of Natural Knowledge. Wilkins' collaborators Francis Willughby and John Ray, a fellow commoner and a former fellow, respectively, duly joined him as members.[160] Other members of Trinity followed the publications that emerged with the new Society's imprint, above all the young Isaac Newton, who made extensive notes on Robert Hooke's *Micrographia* (1665), Thomas Sprat's *History of the Royal Society* (1667), and on early numerous numbers of the *Philosophical Transactions of the Royal Society* (1665 onwards).[161] Though it has since been transformed out of all recognition, Trinity's natural scientific tradition can be traced back to the academic study of natural philosophy of the sixteenth and seventeenth centuries; and, perhaps more specifically, to the experimental and natural historical interests of the generation that immediately preceded the arrival in the college of the young Isaac Newton.[162]

---

[156] TCM, Conclusions and Admonitions, 1607–1673, p. 255; East Sussex Record Office, Lewes (hereafter ESRO), DAN/352 (John Ray to Peter Courthope, 26 Nov. 1661).

[157] ESRO, DAN/361 (John Ray to Peter Courthope, 20 Jan. 1663). On Nidd, see further Christopher D. Preston, 'Using John Nidd's annotated books in the Wren Library to reassess his contribution to John Ray's *Catalogus* (1660)', *Archives of Natural History*, 44 (2017), 275–91.

[158] See further Tim R. Birkhead et al., 'Willughby's Ornithology', in *Virtuoso by Nature*, ed. Birkhead, 268–304.

[159] ESRO, DAN/2231 (Francis Willughby to Peter Courthope, [Feb.–Apr. 1660]); Willughby, 'Another extract of a letter', in *Philosophical Transactions of the Royal Society*, 6 (1671), 2221. See further Brian W. Ogilvie, 'Willughby on Insects', in *Virtuoso by Nature*, ed. Birkhead, esp. 353.

[160] See further Richard Serjeantson, 'Wilkins in Cambridge', in *John Wilkins: Quatercentenary Essays*, ed. William Poole (Leiden, 2017), 66–96.

[161] CUL, MS Add. 3958, item 1.

[162] On this point, see also Feingold, 'Isaac Barrow', esp. 22–36.

MATHEMATICS

The same point holds in the related but slightly outlying case of mathematics. Though neither obviously a part of philosophy or of humanity, by the mid-eighteenth century mathematics was coming to take on the enormous significance, in Trinity and in Cambridge more generally, that it would hold for the next hundred years.[163] At the beginning of the seventeenth century, however, mathematics did not play nearly so central a role in the College's studies. The question therefore arises as to how the mathematical tradition at Cambridge in general, and at Trinity in particular, came into being. The legacy and influence of Isaac Newton has often seemed important here. Yet the argument that will be made here is that, while Newton certainly encouraged Trinity's later mathematical tradition, he was not its inaugurator.

A significant document here is a notebook kept by Edward Hyde in the later 1630s. This modest leather-bound volume records Hyde's study of the subject, in its broader acceptation, as including, in addition to arithmetic, not only geometry, but also music, optics, and astronomy as well. He records readings from the treatise on astronomy written by the thirteenth-century teacher at the university of Paris, Johannes de Sacrobosco, the *Tractatus de sphaera*—a work still very widely taught from into the seventeenth century.[164] He also takes notes from a more recent work by the foremost Jesuit mathematician of the early seventeenth-century, Christoph Clavius, who had edited the Sacrobosco.[165] The document as a whole is prefaced by some notes on solar eclipses,[166] and also by a copy of the oration that he delivered when he took up the office of Praelector in Mathematics at the college in October 1639.[167] Importantly, this early entry dates the composition of the notebook to the period of Hyde's tutorship, not that of his own studies: he was taking notes on mathematics, therefore, in order to teach his own pupils.[168] The remainder of the notebook contains material relating to Hyde's pastoral work in the parish of Brightwell, in Suffolk, to which he was collated in 1643.[169]

---

[163] Gascoigne, 'Mathematics and Meritocracy'.
[164] PLM, MS MA0079 (unfoliated), fols. [26]v ff.
[165] PLM, MS MA0079 (unfoliated), fol. [17]v: 'Brevis Notatiunculæ in Clauium'.
[166] PLM, MS MA0079 (unfoliated), fol. [1]r.
[167] PLM, MS MA0079 (unfoliated), fols. [2]r ff.: 'Oratio Mathematici Prælectoris an. 1639.'
[168] This is not to say, of course, that other pupils did not take notes on mathematical subjects themselves. Detailed notes on arithmetic taken by Hyde's younger friend Thomas Plume during his time as a Pensioner at Christ's College survive in PLM, MS MA 0007, pp. 19–36.
[169] PLM, MS MA0079 (unfoliated), fols. [71]r, [87]r, and (at the rear of the volume) 'A prayer before sermon, made anno i644 [*sic*]'.

Given the importance of mathematics in Newtonian and eighteenth-century Trinity, we may ask whether how far back its origins may be traced. John Wallis, who later became Savilian Professor of Geometry at Oxford, was a student at Emmanuel College, Cambridge, in the later 1630s; he claimed that he received no teaching in mathematics there at all. Moreover, in the two surviving 'Directions for study' written in the pedagogic context of Emmanuel College—by Richard Holdsworth (*c.* 1648), and Nathaniel Sterry of Emmanuel (*c.* 1650), say nothing about mathematics.[170] More pertinently, nor does James Duport of Trinity mention mathematics in his 'Rules' (1660)—although these are not especially discipline-specific.[171]

Yet there is some evidence to indicate that mathematics already held a place of esteem in Trinity College in the early seventeenth century. Hyde's notebook, including the Praelector's oration from 1639 that he copies, suggests as much. In 1648 the Trinity fellow commoner James Master purchased from a Cambridge bookseller a book entitled *Mathematical Magic*, a treatment of mechanical devices and tricks; its author was John Wilkins, who in 1659 would briefly become Master of Trinity.[172] The young Isaac Barrow, in an illustration of the principle of the interconnection of disciplines that unpinned the idea of general learning, found that:

> When he read Scaliger on Eusebius, he perceived the dependence of Chronology on Astronomy, which put him on the study of Ptolemy's *Almagest*; and finding that book and all Astronomy to depend upon Geometry, he applied himself to Euclid's *Elements*, not satisfied till he had laid firm foundations; and so he made his first entry into the Mathematics.[173]

Thus by the 1650s the evidence for the importance of mathematics at Trinity is becoming deafening. In 1654 or so Isaac Barrow praised the University for its 'recent' inclination towards the mathematical sciences: you academics shall be honoured, he says, for such distinguished and praiseworthy studies.[174] Barrow himself published a teaching edition of Euclid in February 1656, which he dedicated to three of the higher-ranking students at the College.[175] One of these students was Francis Willughby (at Trinity 1652–1660), who was celebrated in his lifetime as a mathematician, although only limited evidence now survives to verify this

---

[170] Holdsworth, 'Directions'; OB, MS Tanner 88, fol. 5r.
[171] Preston and Oswald, 'Duport's Rules'.
[172] Robinson, 'Expense-Book of James Master', 172.
[173] Hill, 'Some Account', xlii.
[174] Barrow, 'Oratio ad Academicos', 41. See also Whewell, 'Barrow', iii.
[175] Euclid, *Elementorum libri xv. breviter demonstrati*, ed. and trans. Isaac Barrow (Cambridge, 1655). The dedicatees were Edward Cecil, a younger son of earl of Salisbury; John Knatchbull, whose father was a significant gentleman scholar; and Francis Willughby.

reputation.[176] In the autumn of 1661 Isaac Newton's tutor, Benjamin Pulleyn, read Kepler's *Optics* with some of his fellow commoner tutees, and invited the young Newton to joint them.[177] The soil in which the young Isaac Newton planted himself in June 1661 was therefore unusually fertile for the fostering of his prodigious mathematical talents.

Newton's physical studies in their turn considerably shaped the direction of eighteenth-century undergraduate teaching in Trinity and in the University as a whole. Already by 1680 Newton's theory of colours (published in 1672) was being defended in the philosophy act, though by a member of Jesus College.[178] By the middle years of the eighteenth century the topics treated in the undergraduate act had become much more mathematical in nature than they had been in the seventeenth century, though they were still decanted into the structures of a philosophical disputation. Richard Cumberland recalled with pride his youthful success in vanquishing a 'North-country black-bearded philosopher' who also gave private tuition in mathematics in a disputation on questions drawn from Newton's *Principia* when he first 'kept an act' as a sophister in about 1750. Their debate was so 'purely mathematical' that Cumberland had some difficulty in discovering where his opponent's syllogisms 'pointed', since the use of diagrams was not permitted. In preparation for his work Cumberland had mastered the 'best treatises' (unspecified) 'in the several branches of the mechanics, hydrostatics, optics and astronomy.' Although, as we have seen, these subjects had been studied a hundred years earlier, they were now being formally examined to the exclusion of questions on the soul or in moral philosophy which had formerly predominated. Cumberland, for his part, regarded these studies as thoroughly intellectually beneficial and indeed useful, and chided the Eton scholars at King's College for being exempted from the study of mathematics; 'Under-graduates of Trinity College, whether elected from West minster or not, have no such exemptions.'[179]

---

[176] Benjamin Wardaugh, 'Willughby's Mathematics', in *Virtuoso by Nature*, 122–41.

[177] Newton Papers Project, KCC, MS Keynes 130.10, fol. 2r. Westfall, *Never at Rest*, 83 n. 51, chose to discount this story. But given what we now know about the depth of mathematical and natural philosophical culture in the College during the 1650s he was surely mistaken to do so. The recent English edition of Johannes Kepler's *Dioptrice* (London, 1653), was easily available.

[178] Isaac Newton, 'A Letter...containing his new Theory about Light and Colors', *Philosophical Transactions*, 80 (1672), 3075–87. Hall, *Act and Tripos Verses*, 177 (1680.3.com. phi): Thomas Man defended the thesis that 'Newtoniana hypothesis rectè explicat rationes colorum'.

[179] Cumberland, *Memoirs*, 74–76, 84–85.

CHYMISTRY AND ASTRONOMY

But the study of nature was not treated at Trinity as an exclusively philosophical, let alone mathematical, endeavour. It does not even seem to have been especially closely associated with the study of medicine. From the earlier seventeenth century onwards there is evidence for interest among certain members of the college in the art (it did not yet count as a science) of 'chymistry', or alchemy. Thomas Nevile (*d.* 1615) donated a single fifteenth-century alchemical manuscript.[180] But when Thomas Whalley died as Vice-Master in 1637 he bequeathed to the College a number of more recent chymical manuscripts, as well as a number of printed books on chymistry.[181] Though not comparable with the unparalleled collection of an earlier fellow of Trinity, John Dee, Whalley's collection testifies to a thoroughly developed interest in the subject at Trinity in the earlier years of the seventeenth century. This interest is confirmed by the oration delivered before the university by the young James Duport in 1631. Duport had been appointed 'praevaricator', a licensed jester chosen from among the recent MAs (he had taken his own in 1630). Duport took as the subject of his ludic oration the thesis that 'it is possible to produce gold by means of the art of chymistry'. His speech (if not his scientific methods) was sufficiently effective that his oration circulated widely in manuscript as a model of the genre.[182]

Though there was no formal curricular encouragement to explore it, the evidence suggests that a chymical tradition subsequently developed in Trinity prior to the institutionalisation of the subject in the University in the early eighteenth century.[183] During his time at Trinity in the later 1650s John Ray also engaged in experiments in what was known as 'Chymistry', exploring the properties of metals, elements, and crystals. In 1658 or so he and his friend Thomas Pockley, another fellow of the College,

---

[180] TCC, MS R. 14. 37 (James no. 909).

[181] Anke Timmermann, *Verse and Transmutation: A Corpus of Middle English Alchemical Poetry* (Leiden, 2013), 144–55. TCC, MS R. 14. 56, bequeathed by Whalley, is signed by the sixteenth-century chymist Richard Eden.

[182] GCC, MS 627/250, unfoliated [fols. 2r–9v]: 'Prævaricatio Mri Duport Trin: Coll: Socij: Anno: Dom. 1631. Quæstio sic se habet. Aurum potest producj per artem Chymicam'; BL, MS Add. 44963, fols. 22v–26r (copied by Anthony Scattergood while at Trinity); OB, MS Rawlinson D. 1026, fols. 1r–7v; OB, MS Tanner 461, fol. 146r; CCO, MS 288, fol. 99r. As late as the early eighteenth century Thomas Baker copied it as 'an example of the wit of the previous age' (*specimen ingenii prioris seculi*), BL, MS Harley 7045, fo. 231.

[183] See further Anna Marie Roos, 'The Chymistry of Francis Willughby (1635–72): The Trinity College, Cambridge Community', in *Virtuoso by Nature*, 99–121.

carried through a programme of executing 'all the easie & usefull chymicall experiments which we‹e› find in bookes'. They drew especially on the writing of the important mid-century chymist Johann Rudolph Glauber. They spent the ample sum of 40 shillings in this work, but felt the want of an iron retort with which to operate.[184] Detailed accounts of experiments by John Ray appear in Francis Willughby's commonplace book in a hand that belongs to neither of them.[185]

Most interestingly, a Greek chymist called Constantine Rhodocanacis seems to have been engaged on a semi-formal basis at Trinity at this time to perform experiments. In March 1660 he performed in the Combination Room at Trinity an experiment in which Isaac Newton was later interested, known as 'the *Experiment* of the *Tree*'.[186] Rhodocanacis thus constitutes a previously unknown precursor to another foreigner who worked on chemistry at Trinity, Giovanni Francesco Vigani (*c.* 1650–1713).[187] Vigani was the first person to be 'honoured' with the title of 'Professor of Chemistry' in the University, in 1702—albeit without any formal emolument. In 1707 Richard Bentley provided a laboratory for Vigani in the north range of Great Court, probably in the room that is known to this day as 'Vigani's Room'.[188] Students from throughout the university attended the courses he gave there. Hence like Rhodocanacis, only with more lasting success (since the Greek scholar migrated to Oxford and then to London after the Restoration) Vigani maintained himself in Cambridge by lecturing on chemistry and *materia medica*, and by demonstrating experiments. A number of manuscripts recording the courses he gave survive.[189] Yet students did not rely on Vigani for their chymical knowledge: in 1702 a dedicated fellow commoner, John Yardley, compiled for himself an entire 'Course of Chymistry in Four Books' from Nicolas Lémery's *Cours de chimie* (1675).[190] Yardley evidently undertook this work as part of his

---

[184] ESRO, DAN/345 (John Ray to Peter Courthope, 3 Jan. 1659).
[185] NUL, MS Mi LM 15/1, pp. 404–15.
[186] William Derham (ed.), *Philosophical Letters* (1718), 357–58 (Courthope to Willughby, 17 Mar. 1660). For Newton's interest in chymical 'trees', see KCC, MS Keynes 51 (notes on Ripley), and KCC, MS Keynes 55 (notes on Starkey), both published at *The Chymistry of Isaac Newton*, ed. W. R. Newman (2006) (purl.dlib.indiana.edu/iudl/newton).
[187] Rhodocanacis' contribution to the study of chymistry in Cambridge goes unnoticed in Mary D. Archer and Christopher D. Haley (eds.), *The 1702 Chair of Chemistry at Cambridge* (Cambridge, 2005).
[188] Antonio Clericuzio, 'Vigani, John Francis (*c.*1650–1713)', *ODNB*. The chamber overlooks the fellows' bowling green.
[189] Simon Shaffer and Larry Stewart, 'Vigani and After: Chemical enterprise in Cambridge 1680–1780', in *The 1702 Chair of Chemistry*, 31–56.
[190] GCC, MS 460/631. Christopher Wordsworth and R. W. T. Gunther had claimed that this manuscript reflects Vigani's teaching, but the relation to Lémery's writing is more plausibly made by L. J. M. Coleby, 'John Francis Vigani', *Annals of Science*, 8 (1952), 55.

medical studies, for although he did not take either the BA or MA, in 1704 he did take the degree of MB.

Hence the most celebrated person to pursue chymical studies in later seventeenth-century Trinity, Isaac Newton, joined a well-established community of investigators. Newton's very well-thumbed copy of Martin Ruland's *Lexicon Alchemiæ* (Frankfurt, 1612) survives among that portion of his library now possessed by the college.[191] Newton profited from his reading of a copy of Vigani's *Medulla Chymiæ* in the 1683 London edition, and Vigani profited from Newton's expertise in making ovens.[192] Vigani's successor in the chair of Chemistry, John Mickleburgh (*c*.1692–1756) may have drawn upon personal knowledge rather than merely reputation when he spoke in a lecture of the 'Furnaces and utensils' that Isaac Newton 'had and made use of whilst he lived in Trin. College'.[193]

Richard Bentley regarded his support for chemistry following his ally Newton's departure for London in 1696 as going along with his promotion of astronomy, for which he also provided a home in the form of an observatory and its accompanying accommodation over the Great Gate. This was to house the first Plumeian Professor of Astronomy, Roger Cotes. This chair was endowed by the will of Thomas Plume, an Essex clergyman who had taken his BA from Christ's in 1650 but who was acquainted with a number of older former fellows of Trinity (Edward Hyde and Robert Boreman) who have also appeared in this account.[194] Cotes, for his part, was a brilliant young mathematical scientist who was appointed to the chair by Bentley at the age of twenty-four in the year in which he was elected to a fellowship at Trinity.[195] The clergyman Plume's well-developed interest in astronomy (he was friendly with the astronomer of the Royal Observatory at Greenwich, John Flamsteed), reflects the growing intellectual and maritime significance of that science in later seventeenth-century England, a significance that Bentley's patronage of the subject also indicates. Thus in both chymistry and astronomy early eighteenth-century Trinity succeeded in engrossing to itself some of the most able and prominent professors in the University, some external, some home-grown, a habit it has often continued since.

---

[191] TCC, classmark NQ.16.102.

[192] Shaffer and Stewart, 'Vigani and after', 43–44 and n. 46, reporting Newton's copy at in the Library of the University of Wisconsin–Madison (shelfmark LNI T67 Cutter).

[193] L. J. M. Coleby, 'John Mickleburgh, Professor of Chemistry in the University of Cambridge, 1718–56', *Annals of Science*, 8 (1952), 165–74, at 171; see further Shaffer and Stewart, 'Vigani and after', 45.

[194] The manuscripts of Hyde and Boreman came into Plume's possession following their deaths, and have therefore survived by virtue of their presence in his library at Maldon, Essex.

[195] Domenico Bertoloni Meli, 'Cotes, Roger (1682–1716)', in *ODNB*.

ARTS COURSE STUDIES: 'HUMANITY'

But philosophical studies, together with their experimental and extra-curricular offshoots, together with mathematics, only constitute a portion of the teaching and learning that was pursued in Trinity before 1750. Another very significant area of studies involved the study of what was called 'Humanity'—that is, what might now be called literature, but which was then distinguished into poetry, oratory, comedy, tragedy, and history. These studies were not formally assessed by the University exercises required by statute, which focussed on disputations in philosophy and the higher disciplines. But 'humanity' was evidently taken very seriously at Trinity, and also served (as we shall see) as a significant means of advancing the studies of its members by the award of scholarships and fellowships. As with the philosophical disciplines, the study of humanity can also be reconstructed from surviving manuscript notebooks, accounts, and other sources.

At Trinity, as also throughout the University, as also indeed throughout the world of learning until the latter part of the seventeenth century, Latin was (at least in principle) the dominant language. Indeed, Latin was so important that students, at least in principle, learned it with complete facility before arriving at Trinity. The university notebooks that some of them kept sometimes also document their studies at grammar school. A rhetoric notebook that was kept by the young Robert Boreman has the distinct feel of a schoolboy, rather than an undergraduate, production, and would therefore have been made in the course of his time as pupil at Westminster School in the mid-1620s.[196] In the case of Isaac Newton, too, we can be confident that the rules of Latin prosody that he dated to 1659 were made during his schooling at Grantham prior to coming up to Trinity in June 1661.[197] The library at Trinity also holds four small notebooks (now in a dreadful condition), which were found under the floorboards of a room in Great Court in the twentieth century. They contain Latin phrases from authors such as Ovid, Terence and Livy, and also a few Greek verses, among other more miscellaneous items. Two of them are signed by Francis Gregory, who was probably responsibly for bringing them to Trinity when he arrived from Westminster School in 1641.[198]

---

[196] PLM, MS MA0091 (unfoliated; handwriting of Robert Boreman). The somewhat jejune quality of the rhetorical materials in this notebook suggests school- rather than university-work, an impression confirmed by the decorative coloured binding prominently bearing Boreman's initials.
[197] TCC, MS R. 4. 48c, fols. 3r–20v. The remainder of the notebook contains financial accounts made following his arrival at Trinity.
[198] TCC, MSS Add. c. 227–230 (all unfoliated). Venn, *Alumni Cantabrigienses*, ii. 262. See further Hammond, 'Dryden and Trinity', 36–37. MS Add. c. 228, at least, appears to have been maintained beyond Gregory's arrival at Trinity, as it also contains a number of philosophical positions.

Yet once a student arrived at Cambridge, Latin became something much more than the language of Roman poetry and drama: it was also the functional language of the university. All university exercises were conducted in Latin: the books in logic and philosophy that students read were written in Latin, while disputations were argued, orations were delivered, and verses were composed in the language. The University Orator addressed visiting monarchs and ambassadors in Latin; plays were performed in Latin. Thus James Duport had good cause to adjure his charges to 'Speake Latin always in *th*e hall, if not elswhere, & at other times.'[199] The studious Richard Cumberland recalled that in preparation for his undergraduate Act in 1751 he had learned to form 'all my minutes, and even my thoughts, in Latin'.[200]

Hence the great majority of teaching, in the seventeenth century, at least, appears to have taken place in Latin. The books in the College Library, as also in the private libraries maintained by fellows, were overwhelmingly in Latin.[201] A conscientious student like Francis Willughby took notes in Latin even when he was reading books in English or French.[202] Latin was a supremely functional language, which permitted the existence of a shared European intellectual culture transmitted by means of printed books, but also permitted educated people to talk to each other even when they did not share a vernacular; when Willughby and Ray travelled across Europe in 1663–65 after leaving Trinity it was by means of Latin that they often communicated with others, and it was Latin that served as the key to the vernacular terms—in Dutch, German, Walloon, Hungarian, and Polish—that they systematically recorded.[203] Latin also served both of them quite naturally as the language by which to communicate their respective findings in natural history.

But Greek, too, was the language of philosophy as well as poetry and drama; of Aristotle as well as of Homer; and it is clear that, in the earlier part of the century at least, there was a prejudice in favour of reading him in his original tongue, rather than in one of the numerous Latin translations that were available by that point. (Very few of Aristotle's writings were available at this point in English translation—only his *Ethics* (from 1547), his *Politics* (from 1598), his *Rhetoric* (from 1637) and the

---

[199] Preston and Oswald, 'Duport's Rules', 345.
[200] Cumberland, *Memoirs*, 74.
[201] Elisabeth Leedham-Green, *Books in Cambridge Inventories*, 2 vols (Cambridge, 1987), ii. 576–84.
[202] Serjeantson, 'Education of Willughby', 67.
[203] Mark Greengrass et al., 'Science on the Move: Francis Willughby's Expeditions', in *Virtuoso by Nature*, ed. Birkhead, 142–225; David Cram 'Francis Willughby and John Ray on Words and Things', in ibid., 250.

pseudo-Aristotelian *Problems* (from 1607). The heart of the Aristotelian corpus—the logic, the natural philosophy, the metaphysics—had to wait until much later to be translated into English.) James Duport required that when his charges 'use the Authority of Aristotle' in disputations they should 'bring his owne words, & in his owne language'—that is, Greek.[204] Richard Holdsworth from St John's assigned 'Aristot*elis* Organ*um*' ('Aristotle's Organon') to the second quarter of the third year of BA study.[205] He also observed that the 'reading of Aristotle, will... help you in Greeke'. And he went on to instruct his charges to 'Gather short memorial notes in Greek out of him, and observe all his termes.'[206] We have already found several students, including the young Newton, doing precisely this. No doubt Newton was aided in this by one of his first purchases upon arriving at Trinity, Cornelius Schrevel's Greek–Latin dictionary.[207] Trinity students who came up from Westminster School had already studied Greek in depth (as we shall see, they practically monopolised the Regius Professorship in that language), and it seems likely that most others would have done so as well.[208] Edward Hyde, in particular, faithfully observed the instructions Holdsworth offers. One of his surviving manuscripts might be characterised as his 'philological' notebook. It contains an extensive 'Table of those terms found in my notes from Aristotle'. It is in Greek, and contains references to the relevant Aristotelian work in which the term is found.[209]

But Homer vied with Aristotle as the most important Greek author. Richard Holdsworth proposed Homer's *Iliad* for the end of the student's third BA year, and both the *Odyssey* and the *Iliad* for the conclusion of their fourth.[210] There is much evidence to suggest that reading Homer was standardly expected of BA students, and indeed fellow commoners who might not expect to take even that degree. At Trinity, James Duport read

---

[204] Preston and Oswald, 'Duport's Rules', 349.
[205] Holdsworth, 'Directions', 630. Holdsworth further recommended that it be studied together with the commentary by Edward Brerewood from which we have already found Edward Hyde taking notes.
[206] Holdsworth, 'Directions', 643.
[207] TCC, MS R. 4. 48c, fol. 25r (it cost 5s 4d).
[208] The intensity of Greek teaching at Westminster is verified by [William Camden], *Institutio Graecae grammatices compendiaria, in usum Regiae Scholae Westmonasteriensis* (numerous editions from 1595); BL, MS Harley 6462 (a handsome seventeenth-century copy of a similar 'Compendium Graecæ Grammaticæ in usum puerorum in Scholâ Regiâ Westmonasterii'); Simpson, *Chronicon*, sig. A5v; and by the work of its head, Richard Busby, for over 50 years between 1639 and 1695.
[209] PLM, MS MA0009 (unfoliated), 'Tabula eoru*m* uocabuloru*m* quæ in collectionibus nostris quæ sunt ex Aristotele*m* reperiuntur'.
[210] Holdsworth, 'Directions', 630, 632.

Homer with his pupils Edward Cecil, John Knatchbull, Henry Puckering and Francis Willughby, as the dedicatory epistle to them of his collection of Homeric quotations explains.[211] Yet Hyde's facility with Greek is evident from his surviving commonplace book: in this full and well-indexed volume Greek, unusually, predominates over Latin in the entries.[212]

Nathaniel Sterry, who was probably a young MA at Emmanuel College when he put together his concise 'direction for a good, & profitable proceeding in study', directed students to 'First read over Homers two bookes, with a peircing into all his sense, & the reason of his Epithetes. & let not any thing passe till you know the meaning of it.' By this means 'you shalbe master of *th*e autho*u*r either to correct, or give a reason of any thing in him.' He further stipulated that any reader studious of the grammar of Homer's Greek should 'passe not a word, whose derivation you know not'. The happy outcome of this demanding process, if a student 'be serious in it', was that he would arrive at 'such a facility of the tongue' that he would be able to read 'an Iliad in an afternoone.'[213] Again we find Edward Hyde's notebooks following such directions. He collected 'phrases and quotations' from Homer's *Iliad* in Greek, with side-notes in both Latin and English glossing the meaning.[214] More impressively, he also took very detailed notes from the commentary on the *Iliad* by the twelfth-century author Eustathius of Thessalonica, and an index of terms in Eustathius.[215] Evidence from contemporary book-collections confirms that Eustathius was an established author, probably among the more serious sort of student, in early seventeenth-century Cambridge.[216]

The efforts of students to understand, appreciate and apply Greek and Roman literature went along with their own efforts to learn to use language eloquently and persuasively. This was the province of the art of rhetoric, which some students (our evidence relates to Westminster School) clearly often encountered before they came up to Cambridge, but then consolidated once they had arrived. Robert Boreman's meticulous collection of rhetorical figures, followed by an exacting rhetorical analysis of a theme on the subject of 'Sobriety must be observed' (*sobrietas est sequenda*) surely derives from his schoolboy studies.[217] But the notes that

---

[211] James Duport, *Homeri...gnomologia* (Cambridge, 1660), sig. (a2)r.
[212] PLM, MS MA0057 (Commonplace book of Edward Hyde).
[213] OB, MS Tanner 88, fol. 5r.
[214] PLM, MS MA0009 (unfoliated), 'Phrases et sententiæ ex Homeri Iliadum collectæ'.
[215] PLM, MS MA0009 (unfoliated), folio headed 'Notæ ex Eustathio in Hom. Il.', and folio headed 'Tabula vocu*m* [or possibly voca*bulorum*] ex Eustathio'.
[216] Leedham-Green, *Books in Cambridge Inventories*, ii. 328.
[217] PLM, MS MA0091 (unfoliated).

Boreman's slightly older contemporary, Edward Hyde, made on the Greek text of book 1 of Aristotle's *Rhetoric*, in a notebook which also contains a high-level account of propositional logic, would rather appear to belong to his time at Trinity.[218] In 1661 Isaac Barrow's second course of lectures as Professor of Greek on Aristotle's *Rhetoric* proved much more popular than his first course on the tragedies of Sophocles had been.[219]

Nonetheless, the classical languages were not the only ones that were studied. Modern languages were also studied. Giacomo Castelvetro, who taught Italian in Cambridge in the second decade of the seventeenth century including to members of Trinity specifically, perhaps including George Stanhope, who inscribed his *album amicorum* with an Italian inscription; it may be among Stanhope's manuscripts that Castelvetro's pedagogic 'Libretto De varie maniere di parlare della Italica Lingua' survives.[220] In 1659 the Master and Seniors voted two pounds on the Steward's account to a different 'Italian teacher', one 'Alex. Amideus'.[221] In an oration he delivered before the University in about 1654, Isaac Barrow claims that the study of the 'light, but not useless' foreign languages of Italian, Spanish, and especially French, was greatly increasing.[222] Francis Willughby may have learned informally at Trinity the French that he seems to have read with some facility, but, good student that he was, he kept his commonplace book almost exclusively in Latin, even when he had been reading books in French. That language was studied by the undergraduate Henry Campion, who entered Trinity in 1697, and who kept a notebook documenting his studies in two fields: mathematics, and French. Among his notes on 'L'art de Plaire dans la Conversation' Campion learned to say (a little equivocally) that Paris 'n'est pas seulement la Capitale dune [*inserted* florissante] Monarchie florissante' but was in fact 'la ville dominante de toute l'Europe'.[223] The geo-political power of the universal monarchy of France was coming to shape the studies even of students at Trinity.

Though it locked its doors against the world every night, therefore, the studies that took place within Trinity's walls did not take place in a political void. Some students at the College sought to understand the politics

---

[218] PLM, MS MA0097 (unfoliated).
[219] Mordechai Feingold, 'Barrow, Isaac (1630–1677)', *ODNB*. On Barrow's lack of success in attracting an audience to the first course, see further M. L. Clarke, *Classical Education in Britain, 1500–1900* (Cambridge, 1959), 65.
[220] Trinity College, Cambridge, MS R. 10. 6. See further John Gallagher, *Learning Languages in Early Modern England* (Oxford, 2019), pp. 20–24.
[221] TCA, Steward's Audit pro anno 1659, fol. 467r.
[222] Isaac Barrow, 'Oratio ad Academicos in Comitiis', in *Theological Works*, ix. 38: 'leve quidem sed non inutile studium.' For the date, see Whewell, 'Barrow', i.
[223] CUL, MS Add. 3455, fol. 43r.

of their own moment by reading the history of the ancient and more recent modern past. Robert Boreman made careful notes on the *History of Italy* by Machiavelli's friend Francesco Guicciardini during the turbulent 1640s.[224] And alongside the notes on Demosthenes' Greek oratory that he made at the end of that decade, Thomas Millington read book 1 of Tacitus' *Histories* and the treatise on princely government, framed as an account of the life of the Roman founder Romulus, by the contemporary Italian author and ambassador to England, Virgilio Malvezzi (1595–1654).[225] Isaac Barrow, for his part, undertook a comprehensive plan of reading the ancient Greek historians: Herodotus, Thucydides, Diodorus Siculus, and Polybius. Like his contemporary John Smith, at Queens' College, Barrow preferred to take his notes in alphabetical form.[226] His ambition of making an alphabetical index of notes from Plutarch's *Lives* failed him, but extensive Greek notes from individual lives do survive.[227] Following the award of his BA degree in 1751 Richard Cumberland undertook nothing less than the compilation of a 'Universal History, or at least for that of the Great Empires in particular.' Yet finding himself hampered by his ignorance of the 'Oriental' languages he turned to a comprehensive review of 'all the several systems of the Heathen Philosophers'.[228]

TUTORIAL TEACHING

By virtue of the surviving pedagogic notebooks it is relatively straightforward to establish the books from which students at Trinity worked. It is rather harder to reconstruct the nature of the day-to-day teaching experience within and beyond the College. The primary pedagogic experience encountered by students in the first few years of study was with their tutor. The 1560 Statutes required that no Bachelor, scholar, pensioner, sizar, or subsizar should lack a tutor, and this regulation appears to have been

---

[224] PLM, MS MA0106: 'Notes out of Guiccardin. Collected in ye yeere 1646.'

[225] OB, MS Rawl. D. 1041 item 1, noting the Latin translation of Virgilio Malvezzi, *Il Romulo* (Bologna, 1629), i.e. *Princeps, eiusque arcana: in vita Romuli repræsentata*, trans. Johannes Kruuss (Leiden, 1636).

[226] John Smith's impressively thorough alphabetised historical commonplace book is now CUL, MS Dd. 9 44.

[227] TCC, MS R. 9. 38, consists of Barrow's extensive 'Excerpta historiarum'. While an extensive alphabetical template prepared to receive notes 'E Plutarcho', remains entirely empty, full notes by Barrow from Plutarch's *Lives*, in their original Greek, may be found in TCC, MS R. 10. 16, fols. 3v–35r.

[228] Cumberland, *Memoirs*, 85–86.

observed.[229] By the later eighteenth century a situation had emerged whereby a few fellows succeeded in engrossing tuition in colleges to themselves, with other fellows serving as locum lectures and private teachers. In the seventeenth century, however, the situation was more varied. Although James Duport took on an unusually large number of pupils between the 1630s and 1660s, tuition was fairly widely spread across the body of the major fellows, although in 1648 the Master, Thomas Hill, delivered himself of the view that the Senior Fellows 'need not trouble themselves with taking Pupills, their Colledg businesses beeing so many'.[230] Tutors seem to have been responsible not only for providing teaching to their charges, but also for tailoring it to their interests and aptitudes. Thomas Hill again spoke of the need for tutors to discharge conscientiously the 'great Trust' committed to them, which involved the 'large Tuition' of the deserving and turning away from and giving 'little care' to those that were not; the stakes were high, for Hill was confident that Hell itself was full of pupils who had been abused by their 'negligent, yet covetous Tutors'. This responsibility was particularly acute in the case of 'young Nobles and Gentry', whose influence might make or mar 'many persons, yea and possibly Countries.'[231] As this suggests, a tutor's responsibility for his charges' studies was inseparable from his morals and especially his religion.[232]

Being responsible for his pupils' finances, tutors were also responsible to the college for his pupils' debts towards it. A tutor might thereby find himself caught between a profligate son and a censorious parent—or, in the case of a son of the earl of Salisbury, the father's agent.[233] A tutor's obligations to his pupil would therefore involve correspondence, sometimes of a ticklish nature, with a father or mother.[234] At worst, it might involve writing to a parent to inform them of the death of a son, as John Ray had to do in the case of the seventeen year-old Edward Goring in 1661. The boy had scarcely been entered at Trinity as a fellow commoner under Ray before he fell ill from smallpox and died. 'This Gentleman never came into the hall, nor wore his gowne after his admis*sion*', wrote Ray melancholically, and in careful self-justification of his actions.[235]

---

[229] 1560 Statutes, p. 23 (cap. 10).
[230] Thomas Hill, 'A Letter to the Seniors of Trinitie-Colledg in Cambridge', in *The Best and Worst of Paul* (Cambridge, 1648), sig. A3v.
[231] Hill, 'A Letter', sigs. A4v–a1r.
[232] Hill, 'A Letter', sig. a1r, reminded his readers that 'The blind Mahumetans do begin their very sports with prayer'.
[233] *Calendar of the manuscripts of the most Hon. the Marquis of Salisbury*, vol. XXII: *1612–1668*, p. 394.
[234] TCC, MS O. 11a. 5(9), drafts of correspondence with the mother of an (unidentified) pupil.
[235] ESRO, DAN/349 (John Ray to Peter Courthope, 11 June 1661). Venn has Goring entering the College in 1660, but it is clear from Ray's letter that he first arrived in 1661 and died within a week.

Duport's 'Rules' provide some insight into how tutorial teaching worked. He charges his students to 'Be carefull to observe duely those houres, your Tutor hath appointed you to com unto him'. He further demanded that pupils carry themselves civilly in their tutor's chamber, 'not laughing or lolling, or leaning or whispering, or using any other childish gesture or posture'. Furthermore, 'When you reade or speake in your Tutors chamber, or elsewhere, take head of picking *you*r nose, or putting *you*r hatt or hand to *you*r face, or any such odd, uncouth, unseemly gesture.' Among the exercises he mentions as taking place in a tutor's chamber were 'read[ing] a chapter'; 'rehearsing sermons'—that is, recalling the arguments made by a particular preacher; disputing; and answering questions. These tasks were all to be uttered 'with a distinct and audible voice'.[236]

A further primary method of teaching consisted of tutors 'reading' books with, or rather to, their pupils. A mid-eighteenth century story is told about Isaac Newton's tutor, Benjamin Pulleyn, who found Newton to be 'so forward' in mathematics, that he 'told him he was going to read Kepler's opticks to some gentlemen com*m*oners & that he should come to those lectures.'[237] This suggests not only that Newton's specific interests were being catered for, but also that teaching might be given to groups consisting of different classes of student. Yet in its very nature these class divisions cannot have been impermeable, for the sub-sizar Newton was invited to join the group of fellow-commoners. Other sources paint comparable pictures of fellow commoners (and no doubt also other students) reading with their tutors: in dedicating his collection of Homeric wisdom to four of his former fellow-commoner pupils, James Duport recalled reading Homer with them both individually and as a group.[238]

The account that tells us of the freshman Isaac Newton reading Kepler upon his arrival at Trinity with fellow-commoners also recalls his experience of studying Robert Sanderson's *Art of Logic* with Benjamin Pulleyn: 'when he came to hear his tutour's lectures upon it [he] found he knew more of it than his tutour.'[239] One way in which a diligent tutor might stay ahead of their brighter pupils was to produce their own 'system' of logic, or natural philosophy, which they would dictate to their pupils in the

---

[236] Preston and Oswald, 'Duport's Rules', 350, 343.
[237] Newton Papers Project, KCC, MS Keynes 130.10, fol. 2r (also Newton Papers Project, KCC, MS Keynes 130.04, fol. 1r).
[238] Duport, *Homeri Gnomologia*, sig. a2r: 'Iterum ecce ad vos redit (Nobilissimi Juvenes) *Homerus* vester, quem non ità pridem in Academia vos quatuor simul, & unà cum mecum legistis.' The dedicatees were the hon. Edward Cecil, the hon. John Knatchbull, the hon. Henry Puckering, and Francis Willughby.
[239] Newton Papers Project, KCC, MS Keynes 130.10, fol. 2r.

course of teaching them. It was from this kind of teaching, indeed, that Sanderson's book had itself arisen. (Robert Burton, an experienced tutor at Christ Church, Oxford, in the earlier years of the seventeenth century, parodies the expectation that tutors will teach philosophy from their own 'systems' in his play *Philosophaster*.[240]) In the later seventeenth century in Oxford, manuscript systems circulated that were specific to particular colleges.[241] What may be Trinity versions of two such private systems are found in two of the notebooks kept by Edward Hyde during his time at Trinity (1625–1643), one of logic, the other of natural philosophy. It is quite possible that they arise not from Hyde's early studies as a student, but from his later function as a teacher of students.[242]

Thus the tutor guided both his pupils' morals and their studies. It was a mark of distinction to be told by him that one studied too hard, as John Hacket's tutor Edward Simpson is reported to have done: he 'was forced rather to restrain than to incite him to his study'.[243] Francis Willughby was also drolly castigated in verse by his former tutor, James Duport, for his excessive application to his studies ('Slow down a bit! Give knowledge a rest').[244] But not all undergraduates were so fortunate in their tutors. In the mid-eighteenth century Richard Cumberland was placed in the hands of two successive tutors, the first of whom was indolent and the second of whom—Philip Young, later Bishop of Norwich—was wholly negligent: 'from him I never received a single lecture'.[245] The choice of tutor might therefore be the single most determining factor in a student's educational experience.

COLLEGE LECTURESHIPS

But students did not receive all their teaching from their tutor. The College also provided an extensive programme of teaching by college lecturers (*praelectores*).[246] It possessed a lecture-room dedicated to the purpose,

---

[240] Robert Burton, *Philosophaster*, ed. and trans. Connie McQuillen (Binghamton, NY, 1993), 64/65 (act I, sc. vi): 'Audîn, docebo filium tuum | Artem dicendi et disputandi tribus hebdomadis, | Vno mense totius systema philosophiae | Ad meam methodum.'

[241] William Poole, 'A New Manuscript for New College: Thomas Kent's 1674 Curricular Crib for Logic, Ethics, and Metaphysics', *New College Notes*, 3 (2013), art. 11 (www.new.ox.ac.uk/new-college-notes).

[242] PLM, MS MA0086 (unfoliated): 'Physicæ annotationes breuisculæ'; MS MA0087 (unfoliated): 'Annotationes logicæ'.

[243] Plume, 'An Account', vi. Simpson, like Hacket, was a former Westminster scholar.

[244] James Duport, *Musae subsecivae* (Cambridge, 1676), 316: 'Desiste paulum, da moram scientiæ'.

[245] Cumberland, *Memoirs*, 69.

[246] For a parallel study of the lectureships at New College, Oxford, see William Poole, 'Teaching and Learning in Jacobean New College: The Foundation of the Lake Lectureships', *New College Notes*, 9 (2018), art. 5 (www.new.ox.ac.uk/new-college-notes).

which was demolished when New Court was constructed in the 1820s.[247] Trinity's 1560 Statutes stipulated that a *lector primarius* should teach natural philosophy to the Bachelors of Arts and that no fewer than four *sublectores* should be appointed to teach logic.[248] Four further lecturers were to teach the Greek tongue, Latin, mathematics, and Greek grammar to all who had not yet taken their Bachelor's degree.[249] These College Lectureships were characteristically held by recently graduated MAs, perhaps in preparation for becoming a tutor. Trinity's various Admission Books record the holders of the office of *Lector primarius*, of five further lecturers from the first to the fifth *classis*, and of lecturers Greek, 'Humanity or Latin', Greek Grammar, Mathematics, and of an *examinator* in the Greek language.[250] These lectureships tended to be held, if not quite in rotation, then at least in a somewhat piecemeal fashion.[251] The same person might teach very different subjects. Across the 1650s, for instance, the future naturalist John Ray served as the lecturer in Greek language and grammar (1651), in mathematics (1653), in 'humanity' (1655), again in Greek language (1656), and as *praelector primarius* (1657).[252] This last office was best paid, at £1 10*s* a quarter in 1659; otherwise the lecturer in Greek language was paid slightly better (15*s* a quarter), and the lecturer in Greek grammar (10*s*), slightly worse than the others (13s).[253]

A timetable survives for the college exercises maintained at Corpus Christi College, Cambridge, in the later sixteenth century; less systematic evidence indicates that the situation at Trinity was comparable.[254] At Corpus there were three hour-long lectures in a day. There was a lecture in logic or philosophy at 6am (an allusion by Isaac Barrow suggests that the philosophy lectures at Trinity also took place at dawn);[255] a pair of lectures in Greek language and grammar at noon (Trinity elected a pair of lecturers in Greek language and Greek grammar each year); and a rhetoric lecture at

---

[247] Willis and Clark, *Architectural History*, ii. 659. I am grateful to Nicolas Bell on this point.
[248] 1560 Statutes, p. 19 (cap. 9).
[249] 1560 Statutes, pp. 21–22 (cap. 9). The mathematics lecturers at Trinity in the sixteenth century are documented by James Hannam, 'Teaching Natural Philosophy and Mathematics at Oxford and Cambridge, 1500–1570' (unpublished PhD diss., University of Cambridge, 2008), 230.
[250] See TCA, Admissions 1645–1659, pp. 195–209, for the lecturers elected in this period.
[251] Cf. Stewart, 'Fleshy Books', 38.
[252] TCA, Admissions 1645–1659, pp. 199–208. The young Ray is said to have been Isaac Barrow's 'study-fellow' (*socius studiorum*) in the study of mathematics (Hill, 'Some Account', xlii).
[253] TCM, Senior Bursar's Audit, 1637–1659, fol. 342r.
[254] Richard F. Hardin, 'Marlowe and the Fruits of Scholarism', *Philological Quarterly*, 63 (1984), 397–400 (at 388).
[255] Barrow, 'Pro Lectore Humanitatis Oratio', 128–29.

3pm. In addition there were different sets of college disputations for sophisters, scholars, and bachelors of arts. The fellows themselves disputed problems in divinity once a week. And at Corpus, just as at Trinity, the students delivered declamations in the college hall after supper on Saturday evening.[256]

The timing of the lectures led Isaac Barrow, in an oration he delivered in October 1654 upon taking up the Trinity's praelectorship in humanity, to joke that his position was more sought-after than that of the other lecturers. His subject was not dry and sterile, but fertile and flourishing. The philosophy lecturers, by contrast, had to rouse themselves before dawn from their warm beds and explain to an audience recently awakened from their own dreams the more ridiculous dreams of some senile old man—*i.e.*, Aristotle![257] Failure to attend a lecture was punishable by a fine collected from the 'guilty and complaining' culprits, which in turn provided the lecturer with a further reward for his office.[258]

A text survives of the oration that William Lynnet delivered to both the fellows and students upon taking up the office of *Lector Primarius* after the summer vacation in 1656.[259] Turning from his colleagues to addressing the assembled sophisters, Lynnet reminded them that it was for their sake that he upheld the cause of both eloquence and philosophy. In the Hall he would moderate the 'tumultuous brawls of Philosophy'; in the Chapel he would bring order to 'courtroom debates'; and in doing so he would preserve inviolate the friendship between eloquence and wisdom.[260] Drawing attention to the conventional image of logic as the closed fist, and rhetoric as the open palm, he reminded his audience that sweetness of speech softened the severe precepts of philosophy,[261] while warning them against a 'new and stupid' manner of speaking that had apparently come into favour among sophisters in the Schools.[262] A true Ciceronian eloquence was not that which brought gold, but spirit; not that which gave rise to laughter,

---

[256] The continuance of Saturday evening declamations at Trinity down to 1650 is verified by TCA, 29 Trinity College 472.

[257] Barrow, 'Pro Lectore Humanitatis Oratio', 129. See also Whewell, 'Barrow', xvi (whose misdating there to 1659 was later corrected to 1654, see p. liii), and Stewart, 'Fleshy Books', 38, who misdates it to 1653; the true date emerges from the record of Barrow's only election as *humanitatis praelector* in 1654 (TCA, Admissions 1645–1659, p. 202).

[258] I infer this from Barrow, 'Pro Lectore Humanitatis Oratio', 130, who writes of collecting money 'e pœnis et mulctis nocentium querentium'. See also Whewell, 'Barrow', xvi.

[259] Lynnet was first sworn as *lector primarius* on 1 Oct. 1656 (TCA, Admissions 1645–1659, p. 204).

[260] TCC, MS O. 10a. 33, p. 35: 'In Aulâ tumultuosas Philosophiæ rixas moderatur, in Sacello lites forenses componit.'

[261] TCC, MS O. 10a. 33, p. 36.

[262] TCC, MS O. 10a. 33, p. 37: 'novum & insulsum'.

but to astonishment; not that which flashed and sparkled, but which steadily, levelly, and imperturbably brought the light of understanding to the minds of its hearers.[263] Lynnet fears that his philosophical lectures may not be to the taste of his young audience, accustomed as they are to receiving their food pre-masticated.[264] Nonetheless, he will bring them to the 'sublime regions of Metaphysics' and the 'lovely fields of Moral Philosophy', before they carry themselves in a few years' time to theology; like Promethean fire from heaven, the philosophical disciplines are steps to that holier study.[265] Logic would provide them with a scythe they could use again the rest of the sciences; truth itself was not safe unless it was fortified by logical thorns.[266] Lynnet concludes by painting a picture of his engagement with his audience:

> I especially desire that our early-morning lectures may be worthwhile; that by my daily presence I might call forth your steps into the hall, and that with my own feet I might mark them out; and that I shall haul on every rope that might either lead you, or drag you, to a good result.[267]

Lynnet's impressive oratory spoke so successfully to his audience that his oration was copied as a model of the genre.[268]

UNIVERSITY PROFESSORSHIPS

Members of Trinity also, of course, filled the limited number of lecturing positions that the University offered to its members as a whole. Since Trinity's founding the Regius Professorships of Greek, Hebrew, and Divinity, had been associated with the College, and occasionally a member of a different college, or of none, would migrate to Trinity upon taking up one of these chairs. Thus Robert Metcalfe, Regius Professor of Hebrew, translated himself from St John's College at some point after 1633;[269]

---

[263] TCC, MS O. 10a. 33, p. 38.
[264] TCC, MS O. 10a. 33, p. 39.
[265] TCC, MS O. 10a. 33, pp. 41–42: 'ad sublimes Metaphysices regiones, & amœniores Moralis Philosophiæ campos vos demitto.'
[266] TCC, MS O. 10a. 33, pp. 43–44.
[267] TCC, MS O. 10a. 33, p. 49: 'Curato inprimis ut prælectiones nostræ matutinæ honestentur, meâ vos quotidianâ præsentiâ provocavero, et meo pede signavero vobis ad aulam vestigia, et omnem funem movero, quo vos vel ducam vel traham ad bonam frugem.'
[268] I infer this from its presence in TCC, MS O. 10a. 33, which Mordechai Feingold has identified as being in the hand of James Valentine.
[269] Claire Cross, 'Metcalfe, Robert (1579–1652/3)', *ODNB*, states that 'the exact date of Metcalfe's death is unknown', but records attest that he died in office as Vice-Master in December 1652 (TCA, Admissions 1645–1659, p. 200). He was still a fellow of St John's in 1633: Scot 'The names of all such Noble Persons…' (Cambridge, 1633), *STC* 44897.

while Heinrich Sike, who took up the same chair in 1705, arrived clutching a hastily-acquired degree from Utrecht University.[270]

Trinity provided the University, if not with a monopoly, then certainly with a steady succession of Greek professors across the seventeenth and eighteenth centuries (Table 1). It is notable how many of these had previously had the good fortune to be well grounded in the language at Westminster School. Among these professors, James Duport (who came to Trinity from Westminster) published several books emphasising the congruity of Greek with the Hebrew bible, and several manuscripts arising from his Greek studies also survive.[271] Isaac Barrow (not a Westminster scholar), whose audience consisted in principle of all the Bachelors of Arts,[272] complained that his lectures on Sophocles in 1660–61 had been delivered to the walls.[273]

Table 1. Members of Trinity College elected Regius Professor of Greek, 1546–1750.[274]

1547–49		Nicholas Carr
1562–85		Bartholomew Dodington
1625–39	*	Robert Creighton, Sr.
1639–54	*	James Duport
1660–63		Isaac Barrow
1663–66		James Valentine
1666–72	*	Robert Creighton, Jr.
1672	*	Thomas Gale
1672–74	*	John North
1674–86		Benjamin Pulleyn
1686–95	*	Michael Payne
1712–26	*	Thomas Pilgrim
1726–44		Walter Taylor
1744–50	*	William Fraigneau

* educated at Westminster School

[270] Alistair Hamilton, 'Sike, Henry (*bap.* 1669, *d.* 1712)', *ODNB*.
[271] TCC, MS R. 1. 47 (Duport's notes on Demosthenes and Theophrastus); MS R. 3. 31 (a late-medieval copy of 'Sophoclis Tragoediæ', bequeathed by Duport); MS R. 9. 29 (a seventeenth-century copy of Xenophon's *Anabasis*, bequeathed by Duport); MS R. 9. 34 (his notes on Greek terms and proverbs, dated 12 Dec. 1639); MS R. 9. 35 (his notes on Homer); MS R. 9. 36 (his notes on Homer and Theophrastus). The circumstances in which Duport left the chair are considered by Rosemary O'Day, 'Duport, James (1606–1679)', *ODNB*.
[272] Scot 'The Names of all such Noble Persons...' (Cambridge, 1633), *STC* 44897.
[273] Isaac Barrow, 'Oratio Sarcasmica in Schola Græca', in *Opuscula* (London, 1687), 110–17. For the date of this oration, see John Gascoigne, 'Isaac Barrow's academic milieu', in *Before Newton*, 276.
[274] Sources: J. R. Tanner, *Historical Register of the University of Cambridge* (Cambridge, 1917), 78; *ODNB*.

The ideal of 'general learning' is manifest not only in the capacity of fellows to take up a range of college lectureships, but also to fill more than one university chair. When Isaac Barrow resigned his Greek chair in 1663 it was in order to take become the first incumbent of the newly founded Lucasian Professorship of Mathematics in 1664; versions of his lectures relating to this position survive in manuscript and print.[275] With the greatness of mind that characterises both his actions and his writings, Barrow in his turn gave up this chair in 1669 in favour of the younger Isaac Newton (1642–1727); a number of courses of Newton's lectures also survive, although there are considerable doubts about the relation of some of them to his actual teaching.[276] At so late a date as the early 1770s Richard Watson could contrive to occupy both the chair in Chemistry (a subject of which, at the time of his election, he ingenuously confessed he knew 'nothing at all') and the Regius chair in Divinity.[277]

THE SCHOLARSHIP AND FELLOWSHIP ELECTIONS

By no means every student took even a Bachelor's degree. But even these students clearly undertook study in the various disciplines of the arts course, as the book-purchases of James Master suggest.[278] No doubt he did so under the guidance of his tutor, the future non-conformist Nathaniel Bradshaw, who had taken on a whole raft of pupils as soon as he became a fellow.[279] A further task of the tutor, as Duport's 'Rules' make clear, was to prepare his pupils for the 'scholastic exercises' (*exercitia scholastica*) mandated by the University for those sitting for the BA degree.[280] There were, however, even more consequential examinations within Trinity itself.[281] These were the elections for the College's sixty scholarships and sixty fellowships.[282]

---

[275] TCC, MSS R. 9. 39; Isaac Barrow, *Lectiones habitæ in Scholis Publicis Academiæ Cantabrigiensis* (1683).
[276] Westfall, *Never at Rest*, 211.
[277] Watson, *Anecdotes*, 27.
[278] Robinson, 'Expense-Book of James Master'.
[279] Bradshaw (adm. 1637) was elected a fellow in 1645; he left in 1649 after becoming rector of Willingham, from which living he was ejected in 1662 (Venn, *Alumni Cantabrigienses*, i. 202). He took on 14 pupils in 1645 alone, more than any other tutor (Rouse Ball and Venn, *Admissions to Trinity*, ii. 380–86).
[280] Preston and Oswald, 'Duport's Rules', 345–49.
[281] On this point, see also Gascoigne, 'Mathematics and Meritocracy', 557.
[282] For these numbers, see 1560 Statutes, p. 28 (cap. 12; fellowships), 33 (cap. 13; scholarships).

These are enormous numbers. Other colleges might struggle to support a dozen fellows or scholars. Such positions were often restricted by 'country' (i.e. county). A younger but perhaps more brilliant candidate from the same part of England might therefore be excluded from obtaining a position.[283] At Trinity, by contrast, only the Westminster scholars were locally privileged in the scholarship election.[284] In the fellowship election the 1560 Statutes gave preference (other things being equal) to candidates who originated from those parts of the kingdom in which the College possessed livings; it is unclear how far this stipulation was observed in practice.[285]

The sheer quantity of preferment available at Trinity must therefore have made it a desirable institution to become a member of, and may perhaps account for the occasional migration into it from other College. (But those who changed college in the mid-1640s, such as Isaac Barrow and John Ray, may also have done so to fill the unusual void in numbers created by the civil wars.) Scholarships at Trinity were also worth more than in other college. This condition is hinted at in the letters that one tutor wrote to the importunate mother of a pupil who had clearly threatened to have her son move next door:

> One thing I should adde for caution: that if you remooue him to another College you had need to be well satisfyed whether your assurances be better there than here, for mens words are slippery, the ordinary course is rather to giue euery one hopes than discouragements. Agen your Ladyship will soone understand, that Schollarships in other Colledges are of uery small & inconsiderable ualue: & not comparable to these of our College: either for the credit & honour of them or for the profit:

The profit in question consisted of money (the sum varied but was in the order of a pound a quarter) and, more significantly, free commons until a scholar graduated as a Master of Arts.[286]

Scholarships and fellowships were connected insofar as the right to sit for a fellowship was dependent upon having previously been elected to a scholarship.[287] A great deal was at stake, therefore, from an early stage in a student's career. Failure to jump the first step—scholarships were obtained

---

[283] This happened to John Wallis at Emmanuel College in the later 1630s. See Christoph J. Scriba, 'The Autobiography of John Wallis, F.R.S.', *Notes and Records of the Royal Society of London*, 25 (1970), 30.
[284] 1560 Statutes, pp. 33–34 (cap. 13).
[285] 1560 Statutes, p. 30 (cap. 12).
[286] TCC, MS O. 11a. 5⁹ (unfoliated; undated: later 1650s?). I am grateful to Arnold Hunt for supplying me with his accurate transcription of this crabbed draft correspondence. For scholars' stipends, see e.g. TCA, Senior Bursar's Audit, 1637–1659, fo. 342r–343r (accounts for 1659).
[287] 1560 Statutes, 21–22 (cap. 12): 'Et qui cooptantur, sint minimum baccalaurei artium atque omnes ex discipulis ipsius [*recte* istius] Collegij semper præferantur'.

in the course of studying for the Bachelor's degree—meant the curtailment of any academic ambitions that an undergraduate might possess.

The Statutes vested the power of election in the Master and the eight Senior fellows.[288] The bursary accounts confirm other reports that the Master of Trinity regularly travelled down to London to conduct the annual election of Westminster scholars at the school itself; indeed, the election was the cause of Isaac Barrow's death, insofar as he caught the 'malignant fever' that killed him on that visit to London in 1677.[289] Westminster scholars, such as the future poet John Dryden, therefore arrived already placed in a privileged capacity.[290] Within the College, scholars tended to be elected two or three years after arrival. (In 1645 and 1646 the shortage of members caused by civil war meant that this timing was often advanced.[291]) The 1560 Statutes required that scholars (*discipuli*) were to be chosen on the basis of their 'cleverness, learning, virtue, and need'.[292] They also stipulate that, other things being equal, those who could sing were to be preferred over those who could not.[293] The election was to take place within twenty days of the second Sunday after Easter. From eight to ten in the morning, and from two to four in the afternoon, the candidates were to be examined in grammar and humane letters, and their singing assessed; they were also required to have exercised themselves in logic in the hall.[294] Students from England (*domestici*) were to be preferred, other things being equal, to foreigners (*externi*).[295] The Statutes also excluded from a scholarship those whose might expect to inherit more than ten pounds per annum.[296] It seems likely that this restriction was allowed to lapse across the seventeenth and eighteenth centuries, but it is nonetheless the case that those who entered the College as fellow commoners do not tend to be elected to scholarships, and therefore did not become fellows. Those elected were required to make a lengthy oath swearing to uphold the good of the College in all things.[297]

---

[288] 1560 Statutes, 29 (cap. 12): 'Eligendi potestas sit penes magistrum... et penes octo seniores: Locus eligendi Sacellum esto. Tempus hora octaua antemeridiana.' Ibid., 33 (cap. 13): 'Idem sit electionis modus, qui et sociorum, et electores ijdem, locus et hora eadem.'

[289] Mordechai Feingold, 'Barrow, Isaac (1630–1677)', *ODNB*.

[290] In 1659 the Master, then John Wilkins, received £5 for the 'Westminster Election' (TCA, Senior Bursar's Audit, 1637–1659, fol. 346r). See further Whewell, 'Barrow', xliv. Westminster scholars might also be elected in the year following their arrival at the college, as in the case of Francis Gregory, who was admitted in 1641 but elected in 1642.

[291] Rouse Ball and Venn, *Admissions to Trinity*, ii. 380 ff.

[292] 1560 Statutes, p. 33 (cap. 13): 'in his eligendis præcipua ratio habeatur ingenij, doctrinæ, uirtutis et inopiæ'.

[293] 1560 Statutes, p. 33 (cap. 13): 'Et qui cantare norunt, modo cæteris, qui petunt, uirtute et doctrina pares sint, præferantur.'

[294] 1560 Statutes, pp. 33–34 (cap. 13).   [295] 1560 Statutes, p. 34 (cap. 13).

[296] 1560 Statutes, p. 34 (cap. 13).   [297] 1560 Statutes, pp. 34–35 (cap. 13).

These requirements are fleshed out by a further letter by a tutor to the importunate parent of one of his pupils. He explains that in order to obtain the 'preferment' of a scholarship at Trinity a candidate 'must sit 3 daies in the chappel & undergoe publike & private examination', in order that the places might be 'duly disperst' according to candidates' 'proficiency in learning'. The pupil in question was 'the senior of his yeer & of the election, which the electioners have always respect to.' Moreover (the tutor went on), 'of late' elections had not been 'carried as formerly', that is, with 'particular favour & private respects' but were now rather conducted 'with a general & common case to all the candidates that deserue fauour.' (The question of equity and even of corruption will loom even larger in the case of the fellowship election.) Regrettably, however, the pupil in question, who had been absent from the College for much of the previous year, had declined to put himself forward as a candidate; perhaps (the author suggested) from fear of diminishing his reputation in case of failure; 'what other priuate reasons he had I know not'.[298]

The annual fellowship election was, in effect, a more demanding version of the scholarship election, with higher stakes. As it did until the early twenty-first century, the election took place at the beginning of Michaelmas each year.[299] It was prevented from taking place only by plague, civil war—or a lack of places to fill. As we have seen, candidates for fellowships had already to be scholars; they were also required to be Bachelors of Arts, and a person who, in the opinion of the Master and eight Senior fellows, was upstanding in religion, learning, and morals. In general, elections to fellowships occurred in the year or two after a student took his BA degree. Fellows were further required to be people who might be hoped to make successful progress in the study of the sacred scriptures; that is, who might go on to take holy orders. Two fellowships alone were reserved for prospective students of civil law and of medicine.[300]

The 1560 Statutes mandated a detailed scheme of examination. Four days were set aside for the purpose. On the first day, between the hours of seven and ten in the morning and one and four in the afternoon, candidates were to be assessed on their knowledge of logic and mathematics. The second day was devoted to natural and moral philosophy. The third days tested the candidates' knowledge in languages, and history, poetry, and 'all kinds of humane letters' (*in toto genere humanioris literaturæ*). Finally, on the fourth day, candidates were to compose a 'theme' (what might now be thought of as an essay) and also a poem—and like the scholars were also, according to

---

[298] TCC MS O. 11a. 5(9) (unfoliated).
[299] 1560 Statutes, p. 29 (cap. 12).   [300] 1560 Statutes, pp. 28–29 (cap. 12).

the Statute, to be assessed on their singing.[301] The election itself took place (as formally it still does) in the chapel.[302] Successful candidates were elected to a so-called 'minor' fellowship, which upon award of an MA became a 'major' fellowship.[303] Like the scholars, and as they must still today (though less elaborately), new fellows were required to swear an oath to uphold the good of the College.[304] An account of the election dating from the middle or later years of the seventeenth century confirms that the statutory regime was still being followed quite closely at that point.[305] In 1649 the Master adjured the senior fellows to make election frequently, 'with strict Examinations', and 'and as publick as may bee'.[306]

Thus the drama generated by the scholarship election was as little compared to that of the fellowship election. There was a relatively rapid turnover of scholars, as they left, or took their MA degrees, or were elected to fellowships.[307] By contrast, the right of fellows to retain their office (subject to certain statutory requirements) for as long as they wished meant that significantly fewer fellowships opened up in any one year. In 1656, twenty-five candidates competed for ten positions. [308] In 1659, twenty-four candidates are said to have competed for four places.[309] The emoluments of the position, and the limited obligations of those who received them, meant that success or failure in the election was closely watched, and was also remembered with satisfaction in later life.[310]

---

[301] 1560 Statutes, p. 30 (cap. 12). It seems possible that this 'theme' was what one later finds referred to as the 'epistle' composed by candidates for election: TCC, MS O. 10a. 33, pp. 26, 27.

[302] 1560 Statutes, p. 29 (cap. 12).   [303] 1560 Statutes, p. 28 (cap. 12).

[304] 1560 Statutes, pp. 31–32 (cap. 12)

[305] J. Edleston, 'Synoptical View of Newton's Life', in *Correspondence of Sir Isaac Newton and Professor Cotes* (1850), xlii–xliii, quotes what he calls an 'MS. calendar... of the routine events of an academical life' by William Lynnet: 'The fellowes on the 3d day of their sitting must have a theme given them by the Master, which the chappell-clerk fetcheth for them: they sit 3 days being excused the 4th for their theme. They sit from 7 till 10, & from one to 4, each writing his name his age & his country; as doe the scholars, & also the Masters of Arts, which papers are carried to the Master & Vice-Master, the first morning so soon as all have written... Octob. 1... by the tolling of the little bell at 8 in the morning the seniours are called & the day after at one o'clock to swear them that are chosen.'

[306] Thomas Hill, 'A Letter to the Seniors of Trinitie-Colledg in Cambridge', in *The Best and Worst of Paul* (Cambridge, 1648), sig. A4v.

[307] TCC MS O. 11a. 5⁹ (unfoliated): 'Schollarships are uoided 3 waies either by an election of fellowes or else by the commencing of Master of arts, or by causall remotion.'

[308] TCC MS O. 10a. 33, p. 16.

[309] Edmund Calamy, *The Nonconformist's Memorial*, 3 vols (London, 1802–03), i. 277, quoting the testimony of John Hutchinson (elected 1659). But Innes, *Fellows of Trinity*, 35, has seven elected that year.

[310] Such as by John Hutchinson (n. 313, above); by Robert Creighton (see Serjeantson, 'Wilkins in Cambridge', 78–79); or by Cumberland, *Memoirs*, 105–111.

As we have seen, the reading and also the writing of verse was both encouraged by tutors and indeed, in the case of 'act verses', mandated by the university. It is therefore not a surprise to find the annual fellowship election being memorialised in satirical verses in both English and Latin. These verses—which are perhaps better thought of as ballads—are undistinguished, but the circumstantial detail of their invective is invaluable for establishing the standing of the election in the life of the College. We find jokes about the elections related to the most pressing theological and philosophical issues of the time: predestination, and the motion of the earth.[311] We meet the former sizar, Edward Trott, who 'trots to Chappell his Theame for to make' carrying a pair of dictionaries under his arm and whose wit is unfavourably compared to that of his father, a Cambridge barber.[312] We encounter John Henshaw, who rode post back from France, 'preferment to gaine'—but for whom it would have been better if he had found a horse 'to goe back againe'.[313] Robert Bloyse returned to Cambridge too late and missed the election.[314] Robert Stubbs's dream of a fellowship is said to be as distant as his theme was from the subject he was set.[315]

Our poet is also liberal in expressing his national prejudices. The Irishman Thomas Bunbury is said to be 'stuck like one in a bogg' and is accorded the opprobrious epithet of 'Scalogue' (a corruption of the Irish *scalóg*, meaning peasant).[316] A Welsh student is simply referred to as 'S*ir* Taffie'; this unidentified 'Cambrobrittaine', however, was 'repuls'd' in his hopes.[317] Others the poet simply dislikes. David Jenner, who was not elected, is said to be 'as uery a rogue as euer pist', who roused the electors *bilis* (bile) by mispronouncing *miles* (soldier).[318] And of Augustine Plumstead, who was elected, the poet (who may himself be the person alluded to) delicately writes,

> And now Poet Darly may hold his tongue,
> Who without feare or witt hath oft said,
> That Plumsteds nurse when he was young,
> Had suckt out his braines, & shit in his head.[319]

---

[311] TCC, MS O. 10a. 33, pp. 16, 18.
[312] TCC, MS O. 10a. 33, p. 17. Venn, *Alumni Cantabrigienses*, iv. 267.
[313] TCC, MS O. 10a. 33, p. 17.   [314] TCC, MS O. 10a. 33, p. 25.
[315] TCC, MS O. 10a. 33, p. 18.
[316] TCC, MS O. 10a. 33, p. 26. Bunbury's nationality is confirmed by Venn, *Alumni Cantabrigienses*, i. 254. See further J. O. Bartley, *Teague, Shenkin and Sawney: Being an Historical study of the Earliest Irish, Welsh and Scottish Characters in English Plays* (Cork, 1954), 274.
[317] TCC, MS O. 10a. 33, p. 27. I have not identified this student.
[318] TCC, MS O. 10a. 33, pp. 26–27. On Jenner, see further Serjeantson, 'Wilkins in Cambridge', 78–81.
[319] TCC, MS O. 10a. 33, p. 26. 'Poet Darly' is Benjamin Darley, who was admitted as a pensioner on 9 June 1656 and who died in 1659 without taking a degree (Venn, *Alumni Cantabrigienses*, ii. 10).

The poet is also free with sexual innuendo. Several candidates are referred to as women, including 'Mayden Crichton' (Robert Creighton the younger, who was elected).[320] Francis Bridge is said to be as big with hope as his laundress was previously big with child:

> His course for a Fellowship rightly doth steere,
> But something there is that is laide at his door,
> Besides he hath an hundred a yeere.[321]

Neither accomplishment prevented Bridge being elected two years later, in 1661. For his part, William Budgen is said to be the illegitimate offspring of his father's liaison with a sexton's wife, 'Who by the uirtue of two good grave stones, | And a Church yard produced this skin & bones.'[322] But only Latin will suffice for the most scabrous claim about this candidate, who rejoiced that the College was celibate, since he would otherwise certainly have been slept with.[323]

The stakes of the fellowship election were sufficiently high that the disturbing spectre of corruption frequently arises. In a published letter that the Master, Thomas Hill, addressed to his Seniors in 1649, he required that the fellows let candidates know that 'you understand not how to bee mercenarie, or to pass *venalia suffragia*, which hath filled many Societies with Drones.'[324] The 1656 poem begins with allusions both towards Aristotelian categorical logic and towards nepotism when it suggests that, 'a scheme of Phylosophy in there was brought, | To judge of mens Qualities by theire Relation.'[325] This is borne out at the end of the poem when we encounter one Thomas Arrowsmith, who was duly elected to a fellowship in that year:

> *Sir* Arrowsmith prooved that the earth stood still;
> Confuteing Des Cartes by Zabarell.
> But by his good will he disputed but ill
> For with him we know that the world goes well.[326]

The reason for Arrowsmith's success, as every contemporary reader of the poem would have known, was that this particular Bachelor of Arts was also the son of the then Master, John Arrowsmith. We have already heard a tutor claiming in the 1650s that corruption was less prevalent at the point he was writing than 'formerly'. A similar assertion was made about the Mastership of John Wilkins, whom John Aubrey claimed 'revived learning

---

[320] TCC, MS O. 10a. 33, p. 28. See also ibid., p. 16.
[321] TCC, MS O. 10a. 33, p. 28.   [322] TCC, MS O. 10a. 33, pp. 25.
[323] TCC, MS O. 10a. 33, pp. 26: 'Gaudeat Collegium Cœlibes erunt, | Nam certè hic mansuri'.
[324] Hill, 'A Letter', sig. A4v.   [325] TCC, MS O. 10a. 33, pp. 16.
[326] TCC, MS O. 10a. 33, p. 18.

by strickt examinations at elections'.³²⁷ These assertions of improvement suggest that there is something in the charge that corruption had existed. The 1656 poem alludes to the purchase of fellowships, and the suggestion is further made in a not unfunny joke dating from the Mastership of John Richardson (1615–1625). It was told by a member of college whose rank placed him above the fray:

> A Fellow Commoner of Trinity Colledge said, of the Batchellers sitting in the Chappell for Fellowshipps; That Mr Harrison became, and asked some like Question; Quid est physica ['what is physics']? Quid est Natura ['what is nature']. Then came Dr Cumber, and he asked more grauely; Quid est anima ['what is the soul']? Then came Dr Richardson, and he asked 40£.³²⁸

The emoluments of a fellowship in 1620 were about £50 a year; this stiff bribe might therefore have been a tolerably sound investment for a few year's income.³²⁹

Though it was the largest Cambridge college, Trinity was, after all, still a relatively contained society, and the reputation of an especially clever student might travel before him, as Thomas Plume says it did in the case of John Hacket: 'The first proofs he gave of his ability *Logick, Philosophy,* and *Oratory*, were so much above the common sort, that his Preferment was soon presaged in that *Society*, which he obtained by his own merits, without the intercession of Friends to hoist or heave him up. He was chosen *Fellow* of the *Colledge* as soon as he became capable by virtue of his *first degree*' (i.e. taking his BA).³³⁰ Just as in the modern academic world, therefore, what might look to some observers like special favour appeared to others to be merely the just reward of ability and promise.

MEDICINE, LAW, AND DIVINITY

What were the goals of a fellowship? Although some fellows of Trinity pursued investigations into history, biblical or classical scholarship, or natural philosophy, and published their findings, there was no ideal of

---

³²⁷ John Aubrey, *Brief Lives*, ed. Andrew Clark, 2 vols (Oxford, 1898), ii. 301.
³²⁸ LPL, MS 2086, fol. 32r (notebook of William Rawley, a graduate of Corpus Christi College, rector of Landbeach (just north of Cambridge) and former chaplain to Francis Bacon). Thomas Harrison was a fellow from 1579 to 1631 and served as Vice-Master, 1611–1631. Thomas Comber became a fellow in 1597 and was Master, 1631–45; he was made a Doctor of Divinity in 1616, so this story must postdate that event. John Richardson took his DD in 1597 and was Master of Trinity, 1615–1625.
³²⁹ On the emoluments of a fellowship, see further Robert Neild, *Riches and Responsibility: A Financial History of Trinity College Cambridge* (Cambridge, 2008).
³³⁰ Plume, 'An Account', vi.

'research' that became a principal motivation of the twentieth- and twenty-first century university. To remain in the College, and the University, beyond a students' studies of the arts course was done with a professional or at least a vocational goal in view.

Hence the overwhelming focus of the fellows' own studies was—in principle at least—religion. It was to this end that the great majority of academically persistent students acquired 'the preparatory learning' of '*Logick, Physick, Metaphysicks,* and *Ethicks*'.[331]

The 1560 statutes required that fellows had to take holy orders within seven years of taking the degree of Master of Arts. Failure to do so would result in expulsion. The only exceptions were the two fellowships designated for medicine and civil law.[332] In the singular ecclesiastical circumstances that followed the successive abolition in England of episcopacy in 1645 and of the presbyterian classes in 1650, this requirement to take holy orders was suspended for some years.[333] But it was re-imposed in principle in 1658, and insisted upon following the Restoration (which helps to account for John Ray's intensely reluctant decision to take holy orders in December 1660), and on several occasions the College ejected those who had failed to comply.[334] The royal dispensation that Isaac Newton received from this obligation in 1675 was extremely unusual.[335]

In less tumultuous times, however, a fellowship therefore offered a secure opportunity to undertake further study of divinity prior to undertaking the cure of souls. In so doing, of course, fellows might also take on the office of tutor, and deploy their own hard-won knowledge of the arts course in teaching their pupils. But there were also incentives to vacate a fellowship and move on. If a particular fellow did not feel able, for whatever reason, to take holy orders, then he had to leave. More usually, perhaps, departure was occasioned by securing a living—although it was also possible, and more remunerative, to hold a fellowship in conjunction with a nearby living.[336] If the candidate was fortunate, this might bring significantly larger financial rewards than those offered by a fellowship. No less pressingly, perhaps, departure from the celibate college community allowed a former fellow to marry. The consequence of these factors was

---

[331] Plume, 'An Account', vi, describing the case of John Hacket in the 1610s.
[332] 1560 Statutes, 58 (cap. 19).
[333] TCA, Conclusions and Admonitions 1607–1673, p. 212 (conclusion of 17 Jun. 1650), rescinded by a conclusion of 2 Oct. 1656, later altered to 1658 (ibid., p. 244). See further Whewell, 'Barrow', xi–xiii.
[334] *Pace* Charles E. Raven, *John Ray, Naturalist*, 2nd edn (Cambridge, 1950), 57–59.
[335] Westfall, *Never at Rest*, 330–34.
[336] As John Hacket held the Trinity living of Trumpington before going on to greater things (Plume, 'An Account', vii).

that the average tenure of a fellowship at Trinity across the seventeenth century has been calculated at fourteen years—and the median duration was probably rather less.[337]

Nor was every Master of Arts associated with a college necessarily a fellow. There is evidence that some colleges provided opportunities for members without a fellowship to remain and pursue their studies in divinity, and this may also have happened at Trinity, for instance in the case of the (admittedly aristocratic) John North.[338] Trinity also retained several chaplains. It is possible that these positions served to reward members who had been *proxime accessit* for a fellowship. On occasion, chaplains might even serve as tutors. Anthony Scattergood (1611–1687), for instance, as his surviving Cambridge notebook testifies, was a serious student, who went on to edit biblical commentaries and was awarded a doctorate in divinity following the Restoration. Though he was never elected to a fellowship, he became one of Trinity's four chaplains in 1637, the year following the award of his MA degree, and in 1640 served as a tutor.[339]

Nor indeed was it even necessary to take an MA to enter holy orders. Oliver Heywood, who became a prominent non-conformist preacher in the north of England following the Restoration, explained in his autobiography that he had spent his time at Trinity reading books of practical divinity in preference to works of philosophy: 'All that time I was in the university my heart was much deadned to and in philosophical studys, nor could I as I desired apply my mind so close to humane literature'. Having entered the College in the 'comfortable degree of a pensioner' he was conscious of the burden he placed upon his father, yet being prevented (on his own account) from winning a scholarship by a 'sore and grievous sicknes', he left the College upon taking his BA. While his tutor Alexander Akehurst assumed that he would become a country school-teacher, Heywood himself intended to inch towards the 'weighty calling' of becoming a minister.[340] The question of how to maintain godly students preparing for the ministry was a persistent one: those fortunate enough to be elected to a fellowship at Trinity were at a distinct advantage in the matter.[341]

---

[337] The average figure of 14.32 years is owing to John D. Twigg, 'The Parliamentary Visitation of the University of Cambridge, 1644–1645', *English Historical Review*, 98 (1983), 523.

[338] George Palfrey did so at Sidney Sussex in the 1620s, and John Patrick at Queens' in the 1650s. John North moved to Trinity from Jesus in 1670 as a resident MA (C. S. Knighton, 'North, John (1645–1683)', *ODNB*).

[339] Venn, *Alumni Cantabrigienses*, iv. 29; Hugh de Quehen, 'Scattergood, Anthony (*bap.* 1611, *d.* 1687)', *ODNB*. BL, MS Add. 44963. Duport, *Musæ subsecivæ*, 174, addressed a poem to his old acquaintance praising his critical skills.

[340] Heywood, *Autobiography*, 161–2.

[341] Matthew Poole, *A Model for the Maintaining of Studies* (1658), 5.

Yet it would be a mistake to suppose that the study of divinity was strictly reserved for those who had passed the second 'step' of the MA degree. On the contrary: the study of theology, and especially of the bible, was expected of all scholars in the College from the moment of their arrival. Duport's 'Rules' are instructive here. He instructed his students to 'Keepe a constant course in reading the Scriptures, 2 or 3 chapters a day', together with a commentary upon them. (He recommended the one by the Italian Protestant Giovanni Diodati, which had been translated into English in 1643.) He insisted that his charges seek to read the bible in 'the originall tongues': 'never think you can see clearly into God's word without the 2 eyes of Greek and Hebrew'. He also recommended that his students study English works of devotion and practical divinity, of the sort that Oliver Heywood particularly cherished, by authors such as John Preston, Robert Bolton, and Richard Baxter.[342] At Emmanuel, Richard Holdsworth reserved the mornings of the final term of BA study for a reading of Marcus Friedrich Wendelin's systematic account of Christian theology, a popular work in civil-war era Cambridge, on the grounds that 'It is necessary to have some entrance in Divinity before you commence'.[343] The evidence of the accounts kept by the fellow-commoner James Master, who took no degree and was not ordained, is that catechisms and other works of practical divinity by good Reformed authors played a prominent role in the growing book-collection he made during his time at Trinity.[344]

Divinity remained prominent as one rose through the college hierarchy. Fellows were required to deliver theological 'common-places' in the College chapel three times a week in the morning.[345] In the later sixteenth century these were described in terms of handling 'some place of the scripture', from which the fellow delivering the common-place took occasion 'to entreat of some common place of Doctrine, the which he proueth by the scripture, & doctors.'[346] Very occasionally members of the college were so forward as to print their common-places. Caleb Dalechamp, from Sedan in Protestant Normandy, and made MA (though not a fellow) of

---

[342] Preston and Oswald, 'Duport's Rules', 333, 352, 335, 334.

[343] Holdsworth, 'Directions', 633, 645. See further Stewart, 'Isaac Barrow', 146.

[344] Robinson, 'Expense-Book of James Master', 164–72. Master purchased Johannes Wolleb's *Compendium theologiæ Christianæ* (1s 6d), John Rogers' *The doctrine of faith* (1s 6d), William Ames, *De conscientia* (in a Dutch edition, 2s 4d), William Ames' catechism (1s 6d), Zacharias Ursinus' *Summe of Christian Religion* (9s 6d), William Ames's *Lectiones in omnes Psalmos Davidis* (3s 4d), John Lightfoot's *Harmony of the foure evangelists* (4s 6d), a Latin version of the Bible, and a few sermons by Stephen Marshall, Ralph Cudworth, and others.

[345] John Ray, 'Preface', to *The Wisdom of God* (1691), sig. A6r, explains that in the University of Cambridge the 'Morning Divinity Exercises', are called 'Common Places'.

[346] Hardin, 'Marlowe', 388.

Trinity by a Grace of the University, published in 1632 a treatise on the religious duty of hospitality that he had previously 'handled commonplace-wise' in the college's chapel.[347] John Sherman, a fellow of Trinity who was ejected in 1644, published his meditations on Acts 17:28 in 1641 under the title of *A Greek to the Temple*.[348] Better known, and rather more consequential for the intellectual history of eighteenth-century England, were the common-places that John Ray delivered in Trinity at some point in the 1650s and which he eventually published in revised form as the natural-theological treatise *The Wisdom of God Manifested in the Works of the Creation* (1691). As this suggests, commonplaces provided an opportunity for philosophically and humanistically educated scholars to apply their learning to the exposition of scripture and the elaboration of Christian doctrine.

Very occasionally the result of this work was the publication of a substantial work of scholarship. Edward Simpson's *Chronicle* of world-history from the creation to the death of Christ, only published in full in 1652 following his death, was begun during his time as a fellow at Trinity in the first two decades of the seventeenth century.[349] And the young William Spencer published his edition of Origen's *Contra Celsum* in 1658 a mere four years after taking his MA, both drawing upon and helping to feed the intense interest in Origen's works that is characteristic of certain corners of Cambridge's theological life at that moment—corners that evidently included not only Christ's, but also Trinity College.[350]

Nor was the Master himself exempt from the divine discipline. He was, after all, required by the Statutes to be a Doctor of Divinity. In a paper of 1650 defending Trinity's practices, Thomas Hill noted that he 'expounds *th*e scripture' to members of his college on a weekly basis.[351] He published a specimen of this Sunday evening work in the College chapel alongside some of his other sermons from other more public pulpits: it demonstrates

---

[347] Caleb Dalechamp, *Christian Hospitalitie* (Cambridge, 1632), title-page. The dedication to John Williams, the bishop of Lincoln, describes Trinity as 'the most hospital [*i.e.* hospitable] Societie that I know' (sig. A3r). He was allowed the degrees of BA and MA by Grace of 3 March 1624 (CUL, MS Mm. 1. 36 (Baker MS 25), p. 256).

[348] John Sherman, *A Greek to the Temple* (Cambridge, 1641). See also Duport, *Musae subsecivae*, 359.

[349] Simpson, *Chronicon historiam catholicam complectens*, sig. A5v.

[350] William Spencer (ed.), *Origenis contra Celsum libri octo* (Cambridge, 1658). Marialuisa Baldi (ed.), *Mind Senior to the World. Stoicismo e origenismo nella filosofia platonica del Seicento inglese* (Milan, 1996); Alfons Fürst and Christian Hengstermann (eds.), *Die Cambridge Origenists* (Münster, 2013).

[351] LPL, MS 804 ('An answer to a paper concerning Trinity College', 1650), fol. 42v.

that, although it was delivered in English, a college commonplace was more explicitly didactic, more self-consciously argumentative (raising and dissolving objections), and more doctrinally technically than his non-scholastic preaching.[352]

Of all the studies undertaken in the early modern English universities, those that were made towards the degree of Bachelor of Divinity have been the most elusive to reconstruct. One reason for this is that they seem to have been highly informal and personal in nature. MA students were already largely liberated from the guidance of their tutors; BD students, no longer *in statu pupillari* and often indeed fellows and tutors themselves, were even freer. Another reason for the elusive quality of such studies is that a higher degree was not necessary (as we have seen) to enter holy orders. Thus manuscript notes on theological subjects might document a formal course of study, or they might instead bear witness to the piety applying itself to learning, without the goal of a degree in sight. What is clear is that members of the university actually taking the BD degree were required to preach a Latin sermon before the University (a *concio ad clerum*), or to pay a caution money towards a promise to do so in future.[353] Such sermons were sometimes delivered before the annual Ash-Wednesday disputations.[354] But this came at the end of a long, though ill-defined period of study, some portions of which might be undertaken out of residence from the University itself.

At the apex of the few academic positions offered by the University, rather than by the colleges, were the two professors of Divinity, the Lady Margaret, and the Regius. Notwithstanding its size, Trinity only laid claim to four holders of these positions across the period from 1600 to 1750: John Richardson (Regius, 1606–17), John Arrowsmith (Regius, 1651–1659), John Pearson (Lady Margaret's, 1661–1672), and Richard Bentley (Regius, 1717–1742). The professors of divinity were not expected to publish extensively, but they did play a pivotal role in the Divinity School of the University, 'determining' theological disputations and assessing candidates for the higher degrees of BD and DD. All Masters of Arts in their first year were, in principle, to attend their lectures.[355] In his life of Archbishop John Williams, John Hacket painted an approving pen-portrait of Richardson's intellectual capacity in the course of describing

---

[352] Thomas Hill, *The Best and Worst of Paul* (Cambridge, 1648), also collected in *Six Sermons* (London, 1649).
[353] For instance, in the case of George Rust of Christ's in 1659 (Cambridge University Archives, Grace Book Eta, p. 198).   [354] Buck, 'Extracts', lxix.
[355] Scot, 'The names of all such Noble Persons…' (Cambridge, 1633), *STC* 44897.

the young Williams' encounter with him upon defending his theses for BD in 1613:

> Dr. *Richardson*, who received from him these *Theses*, as it were the Chartel of Challenge, met him in the Schools. He was a profound Divine, as famous in the Pulpit as in the Chair, (which is not usual) a great Linguist, noted for a kind of Omnisciency in Church Antiquities, of pure Language, yet used not his Pen to Compose his Lectures but brought his Memory with him, and dictated his Mind with great Authority. We that frequented at his Polemical Exercises observ'd, That if the Respondent that stood before him were not a lusty Game-Cock, but of a Craven kind, he would shake him a little, but never cast him on his back: But if he were one of the right Brood, that would strike Spur for Spur, he would be sure to make him feel the weight of a Professor's Learning before they parted. Therefore did he not dally with Mr. *Williams* at this time, but laid at him with all his Puissance. Nothing could be more delightful for two long hours and better to us that were the Lookers on.[356]

As Hacket's language attests, disputations were often regarded as a kind of instructive sport—even in the case of the divine science of theology.

CONCLUSIONS

An effective though admittedly partisan way of assessing the condition of learning at Trinity in this period is to consider the comparisons that its members made of it with other universities in Europe. When Isaac Barrow travelled to Paris in 1655 he bemoaned the condition of learning there to his colleagues at Trinity. The Jansenist Antoine Arnauld stood out; but among mathematicians careful inquiry had revealed only Gilles Personne de Roberval. Otherwise the giants of the previous generation were all dead: Denis Pétau, the great Jesuit chronologer; Jacques Sirmond, the scholar of ecclesiastical history, and another Jesuit; Marin Mersenne, the Minim friar, philosopher and savant; and Pierre Gassendi, widely regarded as the greatest general scholar of his age. Visiting Paris's numerous colleges he had seen nothing that Cambridge need envy. 'Even if the Sorbonne itself, together with the Collège de Navarre, was put together with the Jesuit Collège de Clermont the whole lot of them would scarcely equal Trinity College in greatness or magnificence, still less exceed it.'[357]

---

[356] John Hacket, *Scrinia Reserata* (London, 1693), 25.
[357] Barrow, 'Epistola' (1655), in *Theological Works*, ix. 118–19.

During their European journey of 1663–64 the former members of Trinity, Francis Willughby and John Ray, were impressed by the universities of Leiden, Heidelberg, and Padua.[358] But when Willughby concluded his grand tour in 1664 by circumnavigating Spain he was taken aback by the University of Valencia: 'None of them understood any thing of the new Philosophy, or had so much as heard of it. None of the new books to be found in any of their Booksellers shops.' In a word, Willughby concluded, 'the University of *Valence* is where our Universities were 100 years ago.'[359]

Fifty years later, the comparisons that occurred to Richard Bentley were now Dutch, reflecting the translation of studies away from northern Italy and war-torn Germany and towards the Netherlands that had taken place across the seventeenth century. Extolling the flourishing condition of Trinity at a moment when his governance of it was most in question, he vaunted that 'we were grown like an University within ourselves, having within our own walls better instruments, and lectures for Astronomy, Experimental Philosophy, Chymistry, &c., than Leyden, Utrecht, or any University could shew.'[360]

These self-interested observations are best taken as a reflection of the intellectual self-confidence that members of Trinity had about their college. The precise merits of the comparisons are less significant. But these comparisons also provide an opportunity to challenge received opinions about the nature of intellectual life in the College in this period. A conventional view of intellectual life at Trinity in the thirty years before Newton came up in 1661, expressed by his great biographer Westfall, has been that the college was untouched by the transformation in knowledge that occurred across Europe in the mid-seventeenth century.[361] More generally, seventeenth-century Cambridge stands accused of being buried in 'scholasticism'. It is clear from this account of the richly varied and consistently up-to-date philosophical, humanistic, and mathematical studies that were pursued at Cambridge's largest college in the seventeenth and earlier eighteenth centuries that these are disastrous misapprehensions.[362]

---

[358] John Ray, *Observations... Made in a Journey* (London, 1673), 11–18, 82–91, 208–13.

[359] Francis Willughby, 'A Relation of a Voyage', in Ray, *Observations*, 474.

[360] Richard Bentley to Thomas Bateman, 25 Dec. 1712, in *The Correspondence of Richard Bentley*, ed. J. Wordsworth, 2 vols (London, 1842), ii. 448–49. See also John Gascoigne, *Cambridge in the Age of the Enlightenment: Science, Religion and Politics from the Restoration to the French Revolution* (Cambridge, 1988), 154.

[361] Westfall, *Never at Rest*, 83: 'During those thirty years, the intellectual life of Europe had been turned inside out. As far as Cambridge was concerned, nothing had happened.' See also Hammond, 'Dryden and Trinity'.

[362] I thank Mordechai Feingold, Adam Green, Helen Kemp, Sachiko Kusukawa, William Poole, Jon Smith, Ian Stewart, and Chris Stray for valuable information and advice.

George Costard (1710–1782) on the Book of Job

Orientalism and Sacred History in Mid-Eighteenth-Century Oxford

Natasha Bailey*

I. INTRODUCTION

When historians have explored the relationship between oriental studies and theological scholarship in eighteenth-century England, attention has gravitated towards 'Hutchinsonianism', which refers to the efforts of the supposedly reactionary theologian John Hutchinson and his followers to prove that the unpointed Old Testament contained a latent Trinitarian philosophy.[1] The consequence has been to obscure how scholars of the period grappled with broader developments in oriental lexicography and biblical criticism.

The current article homes in on a now little-known scholar named George Costard (1710–82) who matriculated at Wadham College, Oxford, in 1726, obtained his MA in 1733, became a fellow of his college, and later served as a proctor of the University. As a churchman, astronomer, and biblical critic, Costard was reputed in his day to be 'a man of uncommon learning, and

---

* I am very grateful to Dmitri Levitin, William Poole, and Andrew Burnett for their detailed comments on a previous version of this article. I would also like to thank David Parrott, Lucy Wooding, and Robin Darwall-Smith for their feedback on the material.

[1] Derya Gürses, 'The Hutchinsonian Defence of an Old Testament Trinitarian Christianity: the Controversy Over Elahim, 1735–1773', *History of European Ideas*, 29 (2003), 393–409. See also Scott Mandelbrote, 'Biblical Scholarship at Oxford in the Mid-Eighteenth Century: Local Contexts for Robert Lowth's *De sacra poesi Hebraeorum*', in John Jarick (ed.) *Sacred Conjectures: The Context and Legacy of Robert Lowth and Jean Atruc* (New York and London, 2007), 1–25.

eminently skilled in Grecian and Oriental literature'.[2] Praise continued into the nineteenth century, when a commentator claimed that 'among the many great scholars and truly estimable men' who entered the Church of England few 'excelled the Rev. George Costard, either in extent of erudition, or excellence of heart' despite 'the highly abstruse nature' of his investigations.[3] This last observation may help to explain Costard's neglect among historians of eighteenth-century English intellectual culture. But, in the wake of recent, pioneering work on the relationship between theology and the arts in the *seventeenth*-century universities, it is time that Costard's role in the schematisation of knowledge and the development of an etymologically orientated mode of textual criticism be given due attention.

When discussed at all, Costard has been labelled an historian of astronomy, since his publications include important works such as *The Rise and Progress of Astronomy Among the Ancients* (1746, with a *Further Account* in 1748); *The Use of Astronomy in History and Chronology* (1764); and *The History of Astronomy, with its Application to Geography, History, and Chronology* (1767). Beyond composing these monographs, Costard contributed to the advancement of astronomical knowledge in mid-eighteenth-century Oxford in various ways: he collated the Bodleian manuscript of the Arab astronomer Ibn Younis for Joseph Ames, then Secretary of the Society of Antiquaries; published and added a preface to Edmond Halley's translation of the 'Spherics' of Menelaus; and penned a piece for the Royal Society's *Philosophical Transactions* that took a sober look at Chinese chronology and astronomy (a topic on which he also corresponded with the Oxford linguist Thomas Shaw).[4] Steeped in Oxonian scholarship, Costard went on (in 1760) to co-publish, with the Laudian Professor of Arabic Thomas Hunt, a second edition of the landmark *Historia religionis veterum Persarum* (1700) by the former Laudian Professor of Arabic and Regius Professor of Hebrew Thomas Hyde.[5]

---

[2] For Costard's biography, see Anita McConnell, 'Costard, George (bap. 1710, d. 1782), writer on ancient astronomy', *ODNB*. See also John Nichols, *Literary Anecdotes of the Eighteenth Century* (6 vols, London, 1812), ii. 428–32. Andrew Kippis, *The Lives of the Most Eminent Persons Who Have Flourished in Great Britain* (5 vols, 2nd edn, London, 1789), iv. 294.

[3] John Doddridge Humphreys, *The Correspondence and Diary of Philip Doddridge* (5 vols, London, 1829), iii. 235.

[4] For Costard's role in editing Halley's 'Sphæra Barbarica', see British Library MS. Birch 4440, fols. 91–6 and Edmond Halley, *Menelai Sphæricorum libri III., quos olim, collatis MSS. Hebræis et Arabicis, typis exprimendos curavit…E. Halleius. Præfationem addidit G. Costard* (Oxford, 1758). For Costard on Chinese astronomy, see 'A letter from the Rev. Mr. G. Costard, to the Rev. Thomas Shaw, D. D. F. R. S. and Principal of St. Edmund-Hall, concerning the Chinese Chronology and Astronomy', *Philosophical Transactions of the Royal Society*, 44/483 (London, 1746). See also Costard's letter to Thomas Shaw at Wellcome Library MS 5403/23 and a brief discussion in Geoffrey Cantor, *Quakers, Jews, and Science: Religious Responses to Modernity and the Sciences in Britain, 1650–1900* (Oxford, 2005), 122.

[5] Thomas Hyde, *Veterum Persarum et Parthorum et Medorum religionis historia*, ed. Thomas Hunt (Oxford, 1760). Costard was the author of the 'To the Reader' [Lectori Benevolo] and assisted Hunt. See *The Encyclopaedia Britannica: A Dictionary of Arts, Sciences and General*

Yet the extent of his learning and its implications for understanding mid-eighteenth-century historical scholarship and textual criticism only become fully apparent when viewed in light of his early commitment to debates over sacred poetry, which is the focus of this article.

The first part of what follows reconstructs the pedagogic context from which Costard's works emerged, particularly with regard to oriental languages. I then analyse his first major theological publication, *Some Observations Tending to Illustrate the Book of Job* (1747), tracing his inventive argument for why the Book of Job dated from around the time of the Babylonian captivity (597–38 BCE). His thesis, I show, had some similarities with the works of more ostensibly radical contemporaries including Jean Le Clerc in *Sentimens* (1685) and William Warburton in his hugely popular *Divine Legation of Moses* (1738–42).[6] But while Costard partially corroborated one of Warburton's most notorious theses by affirming his late dating of Job, he rejected Warburton's overarching allegorical interpretation of the text and attribution of it to Ezra the Scribe, and drew a rather different conclusion about its form. With Costard's less overtly polemical and more technical, stylistic analysis, he could remain within the bounds of a surprisingly expansive orthodoxy.[7]

Even if Costard's challenge to the standard dating and authorship of Job was less inflammatory than Warburton's, he made some striking departures from accepted practices when it came to methodology. Perhaps most notably, he was willing to emend biblical terms and phrases in light of oriental lexicography and etymology rather than manuscript evidence. Such an approach, I conclude, rendered his theological arguments less convincing to contemporaries than his astronomical, chronological, and mythological ones, and, by the mid-1750s, he ceased publishing on religious topics altogether, dedicating his energy to the history of astronomy instead.

II. OXFORD 'ORIENTALISM'

In a 1714 inaugural lecture upon taking up the Hebrew chair at the University of Franeker, Albert Schultens announced that Arabic was among the most fundamental propaedeutics to biblical studies, being 'the

---

Literature (25 vols, 9th edn, Philadelphia, 1894), xii. 443. An MS letter from James Merrick to Hunt from 1763 (at Bodleian Dep. c. 254/2, which is unfoliated) informs us that Hunt was actively engaged in editing Hyde's work: 'D^r. Sharpe will be likewise obliged to you for your kind notice of the correction recommended in Cap. 18. P. 214 of the *Relig. Vet. Persarum*'.

[6] John S. Watson, *The Life of William Warburton, Lord Bishop of Gloucester* (London, 1863), 78–9. See also Frank E. Manuel, 'The Eighteenth Century Confronts Job', in *History of Universities*, XXII/1 (Oxford, 2007), 164–5.

[7] Costard is referred to as an 'orthodox champion of sacred history' in Colin Kidd, *The World of Mr Casaubon: Britain's Wars of Mythography, 1700–1870* (Cambridge, 2016), 83.

most splendid daughter of Hebrew'.[8] His view was echoed in England when an anonymous author boasted in 1735 that Schultens 'assures us from *Arabian* Writers far more ancient than *Muhammed*' that Arabic and Hebrew 'were once very much alike'. For this reason, the author regarded Arabic as a key means by which to 'reconcile the *Hebrew* and *Greec* Texts' (or the Hebrew Old Testament and Septuagint).[9] In a 1738 inaugural lecture titled 'De antiquitate elegantia utilitate linguæ arabicæ', given at Oxford's *Schola Linguarum*, as well as in a 1743 address 'To the Students in Arabic, and the other Oriental Languages, in the University of Oxford', Hunt confirmed that consulting Arabic lexicographers, moralists, and historians was the surest way to illustrate '*the several books of the* Hebrew *scripture*'.[10] Going further than Schultens, he held that it was Arabic, rather than Hebrew, that resembled a '*vast* ocean' from which all other eastern 'dialects' were '*so many rivulets*', and he accordingly looked to Arabic to perfect the Hebrew tongue.

There was nothing new about recognising the theological potential of oriental versions of scripture, not least in England where such outlay bore fruits no less significant than Brian Walton's Polyglot Bible of 1652–7.[11] As was generally accepted by the late seventeenth century, future theology students should learn to read critically not just in Hebrew but also in 'those Tongues, which seem at first derived from it, as most of the *Orientals* are'.[12] The 'oriental' languages had indeed been taught for much of the seventeenth century, with chairs in Arabic being founded in Cambridge (1632) and Oxford (1636), and with various Hebrew lectureships existing even earlier.[13] Keen to preserve and extend these roles, Martin Eagle (or Ædler) – a tutor of oriental languages in Cambridge – urged John Covel, Master of Christ's College, in 1688 and again in 1708, to ensure that future divines received instruction not just in Arabic but also in

---

[8] Han F. Vermeulen, *Before Boas: The Genesis of Ethnography and Ethnology in the German Enlightenment* (Lincoln and London, 2015), 248.

[9] *A Discourse Concerning the Usefulness of the Oriental Translations of the Bible* (London, 1735), 6.

[10] Thomas Hunt, *A Dissertation on Proverbs VII, 22, 23* (Oxford, 1743), iii–iv. Also Thomas Hunt, *De antiquitate elegantia utilitate linguæ arabicæ* (Oxford, 1739). See finally Bodleian MS Rawl. Letters 96, fol. 228r (a letter from Hunt to Richard Rawlinson from 1748). We learn here that Hunt was desperate to get his hands on a 1639 copy of Thomas Greaves' 1737 Oxford oration, *De linguae Arabicae utilitate*, from a book sale in 1744. This also implies that he saw himself as following in distinctly local footsteps, and he gave his oration a strikingly similar title.

[11] See generally Jan Loop, Alastair Hamilton, and Charles Burnett (eds.) *The Teaching and Learning of Arabic in Early Modern Europe* (Leiden and Boston, 2017). See also *Discourse Concerning the Usefulness*, 6.

[12] Henry Dodwell, *Two Letters of Advice* (Dublin, 1672), 194–5.

[13] Mordechai Feingold, 'Oriental Studies', in Nicholas Tyacke (ed.), *The History of the University of Oxford: Volume IV, Seventeenth-Century Oxford* (Oxford, 1997), 458.

Persian, Chaldee, and Syriac.[14] The Cambridge orientalist Simon Ockley echoed this sentiment in *Introductio ad linguas orientales* (1706) – which was addressed to 'Juventuti Academicae' – when he encouraged young scholars to pick up the basics not just of the above languages but also Ethiopic, Coptic, Armenian, and Turkish, partly to help them carry out theological scholarship but also so that they could read and interpret secular texts in these languages.[15]

Largely because the eighteenth-century professors in oriental languages published less than their predecessors, there remains a supposition that eastern learning, along with the ideal of 'learning and enquiry for its own sake', fell out of fashion in enlightenment Oxford and Cambridge.[16] But, in reality, the spotlight merely shifted in the eighteenth century away from a general interest in eastern texts and towards a concern with their linguistic features and their potential to enable greater philological exactitude. Hunt, for one, not only elevated Arabic as an elegant, living language, but he also stressed that it had evolved to incorporate many transliterated Hebrew words. For this reason, he was confident that orientally proficient students would 'meet with very few words' in the (Hebrew) Bible that they could not understand, which he argued was even (or perhaps especially) the case in instances where scripture contained 'no parallel instances' of the same word.[17] Shortly after arriving at Oxford in 1726, Costard befriended Hunt, who undoubtedly instilled in the young scholar a sense of the urgent need to justify the theological payoff of marrying oriental scholarship with philological approaches to scripture.

How exactly students went about acquiring their linguistic skills is another matter. It is difficult to say for certain in Costard's case, though Hunt likely taught him. That is, while Costard was no longer a student during the 1740s when Hunt delivered 'the Arabick Lecture, as my Predecessors D^r. Pocock and D^r. Hyde did', Hunt taught regularly in his college (Hart Hall) from 1718 onwards when Costard *was* a student.[18] As he informed his friend, the book-collector and clergyman Richard Rawlinson, in November 1740, Hunt tended to begin his lectures by 'reading in Hebrew, (as w^t w^d be useful to many young students) and from thence proceed to Arabic'. Obviously a hit, one of Hunt's lecture series, which took place 'in our dining hall', 'every Tuesday and Thursday morning between ye Hours of 9 and 11', was attended by 'upwards of 50 scholars', and the anonymous author of an essay on Arabic learning at Oxford in *The*

---

[14] British Library Add MS 22911, fols. 203r–4v: Martin Eagle to John Covel, 18 May 1709.
[15] Simon Ockley, *Introductio ad linguas orientales* (Cambridge, 1706), A4r–A7r.
[16] The classic study is Gerald J. Toomer, *Eastern Wisdom and Learning: The Study of Arabic in Seventeenth-Century* (Oxford, 1996), esp. 84–115, 147–79, and 212–55.
[17] Hunt, *Dissertation on Proverbs*, v. For discussions of 'Hebraisms', see Hunt to Merrick, at Dep. c. 254/2, fol. 3r.
[18] MS Rawl. Letters 96, fol. 292v.

Student (1750) stated that Hunt 'is as willing as he is able to instruct us'.[19] Costard, in his turn, became a tutor at Wadham soon after graduating, and was almost certainly a driving force behind the rapid progress that Benjamin Kennicott made in grasping the eastern tongues. This is suggested in a 1775 letter that Costard sent to Hendrik Albert Schultens in which he refers to Kennicott as his 'worthy Friend & Pupil', and from Kennicott's acknowledgement of Costard at the outset of his 1747 *Two Dissertations* (a remarkable essay that he published during his BA).[20] Like Hunt, Costard was a popular tutor, though critics lamented that such 'a senseless *Idol* had so numerous an Assembly of zealous Devotees at his Sacrifices'.[21]

Students could also carry out a great deal of work in private thanks not only to the Polyglot Bibles but also the proliferation of lexicons, dictionaries, and critical commentaries.[22] The anonymous author of a *Discourse Concerning the Usefulness of the Oriental Translations* (1735), for example, managed to gain proficiency in the eastern tongues 'without the Direction of a Master' by consulting 'the Works of the learned *Bochart*, wherein one discovers such a Mastery in this Kind of Learning'.[23] In addition to the works of the great French linguist Samuel Bochart, the oriental lexicons of Edmund Castell and the Leiden scholar Jacob Golius were also hugely significant to eighteenth-century divinity pedagogy. In *A Specimen of a New Translation of the Book of Psalms* (1733), Costard frequently called upon all three to validate his translations of selected Psalms, especially when his renditions departed from the authorised (King James) Bible.[24] According

[19] MS Rawl. Letters 96, fol. 38r and '*Of the* Arabick Language', in *The Student* (Oxford, 1750), 46.

[20] Benjamin Kennicott, *Two Dissertations: The First on the Tree of Life in Paradise, with Some Observations on the Creation and Fall of Man; the Second on the Oblations of Cain and Abel* (Oxford, 1747), A2r. See also [Emma Kastelein, 'I shall find you I quite an Englishman? Hendrik Albert Schultens 1749–1793 and Learning English as a Second Language in the Eighteenth Century'], Research Master Thesis (University of Leiden, 2014), 56.

[21] Benjamin Holloway, *A Dissertation upon II Kings x.22, Translated from the Latin of Rabbi C-----d* (London, 1752), 4 and 12.

[22] Hunt was constantly enquiring after and buying oriental lexicons and dictionaries. Usefully, a Wadhamite, John Richardson, from the 1750s went on to produce *A Dictionary, Persian, Arabic, and English* (London, 1777–80) while Leonard Chappelow, Arabic Professor at Cambridge, produced *Six Assemblies; Formerly Published by the Celebrated Schultens in Arabic and Latin, with Large Notes and Observations* (Cambridge, 1767).

[23] *Usefulness of the Oriental Translations*, 6.

[24] See, for example, Costard's analysis of Psalm 104:18 ('The craggy Hills are a Refuge for Wild Goats, and the Rocks for the *Saphans*') in George Costard, *A Specimen of a New Translation of the Book of Psalms* (London, 1733), 16. He decided to reject the King James Bible's rendering of 'לשפנים' (saphans) as 'conies'. To justify his decision, he consulted Golius's *Lexicon Arabico-Latinum*, which interpreted the word as '*Animal quadrupes fele minus; pulveracei Coloris, cauda carens*' (a four-footed, dust-coloured animal, smaller than a cat and with no tail). He then compared this instance with Proverbs 30:26, where the same Hebrew word read in Arabic as 'قنفذ', which Golius and Castell had translated as '*Herinaceus Echinus*' (a variety of hedgehog). Costard was tempted by the Chaldee, which Golius rendered '*Speciem Columba*' and Johannes

to Costard, not only had knowledge of Hebrew become increasingly sophisticated since the publication of the King James Version in the early seventeenth century, but so too had knowledge of other oriental languages. He thus felt equipped, even as a graduate student, to help 'rescue those truly divine Poems, from that Disguise, in which they are at present involved' (that of the KJV).[25]

While most students were reliant on lexicons, they could also call upon a number of staple biblical texts as well as translations of and commentaries on them. As Costard's MA essay suggests, the Psalms were a popular choice for students across Europe not only because they were a frequent subject of paraphrases, sermons, and commentaries, but also because they could be easily approached with a basic grasp of the oriental languages and using a text-critical method. It was for these reasons that the Psalms also formed a core part of the illustrious Dutch linguist Sebald Rau's lectures during his tenure as Professor of Oriental Philology at Utrecht in 1750.[26] While Hunt agreed that the Proverbs could be explicated using Arabic adages, which were storehouses of eastern moral philosophy, he deemed Job even more suited to his method of critical study, writing that the 'language of the book of *JOB* has been allow'd to have a nearer affinity with the *Arabic*, than that of any other part of the *Old Testament*'.[27] Hunt was even poring over a 'little Arabic MS^r', which was 'ill written, both as to the Character and the spelling', but nonetheless 'introductory to the reading of Job's letters, of wch I have some'.[28] Hunt, perhaps more than any of his English contemporaries, made the ideal of critical-oriental study practicable, yet a much wider community of English students and divines shared his basic sentiment. As early as 1715, John Barecroft, for instance, exclaimed in his *Ars concionandi: or, an Instruction to Young Students in Divinity* that 'if we were as well acquainted with the Ancient *Eastern Poetry* and *Eloquence*, as with that of our own Time, what lively Strains of Beauty and Majesty should we find in the Book of *Job*, in the *Psalms*, and in many of

---

Buxtorf read as a turtle (dove?). But he ultimately opted for 'Saphans', preferring to use 'the Eastern Name, only altering the Termination'. See Jacob Golius, *Lexicon Arabico-Latinum contextum ex probatioribus orientis lexicographis* (Lyon, 1653), 1609–10.

[25] Costard, *A Specimen*, 9.

[26] British Library, Add MS 28298, fols. 171r–4v: Sebald Rau 'dictata in Psalmorum loca', dictated by Johann Christopher Brucher.

[27] See the preliminary address to Hunt, *Dissertation on Proverbs*, v. See also British Library MS Harley 2427; a student working through the Psalms, and a fragment of Proverbs 20:14–30:33, in 161 neat folio pages. The main text is in Hebrew with vowel points and accents, accompanied by a parallel Septuagint and a Latin version. The Psalms also have an English translation. There was, more generally, a strong print tradition of the adages in Europe dating back to Scaliger (unlike for other genres). See Noel Malcolm, *Aspects of Hobbes* (Oxford, 2002), 270.

[28] MS Rawl. Letters 96, fol. 160r.

the *Prophets*'.[29] With his attraction to Old Testament poetry (and specifically the Book of Job), Costard was very much of his day.

Another branch of oriental scholarship that was taking shape within Costard's immediate Oxford context was of a more antiquarian, and specifically numismatic, character. Inspired by scholars such as his Wadham college tutor, John Swinton, and Oxford's Lord Almoner Professor of Arabic John Gagnier, Costard realised that studying coins was crucial to understanding civilisations such as the ancient Samaritans and Chaldeans, where we otherwise 'have but little Light to guide us'.[30] In the 1750s, Costard was working with several oriental coins and a 'Mohammedan amulet' with an Arabic inscription that Gagnier had translated into Latin in 1724. This artefact also fascinated Hunt, who was convinced that the 'Mahometans' used it to defend themselves 'from evil spirits'.[31] Teaching ancient oriental history via coins must have been another of Hunt's offerings to BA students, since among the papers that belonged to another Oxford scholar, James Merrick – whom Hunt referred to in 1748 as 'amico meo' – there is 'an Explanation by M*r* Hunt' of a coin owned by 'D*r* Barton' (i.e. Philip Barton, Canon of Christ Church) from 'Jan. 8. 1738' (during Merrick's BA).[32] At the header, Merrick has crossed out 'given' and replaced it with 'drawn up', suggesting that Merrick's notes were based on a lecture or public discussion. The object in question was a brass 'medal or coin', which had apparently been stamped 'by Simon the High-Priest and Prince of the Maccabees on his restoring the Jewish nation to their antient state of Freedom & Independency'. Interestingly, Hunt's dating of the coin to the time of Simon Maccabeus (*d*. 135 BCE) deviated from the consensus that the script originated from the time of Ezra the Scribe (whom, as noted, Warburton argued was the real author of Job).[33] Hunt's belief that the coin had been deliberately stamped with the 'old Samarian character' to make it appear more ancient resounds, as we will see, with Costard's attempt to pinpoint deliberate anachronisms in the Book of Job so as to 'lower' its date. The main point for now, however, is simply that

---

[29] John Barecroft, *Ars concionandi: or, an Instruction to Young Students in Divinity* (4th edn, London, 1715), 10.

[30] George Costard, *Two Dissertations, I. Containing an Enquiry into the Meaning of the Word Kesitah, Mentioned in Job, chap.42. vers.11 [...] II. On the Signification of the Word Hermes* (Oxford, 1750), 2.

[31] See Costard's letters to Charles Godwyn from 1750 (Bodleian MS Godwyn 13), with the Garnier reference at fol. 13v. Gagnier was paid 'ten pound per annum' to read the Arabic lecture at Oxford instead of Dr Barton. For Gagnier's role, see Hunt to Rawlinson, MS Rawl. Letters 96, fol. 31r, and for Hunt on the amulets, fol. 61r.

[32] Bodleian MS Dep. c. 254/2: Merrick's notes on Barton's coin from 8 January 1738. For Hunt on Merrick, see Thomas Hunt, *De usu dialectorum orientalium: ac præcipue arabicæ, in hebraico codice interpretando, oratio habita Oxonii* (Oxford, 1748), 21.

[33] David Jennings, *An Introduction to the Knowledge of Medals* (London, 1764), 11–12.

Hunt, Costard, and their academic circles (including BA students such as Merrick) were engaging actively with oriental antiquities as part of their quest to understand ancient sacred history.

We can finally surmise that, in addition to Hunt, Costard's early education – as exhibited in *Some Observations* – bore the imprint of another, more famous Oxonian: Robert Lowth. Not only was Lowth a friend and mentee of Hunt, but he also held the prestigious title of Oxford's Professor of Poetry. Lowth's frequently cited lectures, *De sacra poesi hebraeorum*, began in 1741 and were attended by none other than Johann David Michaelis during a visit to Oxford that was the 'most delightful time of [his] life'.[34] In these lectures, Lowth broke ground in the study of biblical poetry with his emphasis on parallelisms between Hebrew and Greek verse structures, though it was sometimes said that his specialism lay in classical Latin and Greek, and that his dearth of expertise in oriental languages (and particularly Arabic) prevented him from providing deeper explanations of Hebrew passages.[35] Michaelis, by contrast, was a renowned Arabist, whose German translation transformed Lowth's lectures into 'a rich treasure of Oriental learning'.[36] It is very likely that Costard (like Michaelis) attended Lowth's lectures given his interest in Old Testament poetry; his friendship with Lowth's mentor, Hunt; and the fact that, as we will see, he read the Book of Job as 'an exulted and regular Piece of *Eastern* Poetry, and of the *Dramatick* Kind' (a claim with Lowthian overtones).[37] With this being said, some of Costard's conclusions about Job, particularly his dating of the book, departed considerably from Lowth's (and most other accounts).[38] Though Costard assimilated sources from far and wide, he remained an intrepid thinker, beholden to none.

III. SACRED DRAMA

As Costard was aware, the Book of Job had attracted the 'Attention of the curious' in the decades leading up to his publication. Along with being the subject of numerous printed books, Job was central to the 1714 philological lectures of Christian Benedict Michaelis, Professor of Philosophy at

---

[34] Avi Lifschitz, *Language and Enlightenment: The Berlin Debates of the Eighteenth Century* (Oxford, 2012), 101–5.

[35] See Kristine Haugen, 'Hebrew Poetry Transformed, or, Scholarship Invincible between Renaissance and Enlightenment', *Journal of the Warburg and Courtauld Institutes*, 75 (2012).

[36] Robert Lowth, *Lectures on the Sacred Poetry of the Hebrews*, trans. Calvin E. Stowe (Boston, 1829), x.

[37] George Costard, *Some Observations Tending to Illustrate the Book of Job* (Oxford, 1747), 25.

[38] Robert P. Gordon, *Hebrew Bible and Ancient Versions: Selected Essays of Robert P. Gordon* (Ashgate, 2006), 279.

Halle, and the famous botanist Carl Linnaeus even dedicated his first public lecture at the Swedish Academy of Sciences in 1739 to Job and the 'economy of nature'.[39] But, as Costard realised, much confusion remained about who the historical Job was and how his enigmatic verses should be interpreted. To cite Jerome's famous remark on the book, 'while one thing is said, it does another, as if you would hold tightly an eel or a little murena fish, when you press harder, then the sooner it escapes'.[40]

Particularly significant in the English context was the recent stir caused by Warburton, whose *Divine Legation* boldly described the Book of Job as an allegory of the suffering of the Jews. As one critic, Richard Grey, put it, for Warburton '*Job* is the *Jewish* People, and his Wife their Heathen Wives – that his three Friends are real Enemies and signify the Adversaries of the *Jews*'.[41] While this audacious reading was based on flimsy evidence (or, indeed, cooked up from evidential gaps), the Book of Job formed a core part of Warburton's overarching thesis, according to which the early Jews were ignorant of a future state of reward and punishment. Many divines had summoned the Book of Job to prove that the earliest Jews knew of an afterlife, so Warburton simply had to establish that the text was not in fact written by Moses, or at the time of the Mosaic dispensation, but much later, by none 'other than the great EZRA himself'.[42] He went on to date it to the period immediately after the Jews were restored to their homeland, since he argued that before Captivity the Jews supposed that God distributed his dispensations equally, during Captivity they thought that His dispensations were distributed indifferently, and only after Captivity was this topic hotly debated between Job and his friends.[43] Warburton's landmark work must have been discussed among Costard's Oxford circles, not only because it was sensationally popular but also because several of

---

[39] Michaelis's lectures titled 'Historia Jobi notis perpetuis et necessaria paraphrase illustrata' are in British Library Add MS 4352, fols. 229r–61v. For Linnaeus, see Lisbet Koerner, 'Daedalus Hyperboreus: Baltic Natural History and Minerology in the Enlightenment', in William Clark, Jan Golinski, and Simon Schaffer (eds.), *The Sciences in Enlightened Europe* (Chicago, 1999), 396. For some important works on Job, see Jonathan Sheehan, *Enlightenment Bible: Translation, Scholarship, Culture* (Princeton, 2005), 161 and Jonathan Lamb, *The Rhetoric of Suffering: Reading the Book of Job in the Eighteenth Century* (Oxford, 1995), esp. 110–27.

[40] [Kimberly Susan Hedlin, 'The Book of Job in Early Modern England'], Ph.D Thesis (University of California, 2018), 22–6.

[41] Richard Grey, *An Answer to Mr. Warburton's Remarks on Several Occasional Reflections* (London, 1744), 14. For Warburton's thesis, see *The Divine Legation of Moses Demonstrated* (5 vols, 3rd edn, London, 1742), ii. 509–11.

[42] Warburton, *Divine Legation*, ii. 543. An example of a response to Warburton that rejects his conclusion about the future state but accepts his allegorical reading is William Worthington, *An Essay on the Scheme and Conduct, Procedure and Extent of Man's Redemption* (London, 1743), 494.

[43] Warburton, *Divine Legation*, ii. 503.

Costard's friends were part of Warburton's extended network, including Hunt's and Gagnier's patron, Thomas Parker, 1st Earl of Macclesfield, and Philip Doddridge. One scholar has claimed – rather vaguely – that Costard was 'officially a Warburtonian but by bent a Lowthian'.[44] As we will see, even as he cited several of Warburton's claims, Costard was far from an advocate of the *Divine Legation*'s 'official' line, with *Some Observations* indeed being, in many ways, a *via media* between Warburton's view of the poem as a political allegory and Lowth's more orthodox reading of it as a piece of ancient sacred history. Costard aimed, in short, to bring both clarity and moderation to the debate.

In line with a broader interest during his day in the Bible's historical and literary value, Costard crowned Job 'one of the finest remains of Antiquity'.[45] Quite conventionally, he noted that it described an encounter between three friends who, with profoundly Miltonian overtones, met to debate 'a Question no less important than how – to vindicate the ways of God to Men'.[46] But Costard wanted to drill down a little harder on the nature and meaning of this famous meeting, and began by trying to settle where exactly the 'land of Uz' – Job's homeland – was located. To do so, he seized upon the reference to 'swift ships' in Job 9.26. In the King James Bible, a marginal note stated that this passage referred to 'Ships of Desire', but Costard deemed this 'hardly intelligible' and instead argued that, properly understood, the passage served as a key to Job's whereabouts, exposing his 'acquaint[ance] with Boats and Shipping'. To prove the inaccuracy of 'our English translation' that rendered the passage 'swift ships' ('אניות אבה'), Costard claimed that the Hebrew 'אבה' was much like the Arabic 'اب' or 'aba', which signified 'Arundo. Arundinetum. Papyretum [reed/papyrus]', an idea that he may well have pilfered from Schultens' Arabic-Latin *Liber Jobi* of 1737.[47] The passage in question, Costard confirmed, also had striking similarities to the language used to describe the vessels made from bulrushes in 1 Isaiah 18.2, and he happily noted that Theophrastus's *Historia plantarum* listed boat-building as a chief use of papyrus. Going further, he took the adjective 'swift' to imply that the ships were on a rapidly flowing river (probably the Tigris), which limited the possible locations for Job's place of origin 'to the North of *Babylon*, and in respect of

---

[44] Jonathan Lamb, 'The Job Controversy, Sterne, and the Question of Allegory', *Eighteenth-Century Studies*, 24/1 (1990), 8.
[45] Costard, *Some Observations*, 25. See generally Sheehan, *Enlightenment Bible*, 118–82.
[46] Costard, *Some Observations*, 25.
[47] Albert Schultens, *Liber Jobi cum nova versione ad hebraeum fontem et commentario perpetuo* (Lyon, 1737), 256 and Richard Grey, *Liber Jobi in versiculos metrice divisus, cum versione latina Alberti Shultens* (London, 1742), 64–5.

Judea to the *East*'.[48] Whether they cited Costard or not, later commentators (including the Hebraist Charles Peters) often mentioned Job's maritime upbringing as a key historical detail for determining his location.[49] For our purposes, however, it is most significant that Costard used the nuances of oriental philology to pave the way for a Warburtonian re-dating of the text.

To pin down Job's location more precisely, Costard turned to the descriptions of Job's friends, which also gave him occasion to display his competence in sacred geography, another classic handmaiden to theology. Following 'Dr Hyde', Costard treated Job's friend Eliphaz as a Temanite from the 'Country of *Edom*'. Costard also pointed readers to the student classic, *Geographicae Veteris Scriptores Graeci minores* (1698–1712), by the Oxford scholar John Hudson, which shored up Ptolemy's assertion that the capital of the land of Edom was the city of '*Bosra*'. But this would have placed Eliphaz, who apparently came to assist Job speedily, over 1,000 miles from him, which struck Costard as strange. Moreover, another of the three friends, Zophar, who is described as a 'Naamathite', was said to have come from near the Red Sea, or, more specifically, from Arabia Felix (now Yemen), neither of which would have placed him close enough to Mesopotamia for him to have quickly arrived for the meeting. Such discrepancies led Costard to conclude that the whole episode 'is a Poetical Invention' of an author who eschewed '*Geographical* Niceties'.[50] At this stage, he struggled to determine how much to invest in accurately placing Job using oriental philology (à la Hunt) and how much to assign to narratology (à la Lowth). Crudely put, he was split between historicist and literary modes of criticism.

By the time that he came to assess when Job lived and who he was, Costard had decided that the best approach was to use Lowthian, literary analysis, but to justify such a reading historically. One of Costard's chief arguments for Job being a late production was that it exuded '*Eastern* Figure and *Hyperbole*' while remaining a 'Regular' poem that largely adhered to the rules of the Horatian *ars poetica*. As Costard saw it, the orderly method that gave Job its poetic regularity must have arisen from 'Leisure, Education, and the Establishment of Schools and Academies', which only emerged centuries after Moses.[51] The reference to writing on lead in the poem was also a giveaway, since Costard was convinced that this practice only began when 'the politer Arts of Life, made writing more

---

[48] Costard, *Some Observations*, 7–9.
[49] Charles Peters, *A Critical Dissertation on the Book of Job* (2nd edn, London, 1757), 445.
[50] Costard, *Some Observations*, 12.
[51] Costard, *Some Observations*, 14–17 and 27.

frequent and necessary', and specifically when the Greeks began to contrive elaborate productions such as tragedies that forced them to go beyond the oral.[52] Drawing heavily on Warburton, Costard firmed up this stylistic reading by directing readers to moments in the text where anachronisms were carefully avoided in order to 'preserve the Characters of the Speakers', such as the fact that the word *Jehovah* is mostly left out because it was a name known only to the (later) House of Jacob, and *not* to Abraham's family. According to Costard, it is only at the 'Beginning and the Conclusion, where the Author had no foreign Character to maintain' that the word is 'constantly used'.[53] By reading the replies of Job's friends to his pleas as '*Three* Distinct Acts', with the first and last chapters forming two other acts, Costard could read Job as a five-act classical tragedy.

Moving into the terrain of pre-Greek astronomy and astrology – where Costard had distinct expertise – allowed him to substantiate Job's late date. In this regard, Costard was particularly concerned with the phrase '*hanging the Earth upon nothing*' at Job 27.6. According to him, this implied that the poem's author knew that the earth was a spherical globe, which could 'hardly have been before long voyages were undertaken by sea', 'many Ages after *Moses*'.[54] He also drew attention to the fact that more constellations are mentioned in Job, including 'Aish' and the 'Crooked Serpent', than in the writings of older prophets such as Isaiah and Amos (who were probably the first to mention constellations).[55] As Costard noted, such meticulous naming of constellations only became common with the Chaldeans at the height of the Babylonian Empire.

Costard finally cemented his case by pointing to a range of linguistic anachronisms, such as the fact that Job's author used the word 'Satan' to signify an evil principle, and, as Costard noted, this signification first appears in Chronicles 21.2, which was composed as late 'as the [Babylonian] *Captivity*'.[56] Likewise, the author of Job deployed the Hebrew word 'Ruach' to signify a separate existence (which 'the moderns' know as spirit), and the only similar instance of this is in Kings 22.21, whose author lived 'as late as the 37th Year of *Jehojachim's* Captivity'. These realisations prompted Costard to conclude tentatively that "Twas to living and conversing here [among the Chaldeans], or to keep up to the Characters of the

[52] Costard, *Some Observations*, 22.
[53] Costard, *Some Observations*, 29–30. This hypothesis was lifted from *The Divine Legation*, ii. 492–5.
[54] Costard, *Some Observations*, 28.
[55] Costard, *Some Observations*, 30–3. More generally, see George Costard, *A Letter to Martin Folkes, Esq; President of the Royal Society, Concerning the Rise and Progress of Astronomy Amongst the Antients* (London, 1746).
[56] For a recent instantiation of this kind of argument, see Avi Hurvitz, 'The Date of the Prose-Tale of Job Linguistically Reconsidered', *Harvard Theological Review*, 67 (1974).

Speakers perhaps, that we meet with a number of *Syriac* and *Chaldee* significations of words interspersed throughout this Poem, scarce, if at all, to be met with in the other Books of the old Testament'.[57] Applying his combined knowledge of literary history, astronomy, and oriental grammar, Costard became fully convinced that the only way to read the Book of Job literally was to read it literally. Costard's dating of the Book of Job evidently convinced some of his high-profile contemporaries, for the Cambridge scholar John Garnett, then Lady Margaret preacher, paraphrased his argument in a 1749 publication.[58]

In using historical and etymological details to justify a formalist reading of Job, one can assume that Costard had Richard Bentley's edition of John Milton's *Paradise Lost* at the back of his mind. But a more obvious inspiration still for this hermeneutic mode was the work of Theodore Beza, who argued that Job was so dramatic a poem and so abundantly filled with artful passages that it was closer to fiction and ought to be excluded from the Bible.[59] Lowth, in his turn, dedicated a whole lecture (number 34) to explicating Job's 'acts' based on the principles of Aristotle's *Poetics*. He claimed that 'Though the poem of Job do not contain a plot or fable, it possesses, nevertheless, some things in common with the perfect drama', being an 'anticipation as it were of a genuine tragedy'. This resonates strongly with Costard's view that although the Book of Job, or any '*Eastern* Productions', did not lay 'the foundation for Greek stage', it shared manifold features with classical tragedies.[60]

Having established that the Book of Job was penned soon after the Babylonian exile by a writer who furnished his account with antiquated language for dramatic effect, Costard could pivot to the most difficult question of all: whether the text prefigured the Resurrection. Here Costard's knowledge of oriental philology again proved indispensable. Unlike Warburton, he did not dwell on 'Whether the *Jews* had any Notion of a *State* after *Death*', dismissively observing that such an idea was commonplace in classical literature and was the foundation of 'the whole Story of *Ulyßes*'s visit to the Shades, in *Homer. Odyss.* 11th'. It would have been absurd if the Jews were the only people that God left in a state of total ignorance about the afterlife. Impressed by this assessment, Merrick commended 'Mr Costard on Job' in an undated draft 'Sermon on Easter' for convincingly repudiating the idea that only the Gospels brought the

---

[57] Costard, *Some Observations*, 29–30.
[58] See John Garnett, *A Dissertation on the Book of Job, Its Nature, Argument, Age and Author [...] to which are Added Four Sermons* (London, 1749), 280.
[59] Horace M. Kallen, *The Book of Job as a Greek Tragedy: Restored with an Introductory Essay* (New York, 1918), vii.
[60] Costard, *Some Observations*, 25 and Lowth, *Lectures on the Sacred Poetry*, 282.

doctrine of 'Life & Immortality' into the world.[61] When it came to the apparent prefiguration of Christ's resurrection in Job (19.25), however, Costard was less convinced. The verse read, in the King James Version, 'For I know that my redeemer liveth, and that he shall stand at the latter day upon the earth', yet Costard provocatively claimed that 'the words seem to intend any thing rather than a Resurrection' in the Christian sense.[62] It is notable here that, in the year before Costard published *Some Observations*, the unprolific Richard Brown, soon-to-be Lord Almoner's Professor of Arabic, summoned this very passage in one of the three sermons that he delivered at St. Mary's, Oxford, to bolster his view that '*Job* had the knowledge of a future state and resurrection'.[63] These rather derivative lectures may well have fuelled Costard's efforts to de-Christianise Job using historical criticism.

In a bid to de-Christianise Jewish history further, Costard proceeded to underscore that most heathens rejected the idea of Christ's *bodily* resurrection, drawing attention to Pliny's *Natural History*, for example, which recorded how, when the Athenians heard the Apostle Paul mentioning the event, ''tis said *they mocked*' him. Merrick, in his sermon draft, also remarked that the heathens 'mocked when they heard of it [the Resurrection]', since 'they could not confirm it by certain proofs'.[64] But Costard soon retreated into philological territory, spurred on by a conviction that the editors of the King James Bible had deliberately made the relevant Hebrew lines in Job more overtly prophetic. Specifically, he claimed that the translators had sneakily added 'day' to verse 25 (the redeemer 'shall stand at the latter day upon the earth') to give it a more millenarian character. He also pointed to their insertion of 'worms' at Job 19.26 ('And though after my skin worms destroy this body, yet in my flesh shall I see God'). By implying that Job had died and been buried, this translation increased the verse's prophetic quality.[65]

More generously, Costard proposed that 'worms' may have been added to verse 26 due to some confusion surrounding the Arabic, opening up a space for him to demonstrate that the passage in question had a 'very easy and natural Meaning, and perfectly consistent with the carrying on of the *Drama*'. He proceeded to submit to the 'Judgment of the Learned' some emendations as 'Conjectures, which every one may admit or reject as he thinks proper'.[66] Drawing as usual on Golius, Costard's reasoning went that the Hebrew 'נָקַף' or 'nakaph' ('*gravissimo ictu, hasta, fuste*'; 'with a very

---

[61] Bodleian MS Dep. c. 257.   [62] Costard, *Some Observations*, 33.
[63] Richard Brown, *Job's Expectations of a Resurrection Considered* (Oxford, 1747), 10.
[64] MS Dep. c. 257 and Costard, *Some Observations*, 33.
[65] Costard, *Some Observations*, 33.   [66] Costard, *Some Observations*, 34–6.

heavy blow; spear; club') was much like the Arabic 'nakîph' (*exesus à teredine*), and the nominative case of the noun 'teredine' signifies a worm that gnaws wood.[67] After comparing the Arabic with Ethiopic and Syriac versions of the text, Costard could confirm that the 'general Notion' of the Hebrew 'נָקְפ' was to 'wear away', and he thus proposed reading the passage as 'Nay after this Skin of mine is consumed away'. This made sense, he argued, in '*Job's Case*' because he was 'being undoubtedly wasted away with Sores and Grief'. It also buttressed Costard's larger claim that Job was not so much a prophetic as a moral tale of physical and spiritual restoration.[68] While this minor revision would not have shocked many critics, Costard's underlying desire to decrease the prophetic nature of the verse and accentuate the late, quasi-secular character of the text was more disconcerting.

Although Costard's approach to the Book of Job and its dating shared many features with Warburton's – based as it was on locating anachronisms in the text that implied a deliberate attempt to render it archaic – their methods also diverged strikingly. Specifically, whereas Costard mainly analysed the text's language and stylistic features, Warburton was preoccupied with grander themes that substantiated his hypothesis that it was an allegory of the suffering of the Jews. Warburton noted, for example, that the harsh behaviour of Job's comforters jarred with standard Jewish ideas about friendship, and the story must therefore not be about historical individuals but hostility towards the Jewish people in general.[69] In contrast to Warburton, one of Costard's main polemical aims was to demonstrate that Job was *not* allegorical, which was a position that he may well have derived from Schultens, who had made the same argument against Le Clerc.[70] Throughout his career, Costard expressed a general aversion to allegoresis, and ridiculed Philo and the Alexandrian Jews for their 'Allegorical and ridiculous commenting on the Law of *Moses*'.[71] While Warburton's and Costard's narratives were closely aligned, they were, on this basis, juxtaposed by commentators such as Peters, who wryly noted in *A Critical Dissertation on the Book of Job* (1757) that the story is 'neither

---

[67] Golius, *Lexicon Arabico-Latinum*, 2443.
[68] Costard, *Some Observations*, 36–9 and Garnett, *A Dissertation on the Book of Job*, 200.
[69] Lamb, 'The Job Controversy', 4.
[70] Lamb, 'The Job Controversy', 3. For a nineteenth-century summary of this controversy, see Albert Barnes, *Notes, Critical, Illustrative & Practical on the Book of Job, with a New Translation & an Introductory Dissertation* (New York, 1854). For an allegorical reading, see Worthington, *An Essay*, 494: 'Job is set forth as a sort of Representative of *Adam*, or rather of Mankind in general'.
[71] George Costard, *A Further Account of the Rise and Progress of Astronomy Amongst the Antients* (Oxford, 1748), 44.

Allegorical, nor properly Dramatic' but rather a 'plain and orderly relation of facts'.[72]

It should finally be noted that Costard's belief that Job contained many flights of fancy because the Jews were, to cite his MA publication on the Psalms, 'People of warm enthusiastick Heads' and thus more likely to write poetry 'in the Devotional Strain' resonates strongly with the judgment of Hunt, who imputed the origins of abstruse allegoresis not to the Greeks but to the '*the lively imaginations of these* Eastern *writers*'.[73] According to Hunt, the Jews, whom (as we have seen) he deemed to have been heavily influenced by eastern language and culture, were transported 'from one thing to another', and driven to 'overlook those rules of method and connexion, that are observed by *Europeans* of a cooler and more regular fancy'.[74] It was not a Warburton-inspired belief in the latent political message embedded in Job but rather a Hunt-inspired confidence in the rationality of the ancient Greeks over their enthusiastic predecessors and neighbours that led Costard to assume that the regular, structured, and astronomically-advanced Job must have been composed much later than was traditionally supposed.

IV. CONCLUSION

Costard quickly gained a reputation as a biblical critic with a brazen style, who, in the words of a detractor, displayed the 'infinite Stores of a critical Invention'.[75] While his works were positively reviewed as far afield as Germany – in the *Neue Zeitungen von gelehrten Sachen* of 1752 that the Leipzig-based rhetorician and historian Johann Gottlieb Krause had launched in 1715 – they also met with criticisms at the time and among later historians. Alexander Chalmers, for one, claimed in *The General Biographical Dictionary* (1813) that Costard dealt 'too much in conjectures' and possessed 'more erudition than judgement'.[76] As already noted, the mid-eighteenth century was a time when the attempt to alter translations and editions of scripture usually relied on finding or re-reading manuscripts. Even Hunt, in his *Dissertation on Proverbs VII* (1744), explained his own translation of 'stocks' [עכס or ékes] as to 'dance, skip or bound' in verses 22–3 not only by underscoring the remarkable agreement between the '*Chaldee, Syriac,* and *Arabic*' ('so many versions of great antiquity and

---

[72] Peters, *Critical Dissertation*, 94 and Lamb, 'The Job Controversy', 6.
[73] Hunt, *Dissertation on Proverbs*, vi.   [74] Hunt, *Dissertation on Proverbs*, vi.
[75] Benjamin Holloway, *Marginal Animadversions on Mr Costard's Two Late Dissertations* (London, 1750), 21.
[76] Alexander Chalmers, *The General Biographical Dictionary* (32 vols, London, 1812), x. 302.

authority') but also by citing manuscripts 'never yet printed'.[77] John Ward, Professor of Rhetoric at Gresham College, expressed a similar idea in a letter from December 1743 to Merrick when he remarked that even Bentley had not taken 'those liberties, which some persons have apprehended he would have done' in his copy of the Greek New Testament, making 'no alterations of the common reading but from the authority of manuscripts'.[78] In his *Annotations on the Psalms* (1768), Merrick, for his part, offers plenty of conjectures on, and occasionally corrects, the Hebrew text. But he noted that these interventions were just that – conjectures – and that they could only be properly judged as to their worthiness against Old Testament manuscripts. It is unclear exactly where Costard stood on this point. Although he put forth his readings as conjectures and therefore implied that there was nothing definitive about them, he did not show the kind of deference towards manuscripts that was becoming common among his contemporaries, relying rather on the much less substantive and respected evidence of etymologies.

Some of the criticisms of Costard also reflect broader intra-confessional disagreements in mid-century England.[79] Most significant in this regard was the response of Benjamin Holloway, who had been busy drawing up manuscript 'animadversions' on the *Divine Legation* earlier in the 1740s. Holloway was a renowned follower of Hutchinson, and sought to prove that the unpointed Hebrew of the Old Testament contained a latent Trinitarian philosophy.[80] Adopting Hutchinson's belief in the 'native Light and Perspicuity' of Hebrew, Holloway shunned Costard's attempt to read an ancient text such as the Book of Job 'by an *Arabic* Dictionary', which he saw as a wrongheaded replication of the approach of 'the learned and Pious *Pocock*'.[81] In mid-eighteenth-century Oxford, with the influence of Hutchinson lurking in the background, using Arabic sources to understand the Bible had become, whether one liked it or not, a non-neutral move.

---

[77] Hunt, *Dissertation on Proverbs*, 2–6 and 11.
[78] Add MS 6226, fol. 79r.
[79] Johann G. Krause, *Neue Zeitungen von gelehrten Sachen* (Leipzig, 1752), 497–9. In a letter from John Watson to Richard Richardson from April 29th 1757, Costard's dissertations are described as being 'very learned' (see Richard Richardson, *Extracts from the Literary and Scientific Correspondence of Richard Richardson*, ed. Dawson Turner (Yarmouth, 1835), 422). His work is also praised in Edward Ironside, *Miscellaneous Antiquities, in Continuation of the Bibliotheca Topographica* (London, 1797).
[80] D. Gürses, 'The Hutchinsonian Defence'. See also Mandelbrote, 'Biblical Scholarship at Oxford'.
[81] Julius Bate, *Michah v. 2. and Mat. ii. 6. Reconciled; with some Remarks on Dr. Hunt's Latin Oration at Oxford, 1748* (London, 1749), 5 and Mandelbrote, 'Biblical Scholarship at Oxford', 18–20.

As we have seen, however, Costard came to scholarly maturity in a world that valued oriental learning for far more than polemical purposes, and, addressing topics that forced the marriage of astronomy, archaeology, and linguistics, his output can be regarded as the culmination of scholarly traditions that had long flourished in Oxford. With approaches to Hebrew poetry such as Lowth's developing during his days as a young scholar and tutor, and with the mentorship of Hunt, who transformed Arabic and other eastern languages into profuse interpretative resources for biblical critics, Costard could proudly, and, I think, accurately, remark in 1750 that 'few places, if any, in Europe are so well adapted as the university of Oxford' for the studies in which he was engaged.[82]

[82] Costard, *Two Dissertations*, 47. It is fitting, on this score, that Costard maintained correspondences with some of Europe's most renowned orientalists including Michaelis and Schultens the Younger. For his letters to Schultens, see Kastelein, 'I shall find you', 56.

A History of the Concept of the University of Sussex

From Balliol-by-the-Sea to Plate Glass University

David M. Berry

A university cannot be said to have risen to the heights of its obligations until it has so designed its teaching as to ensure for all its students who use their opportunities to become, in words spoken by J. S. Mill more than eighty years ago, 'capable and cultivated human beings'.[1]

In this article I look at the early history of the founding of the University of Sussex in the 1960s and its links to a perceived moral crisis, particularly emerging after the second world war. This crisis is connected, in part, to the shock caused by the collapse of the once-respected German universities into the arms of the Nazi regime, and the consequent importance of a liberal and democratic university system to prevent it happening again.[2] It was also connected to worries within the British establishment that a massification of higher education in the UK could lead to a decline in the moral character of the graduates that were being turned out.[3] Partly this

---

[1] See University Grants Committee in W. G. Stone, 'University Commentary from Brighton', *Higher Education Quarterly* 12, no. 3 (1958): 226, doi:10.1111/j.1468-2273.1958.tb00951.x.

[2] David Phillips, 'Lindsay and the German Universities: An Oxford Contribution to the Post-War Reform Debate', *Oxford Review of Education* 6, no. 1 (1980): 91–105.

[3] Walter Moberly, *Crisis in the University* (London: Macmillan, 1949). The shift in position by the University Grants Committee towards the establishment of new universities in the post-war period, starting with the University College of North Staffordshire and the University of Sussex was influenced by the concerns around the effects of the Nazi regime upon the German universities. This is demonstrated in Moberly's writings, but also it is reflected in Alexander Dunlop Lindsay's experience of being asked to help with the rebuilding of the German universities in the post-war period and his subsequent discussions and

---

David M. Berry, *A History of the Concept of the University of Sussex: From Balliol-by-the-Sea to Plate Glass University* In: *History of Universities Volume XXXVII/1–2 2024*. Edited by: Robin Darwall-Smith and Mordechai Feingold, Oxford University Press. © Oxford University Press 2025.
DOI: 10.1093/oso/9780198946519.003.0007

was seen to be a result of the specialisation of students, and the move, particularly in Red Brick universities towards a more anonymous and lecture-based mode of study, together with concerns about the rising intensity of industrialism and its pressures towards a perceived one-dimensional individual.[4] I argue that these factors are crucial for contextualising the decision by the University Grants Committee in the approval of the creation of the University College of North Staffordshire (now Keele University) and how these eventually led to the approval for the University College of Sussex.[5] But the creation of Sussex (or Keele) was not a

justifications for new universities see Alexander Dunlop Lindsay, 'The Commission on German Universities', *Higher Education Quarterly* 4, no. 1 (1949): 83, doi:10.1111/j.1468-2273.1949.tb02026.x; Moberly, *Crisis in the University*; Phillips, 'Lindsay and the German Universities'; Drusilla Scott, *A.D. Lindsay, A Biography* (Blackwells, 1971). John Fulton was educated at Balliol as a pupil of Lindsay and was influenced by him in matters both philosophical and educational. An interesting outcome of this is that John Fulton retained an interest in what he called the social and political 'psychopathology' of the Nazi period and later supported the establishment of a Centre for Research in Collective Psychopathology at Sussex in the 1960s funded by David Astor, see David Astor, 'Limited Study of Political Psychopathology (David Astor Correspondence)' (1963), SxUOS1/1/1/17/3, University of Sussex Collection, University of Sussex Special Collections at The Keep. This was encouraged both by Fulton and Asa Briggs who had 'taken a keen interest in the project and shown much goodwill towards it,' see Norman Cohn, 'A Brief History of the Columbus Centre and Its Research Project' (1980), http://www7.bbk.ac.uk/thepursuitofthenazimind/Astor/KMBT35020110914164050.pdf. The centre was run by Norman Cohn and later renamed the Columbus Centre (1963-1980), see also David Astor, 'Diary of the Project' (1964), http://www7.bbk.ac.uk/thepursuitofthenazimind/Astor/KMBT35020110914164153.pdf; Cohn, 'A Brief History of the Columbus Centre and Its Research Project'.

[4] Adolf Lowe, *The Universities in Transformation* (London: The Sheldon Press, 1940).
[5] Cragoe claims that Sussex was formed within the context of the Cold War, describing it as a 'university *of* the Cold War' although not strictly a 'Cold War university', see Matthew Cragoe, 'Sussex: Cold War Campus', in *Utopian Universities: A Global History of the New Campuses of the 1960s*, ed. Miles Taylor and Jill Pellew, 1st edition (London ; New York: Bloomsbury Academic, 2020), 56. His argument that there was 'a distinctive alignment between the cultural framing of the new provision at Sussex and the map of Cold War geopolitics' is, however, unconvincing, see also Stefan Collini, 'Utopian Universities: A Global History of the New Campuses of the 1960s', *Reviews in History*, 2021, https://reviews.history.ac.uk/review/2434; Cragoe, 'Sussex: Cold War Campus', 64. Instead, I argue that Sussex's historical formation points to a greater influence of the experience of the founders of Sussex in working class education of the Workers' Educational Association (WEA) (particularly through John Fulton and his experiences leading to the founding of the University College of North Staffordshire in 1949), see Sir James Mountford, *Keele: An Historical Critique*, Illustrated edition (London, Boston: Routledge & Kegan Paul Books, 1972), 54., the second world war (Briggs worked at Bletchley Park, for example, see Asa Briggs, *Secret Days: Codebreaking in Bletchley Park: A Memoir of Hut Six and the Enigma Machine* (London: Frontline Books, 2011). and particularly the collapse of the German universities into the arms of the Nazi's, see W. B. Gallie, *A New University: A.D.Lindsay and the Keele Experiment*, First Edition (London: Chatto & Windus, 1960); Lindsay, 'The Commission on German Universities'; Alexander Dunlop Lindsay, 'The Function of the Universities', *Nature* 166, no. 4233 (December 1950): 1009–1010, doi:10.1038/1661009a0; Moberly, *Crisis in the University*; Phillips, 'Lindsay and the German Universities'; Scott, *A.D. Lindsay, A Biography*. The structure of Sussex's Schools of Study was very much

straightforward process, and there were a number of complicated and difficult hurdles to clear before approval could be given for creating a new university.

As Thomas Arnold wrote, 'no one ought to meddle with the universities, who does not know them well and love them well'.[6] And this is how Sir Walter Moberly's opened his important book of 1949, *The Crisis in Universities*.[7] In it he diagnosed a coming moral crisis for the university in the new industrial societies that emerged after World War II. He drew on others such as 'Bruce Truscot,' the pseudonym of Edgar Allison Peers, a professor at the University of Liverpool, the author of *Redbrick University* in 1943, who called for the return of universities to the advancement of knowledge through research. Approvingly citing the 1945 Harvard Report, *General Education in a Free Society* which argued that universities should contribute to a wider democratic culture in industrial societies. Lastly, he cited J. D. Bernal's 1939 *The Social Function of Science* which argued that the inevitable rise of applied science would lead to a 'Copernican change' in human affairs and human culture. Moberly, who was chairman of the University Grants Committee (UGC) from 1935–1949, drew these strands together in a book that was widely read in government and academia. Of course, his subject matter was as old as the university itself. He was not alone in diagnosing that under conditions of modernity societies were under increased pressure from industrial and political changes that were not being addressed by the universities. But coming from the outgoing Chair of the UGC it made an impression on politicians, academics and the wider reading public.

Moberly identified drift in the existing universities, a lack of any clear, agreed sense of direction and purpose amplified by World War II and

---

influenced by Moberly's dislike of departmentalism, shared by Lindsay and others, see Asa Briggs, 'Drawing a New Map of Learning', in *The Idea of a New University: An Experiment in Sussex*, ed. David Daiches (London: André Deutsch, 1964), 60–80; Collini, 'Utopian Universities: A Global History of the New Campuses of the 1960s'. This was reflected in the approach of Fulton and Briggs, see Briggs, 'Drawing a New Map of Learning'; John Fulton, 'The Shape of Universities', in *The Expanding University: A Report*, ed. W. R. Niblett (London: Faber, 1962), 46–63; Moberly, *Crisis in the University*; Mountford, *Keele*, 289–290.

[6] Thomas Arnold was the Head of Rugby School, a historian and a writer on Church matters. He was the father of the poet, Matthew Arnold. The full quote is 'no man ought to meddle with the Universities who does not know them well and love them well; they are great and noble places - and I am sure that no man in England has a deeper affection for Oxford than I have - or more appreciates its inimitable advantages. And therefore I wish it improved and reformed - though this is a *therefore* which men are exceedingly slow to understand', see Arthur Penrhyn Stanley, *The Life and Correspondence of Thomas Arnold*. Suppl. to the First Five Editions, 1847, 55.

[7] Moberly, *Crisis in the University*.

particularly 'accentuated by the moral collapse of the German universities under the Nazi regime'.[8] He writes,

> Of no universities had the intellectual prestige been higher; during the last century they had been a model to the world. Yet when the stress came, with certain honourable exceptions among individuals, [the German universities] showed little resistance, less indeed than the Churches. They failed to repel doctrines morally monstrous and intellectually despicable... they suffered themselves to become an instrument for manipulating public opinion in the hand of the powers that be.[9]

Moberly argued that because the universities confused appearance and reality, they had become agents of drift and suffered from a lack of values. He quoted Ortega y Gasset who wrote of the university that 'it is vicious to pretend to be what we are not, and to delude ourselves by growing habituated to a radically false idea of what we are... An institution which feigns to give and require what it cannot is false and demoralised'.[10] Moberly argued that 'the universities are not now discharging their former cultural task,'

> the creation, generation by generation in a continuous flow of a body of men and women who share a sense of civilised values, who feel responsible for developing them, who are united by their culture, and who by the simple pressure of their existence and outlook will form and be enlightened public opinion.[11]

He summarised the situation in four points. Firstly, the universities claim to educate 'rounded persons' with 'an understanding of themselves and their place in the cosmos' but in fact a large number of students are narrow specialists with extremely limited horizons. Secondly, the universities claim to develop a liberal and critical attitude to study, but in fact too often produce an attitude which is self-centred and utilitarian. Thirdly, the university aims to cultivate objectivity and impartiality, but increasingly defers to the unexamined assumptions and attitudes of the student, failing to develop their capacity for reason and judgement. Lastly, the university professes to be a community which has a transforming influence on its students and staff, awakening a sense of wonder through contact with inspiring persons. But increasingly there is little vital communication between departments or faculties, or between students and staff, offering only an a la carte menu of study options and little overall sense of unity or coherence in their degree.[12] It was within this context of a diagnosis of

[8] Moberly. [9] Moberly, 22, 23. [10] Moberly, 23.
[11] Moberly, 22. [12] Moberly, 24.

moral uncertainty, combined with a rising birth-rate and a realisation that the applied science of the growing colleges of technology would need to be balanced with a liberal and humanistic education that helped to create the conditions for the government to look favourably on new kinds of university.

Moberly's importance was not only as a former Chair of the UGC from 1935 to 1949, but was also a former Principal of University College of the South West of England (1925–26) and Vice Chancellor of the University of Manchester (1926–34). He was also influential on many of the key thinkers and planners for the new universities who were to emerge during the post-war period whether through his institutional role or through personal connections.[13] These connections were very important, for example, on the foundation of the University of North Staffordshire (later Keele University) by Alexander Dunlop Lindsay.[14] Indeed, W. G. Stone, one of the key architects of the University of Sussex, liberally quoted from Moberly's work in a 1956 Education committee memorandum for the County Borough of Brighton which concerned the foundation of the, then, University College of Sussex, citing, that 'a technocratic society is as repugnant to the tradition of England and indeed of Christendom as is a bureaucratic one'.[15]

---

[13] see Tom Steele and Richard Kenneth Taylor, 'Oldham's Moot (1938–1947), the Universities and the Adult Citizen', *History of Education* 39, no. 2 (March 2010): 183–197, doi:10.1080/00467600902865479.

[14] Alexander Dunlop Lindsay, known as Sandie Lindsay, was Professor of Moral Philosophy at the University of Glasgow, he joined Oxford in 1924 becoming Master of Balliol College and later Vice-Chancellor of the University of Oxford from 1935 to 1938. Lindsay was a key academic supporting the adult education movement and this inspired John Fulton's interest in this area, becoming chairman of the Universities' Council for Adult Education and the council of the National Institute of Adult Education (both 1952–5), see Asa Briggs, 'John Scott Fulton', in *Oxford Dictionary of National Biography*, ed. David Cannadine (Oxford: Oxford University Press, 2004), 1, doi:10.1093/ref:odnb/39987. After he retired in 1949 from Oxford, at 70 Lindsay became one of the founders and the first Principal of the University College of North Staffordshire, later granted a Royal Charter in 1962 to become Keele University. This creation of a new university was a crucial development. The 'difference between Keele and the later batch of new universities', Asa Briggs noted, were 'more than differences of historical period: they were differences of personnel. No later university had its Lindsay. It is a mistake to think that any new university starts with a *tabula ras*' see Asa Briggs, 'Asa Briggs Reviews "Innovation in Higher Education: New Universities in the United Kingdom"', *Focus: The News Magazine of the University of Sussex*, 1969, 8.

[15] Moberly, quoted in W. G. Stone, 'Memorandum to the Director of Education' (1956), SxMs59/7, University of Sussex Collection, University of Sussex Special Collections at The Keep. Moberly returned repeatedly to the theme of academic 'neutrality' when he further writes, 'such an abdication of responsibility [by assuming that universities expert knowledge would be wholly at the disposal of those who sit in the seats of authority] was the fatal error of the German universities during the Hitler regime, and the present revolt of many scientists against it is significant', see Walter Moberly, *The Universities and Cultural Leadership*, Walker Trust Lectures on Leadership, XI (Oxford University Press, 1951).

As can be seen, the idea of a university, at least within the British context, was under scrutiny amongst intellectuals.[16] The government cognisant of demographic growth, together with the funding council, the Universities Grants Committee, was supportive of a projected growth of 10% in student numbers to 135,000 by 1960. The UGC stated in 1957 that 'this expansion... could be achieved in the existing universities, plus one new one, the University College of Sussex'.[17] It is within this background that the Robbins report was commissioned. The Robbins committee met from 1961 to 1963 and was crucial in enabling the acceleration of Sussex's transformation from a university college into a fully-fledged university able to award its own degrees.[18] Robbins 'relied on the right of the individual qualified by ability and attainment to a university education' and 'he thought it impractical to measure the extent of the state's financial responsibility by the yardstick of the future need for different kinds of skilled services'.[19] The government was already communicating with the academic sector and offering hints of the likely direction of the university sector before 1960 and was open to fresh models as demonstrated by the Anderson Report.[20] This opened what I call the *Robbins parenthesis*, a rare moment in academic and governmental thinking that allowed for new ideas to be tried, but also, and importantly, funded by the state and driven by demand from suitably qualified students. Sussex University which by now had a Royal Charter and was teaching undergraduates was, therefore, ideally placed to take the fullest advantage of this shift in thinking in the British establishment.

The idea of a university that infused the Sussex university design was that it looked towards the future with 'maximum possible flexibility and freedom.' The university was, as Lord John Fulton, the first Vice-Chancellor of Sussex was to describe, created with 'a long period of gestation'.[21] In its early conceptualisations it was crucially understood as being a national university, rather than being based in new or old towns, in large industrial

[16] Stefan Collini, *Absent Minds: Intellectuals in Britain*, First Edition (Oxford ; New York: OUP Oxford, 2006), 462.
[17] Asa Briggs, 'A Founding Father Reflects', *Higher Education Quarterly* 45, no. 4 (1991): 313, doi:10.1111/j.1468-2273.1991.tb01575.x.
[18] The Robbins Report was published in 1963.
[19] R. J. Blin-Stoyle and Geoff Ivey, *The Sussex Opportunity: A New University and the Future* (Brighton: Harvester, 1986), 210; Report Robbins, 'Higher Education (Robbins Report)', 1963, https://education-uk.org/documents/robbins/robbins1963.html.
[20] Colin Anderson, 'Grants to Students (Anderson Report)', 1960, https://education-uk.org/documents/anderson1960/index.html; Ourania Filippakou and Ted Tapper, *Creating the Future? The 1960s New English Universities*, 1st ed. 2019 edition (New York, NY: Springer, 2019), 4.
[21] John Fulton, 'New Universities in Perspective', in *The Idea of a New University: An Experiment in Sussex*, ed. David Daiches (London: André Deutsch, 1964), 9.

centres, or small 'cathedral cities'. Sussex, from its beginning was intended to be a national university that would recruit students from the country as a whole. By locating the university on a 200-acre site 4 miles outside Brighton with a proposed 3000 student cap, it was a deliberate policy to encourage the members of the university to think 'upon problems for whose solution another perspective, another time-scale is needed'.[22] That is, that Sussex should aim to draw students 'for a few years aside from the distractions of the here-and-now'. For this, a sense of community between scholars and students was considered crucially important, with undergraduates in particular '[being] able to work with distinguished scholars to create the conditions for achieving high academic standards'.[23] Here we can hear the echoes of Fulton's early educational training in Platonic philosophy and Cartesian rationalism, the notion of 'clear and distinct' ideas, which he was taught at St Andrews and Balliol College. Fulton believed that education is 'making the future' and as such this raised the question as to whether the '"future" is to be a tailor-made society whose features are clearly imprinted and pre-determined by [people's] decisions in the past or laid down by present authority' or whether the 'teacher's responsibility for the future [is] discharged when [they] have done all that can be done to raise the powers of the individuals committed to [their] charge to their highest capacity, in the confidence that, if they have been so prepared, the future which they shape will be the best attainable'.[24] For a world envisaged as being of rapid technological change, early proponents of the University of Sussex thought that traditional educational practices were no longer appropriate and would need to be changed so that 'we are…saying our say about the future'.[25] As such, Sussex was to be 'born into a society' of institutions that 'accept as final the arbitration of human reason together with all the implications of that acceptance'.[26]

Early thought about Sussex university was therefore concerned with mobilising and arranging a set of values, ideas, and norms around which the new university community was to orient itself. These early debates took in a range of influences, from the traditional, such as John Henry

---

[22] Fulton, 15. According to Briggs, Fulton 'attached an almost mystical significance to the figure of 3000', and Briggs was 'unhappy both about the argument and its consequences for Sussex…[and he] wanted a university of more than 3000, a university with a broad span of interests', see Briggs, 'A Founding Father Reflects', 329. Sussex in 2021/22 had 19,835 students HESA, 'Where Do HE Students Study? | HESA', 2023, https://www.hesa.ac.uk/data-and-analysis/students/where-study#provider.
[23] Fulton, 'New Universities in Perspective', 16.
[24] Fulton, 17.   [25] Fulton, 17.
[26] Fulton, 18. As previously described, Fulton was greatly influenced by his progressive mentor Alexander Dunlop Lindsay at Oxford, who was a Labour party member as well as an academic.

Newman and, as mentioned above, more recent critics such as Bruce Truscot and Walter Moberly, who sought to diagnose problems with existing teaching at Oxbridge and Redbrick universities. However, the mobilisation of theories and ideas of the university were nonetheless particularised due to the very specific historical and material conditions under which Sussex was to emerge. Envisaged as a new university that would address certain shortcomings in the university sector, but without treading on the toes of the technical colleges with their emphasis on applied science and technology, Sussex was seen as an experimental institution and this was very much taken in mind by the people responsible for its early inception and development. Crucially, Sussex was not to be a civic university, in the Redbrick tradition, nor a collegiate university, such as Oxbridge, but a *new* university built ex nihilo on newly purchased land. This was agreed not only with the founders of the university but also with the government and the university grants committee.

In terms of the study and scholarship within the university this would have necessary implications for the 'duty of the university' to 'ensure that its studies involved exacting, disciplined work', that was 'in depth' and that 'flexibility of mind would be a necessary condition of a fully effective intellectual contribution by the graduates-to-be'.[27] The structure of these studies was influenced by Oxford's Greats, through the idea of a main discipline studied in depth alongside cognate, 'minor', 'contextual' studies 'which would naturally illuminate and be illuminated by the "major" subject and by one another'.[28] Early on, the question of 'how to teach?' was answered by a commitment to the tutorial system rather than the lecturing system. Lectures were seen as voluntary but that the 'university holds to be of prime importance... that a strong element of individual tutorial teaching (based on undergraduate written work) should be part of the experience of every student'.[29] For Fulton this would have three 'outstanding virtues',

> First, it makes the [student] active and forces [them] to measure [their] own identifiable work against that of a professional in the particular field of study. Second, it prescribes that such activity should be regular (week by week) and not spasmodic or belated. Third, it offer the possibility (not unerringly but largely with success) of a special and valuable relationship between teacher and [student].[30]

As J. P. Corbett, the Professor of Philosophy at Sussex, explained, 'our intention at Sussex is therefore to make the tutorial, rather than either the lecture or the [seminar] class, the main means of undergraduate instruction.

---

[27] Fulton, 18. [28] Fulton, 18. [29] Fulton, 19. [30] Fulton, 19.

This is a drastic departure from the practice of modern English universities, though not, of course, from that of Oxford and Cambridge; one can indeed say that what we are doing is to adapt the principle of a tutorial system, as developed at [Oxbridge], to the conditions of a modern university'.[31] For Sussex, this modern tutorial system consisted of 'an arrangement under which each undergraduate attend one or two sessions each week with a tutor in groups of not more than five members', so that 'the system therefore counters perhaps the greatest enemy of intellectual progress amongst undergraduates: the passive collection of unanalysed material'.[32] This tutorial system was aimed towards the first year in particular as 'the main effort should be devoted to students who are just beginning their course rather than to those who are concluding it' and has the added value of developing personal contact between teacher and student in such a way as to encourage them to ask for help or for the teacher to notice when a student is struggling. A secondary value was placed at Sussex on the commitment to academic democracy that the tutorial system engendered by sharing teaching across both junior and senior faculty allowing for a 'certain independence of the university hierarchy'.[33]

Sussex was to be able to give an 'education of taste' through 'the architecture of the new university; its landscaping; furnishing and decoration; the pictures on the walls, the musical life of the place)'.[34] It was for this reason that Basil Spence was appointed, who, it was thought, could translate these ideas into a new university estate. Although this would be a rather difficult relationship due to his disregard for financial constraints, indeed, Spence was also famously nicknamed 'Sir Basil-Expense' due to his cost over-runs and expensive designs.[35] Sussex aimed to 'ensure for its undergraduates the fullest development of their whole personalities on which their effective membership in the future of the free society depends'.[36] This was to be done by the careful selection of students to ensure that they form a 'richly diverse body, stimulating the whole university through differences of social origin, of educational background, and of vocational motive… and appropriate proportions of men and women, overseas students… and so on'.[37] Thus, an orderly tutorial framework for teaching would allow for 'maximum freedom for personal intellectual development' and which would allow for a 'humane and satisfactory

---

[31] J. P. Corbett, 'Opening the Mind', in *The Idea of a New University: An Experiment in Sussex*, ed. David Daiches (London: André Deutsch, 1964), 27.
[32] Corbett, 28.   [33] Corbett, 32.
[34] Fulton, 'New Universities in Perspective', 19.
[35] William Whyte, *Redbrick: A Social and Architectural History of Britain's Civic Universities*. (Oxford: Oxford University Press, 2016), 150.
[36] Fulton, 'New Universities in Perspective', 20.   [37] Fulton, 20.

examination system'. For Fulton this would enable students to contribute to a university society marked by 'its insights, liveliness and vitality' and able to 'emerge armed against the encroachments of uncritical uniformity which are the result of the modern mass media of communication and entertainment'.[38]

These ideas were bought together for the University of Sussex and formally organised with a series of documents titled 'Logistics of Development' from the 'building committee' which first met at Marlborough House on Old Steine in Brighton in December 1961.[39] The committee was chaired by Lord Shawcross in the early years, who was later to become the second Chancellor of the University, and were often lively affairs. But the actual conceptualisation of the idea of a university of Sussex, or rather as a university college as it actually started out, began some years before this.

Although the University's Royal Charter was granted on the 16 August 1961, it was first registered as a limited company under the name the 'University College of Sussex.' The application for a Royal Charter stemmed from proposals 'formulated in the winter of 1955 and approved by Brighton Town Council in March 1956'.[40] But in actuality the idea of a university college in Sussex had been first proposed as far back as in November 1911 at a mayoral banquet at the Royal Pavilion by Charles Edward-Clayton who in a vote of thanks 'took the opportunity to put in a powerful and eloquent plea for the founding of a university in Brighton'. The following week, the chairman of the Education Committee at Brighton council strongly supported a proposed motion and a month later on a cold and damp day on 12th December, 1911, the mayor of Brighton convened a public meeting.[41] The mayor argued that 'we want to bring the possibility of university education to [Sussex student's] doors; we want to put the coping stone on the excellent education already provided'.[42] Indeed, a Mr Hannah, the son of the Dean of Chichester, argued that he wanted 'to show the North that we are just as good as they are'.[43] The enthusiasm of the public meeting led to a resolution being passed that 'in the highest degree desirable that a college of university rank should be established for the county of Sussex with a view to such institution becoming recognized as a college of the University of London, or in combination with other

---

[38] Fulton, 20.   [39] Blin-Stoyle and Ivey, *The Sussex Opportunity*, 5.
[40] W.G. Stone, 'Steps Leading to the Foundation of the University', in *The Idea of a New University: An Experiment in Sussex*, ed. David Daiches (London: André Deutsch, 1964), 168.
[41] Stone, 'University Commentary from Brighton', 224; Stone, 'Steps Leading to the Foundation of the University', 169.
[42] Stone, 'Steps Leading to the Foundation of the University', 169.
[43] Stone, 169.

similar institutions on the south coast forming part of a separate university'.[44] The Bishop of Lewes proposed the formation of a committee of local leaders with an executive formed by Mr Hannah, Mr F. Bentham Stevens and the Education Officer for Brighton, Mr Hackforth (later replaced by Mr Thomas Eggar).

This committee acted quickly and agreed to develop a proposal for incorporation within the University of London and which would have required an extension of the 30-mile limit imposed on the University by its Charter. The executive committee had examined the establishment of '(i) an independent university, (ii) a university college, forming in conjunction with other institutions a university for the south coast and (iii) a university college associated with an existing university'.[45] The first option was dismissed as the money required was not forthcoming or available, the second option was rejected due to the communication issues thrown up by a network of south coast institutions, not to mention the lack of prestige it might have. Finally, the third option would have the option of taking support and guidance from an established university and this would also help with developing standards and educational policy. Oxford and Cambridge were dismissed as possible collaborators as they tended not to work very well with new institutions, and where they had they had tended to be ineffective, if not actively blocking new competitors. So London was the most compelling partner and as a Royal Commission had been formed which was considering removing the 30-mile restriction on its ability to form new colleges within its federal structure, it made sense for the committee to try to pursue that idea.

The proposed university college was planned to have departments of arts, science, engineering and mathematics and later law, medicine, commerce and agriculture. It would have a similar structure to other colleges, 'a supreme Court, consisting of representatives of the local education committees, of universities and of the college teachers, as well as donors and co-opted members; a Committee to be appointed by the Court; and an academic Council'.[46] To the relief of the Executive of the Committee, the Royal Commission recommended in April 1913 for the 'recognition of Schools of the University London should include the County of Sussex. The Committee began an appeal for funds but unfortunately a year later the first world war broke out and the country was plunged into a war.[47] Of the £8000 that had been promised (£772,093 in 2023 adjusted for inflation), only £2800 had been received (£270,232 in 2023) and after the Armistice the original plan was made too difficult by new conditions that

---

[44] Stone, 169.   [45] Stone, 171.   [46] Stone, 172.
[47] Stone, 'University Commentary from Brighton', 224.

had been established for new university colleges with the University Grants Committee 'recommending economy and concentration on "consolidating existing activities" '.[48] A consequence of which, the university planned for Sussex narrowly missed being brought into existence in 1914.

In 1925 a new attempt was made to try to take forward the university idea, building on a Sussex University College lectureship which had been formed from the previous monies within the existing Brighton Technical College.[49] However, the estimated £250,000 that was calculated to be necessary (£12 million in 2023) was difficult to find in the new climate and there were few contributions. Instead, the new money collected was again redirected to the Technical College in Brighton.[50] In 1934 the Board of Education created a scheme for the Brighton and Sussex Student's Library and Education Foundation using £4,950 (£290,268 in 2023) to form a library for local students and promoting lectures, the books of which were housed in the Technical College.[51] Attempts were meanwhile made in 1947 to change the Brighton Technical College into a university and following a meeting with the Chair of the University Grants Committee, Sir Walter Moberly, it was clear that the UGC was not interested in turning a successful technical college into a new university, even if it had by now begun teaching the University of London degrees, with over 400 students having passed the degree.[52] A Ministry of Education official informed the Technical College that it would not want to implement a change that might be detrimental for technical education and teacher training. In 1947–48 a new proposal was made in the *Brighton Draft Scheme of Further Education for a University College* to be built adjoining the rehoused Technical College, with halls of residence, common rooms and libraries, but the relationship between these two colleges were found to be unconvincing, and there was the added problem of a proposed regional technical college. Even later in the 1950s it was still not clear to funders and the government that more university colleges were needed, particularly as the purpose and nature of a university for the post-war world had still not been convincingly articulated. Indeed, in 1954 the Parliamentary and Scientific Committee noted that 'for the time being there is no need to envisage any further expansion of the university student population'.[53]

---

[48] Stone, 'Steps Leading to the Foundation of the University', 172.

[49] The Technical College was founded in 1897.

[50] The Technical College was later to merge with Brighton Art College to become Brighton Polytechnic in 1970 and later the University of Brighton in 1992.

[51] At the last meeting of the Trustees for the Brighton and Sussex Student's Library and Education Foundation the remaining funds and the books were transferred to the new University of Sussex.

[52] Stone, 'University Commentary from Brighton', 225.

[53] Stone, 'Steps Leading to the Foundation of the University', 177.

The local council got the message and replied to a query by Councillor Cohen in early 1954 that the idea of upgrading the Technical College to university status was unlikely as 'the winds were unfavourable and the barometer low'.[54]

But in December 1954, Lord Salisbury announced a surprising new government policy on these matters, he stated, 'there is room for advanced work in selected Technical Colleges...but for work complementary to that provided by the universities: advanced courses in close association with industry and in close relation to the less advanced work in the technical college system'.[55] New technical qualifications were planned, equivalent to degrees, with the aim of producing new colleges of technology that concentrated on professional studies. By 1955, Brighton Council was beginning to sense that the tide was turning and with a growing birth rate argued, 'for those who are convinced of the need for a University College of Sussex and who wish to see their dreams become a reality the position today...is more favourable than at any time since 1911...It may be that both employers and future employees can be persuaded that a university education has something far more valuable to offer than mere technical training for a career, and that the nation may become increasingly educated as well as instructed'.[56] Brighton and Sussex could certainly claim 'a long history of ambition and endeavour', and with the new focus on technical training at the Technical College which had withdrawn University of London degree courses, it was felt that a complementary research institution with good liberal arts education provision was made more necessary. Whilst the Technical College could provide the practical training needed for technically trained employees, the university college could focus on basic science, social sciences, and the humanities. Indeed, the South East was one of the few counties in the UK without a university and with the growing social and cultural developments in Brighton and Sussex it was ideally placed for such an institution.

Initially, the university college of Sussex was understood in the context of a 'small university'. Recent universities had small numbers of students, Exeter had 932, Southampton had 863, Hull 715, Leicester 650, North Staffordshire 495.[57] The small university concept was based on the idea that they would help to engender a sense of community, and with little funding available for large scale expansion of student numbers, proposals for the university college of Sussex settled on 800 students. At the time a college of 800 student would need income of approximately £200k

---

[54] Stone, 177.   [55] Stone, 177.   [56] Stone, 179.   [57] Stone, 180.

(just over £4 million in 2023).[58] The cost to build the college was estimated at £1 million (just over £12 million in 2023), with an expectation that the Treasury would fund 90% of the initial cost, the rest being met from the local authorities. Suggestions were made for an experimental college, such as established in North Staffordshire, particularly in relation to a student's right to be 'a capable and cultivated human being' rather than being oriented towards the 'prevailing vocationalism and its attendant specialism'.[59] However, the University College of North Staffordshire's style of organisation was expensive with a low staff-student ratio and a four-year degree with a general foundation in the first year, instead a more traditional organisation of teaching in relation to the University of London's degrees was considered more appropriate. By June 1956, Brighton Council had agreed to make available 145 acres at Stamner park on a 999 year lease at £1 per annum (about £20 a year in 2023).[60] Lord Hailsham made clear in a speech to the Royal Pavilion, 'there could be no continued advance in technology without reference to science which was a vocation of the universities'.[61] The University Grants Committee wrote to the proposers, 'while the committee [the UGC] would not wish to limit the ultimate development of the university college they would envisage it as covering initially a range of pure science and the humanities but not applied science'.[62]

On 20th February 1958 the Chancellor of the Exchequer announced a new programme of over £60 million for new university buildings in 1960-63 (£1.2 billion in 2023), of that £1.5 million had been allocated to the University College of Sussex (£29 million in 2023). A condition of the funding was that of a grant of a Royal Charter which would be assessed by an Academic Advisory Committee. Due to restrictions imposed by the *Education Act* of 1944 it was actually difficult to give approval to transfer money from the local councils to the University College until it was a legal entity, however due to 'benevolent sophistry' the Minister agreed that if the College Council, which by this point had been formalised, were incorporated into a company with the name University College of Sussex,

---

[58] By comparison the University of Sussex had an actual income of £346.2 million in 2021/22.
[59] Stone, 'Steps Leading to the Foundation of the University', 181.
[60] The '999 years and the rent is a peppercorn' was confirmed by the University of Sussex's Director of Finance in 2023, 'it started as £1, and is indexed, so this year is the princely sum of £361' to Brighton and Hove County Council, quoted from Allan Spencer, Email correspondence (13 October 2023). The extra acres to make up the 200-acre requirement were endowed with part of the Chichester estate which now comprises the Innovation Centre land and part of Falmer village.
[61] Stone, 'Steps Leading to the Foundation of the University', 182.
[62] Stone, 185.

he would consent to funding of the nascent university college. On 20th May 1959, a company of that name was registered with the Board of Trade, with its registered offices at Brighton Council.

The University Grants Committee was sympathetic to the idea of a new approach to university studies, part of which would be a move away from the traditional departmental organisation which was seen as rigid and which was thought to over emphasise excessive specialisation or syllabuses which were overloaded.[63] As a consequence, in Brighton an advisory committee was formed to look into the matter of the structure of teaching at the new university. This became known as the Academic Planning Committee and had a general agreement that the studies at the university college should be complementary to the Technical College, that they 'should range over the arts and social sciences (which should be read by half the students) and pure science, and that any engineering course should be of a more general nature than those at the Technical College'.[64] In September 1959 John Fulton, who was Principal of the University College, Swansea, was appointed as the first Principal of the new University College of Sussex.[65] Fulton had seemed likely to become the 'Master of Balliol College, Oxford… instead he choose the challenge of creating a modern university'.[66] But this remained the case only for a short while, as the idea of a self-standing university was now preferred by the UGC and the university college was granted full university status and so by the time the university opened in 1961 Fulton had become the first Vice Chancellor of the University of Sussex.

John Fulton was keen to take onboard the suggestions for how a university might function, and particularly the importance of a 'new type of curriculum as well as residence and tutorial-type teaching' where he was in broad agreement with a desire for Sussex to have the 'prime objectives… to offset the stress on vocationalism and to offer something more than

---

[63] Briggs, 'A Founding Father Reflects', 313. Interestingly, Asa Briggs was on this committee from 1959 to 1967. Briggs was also appointed in 1959 to the 'New Universities Committee' of the UGC, which recommended that 'new universities should be chartered', see Briggs, 312. This was before he was offered a Professorship at Sussex by Fulton in 1960, which he took up later in 1960.

[64] Stone, 'Steps Leading to the Foundation of the University', 188.

[65] The shortlist of candidates for the role of Principal of the University College of Sussex noted in Council Minutes from 6 Jan 1959 were: Mr J. S. Fulton – Principal of the University College, Swansea, Mr J. S. Morrison – Fellow and Tutor of Trinity College, Cambridge, and Mr J. A. Radcliffe – Reader in Physics, Cambridge, University, Fellow of Sidney Sussex College. The agreed salary was £3500 per annum (£67,660 in 2023) plus 'a house and usual expenses', see Ted Shields, 'COUNCIL I: Council Minutes' (1961), SxUOS1/1/2/31/2, University of Sussex Collection, University of Sussex Special Collections at The Keep.

[66] Fred Gray, ed., *Making the Future: A History of the University of Sussex* (Falmer: University of Sussex, 2011), 7.

training for specific qualifications'.[67] As Fulton explained at a conference on new universities in 1961,

> At Sussex we are going to move away from the single-subject honours course. In Arts, we propose to have no Departments. Professors and lecturers will be appointed in subjects but not to departments. After a common first part (taken at the end of one year) the student in Arts will work in one of several Schools. Of these there will be three and soon afterwards, we hope, four. First, a School of European Studies. The student will do a modern language and literature, and do it thoroughly... Secondly, there will be a School of English Studies, similar in structure to the first. Thirdly, a School of Social Studies, a modified P.P.E... In science we shall have a three-year honours course in which three subjects out of four must be taken: i.e., three out of Mathematics, Biology, Chemistry and Physics.[68]

He further explained,

> We would like to see what can be done about teaching methods. It is possible that, with this system of schools, we could have a fairly exiguous lecture system, so that we would not offer students lectures on every aspect of their departmental courses. Perhaps we might offer them broad lecture courses, and then by seminars and tutorials give them the slant they want in their particular field.[69]

Fulton was born in Dundee in 1902, the son of Angus Robertson Fulton, Professor of Professor of Engineering and Drawing and 1939-46 the interim Principal of University College, Dundee. He had attended St Andrews in 1919, as an undergraduate, and due to small classes, as an Honours student he would have experienced something of the 'democratic intellect' which in Scotland universities tended to aim for a general education over a specialised one, and certainly not a classics-oriented Oxford style structure.[70] John Burnet, who taught Fulton, described the system at St Andrews in 1917, stating, 'it is extremely desirable that the students of the Humanities should know something of Science, and that the students

---

[67] Norman Mackenzie, 'Starting a New University', *Higher Education Quarterly* 15, no. 2 (1961): 151, doi:10.1111/j.1468-2273.1961.tb00170.x.
[68] Mackenzie, 150. [69] Mackenzie, 150.
[70] George Elder Davie, *The Democratic Intellect: Scotland and Her Universities in the Nineteenth Century*, Third edition / edited by Murdo Macdonald., Edinburgh Classic Editions (Edinburgh: University Press, 1961), 10. As Fulton notes, 'the Scottish university tradition owes a great deal to the medieval German university. It was no part of that tradition to teach the undergraduate by the tutorial methods which have become associated with Oxford and Cambridge. But when I was at St. Andrews at the end of the first war (I went up when I had just become 17) the numbers in the Honours classes were very small, and there was contact with the professor beyond what would normally have been expected in the Scottish universities at any rate at that time', see Fulton, 'The Shape of Universities', 50.

of Science should know something of the Humanities'.[71] In 1924 Fulton moved to Oxford, reading Greats, and it was at Balliol he experienced in full the Oxford tutorial system taught by distinguished scholars who devoted themselves to their subjects and teaching. After finishing his degree, he worked for 'two years as a lecturer at the London School of Economics (1926–8), [and] he returned to Balliol in 1928 as a fellow and tutor in philosophy. In 1935, when "modern Greats" (philosophy, politics, and economics) had established itself, particularly in Balliol, the "philosophy" in his title was changed to "politics" '.[72] He left Balliol in 1947 and was appointed Principal of the University College, Swansea, where between 1947–59 he tried to adapt the university to be less homogenous, recruiting from a wider geographical spread to create more social diversity. His reforms, 'not to universal acclaim,' introduced a 'liberal approach to higher education...and remoulded the curriculum as a result' and he 'also put in place plans to revolutionise campus life at the College'.[73] Whilst at Swansea he served 'two spells, in 1952–4 and 1958–9, as vice-chancellor of the University of Wales' and 'encouraged university expansion and furthered his interest in adult education, which had been stimulated in the past by his mentoring by Lindsay'.[74]

Fulton used the metaphor of shape, or sometimes pattern, when thinking about the new university.[75] Although Fulton does not tend to refer to abstract geometric forms, such as the circle, triangle, rectangle, he did tend to talk in a Platonic key when outlining the 'shape' of Sussex.[76] For example, Fulton argued for the merits of an abstract notion of the Oxford tutorial system as a basis for Sussex's approach to innovative teaching methods, which became the 2–5 person Sussex tutorial. He argued, this 'made the [student] active, instead of passive: [they are] forced to show [their] hand. It made [them] regular in his habits, because [their] work could not be postponed to the end of term or of the year'.[77] This was because there was an 'attempt to stop the flood of numbers turning

---

[71] John Burnet, *Higher Education and the War* (London, MacMillan, 1917), 227, http://archive.org/details/highereducationw00burnuoft. Fulton was taught at St Andrews under Prof. John Burnet (Classics), Prof. Wallace Martin Lindsay (Classics), Prof. George F. Stout (Philosophy and Psychology), and Prof. Alfred Edward Taylor (Moral Philosophy).

[72] Briggs, 'John Scott Fulton'.

[73] Briggs. See also, Swansea University, 'John S Fulton - Swansea University', John S Fulton, 2023, https://www.swansea.ac.uk/centenary2020/century-of-inspiring-people/js-fulton/

[74] Briggs.   [75] Fulton, 'The Shape of Universities'.

[76] Fulton, 46. Bradbury observed that 'Vice Chancellors, all share in common a Platonic ideal for a university. For one thing it should be big...There should be big sports grounds, a science building designed by Basil Spence, and more and more students coming every year', see Malcolm Bradbury, *Eating People Is Wrong* (London: Secker & Warburg, 1976), 170.

[77] Mackenzie, 'Starting a New University', 150.

university teaching into a conveyor-belt system on the American model, where undergraduate teaching is now in a desperate crisis'.[78] Fulton, 'referred both to Scotland and to Classical Greats and Modern Greats at Oxford' when discussing the need to bridge general and specialised education, with Briggs noting the importance of Davie's work *The Democratic Intellect* which argued that 'speciality need not be inconsistent with unity of learning'.[79] These early ideas are shown in an early 1960 publication titled, *The University College of Sussex: An Appeal*, which argued,

> A new University has two obligations: on the one hand it must have due respect for the long traditions of its sister universities and seek to emulate their high academic standards; on the other, it has a duty, as a newcomer, to try and illuminate some of the difficult contemporary problems of higher education... Among other problems, what is described as 'over-specialisation' has of late come under considerable criticism. If over-specialisation exists in the educational system, the remedy is not to be found in discarding all the virtues and advantages of a healthy measure of specialisation; but, rather, in retaining the discipline which comes from specialisation while, at the same time, broadening the base of specialised studies in such a way as to enlarge the mind of the student.[80]

One of the key decisions by John Fulton was to offer in 1960 the Dean of Social Studies and Professor of History to Asa Briggs, and later in 1964 Pro-Vice Chancellor (Planning).[81] Briggs, accepted the post literally as he set sail to Australia to give a lecture titled *The Map of Learning* to the Research Students' Association of The Australian National University.[82] Briggs shared many of Fulton's aspirations to excellence at the University of Sussex, writing that 'universities are only universities if they provide access to the best'.[83] However, Briggs's notion of a 'new map of learning' was more empirical, more historical and more bottom-up in its conceptualisation. For Briggs, as for Fulton, teaching and research were to be of the highest quality in the new university, as Briggs wrote prior to taking up his appointment,

---

[78] Mackenzie, 150.   [79] Briggs, 'Drawing a New Map of Learning', 68.
[80] University College of Sussex, 'The University College of Sussex: An Appeal' (1960), SxUOS1/1/1/15/4, University of Sussex Collection, University of Sussex Special Collections at The Keep.
[81] Asa Briggs was elected the second Vice Chancellor of the University on 29 May 1966 taking up the post in the 1967 academic year.
[82] Asa Briggs, *The Map of Learning*., Research Students' Association. 1st Annual Lecture, 1960 (Canberra: Australian National University, 1961), https://catalog.hathitrust.org/Record/001735715.
[83] Briggs, 22.

teaching and research are not substitutes for each other in a university but two aspects of the advancement of learning. The pursuit of knowledge and its communication to others are of equal importance in any institution meriting the name of university.[84]

Briggs mobilised a rather unusual set of sources for his idea of a new map of learning. He drew on geographical metaphors, influenced by Francis Bacon, the 17th century empiricist, the idea of personal knowledge drawn from Michael Polanyi, the renowned physicist and social scientist, the notion of two cultures from C. P. Snow, and the importance of bringing together the general and the particular from F. M. Powicke, the medieval historian, amongst others.[85] He argued that universities had to 'cross the Snow line,' so that 'a more general degree with the same prestige as single honours but with connections to related areas of knowledge and the world of thought beyond, not as a substitute for specialization but as a preliminary to it'.[86] Briggs was also highly critical of what he called 'departmentalism' and argued strongly for a new 'school pattern for the university' which would avoid the insularity of the disciplinary system.[87] Briggs noted that Francis Bacon, 'was writing in the light of the far-reaching changes in the organisation of the "map of learning" in the fifteenth and sixteenth centuries, changes to which historians have attached the phrase "the new learning"'.[88] Briggs explained that universities often contained,

> students and teachers in science and the humanities, literature and social sciences all too often figure as inhabitants of separate continents. A few boats pass between them, fewer still on regular service; there are a number of distinguished travellers and a diminishing number of visitors... their ideas of what happens in more distant regions are usually imprecise, frequently prejudiced, and often wrong. Occasionally joint ventures of discovery are made by outstanding explorers within the universities who care little, if at all, for local allegiances.[89]

Sussex at its foundation was given four major schools of study, the School of Social Studies, the School of European Studies, the School of English and American Studies, and the School of Physical Sciences followed by the School of African and Asian Studies in October 1964.[90] For this new university to function Briggs was concerned that academics were well-paid

---

[84] Briggs, 30.
[85] Briggs, *The Map of Learning*.; Briggs, 'A Founding Father Reflects', 319.
[86] Harold Perkin, 'Dream, Myth and Reality: New Universities in England, 1960–1990', *Higher Education Quarterly* 45, no. 4 (1991): 298, doi:10.1111/j.1468-2273.1991.tb01574.x.
[87] Briggs, 'A Founding Father Reflects', 321.
[88] Briggs, *The Map of Learning.*, 7.
[89] Briggs, 'Drawing a New Map of Learning', 73.
[90] Blin-Stoyle and Ivey, *The Sussex Opportunity*, 9. Queen Elizabeth the Second opened the library on 13 November 1964. Additionally the Centre for Multi-Racial Studies (CMRS) was also established at Sussex in 1964 led by Professor Fernando Henriques.

in order to be able to focus properly on their university research and teaching. Bacon, Briggs noted, had argued that 'university teachers deserved more pay and the cost of university equipment needed to be more generously subsidised by the government' quoting Bacon that 'as secretaries and spials of princes and states bring in bills for intelligence, so you must allow the spials and intelligencers of nature to bring in their bills; or else you shall be ill advertised'.[91] For Sussex to attract the very best faculty and to be at the cutting edge of research, Briggs argued that it was critical that it treat its academic staff with the respect it deserved, both in terms of inclusion in decision-making in shaping the university, but also in terms of directing their research out into the world. He was keen to avoid the mistakes of the Redbrick universities which with their hierarchical departmental structures tended to develop control mechanisms that disincentivised initiative both by individuals and their departments.[92]

Drawing on Polanyi, Briggs wrote, 'there was the recognition that a university education involves not merely the acceptance of information or ideas, but a personal quest which, if entered upon with zest, continues far beyond the three years of undergraduate study'.[93] He continued, 'being explorers ourselves in a new university, explorers with ample maps of other universities but with none of our own, we wanted to make the students into explorers also'.[94] As Briggs explains, 'sometimes indeed the decision to create a new university is taken before adequate thought has been devoted to essential facts, let alone values'.[95] For Briggs, to redraw the new maps of learning required that the explorers are able to break with convention and be innovative.

It was on 16 August 1961, Fulton announced the Royal Charter of Incorporation of the University of Sussex in *The Times*, in an article titled

---

[91] Briggs, *The Map of Learning.*, 8.
[92] see Michael Shattock, *Managing Successful Universities* (Berkshire: Society for Research into Higher Education : Open University Press, 2003), 19, http://site.ebrary.com/id/10175236. It is interesting to note that at Senate on 10 October 1961, Sussex debated whether faculty members should wear gowns when lecturing (it was agreed that they should) and that the word 'students' should not be used, but rather that 'the terms "undergraduates" and "graduate students" are substituted' as 'students' was seen as a term for extramural education. At Senate 11 December 1962, it was also confirmed that the practice that students have to wear gowns for examinations would continue, see Ted Shields, 'Senate Minutes' (1962), SxUOS1/1/2/27/3, University of Sussex Collection, University of Sussex Special Collections at The Keep. Truscott, the pseudonym of Edgar Allison Peers, Professor in Hispanic Studies at the University of Liverpool, was critical that Sussex and Keele debated these type of relatively trivial decisions whilst having 'constitutions...which leave everyone guessing whether a university teacher is a member of a society or an employee in a hierarchy?', see Bruce Truscot, 'Academic Screwtape', *Nature* 194, no. 4829 (May 1962): 616–617, doi:10.1038/194616a0.
[93] Briggs, 'Drawing a New Map of Learning', 66.
[94] Briggs, 66.   [95] Briggs, *The Map of Learning.*, 11.

'Balliol by the Sea Faces its Future'.[96] Sussex, he wrote, opened in October 1961 to 52 students in the Arts (both female and male), and was based in two Victorian houses on Preston Road, Brighton, with lectures in a nearby church hall.[97] Fulton outlined how the Sussex undergraduate multi-subject degree was to be modelled on Philosophy, Politics and Economics, or Modern Greats, at Oxford and in the sciences through the combining of fields, such as Chemistry and Engineering as Chemical Engineering, or Physics and Biology as Biophysics. As a consequence of this Sussex was to have no departments, instead there were to be Schools, which by bringing together multiple knowledges would meet Asa Briggs's notion of 're-drawing the map of learning'.[98] Fulton therefore argued,

> For students to be asked to integrate their subjects is a challenge to a difficult task: for this among other reasons the university is committed to a tutorial system in which the undergraduate learns by writing; and by submitting the fruits of [their] writing to the rigorous, though friendly, criticism of [their] teachers.[99]

Briggs writing in *The New Statesman* developed this line of thought, explaining,

> basic study throughout the three years will be through the tutorial. Lectures will be ancillary and voluntary, but given a considered place within the system. The first two terms, which fix the 'image' of the university in the mind of the undergraduate (often, and to a still increasing extent, an undergraduate with no family experience and little previous knowledge of universities), will firmly establish the central significance of the tutorial system (guided individual reading, one essay a week and regular encounters with a tutor). During the second and particularly the third year, tutorials and lectures will be augmented by seminars, some of which by present criteria would be interdisciplinary.[100]

With these safeguards for excellence in teaching and learning given by the tutorial system, Briggs argued that 'it is just as important to decide what not to teach as what to teach'.[101] He stated that at Sussex 'here is a kind of

---

[96] John Fulton, 'Balliol By The Sea Faces Its Future', *The Times*, 1961, The Times Digital Archive. Briggs argued that Sussex 'was sometimes called, though it never was, 'Balliol by the sea', proved highly attractive to applicants' and that it 'came to symbolize the spirit of the 1960s'. Fulton, Briggs also noted, 'inspired the institution rather than managed it, winning friendship as well as loyalty', see Briggs, 'John Scott Fulton'. Briggs, of course, had been appointed by Fulton as Pro-Vice Chancellor (Planning) at the university.

[97] Gray, *Making the Future*, 9.   [98] Fulton, 'Balliol By The Sea Faces Its Future'.
[99] Fulton, 9.
[100] Asa Briggs, 'Maps of Learning', *New Statesman*, January 1961, 338, Periodicals Archive Online.
[101] Briggs, 340.

university education which does not depend on premature specialisation, but on curiosity, interest and the desire to probe and to relate'.[102] For Fulton, Sussex teaching was to be similar to 'Modern Greats at Oxford... a multi-subject Honours course in which three aspects of civilization—philosophy, politics and economics—are studied together. Here the unity is to be found in their inter-relation and their influence upon one another'.[103] From this Fulton believed that the university would give 'the gift of a new perspective' by encouraging the student to acquire the habit of mind to 'learn to think independently and resourcefully' catching 'something of the spirit' of 'quite another world from the daily practical one' to 'encourage them to free themselves from the partial, the prejudiced, the uncritical view'.[104] Indeed, Daiches described Sussex as having a 'curiously illogical combination of establishment image and reputation for being new and rebellious'.[105] Fittingly, the university motto chosen by John Fulton in 1961, from Psalm 46, verse 10, was 'be still and know'.[106] Fulton noted that it 'seemed to sum up his view of undergraduate life, i.e. a three year period away from the distractions of normal life; he felt it particularly apt for education on the new green campus at Falmer' and also 'its relation to Cartesian logic of doubt, etc.'.[107] Fulton made an explicit link to Descartes method, where a sceptical approach to the search for truth has to take place out of this world, to use scepticism to help in acquiring knowledge. As Williams explains,

[102] Briggs, 340. As was noted even as late of 1991, 'Sussex made the two-student tutorial the basis of teaching and has stuck to it in the more Socratic schools', although sadly this is no longer the case today, see Perkin, 'Dream, Myth and Reality', 299.
[103] Fulton, 'The Shape of Universities', 56.   [104] Fulton, 62.
[105] David Daiches, 'One Day This Summer They Moved a Piece of Sussex History', *Focus: The News Magazine of the University of Sussex*, 1969.
[106] Geoff Lockwood, 'University Motto' (February 1985), SxUOS1-1-1-15-7, University of Sussex Collection, University of Sussex Special Collections at The Keep; Geoffrey Victor Whitfield, *The Transformation of an English University from the 1960's: Fifty Years of Societal and Religious Developments at the University of Sussex* (Lexington, Kentucky: Emeth Press, 2013), 66. Briggs notes, 'the motto of the University of Sussex of [Fulton's] own devising had been 'Be still and know', but to the end Fulton had little wish to be still. He was always full of vitality', see Briggs, 'John Scott Fulton'. It was taken from Psalm 46:10. It is interesting that the motto has particular resonances with the critique of a sense of drift and a lack of values in the university identified by Moberly discussed above, see Moberly, *Crisis in the University*. As to why Fulton cut half the full biblical verse, 'he has been asked the question about the omission of 'that I am God' before and has refused to answer', see Lockwood, 'University Motto'.
[107] Lockwood, 'University Motto'. This is recorded in the University archives as a conversation with Fulton noted in a University of Sussex memorandum dated 4 Feb 1985, see Lockwood. The document notes that Fulton explained, 'it was his decision to have [the motto] in the native language; others would have preferred Latin' and that 'he decided if English it had to be from the Bible or Shakespeare, and he chose the Bible' and that 'walking on the Scottish hills he discussed the issue with friends, 'Be Still and Know' came to mind, and he stuck with it for a variety of reasons', see Lockwood.

Descartes conceived of a project that would be purely the search for truth, and would be unconstrained by any other objectives at all. Because it temporarily lays aside the demands of practical rationality, it has to be detached from practice; and because it is concerned with truth and nothing else, it has to raise its requirements to the highest conceivable level, and demand nothing less than absolute certainty.[108]

For Fulton, education starts using a methodical sceptical approach that questions every step in our thinking, a refusal to take things for granted.[109] But Sussex was not just to be a teaching university, research was also key to its idea and ethos.[110] As Blin-Stoye writes, 'those of us responsible for bringing the university into being were always absolutely clear (unlike some in high places today) that a high level of research and scholarship contribute so much to the general ethos of a university, but also because, without them, teaching at a university level can become lifeless, uninspired and dated'.[111] Briggs agreed, 'the sense of the University of Sussex [was] as a research university (with the research, when possible, linked to teaching), where institutes, [and] centres…would concern themselves with major national and international themes, where appropriate, in an interdisciplinary way'.[112] Interestingly, most of the changes that took place between 1961–1967 were not influenced by students and the innovation in the university was led by faculty, this included the success of the Institute of Development Studies being located at Sussex in 1965, against Oxford's attempt to lay claim to it, and the foundation of SPRU in 1966.[113]

---

[108] Bernard Williams, 'Introductory Essay', in *Meditations on First Philosophy with Selections from the Objections and Replies*, ed. John Cottingham. (Cambridge: Cambridge University Press, 2003), 6.

[109] The theological basis of Descartes method is also, I believe, important in accounting for Fulton's belief in the necessity of a moral compass for a university.

[110] To ensure academic quality it was noted in Council Minutes of 8 Dec 1961 that an Academic Advisory Council was appointed by the Privy Council to Sussex including, Sir Isaiah Berlin, Sir James Duff, Dr. R. Holroyd, Prof. P.B. Medawar, and Prof. N.F. Mott, see Ted Shields, 'COUNCIL II: Council Minutes' (1961), SxUoS1/1/2/31/5/1, University of Sussex Collection, University of Sussex Special Collections at The Keep.

[111] Blin-Stoyle and Ivey, *The Sussex Opportunity*, xv.

[112] Blin-Stoyle and Ivey, 12. As Perkin noted, 'In the UFC research rankings in 1989, five of [the Plate Glass Universiites] were placed in the top twenty: Warwick was 5th out of 55 institutions, behind only Cambridge, Imperial College, Oxford, and University College London; York was 9th, Essex and Sussex 11th and 12th, Lancaster 17th, East Anglia was 22nd and Kent 38th' see Perkin, 'Dream, Myth and Reality', 308.

[113] Martin Trow joined Sussex in 1965 and made this observation which rings true at Sussex till this day, 'one strong impression is that the faculty at Brighton spend a quite prodigious amount of time meeting with one another on academic business. Besides the many regular committees and conferences, the staff seems always to meeting about some question or other…my first thought at Brighton was 'My God, how does the faculty manage to get any work done?' see Martin Trow, 'Notes From The Notebook Of An Educational Anthropologist', *Bulletin* 10/3/1965, no. 22 (1965): 14–15.

Fulton stood down as Vice Chancellor in 1967. Sussex existed up to this point in what I earlier referred to as the *Robbins parenthesis*, but this parenthesis was soon to close. Change was already coming as higher education policy swung away from Robbins. In 1965 a sense of the coming shift was signalled by the so-called 'Woolwich speech' speech given by Antony Crosland and the subsequent publication of Toby Weaver's white paper, 'A Plan for Polytechnics and Other Colleges,' which established a binary system in British higher education. Crossland argued that

> there was a public sector of higher education, with distinctive principles and purposes, alongside the universities. If the universities could be said to be in an 'autonomous' tradition, the public-sector colleges were in a 'service' tradition, which was valuable in itself and should not be subsumed by the other.[114]

In 1967, Asa Briggs prepared to take over as Vice Chancellor of the university. A shift in higher education policy was now well under way within government. As a consequence, the University Grants Committee agreed a grant to Sussex 'considerably less than we had hoped, and in the light of our budget we had to make substantial changes to the academic plans which we had drawn up, we believed, not unrealistically'.[115] Briggs observed that there was unlikely to be any further large-scale developments until after 1972 based on the funding plans of the UGC, and consequently Sussex would need to seek development funds from elsewhere. As a result, Fulton (then in the final months of his Vice Chancellorship) and Briggs commissioned a McKinsey report in the government, organisation and administrative methods of Sussex. The result was a proposal for 'streamlining of committees, an increase in participation, a clearer definition of administrative responsibilities, greater devolution, a strengthening of the planning process and an improved system of internal communication'.[116] The effect of this was that the administrative centre was removed from most academic matters, including academic planning. Interestingly, up until this point students had not been much involved with university matters, but student attitudes were beginning to shift, especially following student protests in 1968. One of the more famous of these was when red paint was thrown over Robert Beers, spokesperson for the US embassy, who talked at Sussex about the Vietnam War, by self-described anarchists

---

[114] Tyrrell Burgess, 'Sir Toby Weaver', *The Guardian*, June 2001, sec. Education, https://www.theguardian.com/news/2001/jun/13/guardianobituaries.highereducation.
[115] Blin-Stoyle and Ivey, *The Sussex Opportunity*, 15.
[116] Blin-Stoyle and Ivey, 16.

Sean Linehan and Merfyn Jones.[117] But Sussex in actuality was less radical in political matters in the late 1960s than it appeared either in the media, or in nostalgic accounts of the university, as Crouch argued,

> disciplinary action was taken against the individuals concerned with, apparently, the approval of the student body. This was the only major incident of student disruption at Sussex, which had an elaborate system of disciplinary procedure involving proctors (youthful members of academic staff) and students, with a clear and explicit structure of appeals...in this way discipline seems to have a different image at Sussex than in less fortunate institutions, where it still appears as a remote and magisterial authority.[118]

After 1967, with Fulton no longer at the helm, Sussex's identity as 'Balliol-by-the-Sea' was waning, as the 'original Oxbridge trappings...dwindled in significance. Gowns...disappeared, and formal leave-taking [was] vanishing. Proctorial authority [was] not the despotism tempered by expediency of the Oxford model but something far more limited'.[119] Whitfield wrote in 2013 that 'in some quarters, the University of Sussex was sometimes expected to be akin to "Balliol by the Sea" but it came well below such inappropriate expectations'.[120] However, according to Beloff, the commitment to small-group teaching that was 'a true echo of the Oxford ideology' remained. The Sussex philosophy stressed 'the interdependence rather than the independence of traditional subjects...the notion of the school rather than the department as the basic academic institution' as the organisational reflection of the underlying philosophy.[121] The tutorial system which gave greater concentration at the start of the undergraduate degree strengthened the weaknesses apparent in this interdisciplinarity. But as the funding environment began to tighten it became inevitable that Sussex's self-identity as an experimental laboratory for university education would become more aligned with the broader notion of the other 'Plateglass Universities', a term that Beloff introduced in 1968.[122] Sussex

---

[117] Merfyn Jones later became Vice Chancellor of the University of Bangor from 2004 to 2010.
[118] Colin Crouch, *The Student Revolt* (Bodley Head, 1970), 100.
[119] Michael Beloff, *The Plateglass Universities* (Secker, 1968), 82.
[120] Whitfield, *The Transformation of an English University from the 1960's*, 23.
[121] Beloff, *The Plateglass Universities*, 83. The notion of the School was key to the way in which Sussex understood itself. Professor Hugh F. Kearney, writing in 1964, reflected in the University magazine, *Bulletin*, that 'the original idea behind the School should be developed so as to make it a reality. No one at Sussex regrets the passing of the department with all its narrow loyalties...this is the point at which the Schools have their own contribution to make. I believe that each School should work as far as possible as an independent unit, on the analogy, *mutatis mutandis*, of an Oxford college' see Hugh Francis Kearney, 'When Is a School Not a School?', *University of Sussex Bulletin*, 1964.
[122] As Beloff quoted of an academic from another university, 'if Sussex had not existed, it would not have been necessary to invent it' see Beloff, *The Plateglass Universities*, 81.

was changing due to pressures from its funding body, the UGC, faculty and student demands, and a new regime under Asa Briggs.[123] Indeed, as it matured it began to look more like its sister universities created in the 1960s, and less as a radical experimental lab for new academic ideas. But the questions posed by Moberly and others remained vital, for as John Fulton remarked, looking back on the history of the University of Sussex in 1986, it remained important to ask: who are 'the keepers of the university's conscience?'[124] Sussex's guiding vision, its idea of a university, remained important throughout this period.

Sussex was concerned with the ability to combine the particular and the general, both in research and teaching, to create new ways of situating specialisms in contexts through interdisciplinary approaches. Sussex offered, not the final map of knowledge, but rather the institutional context within which the practice of drawing and redrawing these 'maps of learning' were made possible. Sussex could be said, therefore, to have had a compass that gave a sense of the general direction for academics in research and teaching. But it also had a strong sense of identity which translated into everything the University did. These freedoms in research and teaching that Fulton and Briggs had created attracted the best academic researchers and students to Sussex and it soon overtook many of the civic universities in terms of research excellence. This legacy further resulted in excellent research outcomes when a research assessment exercise was introduced from 1986-2001 (later called the REF). Sussex was rated in the top 15 universities for research in the UK during this period.[125] Donald Winch, who came to Sussex in 1962 and was Professor of the History of Economics, spoke for many when he explained, 'those of us

---

[123] In 1967 Sussex was a remarkably popular choice for applicants to study. For example in 1967–68 "the university received 13,632 applications for the 908 places which were available". Cox further claimed a "marked tendency for Sussex to figure as a very strong alternative institution for those who were unable to secure places at Oxford or Cambridge" see Edwin H. Cox, 'How Admissions Cope with the Demand for Places', *Focus: The News Magazine of the University of Sussex*, 1969.

[124] Blin-Stoyle and Ivey, *The Sussex Opportunity*, 207.

[125] Shattock, *Managing Successful Universities*, 6. Sussex had an average ranking of 12 from 1986–2001. As noted in 2003, by Shattock, 'Sussex seem to be slipping down the rankings and must be hoping to recover their positions next time' see Shattock, 7. It has since dropped to 33 in the 2021 REF tables, see Jack Grove, 'REF 2021: Quality Ratings Hit New High in Expanded Assessment', Times Higher Education (THE), May 2022, https://www.timeshighereducation.com/news/ref-2021-research-excellence-framework-results-announced. As Shattock noted, 'universities performing at the highest levels in research success is paralleled by success in student related measures, including teaching, see Shattock, *Managing Successful Universities*, 9. Although it should be noted that Sussex was the only university in this set to have poor league table position in teaching, which may be a hangover of the inability of the original School system to meet new demands after 1986 from students for departmental support and teaching, see Shattock, 10.

who retain the privilege of teaching... at Sussex will, therefore, as in the past, have to stand by a calling that avoids the over-responsiveness to external interests. I can think of no better way of doing this than to cultivate, in due measure, those more fundamental issues which are nobody's business, if not our own'.[126]

School of Media, Arts and Humanities,
University of Sussex,
Falmer,
East Sussex, BN19RH.

This article was made possible by funding from The British Academy reference MD160052. The author would also like to thank the Rector and Fellows of Lincoln College for the kind invitation to become a member of the College Senior Common Room during 2017 whilst researching the project.

BIBLIOGRAPHY

Anderson, Colin. 'Grants to Students (Anderson Report)', 1960. https://education-uk.org/documents/anderson1960/index.html.
Astor, David. 'Diary of the Project' (London, 1964). http://www7.bbk.ac.uk/thepursuitofthenazimind/Astor/KMBT35020110914164153.pdf.
———. 'Limited Study of Political Psychopathology (David Astor Correspondence)' (Falmer, 1963). SxUOS1/1/1/17/3. University of Sussex Collection, University of Sussex Special Collections at The Keep.
Beloff, Michael. *The Plateglass Universities* (Secker, 1968).
Blin-Stoyle, R. J., and Geoff Ivey. *The Sussex Opportunity: A New University and the Future* (Brighton: Harvester, 1986).
Bradbury, Malcolm. *Eating People Is Wrong* (London: Secker & Warburg, 1976).
Briggs, Asa. 'A Founding Father Reflects'. *Higher Education Quarterly* 45, no. 4 (1991): 311–332. https://doi.org/10.1111/j.1468-2273.1991.tb01575.x.
———. 'Asa Briggs Reviews "Innovation in Higher Education: New Universities in the United Kingdom"'. *Focus: The News Magazine of the University of Sussex*, 1969.
———. 'Drawing a New Map of Learning'. In *The Idea of a New University: An Experiment in Sussex*, edited by David Daiches (London: André Deutsch, 1964), 60–80.
———. 'John Scott Fulton'. In *Oxford Dictionary of National Biography*, edited by David Cannadine (Oxford: Oxford University Press, 2004), 1. https://doi.org/10.1093/ref:odnb/39987.
———. 'Maps of Learning'. *New Statesman*, January 1961. Periodicals Archive Online.

---

[126] Blin-Stoyle and Ivey, *The Sussex Opportunity*, 93.

———. *Secret Days: Codebreaking in Bletchley Park: A Memoir of Hut Six and the Enigma Machine* (London: Frontline Books, 2011).

———. *The Map of Learning*. Research Students' Association. 1st Annual Lecture, 1960 (Canberra: Australian National University, 1961). https://catalog.hathitrust.org/Record/001735715.

Burgess, Tyrrell. 'Sir Toby Weaver'. *The Guardian*, June 2001, sec. Education. https://www.theguardian.com/news/2001/jun/13/guardianobituaries.highereducation.

Burnet, John. *Higher Education and the War* (London, MacMillan, 1917). http://archive.org/details/highereducationw00burnuoft.

Cohn, Norman. 'A Brief History of the Columbus Centre and Its Research Project' (Sussex, 1980). http://www7.bbk.ac.uk/thepursuitofthenazimind/Astor/KMBT35020110914164050.pdf.

Collini, Stefan. *Absent Minds: Intellectuals in Britain*. First Edition. (Oxford ; New York: OUP Oxford, 2006).

———. 'Utopian Universities: A Global History of the New Campuses of the 1960s'. *Reviews in History*, 2021. https://reviews.history.ac.uk/review/2434.

Corbett, J. P. 'Opening the Mind'. In *The Idea of a New University: An Experiment in Sussex*, edited by David Daiches (London: André Deutsch, 1964), 22–39.

Cox, Edwin H. 'How Admissions Cope with the Demand for Places'. *Focus: The News Magazine of the University of Sussex*, 1969.

Cragoe, Matthew. 'Sussex: Cold War Campus'. In *Utopian Universities: A Global History of the New Campuses of the 1960s*, edited by Miles Taylor and Jill Pellew, 1st edition. (London ; New York: Bloomsbury Academic, 2020), 55–72.

Crouch, Colin. *The Student Revolt* (Bodley Head, 1970).

Daiches, David. 'One Day This Summer They Moved a Piece of Sussex History'. *Focus: The News Magazine of the University of Sussex*, 1969.

Davie, George Elder. *The Democratic Intellect: Scotland and Her Universities in the Nineteenth Century*. Third edition / edited by Murdo Macdonald. Edinburgh Classic Editions (Edinburgh: University Press, 1961).

Filippakou, Ourania, and Ted Tapper. *Creating the Future? The 1960s New English Universities*. 1st ed. 2019 edition. (New York, NY: Springer, 2019).

Fulton, John. 'Balliol By The Sea Faces Its Future'. *The Times* (1961). The Times Digital Archive.

———. 'New Universities in Perspective'. In *The Idea of a New University: An Experiment in Sussex*, edited by David Daiches (London: André Deutsch, 1964), 9–21.

———. 'The Shape of Universities'. In *The Expanding University: A Report*, edited by W. R. Niblett (London: Faber, 1962), 46–63.

Gallie, W. B. *A New University: A.D.Lindsay and the Keele Experiment*. First Edition. (London: Chatto & Windus, 1960).

Gray, Fred, ed. *Making the Future: A History of the University of Sussex* (Falmer: University of Sussex, 2011).

Grove, Jack. 'REF 2021: Quality Ratings Hit New High in Expanded Assessment'. Times Higher Education (THE), May 2022. https://www.timeshighereducation.com/news/ref-2021-research-excellence-framework-results-announced.

HESA. 'Where Do HE Students Study? | HESA', 2023. https://www.hesa.ac.uk/data-and-analysis/students/where-study#provider.

Kearney, Hugh Francis. 'When Is a School Not a School?' *University of Sussex Bulletin*, 1964.

Lindsay, Alexander Dunlop. 'The Commission on German Universities'. *Higher Education Quarterly* 4, no. 1 (1949): 82–88. https://doi.org/10.1111/j.1468-2273.1949.tb02026.x.

———. 'The Function of the Universities'. *Nature* 166, no. 4233 (December 1950): 1009–1010. https://doi.org/10.1038/1661009a0.

Lockwood, Geoff. 'University Motto' (Falmer, February 1985). SxUOS1-1-1-15-7. University of Sussex Collection, University of Sussex Special Collections at The Keep.

Lowe, Adolf. *The Universities in Transformation* (London: The Sheldon Press, 1940).

Mackenzie, Norman. 'Starting a New University'. *Higher Education Quarterly* 15, no. 2 (1961): 139–151. https://doi.org/10.1111/j.1468-2273.1961.tb00170.x.

Moberly, Walter. *Crisis in the University* (London: Macmillan, 1949).

———. *The Universities and Cultural Leadership* Walker Trust Lectures on Leadership, XI (Oxford University Press, 1951).

Mountford, Sir James. *Keele: An Historical Critique.* Illustrated edition. (London, Boston: Routledge & Kegan Paul Books, 1972).

Perkin, Harold. 'Dream, Myth and Reality: New Universities in England, 1960–1990'. *Higher Education Quarterly* 45, no. 4 (1991): 294–310. https://doi.org/10.1111/j.1468-2273.1991.tb01574.x.

Phillips, David. 'Lindsay and the German Universities: An Oxford Contribution to the Post-War Reform Debate'. *Oxford Review of Education* 6, no. 1 (1980): 91–105.

Robbins, Report. 'Higher Education (Robbins Report)', 1963. https://education-uk.org/documents/robbins/robbins1963.html.

Scott, Drusilla. *A.D. Lindsay, A Biography* (Blackwells, 1971).

Shattock, Michael. *Managing Successful Universities* (Berkshire: Society for Research into Higher Education : Open University Press, 2003). http://site.ebrary.com/id/10175236.

Shields, Ted. 'COUNCIL I: Council Minutes' (Falmer, 1961). SxUOS1/1/2/31/2. University of Sussex Collection, University of Sussex Special Collections at The Keep.

———. 'COUNCIL II: Council Minutes' (Falmer, 1961). SxUoS1/1/2/31/5/1. University of Sussex Collection, University of Sussex Special Collections at The Keep.

———. 'Senate Minutes' (Falmer, 1962). SxUOS1/1/2/27/3. University of Sussex Collection, University of Sussex Special Collections at The Keep.

Stanley, Arthur Penrhyn. *The Life and Correspondence of Thomas Arnold. Suppl. to the First Five Editions*, 1847.

Steele, Tom, and Richard Kenneth Taylor. 'Oldham's Moot (1938–1947), the Universities and the Adult Citizen'. *History of Education* 39, no. 2 (March 2010): 183–197. https://doi.org/10.1080/00467600902865479.

Stone, W. G. 'Memorandum to the Director of Education' (Falmer, 1956). SxMs59/7. University of Sussex Collection, University of Sussex Special Collections at The Keep.

———. 'University Commentary from Brighton'. *Higher Education Quarterly* 12, no. 3 (1958): 223–227. https://doi.org/10.1111/j.1468-2273.1958.tb00951.x.

Stone, W.G. 'Steps Leading to the Foundation of the University'. In *The Idea of a New University: An Experiment in Sussex*, edited by David Daiches (London: André Deutsch, 1964), 168–192.

Trow, Martin. 'Notes From The Notebook Of An Educational Anthropologist'. *Bulletin* 10/3/1965, no. 22 (1965): 14–15.

Truscot, Bruce. 'Academic Screwtape'. *Nature* 194, no. 4829 (May 1962): 616–617. https://doi.org/10.1038/194616a0.

University College of Sussex. 'The University College of Sussex: An Appeal' (Falmer, 1960). SxUOS1/1/1/15/4. University of Sussex Collection, University of Sussex Special Collections at The Keep.

Whitfield, Geoffrey Victor. *The Transformation of an English University from the 1960's: Fifty Years of Societal and Religious Developments at the University of Sussex* (Lexington, Kentucky: Emeth Press, 2013).

Whyte, William. *Redbrick: A Social and Architectural History of Britain's Civic Universities*. (Oxford: Oxford University Press, 2016).

Williams, Bernard. 'Introductory Essay'. In *Meditations on First Philosophy with Selections from the Objections and Replies*, edited by John Cottingham. (Cambridge: Cambridge University Press, 2003), vii–xvii.

Cornelia M. Rudderikhoff and Hilde de Ridder-Symoens (eds), *Les registres-matricules de la nation germanique de l'ancienne Université d'Orléans, 1602–1689. Avec un supplement 1721–1781* (Leiden and Boston MA: Brill, 2023), pp. xvi + 909

Andrew Hegarty

This is a huge volume by any standards. It will surely be worthwhile sketching in this review some history for potential users. But, first of all, it is essential to schedule for the reader what it contains: a valuable outline of manuscript sources from assorted deposits; then a section listing printed primary sources and secondary works; those followed by an *'Introduction historique'*, pp. 1–32, and after that a very short chapter on *'Sources'* of various kinds, pp. 33–37 (which commences with an indication that many Orléans archival documents were lost in the June 1940 bombardment, but that fortunately the registers specifically of the German Nation here covered had been microfilmed in 1939); then there is an even shorter chapter 3, *'Méthode d'édition'*, pp. 38–39 (which commences with a contextualising indication that this volume is really a continuation of four volumes of *Livres des procurateurs de la nation germanique de l'ancienne Université d'Orléans* published also by Brill between 1971 and 2015, and an explanation of how it has been put together); there is a most interesting Chapter 4, *'Formulaire de serments'*, pp. 40–46, with the texts of oaths to be tendered to those entering the Nation – even if the University gets its mention – in Latin,

German, Dutch and French versions (but notably not – and this is surely indicative of the genuine core clientele of the institution – in English or Scandinavian languages or Polish); the bulk of the content is in a huge Chapter 5, *'Listes des immatriculés et gradués, 1602–1689, avec un supplement 1721–1781'*, pp. 47–744, the supplement significantly amounting only to pp. 737–744 ; finally, as well as usefully, there is an extensive *'Index des noms de personnes'*, generally in more or less Latin forms, provided by the editors, at pp. 745–909.

Orléans had achieved its standing as a University, albeit as a restricted *universitas legum*, built upon a lesser *studium aurelianense*, thanks to a grant in 1306 from Pope Clement V who happened to be an alumnus. An earlier pontiff, Honorius III, had prohibited in 1219 the teaching of the Civil (or Roman) Law in Paris, seemingly to cosset the ecclesiastical faculties of Theology and Canon Law by removing competition that might draw away from them ambitious clerics. There was it appears – although this is not wholly clear – some collusion or overlapping of interests as medieval French kings, starting with Philip Augustus, for their part seemingly preferred not to have 'foreign' or 'imperial' law taught in their capital city. Both Civil and Canon laws were taught at Orléans, and this gave that University a power of attracting students over centuries. Some have even seen Orléans as *de facto* the second Law faculty of Paris, although neighbouring Loire valley universities at Bourges and Angers, too, were well-sited to capitalise on Paris's deficiency. St. Yves (1253–1303) who had studied Civil Law in Orléans was, interestingly, later recognised by many in France and elsewhere as the patron saint of lawyers.

Bologna in Italy was an older university with great Europe-wide appeal, and its organisation certainly influenced Orleans, both institutions being in some senses *universitates studentum* rather than *magistrorum* – although so muddled a matter should not be over-stated – and both notably having important German Nations. Their styles of teaching differed, however, even in medieval centuries which allowed Orléans to sell a scholastic specific difference. Students at Orléans were early on grouped into ten Nations, roughly geographical in origin but quite unequal. A mid-sixteenth-century *reformatio* imposed by *arrêt* of the Parlement of Paris reduced the Nations to only four via more or less happy amalgamations. Those left in being were named for France, Picardy, Normandy and Germany – of which the first and the last were much the most numerous. The *Collegium doctorum regentium et procuratorum nationum* that ran the institution – with one of the *doctores regentes* serving as Rector on a quarterly basis – thereby sustained a change which altered the balance of the institution: instead of ten student *procuratores* sitting with professors on the key governing body, there were now to be only four, such that they no longer possessed an in-built 'super-majority' in the *Collegium*. Notionally, at least from early sixteenth century, there had been five teachers of Civil Law, and three of Canon Law, but by the 1570s there were left four only teaching Civil Law alone, even if degrees *utriusque iuris* continued to be granted. The total of active regents in the whole period 1602–1689 was only seventeen, and some of these remained on the notional strength into the early eighteenth century.

It will be worth noting for potential users that independent Lorraine, not incorporated into France until the eighteenth century, was after the *réformation* to be part of the German Nation, while some Scots, who had formerly been significant as a Nation on their own, but who had had ancient links with the 'Germans', for a time strove against formal amalgamation into the Nation of Normandy and wormed their way into that of the Germans. It was, as ever, one thing to regulate, another to enforce regulation. By the time of the Registers here edited the Scots (and other islanders), were almost entirely missing. The traditional broad division between *Germani superiores* – roughly those coming from within imperial frontiers – and *Germani inferiores* – more or less those from the Low Countries – carried on, with turns arranged for holding offices.

To many familiar with colleges elsewhere Orléans might surprise by its lack of such institutions, and for focusing student life in nations. By the early seventeenth century the German Nation stood out for numbers as well as the organisation of its offer, and that in good measure because of young men sojourning as part of their 'Grand Tour' and because (not quite the same thing) of its drawing power for mere tourists. (It must be allowed that the sheer wealth of detail we have for the German Nation, as in this volume, may do a disservice to less documented others.) Where in Oxford membership of a college or hall had become essential to matriculate, in Orléans the Nation played a like role except that until late in the day matriculation in the University itself as opposed to signing up for the Nation was not required. French kings had long been keen to sustain Orléans' drawing power as a strategic geopolitical asset and vehicle of 'soft power' since youthful élites, above all from territories within the Empire were thereby subjected for a time to a French cultural, linguistic and scholastic experience. The monarchs had distinguished and privileged the German Nation above all others by safeguarding members' free movement and permitting use of arms – all in the Nation thereby benefitting in practice from treatment as nobles.

Nations were umbrellas of protection, but they also facilitated a congenial social life – suited to young gentlemen – around the University quarter of the city in which students were supposed to dwell. There were resident teachers of fencing, equitation, dancing, lute playing and music of other kinds, as well as voice training. Dramatic performances from travelling players were often staged. Teachers of all kinds dwelling in the academic quarter offered private classes to those who could afford them, and were prominent amongst those offering students domestic accommodation for a consideration.

Most interestingly the physical heart of the German Nation from mid/late-sixteenth century onwards was its important Library, which more than matched, at least for legal studies, what many European colleges elsewhere could provide for their students. Useful sets of texts were freely available therein, and the institution regularly received legacies of books. The volume here reviewed notably lists those in charge of the Library with other officers of the Nation. Regular classes of French for men from elsewhere who wished to attain command of the language, as well as meetings of assorted kinds including 'law moots', took place in the building which changed address several times over the years. Funerals of members – for which use of a special ornate pall might be called upon – and annual religious services took place in a couple of Catholic churches. Arrangements were tacitly made not to put the Protestants prominently resident in the late-sixteenth and seventeenth centuries under pressure. They were long able to attend reformed services nearby. It was even made possible for them to obtain diplomas by an unobjectionable route, that is, in the name of Rector and *doctores regentes*, instead of from the Chancellor of the Cathedral representing the Pope.

There was a manifest decline approaching to oblivion over the seventeenth century, but it is difficult to assign blame accurately. The King of Spain's restrictions on his subjects studying abroad certainly reduced numbers coming to Orléans from the Catholic southern Low Countries even in late sixteenth century when Wars of Religion also had their impact, as certainly did later the Thirty Years War that devastated much of the Empire and made religious co-existence precarious. Inscription into the University itself (as opposed to the Nation which had until then given academic status and the capacity to sit examinations) was made compulsory by royal decree only in 1679 when Louis XIV also made obligatory the teaching of French Law which was of little or no interest to those who were not his subjects. The Edict of Nantes of 1598 was revoked by the King in 1685 with obvious consequences for Protestants even if arrangements were in fact quickly made with royal approval to prevent this impacting excessively on students. The real killer in that era, however, was almost certainly the French King's wars from the late 1660s through to 1714 against assorted coalitions of the independent Netherlands and its allies, during which even the Nation's protective royal privileges provided insufficient security. The Nation in fact ceased to exist temporarily in 1689, and started up again modestly in 1721 (with less than 8pp. here), as the lengthy title suggests. After staggering on thereafter – partly perhaps due to hereditary momentum in some families – the University and Nation finally closed in 1793.

There were also endemic, especially from the early seventeenth century until reforms took effect in mid-century after complaints, abuses and multifarious forms of corruption. The 'Grand Tour' undertaken by wealthy young men often 'swung by' Orléans where names were entered in books of the Nation, fees paid to officials and others, and money often freely spent in diversions within the academic quarter. There came to exist a 'fast track' to licence and doctorate for tourists, via payment of higher dues, and nominal examination *in camera*. Some of those involved had, however, undertaken studies in a more genuine manner at home or elsewhere, so that a prestigious Orléans diploma, sometimes obtained almost overnight, was in fact the crowning, however venal, of a deeper process. More serious and public attainment of a diploma continued even for men on the Tour, not all of whom were mere tourists. The Nation of Germany, as this volume shows, was the most organised and best documented, in part because seemingly the most populous for much of the period covered, but the Registers rarely make the full truth clear, even when degree-taking itself was recorded as here by the Nation after a decent interval of supposed study.

This is a magnificent reference work – hardly bed-time reading – that complements earlier volumes published by Brill. The records of the German Nation of Orléans are now printed as well as, or better than, those of almost any comparable institution. One can only hope that what is recorded has been written up more accurately than such matters in other places, but there is little here to render a verdict possible. If this and its companion volumes serve to spell out for those interested enough to tackle them the importance that a Nation might have for so many young men in a medieval and early-modern university, it will have served its purpose. At Orléans in practice the Nation counted for more, in many respects, than the University. There is an enormous amount of information here, for which the superb 165pp. 'finding aid' of the *'Index des noms de personnes'* will be of great assistance to users and potential analysts of the data provided.

Andrew Hegarty
8 Orme Court
London W2 4RL
ajh1954@googlemail.com

Nigel Aston, *Enlightened Oxford: The University and the Cultural and Political Life of Eighteenth-Century Britain and Beyond* (Oxford: Oxford University Press, 2023), pp. xxiv + 819

Robin Darwall-Smith

In his review of L. W. B. Brockliss's one-volume history of Oxford University for the 2017 issue of this journal, Nicholas Tyacke concludes with an observation of how much there still remained to discover, 'especially as regards the terra incognita of the eighteenth century.'

Previous scholars have tended to look upon this unknown territory with disdain, content to follow the usual jibes about the intellectual torpor of the Georgian University. Even Brockliss was, in the main, content to follow this traditional picture in his book.

Serious attempts have been made to rectify this picture, above all Volume V of *The History of the University of Oxford*, published in 1986 and edited by Lucy Sutherland and Leslie Mitchell. More recently, Peregrine Horden and I co-edited for this series a collection of essays (one of them by Aston himself) titled *The Unloved Century: Georgian Oxford Reassessed*. Now Nigel Aston has entered the fray with a veritable leviathan, reflecting a lifetime of work and study of Georgian Oxford. Although the work of one author, it is almost the same length as Sutherland and Mitchell's edited book.

Aston is not afraid to defend Georgian Oxford to the hilt. Early on, he declares: 'Oxford was not condemned to marginality in eighteenth-century national and international life because of its apparent reluctance to introduce a modernising curriculum' (11), and he regularly emphases

Oxford's national and international importance. He has also given his book a provocative title. It has been all too tempting to contrast unenlightened Anglican Oxford with the 'true' secular enlightenment, to be found elsewhere in Britain and in Europe, as if enlightenment and Oxford cannot co-exist. Rather, he says, 'Oxford was a primary locus for the moderate Enlightenment in England' (74). Furthermore, he argues that 'At no point... should Oxford be considered intellectually at a clear remove from what one might call the moderate Enlightenment' (659). Aston rightly observes that contemporary scholarship finds it hard to believe that Christianity was anything other than central to enlightened intellectual activity at this time.

Aston divides his book into three main parts: 'Intellectual Presence', 'Institutional Presence and Interactions', and 'Cultural Constructions, Connections and Tensions'. 'Intellectual Presence' examines what people studied at Oxford. Its first chapter is devoted to theology, which Aston called 'foundational to the whole study' (5). This is a very welcome departure: Aston, who really understands Georgian theology, knows that eighteenth-century Oxford saw its primary duty as being a seminary for the Church of England, and the modern reader who does not appreciate this crucial fact will find Georgian Oxford all the harder to understand. A study like R. G. Ward's *Georgian Oxford* of 1958 which, as seen below, wholly devotes itself to the political life of the university provides a seriously misleading picture by being so one-dimensional. It is therefore a pleasure to see theology here given pride of place.

The two remaining chapters in this part discuss respectively the arts and humanities and the sciences. The former chapter opens with Aston in feisty form: 'This chapter argues for the zestiness, vigour and variety of the arts and humanities in eighteenth-century Oxford... Oxford was not an obscurantist Anglican backwater; it was a university well-connected with the contemporary world' (131). Aston then takes the reader around the different arts and humanities subjects pursued at Oxford, including poetry and literature, alongside history, classics, philosophy and oriental studies. One question that Aston might have explored is the way that many a promising classical scholar at Oxford might publish a fine work of classical scholarship (usually an edition or a commentary), but then put classics aside to ascend the mightier peaks of theology.

There is also a welcome section on music, a subject often overlooked in such studies. Aston, however, is well aware that Georgian Oxford enjoyed a thriving musical culture and attracted composers of the calibre of Handel and Haydn to visit and give concerts. It is therefore regrettable that there is no comparable discussion of painting or sculpture, because some colleges did commission work from major figures of the day, such as New College with Joshua Reynolds and All Souls with James Thornhill and Anton Mengs. As for architecture, Aston rightly says that 'Oxford was a primary site throughout the century for architectural virtuosity' (28), and there is a brief discussion of this in the introduction, but I admit to appearing greedy in regretting that his book does not contain more.

In the next chapter, Aston combats head-on the claims that Georgian Oxford was unsympathetic to the sciences. No, he says: Oxford probably trained one-third of all English pioneers of science in the eighteenth century (17). Later in the century, when the Radcliffe Observatory was built, Thomas Hornsby, the then Savilian Professor of Astronomy, made it arguably the best equipped observatory in Europe (226–9). He reminds us too that the old Ashmolean Museum had a fully functioning laboratory. Aston also considers Oxford's relationship with Sir Isaac Newton (201–5). Oxonians, he suggests, certainly appreciated the importance of Newton's works, but, perhaps because of his Whiggishness and unorthodox beliefs, never let Newtonianism become the dominant force which it was in Cambridge – a sign, he suggests of Oxford's intellectual independence.

The second part of *Enlightened Oxford*, 'Institutional Presence and Interactions,' discusses political matters in three chapters, respectively titled 'Oxford personnel: Offices, interest, and the polity', 'Oxford and the Crown' and 'Oxford, the World of Westminster and the defence of the University's interests.' Here Aston enters the world of political Oxford as discussed in Ward's *Georgian Oxford*. Whereas, however, Ward's book, as said above, portrays a monochrome Oxford, completely consumed with politics to the exclusion of all else, in Aston's book, by this point one has been fully briefed that Oxonians were interested in a great many other subjects, and that politics was not the only thing in their lives.

Rather than providing a simple narrative of Oxford's political vicissitudes, Aston instead provides a thematic discussion, the first chapter studying Oxford's Chancellors, Vice-Chancellors, college heads, and college Visitors, and the second and third respectively examining Oxford's relationships with the Crown, and then with successive governments and the several MPs who represented the university in Parliament.

The basic narrative of this period – ups and downs in 1689–1714; the deep freeze of 1714–60; and the reconciliation under George III – is therefore told from three perspectives. Some inevitable repetition results, but there are benefits, not least from the details which Aston brings to bear. Among the most significant sections is that in which he assesses Oxford's successive Chancellors. Aston shows that each new Chancellor brought something different to bear in their relationships with the University and portrays them as being less passive than previous observers might have had one believe.

Aston also has interesting observations about the Hanoverian dynasty and Oxford. It is well enough known that many at Oxford had reservations about the accessions of George I and George II, but Aston shows that both kings in turn had little hesitation in snubbing Oxford, never visiting it, and generally spurning its overtures (320–1). On the other hand, Aston creates an interesting might-have-been, in that several Oxonians attached themselves to Frederick, Prince of Wales, who was happy to accept their overtures, before Frederick's early death in 1751 (313 and 325–6.). Aston also makes a pertinent point about the gradual disappearance of Jacobitism in Oxford by observing that, by the late 1750s, people had to choose between 'a royal, middle-aged inebriate given to beating up his mistresses, born in Italy, and George, Prince of Wales, the virtuous heir presumptive, born at Kew' (314). Even the arch-Jacobite William King ended his days as a keen supporter of George III.

This thematic approach also pays dividends in Aston's discussion of the university's successive MPs. By considering them all together, it is easier to understand their different personalities and contributions both to Oxford and to Westminster, especially in the case of skilful operators such as George Clarke and Sir Roger Newdigate. Aston also allows himself some barbed fun at the expense of Oxford's Whig community. It is important to remember that there were Whigs in Tory Oxford, mainly based in such colleges as Exeter, Merton, Wadham and eventually Christ Church, and Aston takes an interest in them, not least for their acting as the government's agents in Oxford, on the lookout for any sign of disloyalty. As a result, Aston suggests, they projected 'an increasingly implausible martyred image' (416), and 'failed to produce any new twists in Whig apologetics and preferred instead to be the often pettifogging creators of a victim culture quick to run to ministers' (668).

So far, Aston's book has generally kept within the bounds of the city of Oxford, which is not to say that he has been unaware of the outside world. Far from it: he frequently compares Oxford's story with those of the other universities within the British Isles. In his third part, however, he roves far more widely, exploring in detail the complex links between Oxford and the rest of the country. For him, Oxford is no island, for he shows how its members spread its influence far and wide. I doubt whether any previous study of Oxford has explored this subject so fully.

In Chapter 9, 'Beyond the University', he starts with the environs of Oxford, with the Oxford dons who hold college livings, and the local aristocrats and their details with the university, but then moves out to think about the many estates owned by colleges, or the schools with closed scholarships to Oxford. He gradually works out to Wales, Scotland, and Ireland, to show the links established there, not least the intriguing case of the support given by many Oxonians to the Episcopalian Scots after 1689.

Chapter 10, 'The University as seen from outside', is a more general chapter, discussing how people who were not members of the university saw it, be it in literary or artistic representations. He is also very interested in the visitors who came to Oxford. Not only did the great celebrations of Acts and Encaenia, and the installations of new Chancellors provide opportunities for visitors, but Oxford was in general becoming a tourist attraction, as Aston notes from the several guidebooks to Oxford which were published at this time (493). He also notes the attacks made on Oxford, partly from Dissenters, but also some such disgruntled Oxonians as Edward Gibbon (who, nevertheless, kept his true feelings about Oxford concealed during his lifetime).

This chapter also includes an important section about the relationship between women and the university (524–41). Aston shows how women could and did interact with the university. He provocatively declares at the start of this section that 'Women were actually everywhere in Oxford, but it is primarily from the male perspective rather than from their own surviving testimonies that they have been viewed' (524). Aston also takes the trouble to discuss servants in the university and colleges.

Chapter 11, 'Oxford and the wider world', explores relations between members of Oxford and those of other universities. Here he portrays a lively world in which Oxonians travelled around Europe, establishing friendly relations with other scholars, and, in turn, scholars from the continent regularly visited Oxford, above all to exploit the resources of such treasure houses as the Bodleian Library. For him, Oxford is an important and committed member of the Republic of Letters.

Aston's last chapter, 'Insider trading: Family friendships, connection and culture beyond the University', explores some fresh links between Oxford and the wider world. Here he considers what it means to have so many clerics or members of the gentry and aristocracy living all over the country who had been to Oxford, and the informal associations which ensued. There will have been lifelong friendships established, patronage networks created – and even some marriages, as Oxonians came to meet their friends' families. Many alumni took a continuing interest in their old colleges, even to the point of creating old members clubs (623–4), and sometimes making generous gifts and bequests. There were also ways for Oxonians living at some distance from the city to associated locally, such as meetings for Quarter Sessions and Assizes, as well as local societies. Once again, Aston shows that Oxford is no enclosed space, but held a great influence over the country as a whole.

Without any doubt, Aston's book has transformed our understanding of Georgian Oxford. It is a long read, but it is very well written, and written by someone who really knows and appreciates the Georgian university, and who is eager to make that appreciation known. Perhaps some may wonder whether Aston praises Georgian Oxford too uncritically, but in the light of two centuries of abuse hurled in its direction, it is good at last to find someone who takes it and its ideals seriously. It may well be that Georgian Oxford never quite escapes the sneers of the mockers, but Aston's work has surely shown how unjustified they are. I noted at the start of the review that Nicholas Tyacke wrote of the 'terra incognita' of eighteenth century Oxford: arguably Aston's magisterial work at last equips the reader with a first-rate set of maps and a compass with which to explore, understand, and even enjoy, this terrain.

Unfortunately, this review has to end with a warning. The original printing of this book, which I used to write this review, contains several proofreading errors, above all on the cross-references in the footnotes, none of which actually match with the right text. I understand that a fresh printing has since been issued in which these errors are put right. Readers are advised to ensure that they have a corrected copy. It is just unfortunate that OUP's own proofreaders or copyeditors failed to spot this in time.

Robin Darwall-Smith
Jesus and University Colleges, Oxford

William J. Ashworth, *The Trinity Circle: Anxiety, Intelligence, and Knowledge Creation in Nineteenth-Century England* (Pittsburg: University of Pittsburgh Press, 2021), pp. 256

Sheldon Rothblatt

William Ashworth visits (or revisits) the culture wars - forgive the anachronism - of the first third or more of nineteenth-century England. Gender was not then an issue. Identity politics, however, had social and religious dimensions in the form of social class and faith communities that suffered from civil disabilities. The radicalism of the French Revolution sharpened the sense of grievance and the anger of being outside the institutions where decisions were made. But for the personalities at war, the members of the Trinity Circle and their adversaries, issues were largely stated in the language of competing ideas.

Although the origins of several of the issues can be traced much further back into the final years of the previous century, the culture wars took on greater and broader intensity following the defeat of Napoleon. The macro context was explaining how a society governed by an hereditary landed aristocracy allied to an Established Church would reform itself politically and religiously if at all. Non-Anglicans (protestant sects, Roman Catholics and a tiny community of Jews) were collectively large enough to demand an end to particular privileges. A manufacturing class, often if not always of protestant sectarian origin, certainly wanted to end the unchallenged supremacy of peers and landed gentry. Industrialism moved laboring populations off the land and into factories, creating a multitude of grievances, and metropolitan areas grew swiftly, exposing social difficulties that new professions of urbanists would need to confront.

The combinations of forces that ultimately altered both the appearance and the inherited character of the kingdom amounted to a crisis of historical proportions. At least it appeared to be so for those with either a stake in the old ways or gripped by a feeling that the losses would be far greater than the gains. For them, especially in the 1820s and 1830s, when significant reforms had been made to the parliamentary franchise and the condition of non-Anglicans (except for the small Jewish community), the times were as Ashworth calls it 'an age of anxiety'.

His focus is on a well-known group of academics and churchmen who were either fellows of Trinity College, the largest and most important of the Cambridge colleges, chair-holding professors at the University, leaders in the Church or politicians who were either graduates of Cambridge or influenced by Trinity thinkers and teachers. Most names are familiar, such as Julius Hare, Adam Sedgwick, Connop Thirlwall, F.D. Maurice, but Ashworth adds several who have escaped the attention of historians, Hugh Jones Rose, for example. The leader, so to speak, was William Whewell. He has attracted and continues to attract a great deal of scholarly attention with new writings appearing regularly. Whewell is especially credited with being the founder of the history of science as a scholarly discipline, with a special emphasis on the primacy of the inductive as opposed to the deductive method of scientific reasoning. He was a formidable polymath, both praised and teased for knowing everything.

His particular targets were the ideas at work in transforming England, its inherited institutions of Church and State, its ancient universities, and the moral underpinnings of a society in the process of long-term historic change. In the short term changes were more in the realm of incomplete combustion, but for the Trinity Circle they appeared immediate. Perhaps it is in the very nature of intellectual dispute to elevate certain events into potential calamities. In any case, the challenges were regarded of sufficient magnitude to require a multi-faceted or polymathic approach. All ideas were treated as interconnected rather than as discrete and separate.

Whewell was not an easy man, to say the least. His reign as Master of Trinity was authoritarian. Temperament aside, he saw any challenge to authority as a mark of disorder, whether it was by the students of the college, who were often boisterous and engaged in town and gown disturbances, or the fellows, especially if they held views at variance with his own. Interestingly, he was not to the manor born. He was a prime example of the kind of sponsored mobility characteristic of England's *ancien régime*: a clever youth from the lower orders recognized as talented by parish priests and advanced educationally with the aid of an existing network of scholarships often misused. Curiously, or perhaps not, Whewell easily outgrew his common roots once accepted into the fleshpots of Cambridge when dons lived unusually well. His assimilation was so complete that he never found himself comfortable with ordinary folk and would have been miserable in a country rectory.

He twice married well (both wives predeceased him), inheriting considerable income, and despite his fears that the new manufacturing economy was fundamentally dehumanizing, he invested heavily in railways, the primary symbol of the new economic base. Five percent interest was not to be ignored. Ashworth takes an understandable ironic pleasure in telling us this. Whewell was a generous benefactor to his college, however, and marks of his largess remain for all to see.

The culture wars of the Trinity Circle consisted of two main aspects. The first falls within a sociology of knowledge. How does one know anything and does knowing something make it true? Or make it moral? This argument dates back well before Whewell and the Circle to at least John Locke. The second, of more recent origin, was German biblical criticism, adopted initially with some enthusiasm by Circle members such as Connop Thirlwall, who later, as a bishop in Wales, saw the error of his ways. One day he was alarmed to realize that the very foundations of Christianity and revealed religion were being dangerously questioned.

Perhaps it is laborious for us to tolerate the amount of attention devoted to Locke's writings on mental 'understanding', but since every thinker of note in the first decades of the nineteenth century weighed in on the problem, historians of ideas are always forced into recapitulating the innumerable contests. Whewell and John Stuart Mill, inheritor of his father's version of Locke, exchanged bitter arguments for years, even if they occasionally reluctantly agreed on some logical point or the other. The basic issue derived from Locke and subsequently refined was that knowledge was truth if acquired by experience via our senses. Ergo, political, social and legal reforms and changes - necessary for the school of radical utilitarianism to which Mill belonged - were truthful (and morally correct) since they were environmental in origin. Add a democratic note to all of this and then say that good is to be defined by how many people benefit from a particular cardinal change to the determining environment.

Charles Babbage, the inventor of a calculating instrument and himself a professor at Cambridge, at least for a time, was a continual nuisance for the Circle, advocating positions which Whewell et al strenuously opposed. Babbage thought of the mind as a mathematical machine, and for the Circle this malignant heresy foreshadowed a world where human agency was no longer enriched by Divine intentions.

To refute the 'sensational philosophy,' the school of thought to which Whewell adhered argued that experience was not the primary guide to the understanding. There were truths that were inherent in our minds, principally truths relating to the existence of the Almighty and to religious morality in general. But there was a third position - Ashworth credits Immanuel Kant's influence on the Circle, although Kant's philosophical influence was never thorough. (One Victorian wag called German idealism in England the 'Age of Steam and Cant'.) Sensory phenomena were indeed influential, but the mind itself was never passive. The mind, when awakened by stimuli, possessed an intuitive capacity to transform received data, to shape and direct it, so that presumed appearances were often faulty. A properly educated or instructed mind could be trusted to arrive at the truth. Information derived from sensory phenomena alone could certainly be misleading (Bishop Berkeley's optics had demonstrated this possibility in the century before). The astronomer John Herschel, who figures into the story, found proof of his own third position within the field of algebraic logic.

We might today, with our ongoing work on brain physiology and psychology, decide that the intuitive or intuitionist argument is sometimes plausible, that is to say, we would agree that our senses are often unreliable. The mind, it is popularly said, plays tricks, and without prior preparation, we are easily led astray.. However, our tendency would not be to align with Whewell and his compatriots on one conclusion, namely that the Divine Will had deposited definite ideas into the mind to divert experience into a deeper and more correct channel of truth. Nor would we find many who would move to the next step and employ that conclusion in defense of an Established Church and political status quo. But we are not Victorians. Yet we certainly have our own versions of culture wars, heated, partisan, with their own nomenclature and derivative propositions regarding the moral and social directions that a society should take.

At any rate, the debate was fierce and long-lived. Its abstruse nature notwithstanding, it was widely reported in the literary and philosophical press. Within the 'intellectual aristocracy' of the day, to reference Noël Annan's characterization of an inter-connected network of highly-respected families, civil servants, literateurs, academics, churchmen and hangers-on, a mass circulation media was not required to make certain quarrels less prominent or quiescent.

Taking the argument to a special educational level, Whewell was an indefatigable defender of the teaching of Euclid in the Cambridge University curriculum and system of written competitive examinations. He repeatedly maintained that geometry with its axiomatic proofs best supported the intuitionist position, something that 'French' analytical algebra, which had its English supporters, utterly failed to do. It was too abstract, said the Circle, and as such likely to elide into atheism. And he argued for the method of induction as superior to deduction in the acquisition of truth in support of his explanation of 'Fundamental Ideas', in-dwelling axioms which, when stimulated by experiential data, guided reasoning to correct conclusions. Examples were space, time, number, cause and 'verticality' (gothic architecture). Such fundamental ideas made discovery possible (an issue relevant to debates over whether new knowledge should be thought of as genuinely new, which meant that it could pose a threat to received opinion.) Kepler, to use one example, could not have discovered the elliptical orbital motion of the planet Mars if he did not already have within his mind a fundamental idea of an ellipse. To discover was not to overthrow. The point was critical.

One other relevant area of thought, owing somewhat to the Romantic poet Coleridge, was philology, which Ashworth considers to be at the centre of the Circle's concerns. Language was for its members a profound proof of inner-dwelling ideas utterly remote from sensations in origin. But opposition to this assumption arose from a growing interest in human evolution, with the challengers demonstrating that the primal history of mankind preceded any ability to know words. Towards the end of his life Whewell admitted that the findings of the schools of evolution were substantial challenges to his thinking. Charles Darwin, notes Ashworth, actually disliked Whewell, but he was hardly alone.

In general Whewell's coming of age and his college life coincided with Romanticism. Undergraduates wrote poetry, as did he. A relationship with the Wordsworth family, one of whom preceded him as master, became important. But Romantics could hardly be easily classified according to their political beliefs. Conservatives like Whewell had to choose carefully. Historians have long demonstrated that Romanticism was a double-edged sword, capable of supporting both left and right political movements, and German Romantics had once defended the French Revolution as Ashworth mentions.

Ashworth's return to the culture wars of the late Georgian and early Victorian periods may not be new *en gros*. As his impressive bibliography indicates, a large literature exists relating to the personalities and issues of the post-Napoleonic and Great Reform Bill periods. Cambridge University itself has been much written about. But having worked for years in the library and archives of Trinity College, Ashworth knows his subject well and is in command of many helpful details. To the better-known members of the Trinity Circle he adds personalities who contributed more than previously understood. He has condensed a wealth of material into a short book always to the point. His self-discipline deserves praise, but readers less familiar with the fights over a morality appropriate to a coming industrial and materialistic age may require some assistance. A sentence such as 'emotion was the link between the inside and the outside world with the act of introspection achieved via the imagination' is hard to unpack even with the aid of later discussions. The system of private teaching or coaching at Cambridge, which Whewell disliked but did little to challenge, being himself unable to break the tyranny of the written examination system, is not fully explained, although perhaps Ashworth believes enough has been said about it elsewhere. He does, however, guide us in seeing how the most famous of the Cambridge coaches, William Hopkins, lines up with respect to the fights over the kind of mathematical inquiry best able to advance an ability to reason. 'Faculty,' a word much used in the arguments over brain psychology and epistemology, is mentioned only in passing, and readers may be forgiven for not knowing what is referred to as 'Scottish stage theory'.

Whewell was a conservative, but not a reactionary, favoring the slow and if possible organically-led transformation of the institutions of society. He and those of his Circle, disagreeing at times, defended the England that they knew, and that they feared, not without reason, was being attacked on all sides. The attack was successful in the long run. By the end of the century England was no longer in reality a country that could be described accurately as a union of Church and State, for both the Church and the State were no longer monopolies of the kind that the generation of Whewell had known and cherished. But Whewell's Cambridge was also changed, possessing many more curricular opportunities than once known. New colleges were added to the collection, including women's colleges destined for fame, and a student body drawn from all faith communities could now receive degrees without subscription, without having to take an oath of loyalty to the tenets of the Church of England. Church and University lost their historic intimacy if not in every dimension.

Whewell's conception of a liberal education, based on the epistemology he explored in detail, has not travelled well. It did not, for instance achieve canonical status, whereas other great Victorians such as his contemporaries, a younger Matthew Arnold or John Henry, Cardinal Newman, still find an Anglo-American audience for their ideas of a humanistic education. His huge talents not withstanding, Whewell's prose style, unlike theirs, is not captivating. There are few lapidary lines to quote. His educational philosophy is forgotten.

But wait! Is this truly the final word? Ashworth does not think so. Odd influences pop up here and there. Karl Marx, for example, found the Circle's critique of the hateful David Ricardo's theory of rent to be significant. However, Ashworth has in mind a larger object in recounting bygone intellectual quarrels that in fact provide parallels or lessons appearing afterwards. For one thing, the Circle advocated the humanistic ideal of a well-rounded person, a position generally associated with Arnold and

Newman. Although scholars themselves, they were not advocates of specialized education for undergraduates. Learning to reason with the correct logical methods meant that the mind was trained to make connections between fields of knowledge that were continuing to layer and divide. Above all, university graduates would know right from wrong and truth from falsehood. Or to state the problem differently, relativism was not in good odor.

But in conclusion Ashworth arrives at the location to which he has aimed from the outset. The Circle did not exactly disappear. Another and later generation took up some of their concerns. He closes with a section on Oxford idealists such as T.H. Green and Christian socialists such as R.H. Tawney (a good place to have cited the work of the greatly-distinguished Oxford don, A.H. Halsey). The Trinity Circle was not actually interested in issues of inequality, a primary concern of Tawney, being more focused on the other world, nor were they in pursuit of today's cliché of 'social justice'. But what they held in common with the later idealists and humanists was a fear that the world would become one of disembodied persons, dehumanized, commodified, sold on the present, oblivious of history and tradition, faddist. We arrive at the present, a world where the Babbages have found a means of replacing human intellect with machines. Morality in the Age of Artificial Intelligence, says Ashworth, is now all about calculation. It is not a received and settled way of knowing and living with enduring truths.

And so with the addition of some new insights, he brings the story of the Trinity Circle up-to-date and gives to them a longevity hitherto implicitly denied.

Sheldon Rothblatt
University of California, Berkeley

William C. Kirby, *Empires of Ideas: Creating the Modern University from Germany to America to China* (Cambridge, MA and London: Harvard University Press, 2022), pp. 491

David Palfreyman

Perhaps the sub-title should have a question-mark since the theme of the book is the passing of the baton marked 'leading global universities' - from Germany in the nineteenth century to the USA in the twentieth and so, query, to China in the twenty-first.

Kirby is an academic at Harvard University and he seeks to explore the rise and fall of 'empires' as in the ranking of global universities by looking in detail at representative institutions from each of the three nations: the University of Berlin and the Free University of Berlin; Harvard, Berkeley, and Duke; Tsinghua, Nanjing, the University of Hong Kong.

An obvious question is why Harvard and not The Johns Hopkins University - of which Edward Shils said: 'The establishment of Johns Hopkins was perhaps the single most decisive event in the history of learning in the Western hemisphere.' (quoted in M.T. Benson's 2022 biography of its founding President: 'Daniel Coit Gilman and the Birth of the American Research University' - The Johns Hopkins University Press). The answer seems to be that Kirby knows Harvard as 'A German-English Hybrid' - and even if Harvard's justly famous President Charles Eliot commented that the German research model at the time so keenly being taken up by TJHU would fit Harvard freshmen 'about as well as a barnyard would suit a whale'!

He begins by quoting Sheldon Rothblatt's discussion of 'the history of the idea that a university derives its identity from an idea' in which Rothblatt notes that in fact over the centuries 'a single idea of a university has never truly existed' (*The Modern University and its Discontents*' (1997)). Hence in our *Universities and Colleges: A Very Short Introduction*' (2017) Paul Temple and I talk of 'the changing idea and ideal of the University', noting that as the concept of the university crept into Western Europe in the C11 and C12 centuries there were initially two competing models - Bologna run by the students for the students with the academics firmly under control and a tad later Paris where the Masters had asserted themselves over 'the junior members' (and as copied in Oxford & Cambridge before spreading across Europe and then being carried to all corners of the globe).

Thus, Kirby offers 'a book about the roles, historically and in prospect, of universities in a global context... about the modern research university in three of its most powerful settings... about the future of the university in light of its past... examin[ing] three leading global centres of higher education in the twenty-first century... explor[ing] how they have grown, assess[ing] their greatest challenges today, and estimat[ing] which system (if any single one) is likely to set global standards in the twenty-first century'. He starts with an interesting assertion: 'In the making or breaking of great global universities, perhaps no criterion is more important than the quality of governance' - a theme he returns to through the analysis. He also notes the wise words of Philip Altbach: 'Everyone wants a world-class university. No country feels it can do without one. The problem is that no one knows what a world-class university is, and no one has figured out how to get one'.

So, the book kicks off with a review of the rise, fall, and recent revival of the German universities (invigorated by the 'Bologna Process' that led them 'to streamline antiquated and idiosyncratic degree systems' and by Germany's 'Excellence Initiative' that 'propelled certain institutions forward'. The two Berlin institutions are supplied as case-studies: 'Humboldt [the University of Berlin] is today a living museum of a university, striving to return to distinction' as 'the mother of all research universities'; and the Free University that started with shades of medieval Bologna whereby 'the governing structure of the university entrusted students with a remarkable degree of influence' although soon 'the Berlin Model of faculty-student comity was on life support' and recently has done rather well out of the Excellence Initiative.

Next up the US research universities - the American ascendency explored via the three case-studies and Kirby asks whether American universities can continue to lead the world in the coming decades. Kirby is blunt and honest about the unfortunate episode of Larry Summers as Harvard's President and the faculty passing an 'unprecedented' vote of no confidence in his leadership; and Kirby also notes the egregious nonsense of 'legacy candidates' making up some third of the class of 2022 as 'children of alumni were six times more likely to be admitted than others'! Harvard seemingly has a better chance - helped by a $50b+ endowment - of retaining its world-leading status than Berkeley as an increasingly under-funded public university (although it did afford a $700k fence around the Chancellor's residence which was seen as Chancellor Dirks 'fencing himself off' from Berkeley and its fractious faculty and rebellious students!). Indeed, Kirby asks if 'one of Berkeley's historic strengths, faculty governance, [now makes] it impossible to face inevitably difficult choices? [Has] Berkeley - home to the Free Speech Movement, long traditions of academic autonomy, and insurgent citizenship - finally become both ungovernable and insolvent…?' Kirby is far less gloomy about the success story of Duke whose chapter is titled 'Outrageous Ambitions' - there is extensive 'innovation rooted in relentless planning' that allows Duke to 'grow as a research and global university on its own terms'.

And so to China…A chart on 237 shows the surge in the astonishing growth of HE students: 1984, 2.1m; 2018, 45m (1980, 675 HEIs; 2015, 2560). But, of course, the latest news from China is the inevitable unemployment of graduates arising from their over-production via the over-expansion of HE - a problem also in the UK, although more by way of the under-employment of graduates churned out at the expense of neglecting vocational further education (community college provision in US terms); and indeed in many other mass HE European systems. Kirby noted the success of the Chinese Excellence Initiative driving certain universities up the global rankings - but, back to the mention of governance as above, there is the problem of the fact that 'the Party [has] increased its authority over university governance'… So, have the three case-study universities 'the potential to lead the world of higher education in the twenty-first century'?

Tsinghua as China's MIT or ICL probably can resist 'the resurgence of political repression within China' given its impact via intrusion into university governance is arguably less direct for the sciences and engineering than for the humanities and social sciences - Kirby noting 'the unquestioned success' by 2020 of the Schwarzman Scholars programme aimed at 'the next generation of global leaders' and its having 'so far been insulated from the growing political oversight of the Xi Jinping era'. The programme is presented by TU as 'the Rhodes Scholarship for the twenty-first century' - after all, adds Kirby, 'why should the best and brightest of the world's young leaders go to Oxford' as located within 'a foggy, chilly, self-isolating island, in decline, off the coast of Europe'! So much for the chances of English HE and the case-study of Oxford being any kind of global HE leader in the future... Nanjing, however, is seen as vulnerable to Party interference (a chapter subsection is titled: 'The Party Strikes Back') and hence 'the sun may be setting on the prospects for the great and historical university in China's southern capital'. Nor is the University of Hong Kong much better placed.

So, 'what then are the prospects for Chinese leadership in the twenty-first century?'. We have 'A German Reawakening' but not enough to 'again dominate the global stage'; while in the USA 'The Trials of Public Higher Education' risk pulling US HE off its global pedestal - 'Make no mistake: the slow motion defunding of US public higher education will have consequences also for the private schools, the Stanfords and the Harvards... There is no greater threat to the leading position of American higher education than America's growing parsimony in the support of public higher education'. And in China? On the positive side there is not only the success of TU in the sciences but also the recognition within elite universities of the role of the arts and humanities in providing 'general education' fit for the new century by churning our graduates tutored in 'how to think, to reflect, to analyse, and to become the critical thinkers and problem-solvers of the next generation'.

Hence perhaps why my 'The Oxford Tutorial' collection of essays from Oxford dons on their tutoring of students in 1:2 hour-long tutorials has been translated into Chinese by Peking University Press (English version at Amazon as h/b, p/b, and Kindle download); while our spin-off Centre for Tutorial Teaching Limited as an attempt to spread the Oxford Tutorial pedagogical concept into less well-funded HEIs than Oxford and also down the educational age range into schools is working with entities in a China as well as South Africa and in the USA.

Kirby ends by asking: 'Can China Lead the World of Universities?'. Answer - 'that day will come, but we are not there yet'. Nor is there a 'Chinese model' for universities to be exported along the 'New Silk Road' as 'a university with Chinese characteristics'. Chinese universities follow the global US model of the elite research university, (examples of which are even to be found in England's depressing foggy and chilly environment!). They are successful and competitive because some are very well-funded, but their 'greatest challenge' is 'the obstruction they encounter' from 'the Party' and its presence in their governance: 'At the end of the day, can 'world-class' universities - however they are defined - exist in a politically illiberal system?'. This century will, as for the last century, in terms of the HE gold-standard model continue to dominated by the US research universities - but a few Chinese institutions will be snapping at the heels of those US elite world-class universities (and perhaps even Oxford, Cambridge, ICL, and UCL can remain on the radar, despite being located on an isolated island now deprived of the supposedly warm and stimulating embrace of the EU...).

David Palfreyman, OBE
New College, Oxford, OX1 3BN